# A WISE EXTRAVAGANCE

A John D. S. and Aida C. Truxall Book

# A WISE EXTRAVAGANCE

The Founding of the
Carnegie International Exhibitions,
1895–1901

KENNETH NEAL

UNIVERSITY OF PITTSBURGH PRESS

Published by the University of Pittsburgh Press, Pittsburgh, Pa. 15260
Copyright © 1996, University of Pittsburgh Press

Manufactured in the United States of America
Printed on acid-free paper

10   9   8   7   6   5   4   3   2   1

Library of Congress Cataloging-in-Publication Data

Neal, Kenneth, 1950–
    A wise extravagance : the founding of the Carnegie International
exhibitions 1895–1901 / Kenneth Neal.
        p.   cm.
    Includes bibliographical references and index.
    ISBN 0–8229–3925–8 (cloth : alk. paper).  —  ISBN 0–8229–5584–9
(pbk. : alk. paper)
    1. Carnegie International — History.    2. Art, Modern — 20th century —
Exhibitions.    3. Carnegie Institute.    Museum of Art — History.    I. Title.
N6487.P57C375    1996
759.05 — dc20        95–50881


A CIP catalogue record for this book is available from the
British Library.

*To my mother*

# CONTENTS



*Illustrations begin on page 61*

# PREFACE

The idea for this book came to me several years ago when I was one of
a team of researchers working on the American paintings in the collection of the Carnegie Museum of Art. It became apparent to all of us that
the Carnegie annual exhibitions had been major events in the world of
art; but it became equally apparent that the only readily available accounts of their history — a series of short articles and a catalogue essay,
both published in the 1950s — were far too summary and superficial to
answer many of the questions that arose in the course of our research. We
discovered, for example, that several pictures from the early exhibitions
had been purchased for something called the "chronological collection,"
whose precise nature remained a mystery. Whatever it was, it was apparently discontinued after 1901, and its very existence had been forgotten
by the 1950s. We knew that after 1896 the jury was elected by the con-
tributing artists, but we did not know exactly how the election was conducted or exactly what the elected jury did. The most obvious questions
remained unanswered. At times we suspected the published accounts of
inaccuracy. For instance, they give the impression that the 1895 loan
exhibition had been a modest display of works from local collections; yet
we occasionally stumbled upon documents in the museum's rather disor-
derly archives that suggested that the loan exhibition was a significant
exhibition in its own right, a forerunner of the regular series of exhibitions
that began the following year.

This dearth of precise information is not, unfortunately, peculiar to
the Carnegie Internationals. The standard histories of such important
exhibiting bodies as London's Royal Academy and New York's National
Academy of Design tend to highlight their subjects, concentrating upon
major stylistic trends and the relative handful of artists whose reputations

have survived to the present. They are useful in their way, but they often fail to provide the information scholars are looking for. And for many exhibitions, most notably the Paris Salon, complete histories have yet to be written. Despite the wishful thinking of those who believe that the age of art historical archaeology has ended, leaving us nothing to do but interpret the facts according to various trendy "methodologies," a great deal of digging remains to be done.

My original optimistic intention was to study the Carnegie Internationals from their inception to the present day, but I soon realized that it would be impossible to do this without either writing a book of inordinate length or sacrificing much of the intimate detail that had attracted me to the subject in the first place. It was necessary to focus on a particular phase of their history; and the most interesting phase from my point of view was the earliest, when Pittsburgh, a city that had been of negligible importance to the world of art, acquired almost overnight the most distinguished exhibition in America. This was the critical period during which the Carnegie Internationals' reputation was built, their organization and format developed, their basic purposes and methods most clearly expounded and debated. The year 1901 brought this period to a close: the series of competitive exhibitions that had begun in 1896 was temporarily suspended in 1902, and the founders paused to take stock of their endeavors. When, following a partial revival in 1903, the Internationals were fully resumed in 1904, they were considered a permanent feature of the American art scene, and their character remained virtually unaltered until the first director, John Beatty, retired in 1922.

Despite having limited my topic to a period of only six years, I still found myself embarrassed with riches. I am quite aware that what I have written, although extremely detailed for an exhibition history, will often fail to satisfy those interested in a particular artist or a particular work of art. Hundreds of artists, most of them highly regarded in their day, exhibited at the Carnegie galleries during the period in question, and it is impossible to mention — much less provide a full account of — each and every one. Similarly, it is impossible to locate and illustrate every painting mentioned in the text. As Gabriel Weisberg observed in 1983:

> [Though] some of the paintings exhibited in the earliest shows . . .
> [were] purchased for the permanent collection of the Department of
> Fine Arts, Carnegie Institute, the vast majority of the works shown by

artists once well-known have disappeared from view, often without leaving a trace to enable future generations to judge the quality of a given work or to fully comprehend the tendencies of the time in the art world.[1]

The situation is actually worse than Weisberg indicates, for many of the paintings acquired by the Department of Fine Arts have also disappeared from view, thanks to years of ruthless de-accessioning.

Moreover, the largest private collection formed from the early Internationals, that of Andrew Carnegie, has been dispersed beyond recovery. When in 1991 the New-York Historical Society organized an exhibition of painting and sculpture that had once belonged to Carnegie, it was unable to locate any of the works he purchased from the galleries that bore his name. It is fortunate that halftone photoengraving had come into general use by the 1890s, allowing many of the works from the Internationals to be reproduced in catalogues and illustrated magazines. I have tried to provide an illustration of every painting that receives special attention in the text, as well as of a number of others, in order to give the reader some idea of the nature and quality of the works that were hung in the Carnegie galleries.

*A Wise Extravagance* has been extensively revised from a doctoral dissertation that I presented to the University of Pittsburgh's Department of History of Art and Architecture in spring 1993. I should like to thank my advisor, David Wilkins, and Henry Adams, former curator of fine arts at the Carnegie Museum of Art, for their support and encouragement both during and after the long years of writing—their patience has, I hope, finally been rewarded. I should also like to thank Catherine Marshall and Kathy McLaughlin, my editors at the University of Pittsburgh Press, and Pippa Letsky, a copy editor of uncommon taste, intelligence, and sensitivity, for making the transformation of the dissertation into a book as painless (even pleasant) as possible. The staff of the Carnegie Library of Pittsburgh, especially Maria Zinni and Marilyn Holt, the former and current heads of the Pennsylvania Department, gave me invaluable assistance in my research; they, along with Matthew Roper, curator of visual resources in the Department of Fine Arts and Architecture, University of Pittsburgh, Paul Chew, director emeritus of the Westmoreland Museum of Art, Greensburg (a gem of a museum that deserves to be more widely known), Bill Stover and Nona Martin, former and present coordinators of photographic services at the Carnegie Museum of Art, helped to ease the often frustrating effort of securing photographs. Together with many other authors, I am indebted to John D. S. Truxall and his wife Aida, whose own wise extravagance in endowing the University of Pittsburgh Press has made the publication of this book possible. My warmest thanks must go to my friends, who helped keep my spirits up during the gloomy spells that afflict ever writer: they will not be jealous if I single out my colleague Rina Youngner, who read the manuscript several times, and Phil Morris, who hasn't read a word of it. Above all, I owe a debt of gratitude to my parents that I can never repay.

# A WISE EXTRAVAGANCE

# 1

# The Founders and Their Philosophy

I N THE 1890s, America was ripe for an annual international exhibition of contemporary art. During the last quarter of the nineteenth century, the country had ceased to be an aesthetic backwater: wealthy Americans, often of informed and progressive tastes, had become a major source of patronage for European art, and American artists, trained in the best schools of Europe, had begun to enjoy considerable success abroad. The reputations of such native sons as James McNeill Whistler, John Singer Sargent, and John White Alexander fully equaled those of European luminaries such as Adolphe Bouguereau, Lawrence Alma-Tadema, and Giovanni Boldini. An interest in art was burgeoning among the country's middle classes. There were few large or middle-sized cities that could not boast of a gallery, an art association, or a school of art. Popular magazines such as *Harper's* and *Scribner's* regularly informed their readers of the latest artistic developments at home and abroad. Exhibitions — especially such major international exhibitions as those at the Chicago World's Columbian Exposition of 1893 and the St. Louis Exposition from 1895 to 1897 — were well attended. A yearly exhibition that would assemble the best or most representative work of both continents, allowing comparisons to be drawn between them, was virtually assured of an enthusiastic reception from artists, critics, and public alike.

But who would have expected it to be established in Pittsburgh? The logical home for such an important exhibition would have seemed to be

New York, the art center of the nation, or Boston, or Philadelphia, or perhaps even Chicago, in an effort to build upon the successful exhibition of 1893. Pittsburgh had no reputation as an art center. Like most large cities, it had its artists and its exhibitions, but none that excited more than local interest. In the eyes of the world, Pittsburgh was exclusively an industrial center, from which little in the way of artistic endeavor could be expected. That it became the home of a major international exhibition was due to that most remarkable of nineteenth-century industrialists, Andrew Carnegie (figure 1).

A native of Dunfermline, Scotland, Carnegie emigrated to Pittsburgh in 1848, when he was thirteen years old. His first job, working as a bobbin boy, earned him $1.20 a week; but by 1867, when he left Pittsburgh for New York, he had amassed the sizable income of $50,000 a year, largely through shrewd investments in railway sleeping-car stock. A few years later he entered the steel industry and became a multimillionaire. Although Carnegie was the equal of any late nineteenth-century capitalist in cunning and ruthlessness, his mind was of a far more philosophic temper than was usually encountered among that breed, and he was far less interested in the acquisition of wealth as an end in itself. In a private memorandum of 1868 he wrote: "No idol more debasing than money. . . . To continue much longer overwhelmed by business cares and with most of my thoughts wholly upon the way to make more money in the shortest time, must degrade me beyond hope of permanent recovery." He resolved to retire from business in 1870, secure an Oxford education, then settle in London, where he would involve himself "in public matters, especially those connected with education and improvement of the poorer classes."[1]

Although he failed to adhere to the letter of this resolution (he did not retire until 1901 and received only an honorary degree from Oxford), he succeeded in living up to its spirit. As his millions multiplied, he devoted more of his time to philanthropic and intellectual pursuits. Although he belonged to New York's business-oriented Union League Club, Carnegie preferred to hobnob with the intelligentsia at the Nineteenth Century Club, and he counted among his friends some of the leading American and British thinkers of the age, including Henry Ward Beecher, Matthew Arnold, and Herbert Spencer.

Philosophical considerations, including an idiosyncratic and inaccurate interpretation of the Social Darwinism of Herbert Spencer, deeply influenced Carnegie's theory and practice of philanthropy. In his youth, he recalled in his memoirs, Spencer's writings had affected him with all the force of a divine revelation:

> I remember that light came in as a flood and all was clear. Not only had I got rid of theology and the supernatural, but I had found the truth of evolution. "All is well since all grows better" became my motto, my true source of comfort. Man was not created with an instinct for his own degradation, but from the lower he had risen to the higher forms. Nor is there any conceivable end to his march to perfection. His face is turned to the light; he stands in the sun and looks upward.[2]

Yet, despite his professed faith in Spencer's doctrine, Carnegie owed little to it beyond an optimistic belief in human progress. Many of his ideas were utterly contrary to those of the English philosopher. Social Darwinists opposed philanthropy on the grounds that it interfered with the natural process of evolution, which dictated the survival of the fittest and the extinction of the unfit. The wealthy, whose economic success proved their fitness, were warned against protecting the obviously unfit poor from the consequences of their inferiority, for to do so would be to thwart nature's design and impede the betterment of the species.

Carnegie, who accepted the economic criterion of fitness but recalled his own spectacular rise from poverty to affluence, took an altogether different view of the evolutionary role of wealth. The natural leader of society was not the pampered rich boy but the poor boy possessed of genius and a strong incentive to get ahead in this world:

> Such boys always have marched, and always will march, straight to the front and lead the world: they are the epoch-makers. Let one select the three or four foremost names, the supremely great in every field of human triumph, and note how small is the contribution of hereditary rank and wealth to the short list of immortals who have lifted and advanced the race. It will, I think, be seen that the possession of these is almost fatal to greatness and goodness, and that the greatest and best of our race have necessarily been nurtured in the bracing school of poverty — the only school capable of producing the supremely great, the genius.[3]

It was the duty of the rich, Carnegie argued, to assist and encourage the natural geniuses among the ranks of the poor. The way to achieve this was not through indiscriminate almsgiving or through raising the wages of workers (in this, he agreed with the Social Darwinists, and his employees fared no better than those of less enlightened industrialists) but through educational opportunities. In a speech delivered in 1895 at the dedication ceremony of Pittsburgh's Carnegie Institute, he declared that money spent on education

> is put to better and nobler ends than if it had been distributed from week to week in driblets among the masses of the people. Concentrated in one great educative institution, lasting for all time, its usefulness is forever, and it ministers to the divine in man, his reason and his conscience, and thus lifts him higher and higher in the scale of being; he becomes less and less of the brute, and more of the man. I am not content to pass down in the history of Pittsburgh as one who only helped the masses to obtain greater enjoyment of those appetites which we share equally with the brutes — more to eat, more to drink, and richer raiment. . . . My aspiration takes a higher flight. Mine be it to have contributed to the enlightenment and joys of the mind, to the things of the spirit, to all that tends to bring into the lives of the toilers of Pittsburgh sweetness and light. I hold this the noblest possible use of wealth.[4]

It is clear from this statement that Carnegie's ameliorist ambitions often went beyond the potential geniuses to embrace the masses as a whole.

The "great educative institution" that Carnegie founded in Pittsburgh was an elaboration of his favorite form of philanthropy, the free public library. He first offered to build a library for Pittsburgh in 1881, subject to his usual condition that, whereas he would provide the funds for the actual structure, the community must pay to supply, staff, and maintain it. Because Pennsylvania law did not permit municipal property taxes to be used for such a purpose, the city had to decline the offer. In 1887 the state legislature passed an enabling act that removed the restriction, and in February 1890, Pittsburgh asked Carnegie to renew his offer, which he gladly did.[5]

By this time, his ideas had expanded. In "The Best Fields for Philanthropy," published in the December 1889 *North American Review*, he had suggested that, whenever possible, the free library should include a museum and an art gallery. Some, he admitted, might consider the latter benefaction "fanciful," but, he declared:

> It is better to reach and touch the sentiment for beauty in the natu-
> rally bright minds of this class [that is, the working class] than to
> pander to those incapable of being so touched. For what the improver
> of the race must endeavor is to reach those who have the divine spark
> ever so feebly developed, that it may be strengthened and grow.

The library, however, was to be the core of the institution, whereas the art gallery and museum were to be regarded "as wise extravagances, for which public revenues should not be given. . . . These are such gifts as a citizen may fitly bestow upon a community and endow, so that it will cost the City nothing."[6]

Despite the role that art played in Carnegie's philanthropy, he never became a noted connoisseur or collector as did his business partner Henry Clay Frick. His longtime friend the Pittsburgh artist Martin Leisser declared flatly that Carnegie "didn't really know much about art." Carnegie's own claims to artistic knowledge varied from the bold to the modest. In his autobiography, he declared that his European tour of 1865–1866 had taught him to "classify the works of the great painters" and had made him a highly competent judge of art. Elsewhere, he credited himself with "just a little artistic sense, . . . I can't be fooled all the time, that is, I do know a little."[7]

This latter remark would appear to be closer to the truth. His occasional statements on art, taken all together, show that he was aware of the more important established artists of his time; that he had a basic, though superficial, knowledge of the history of art; and that he knew what he liked. His opinions were often forcefully expressed but breathtakingly ill-informed. Asked to approve a list of names to be carved on the Carnegie Institute's entablature, he complained that Perugino had been omitted and Rubens included: "The latter only a painter of fat vulgar women, while a study of the pictures of Raphael will show anyone that he was really only a copyist of Perugini [sic], whose pupil he was."[8] Carnegie does not, in fact, seem to have taken a deep interest in art, except insofar as it could serve to improve the condition of humanity. According to the wisdom of the age, art was ennobling, uplifting, at once an agent and an index of social progress. Carnegie accepted this view; he regarded art as a powerful instrument for his purposes, and he meant to make use of it.

The idea of the social utility of art became widely current among American intellectuals during the second quarter of the nineteenth century.[9] Travelers abroad contrasted the behavior of the European and American masses, observing that the former were orderly and restrained, the latter often dangerous and unruly. This, they reasoned, was due to Europe's artistic traditions, expressed in common household goods as well as in great works of public architecture and in the art displayed in public museums, which produced a cultural ambiance whose refining influence penetrated to the lowest levels of society. America lacked these traditions yet, as a democratic republic, had a special need of them to ensure public order. Nor was it simply a matter of controlling the masses; the upper classes also required art to prevent them from sinking into gross materialism. Addressing the American Art-Union in 1844, the Reverend Henry W. Bellows declared: "No nation needs its exalting, purifying, calming influences more than ours. We need it to supplant the mean utilitarian tastes which threaten to make us a mere nation of shopkeepers. We need it to soften the harsh features of political zeal, and party strife, the other engrossing business of this people."[10] Nearly sixty years later, these same arguments were being put forth with undiminished force to promote art education in the nation's public schools:

> As a people we are somewhat brusque, and it is difficult for us to get on without more or less friction. Nations with infinitely less natural and acquired intelligence are masters in the art of agreeable intercourse, politeness and consideration. Indeed, they seem to be inborn characteristics of some European nations, notably those in which art is an important part of all things, of public and private buildings, richly decorated without and within, and of all public utilities. Whichever way one may turn he is met by harmonious combinations. Nature and art go hand in hand through the length and breadth of those staid old countries, and the people in daily contact with such agreeable surroundings are unconsciously moulded along similar lines and act in harmony with these outward conditions. . . . Our first efforts must be the amelioration of incongruous conditions, the checking of tendencies towards the bizarre, meretricious and ugly disfigurements which are constant irritants to a nervous people who should be brought into contact only with things harmonious and quieting.[11]

It should be noted that a belief in the moral efficacy of art was, for many, fully compatible with the "art for art's sake" movement of the later part of the century. Although some would argue that art must have an explicitly moral content in order to produce the desired effect, the predominant emphasis, especially after the Civil War, was on beauty, independent of subject matter. In an article published in 1898, the president of the Chicago Women's Club pointed out that the greatest art-producing civilizations of the past (such as Periclean Athens, Renaissance Italy, and seventeenth-century France) were notoriously immoral by modern standards, as, in many cases, were the subjects their artists depicted—for example, the Venuses of Titian. An immoral or simply amoral work of art, however, could still be a great instrument of good:

> Art has a vital relation to morality, but we must seek it not in its didactic teaching, but in beauty, which always exerts a refining influence, tending to soften manners and elevate character. . . . Here is where the moral mission of art is to be sought—in the elevating influence of pure delight filling life with joy and beauty, and by these making the world happier and better. . . . Is it not the distinct mission of painting, poetry and music to soothe the soul weary with the cares of life, to make a city of refuge in the realms of fancy, to give moments of delight in a world of beauty and joy where no moral judgments are demanded of us, and where poise and serenity of mind may be gained; to enable us again to enter the arena of the actual world, from whose struggle no mortal is long released?[12]

For many affluent and cultivated Americans, "the moral mission of art" assumed the character of an evangelistic creed. In *Art's True Mission in America* (1853), Augustine Duganne exhorted his countrymen to bring the blessings of art to "hut and prison." He wrote: "To evangelize men, first give them to eat. To refine a people, make them comfortable and familiarize their minds to the enjoyment of the beautiful." The eloquent Congregationalist clergyman Henry Ward Beecher urged the wealthy, as a Christian duty, to share beauty with the less fortunate masses:

> Nothing can make others so rich, without diminishing our own means, as generosity in the use of art-treasure, of materials of beauty. . . . Nothing can well redeem the possession of beauty in a large degree, from the charge of sinful self-indulgence, but such a use of it as shall confer pleasure on all those who need the solace and ministration of the divine element of beauty.[13]

By the 1890s the aesthetic mission was being carried out by dedicated social workers, who regarded the beneficent influences of art as essential to bettering the lot of the urban poor. Chicago's famed Hull-House, founded in 1889, brought to the inhabitants of the city's slums lectures on the history of art, a circulating collection of fine art reproductions, and frequent loan exhibitions of oil paintings, watercolors, and prints. "There is abundant testimony," wrote cofounder Jane Addams in 1895, "that the lectures and pictures have quite changed the tone of their minds; for they have become, of course, perfectly familiar with the photographs of the best things, and have cared for them, not 'as a means of culture', but as an expression of the highest human thought and perception."[14] In June 1892, the New York University Settlement Society launched a series of free loan exhibitions in the lower East Side; and the university settlements of Boston followed suit a few months later. Noted artists and wealthy collectors gladly lent their paintings to these endeavors, which were closely modeled upon the successful exhibitions held at Toynbee Hall in London's notorious East End slums. As in London, the educational aspects were assisted by cheap explanatory catalogues and free lectures. The results were encouraging. Commenting on Boston's South End Free Exhibition of March–April 1893, a writer for *Harper's Weekly* observed that crowds had averaged fifteen hundred people a day, many of whom had taken an intelligent interest in the pictures. To them, he concluded, "a light has surely come from another world — a world in which sordidness and toil are not the only things of moment, and where it may be seen that there is other work to be doing besides that of brawn."[15]

Working-class art exhibitions were, however, exceptional in late nineteenth-century America. Carnegie's fellow cultural philanthropists, especially those in the rapidly developing cities of the nation's interior, were more interested in preaching the Gospel of Art through public exhibitions and galleries aimed at middle-class audiences. Charles L. Hutchinson, president of the Art Institute from 1882 to 1924, may be taken as representative of the breed — indeed, more representative than the idiosyncratic Carnegie. Like Carnegie, he believed devoutly in the obligations of wealth (the selfish rich, he declared, were "mere sponges, absorbing all and giving nothing . . . no better than burglars") and in the uplifting influence of high culture, but he rarely spoke of "the masses" and "the toilers." His great concern was to rescue businessmen from the degrading effects of rampant materialism.[16] "Are we not losing sight of the being created in the image of God, with heart and intellect and soul?" Hutchinson asked in an 1888 address, "Are we not losing sight of the human being in the business man?" His answer was that we were, and that the remedy for this was art, which "in the midst of this busy material life of our day . . . may call upon us to halt, and turn our thoughts away from so much that is of the earth earthy, and lead us to contemplate those eternal truths which after all most concern the children of God."[17]

Although the Pittsburgh exhibitions were more similar in tone to the annual exhibitions held at the Art Institute from the 1880s on than to the settlement exhibitions of New York and Boston, Carnegie's rhetoric was considerably in advance of Hutchinson's. It was only after the turn of the century that the Chicagoan came round to a more democratic view and could write: "Art is not destined for a small, a privileged class. Art is democratic. It is of the people and for the people."[18]

Carnegie could have received the Gospel of Art from many sources, but his principal source was undoubtedly the English poet and critic Matthew Arnold (1822–1888), whose views were as well known and influential in America as in his homeland. The two men met at a London dinner party in June 1883, at the very beginning of Carnegie's philanthropic career, and they became close friends.[19] Arnold occupied a place in Carnegie's intellectual pantheon that was very little inferior to Spencer's: he was "the man whom I am so thankful for having known and so favored as to call friend . . . the true teacher in advance of his age, the greatest poetic teacher in the domain of 'the future and its viewless things'."[20]

Indeed, the main points of Carnegie's ideas on cultural philanthropy were Arnoldian rather than Spencerian. Arnold passionately believed that "culture"—which he defined as "a pursuit of our total perfection by means of getting to know . . . the best which has been thought and said in the world"—was essential to the improvement of humanity and should be disseminated as widely as possible. "Culture looks beyond machinery," he wrote in 1869:

> Culture hates hatred, culture has one great passion, the passion for sweetness and light. It has one even yet greater!—the passion for making them prevail. It is not satisfied until we all come to a perfect man; it knows that the sweetness and light of the few must be imperfect until the raw and unkindled masses of humanity are touched with sweetness and light.

Like Carnegie, but anticipating him by several years, he recognized among the masses the presence of rare and gifted souls, who might flourish with the right encouragement: "In each class there are born a certain number of natures with a curiosity about their best self . . . persons who are mainly led, not by their class spirit, but by a general humane spirit, by the love of human perfection; and . . . this number is capable of being diminished or augmented." Arnold's creed was at least as optimistic as Spencer's (as it would have to be to hold any appeal for Carnegie), but it allowed more scope for individual endeavor than did the inexorable natural laws of Social Darwinism. The quest for perfection through culture, he assured his readers, "is the master-impulse even now of the life of our nation and of humanity, somewhat obscurely perhaps for this actual moment, but decisively and certainly for the immediate future," and he hailed those who worked for its attainment as "the sovereign educators."[21]

Carnegie and Arnold, however, disagreed sharply in their estimates of the cultural development of the United States. In 1886 Carnegie published his *Triumphant Democracy, or Fifty Years' March of the Republic,* in which he boasted that, owing to its democratic institutions, America was rapidly outstripping Europe in every field of human activity, spiritual as well as material. Those who maintained that the arts could flourish only under the patronage of monarchs and aristocrats were, he argued, utterly mistaken: "The equality of the citizen is the fundamental law upon which is founded all that brings sweetness and light to human life."[22] The arts, by their very nature were republican — individual genius counted for everything, hereditary rank and privilege for nothing — and therefore could be expected to thrive in America. Carnegie claimed they were doing precisely that. In the field of the representational arts, for example, Americans were to be reckoned among the world's shrewdest and most liberal patrons, and American artists, having created a landscape school of unsurpassed excellence, were quickly coming to the fore in other branches of painting as well.[23] He concluded:

> In art and music this nation is advancing with a rapidity which belies the assertion that the tendency of a Democracy is to materialize a people and give it over to sordid thoughts; that the unrestrained exercise of personal liberty ends only in the accumulation of dollars. Republicanism does not withhold from life the sweetness and light which mainly make it worth living. . . . It is now certain that in love of

art and music the Democracy even to-day is not behind the mon-
archy, and evidence is not wanting that it is entering more and more
into, and elevating, year after year, not only the few, but the great
masses which make up the national life of the republic.[24]

The idea that a republican form of government, coupled with mate-
rial prosperity, tends to encourage high culture and promote its spread to
all levels of society enjoyed a high degree of intellectual respectability in
America at that time. This was precisely the position of Charles Eliot
Norton, the nation's leading art historian, who cited the examples of
Athens, Venice, and Florence in its support. However, in his opinion the
United States had hardly begun to live up to its potential; its civilization was vulgar and mediocre, dominated by the uneducated taste of the
masses.[25]

Arnold, who regarded democracy as "acute and energetic, but taste-
less, narrow-minded and ignoble," fully agreed with Norton's assessment
of the American situation. Carnegie's boasts, which from their reiteration
of the Arnoldian catchphrase "sweetness and light" would appear to have
been specifically directed to him, wholly failed to impress him. He urged
his friend Sir Mountstuart Duff to read *Triumphant Democracy* but observed that Carnegie

> and most Americans are simply unaware that nothing in the book
> touches the capital defect of life over here [Arnold was visiting Amer-
> ica]; namely that, compared with life in England, it is so uninterest-
> ing, so without savour and without depth. Do they think to prove
> that it has savour and depth by pointing to the number of public
> libraries, schools and places of worship?

Arnold repeated this criticism at greater length, but without any overt
reference to Carnegie, in an essay published in the *Nineteenth Century* for
April 1888:

> Partial and material achievement is always being put forward as civili-
> sation. We hear a nation called highly civilised by reason of its indus-
> try, commerce and wealth, or by reason of its liberty or equality, or by
> reason of its numerous churches, schools, libraries and newspapers.
> But there is something in human nature, some instinct of growth,
> some law of perfection, which rebels against this narrow account of
> the matter. And perhaps what human nature demands in civilisation,

over and above all those obvious things which first occur to our thoughts — what human nature, I say, demands in civilisation, if it is to stand as a high and satisfying civilisation, is best described by the word *interesting*.

American civilization was emphatically not "interesting"; it lacked "distinction and beauty," especially in the arts. However, in a May 1882 essay Arnold had suggested a remedy — that the American "friends of civilisation" cease "hopping backwards and forwards across the Atlantic" and devote themselves to the cultivation of sweetness and light at home.[26]

The establishment of the Carnegie Institute as a vast cultural complex rather than as a simple public library and the fact that it was founded in Pittsburgh would appear to owe a great deal to the close personal relationship between Arnold and Carnegie, which gave added force to the ideas of cultural philanthropy current at the time. Carnegie's late friend not only inspired him to become one of the "sovereign educators" of humanity; he also challenged him to prove that sweetness and light could flourish in a republic, and that American civilization was, or could be rendered, interesting. And where better to conduct the experiment than in Pittsburgh, the city upon which Carnegie's fortune was founded, the city that he proudly showed to foreign visitors as an exemplar of America's industrial wealth and power, but a city that (measured by Arnoldian standards) was grossly materialistic and wholly uninteresting? Thanks to the Institute, Carnegie predicted,

> not only our own country, but the civilized world, will take note of the fact that our Dear Old Smoky Pittsburgh, no longer content to be celebrated only as one of the chief manufacturing centres, has entered upon the path to higher things, and is before long, as we thoroughly believe, also to be noted for her preeminence in the arts and sciences.[27]

Carnegie's hopes for Pittsburgh may strike us today as utopian, but by 1895 when the doors of the new Carnegie Institute opened an event had occurred that many thoughtful observers regarded as incontrovertible proof that a vulgar, provincial, materialistic American city could rise almost overnight to the heights of cultural eminence: the World's Columbian Exposition held in Chicago in 1893. Prior to the exposition, Chicago's reputation had been at least as bad as Pittsburgh's. "Having seen it,

I urgently desire never to see it again," wrote Rudyard Kipling in 1889, expressing a sentiment that many visitors to the city, both foreign and American, would have endorsed. "It is inhabited by savages. Its water is the water of the Hugli, and its air is dirt."[28] A few years later, John J. Ingalls recalled the incredulity that greeted the idea of holding a world's fair at Chicago:

> The original suggestion of the name was received with mingled derision and disdain. . . . It was not serious. It was a frontier joke, an advertisement, a bid for notoriety. The city was so far inland that failure was inevitable. And after the location was determined, the cynics sneered and the scoffers jeered, and instead of hearty, generous, cordial, patriotic coöperation, there was indifference, jealousy and malevolence.

But Chicago, led by its wealthy elite, exceeded every expectation:

> the men who had built the railroads and warehouses, and grown rich by the barter in cattle and hogs and corn, saw the greatness of the opportunity which stood at their gates. They summoned a congress of artists, architects, painters, sculptors, landscape gardeners, and commissioned them to design and execute a scheme commensurate with the objects for which it was intended: the assemblage of the highest achievements of civilization; the fraternal rivalry of nations; the uplifting of the human race. The conception was Napoleonic, and the result is an epoch in history. Other expositions will be judged as they approach or recede from this ideal. Chicago is no longer provincial. She has established her claim to take first rank among the great capitals of the world.[29]

And, by extension, America established its claim to take first rank among the great nations of the world. "Chicago, the enormous town we see expanding, the gigantic plant which grows before our eyes, seems now in this wonderfully new country to be in advance of the age," wrote the French novelist and critic Paul Bourget. "But is not this more or less true of all America?"[30]

Many visitors to the fair's White City were most impressed by the indications of technological and scientific progress, whereas some found compelling evidence for actual or potential excellence in the arts. "Art and Music and Poetry belong to Chicago," proclaimed the English novelist Walter Besant, "the Hub of the Universe is transferred from Boston to Chicago; this place must surely become, in the immediate future, the center of the nobler world — the world of Arts and Letters."[31] To others it was less a matter of Chicago and Boston than of America and the world:

> When the White City was built in 1893 art assumed a definite place in our national life. Then for the first time we awoke to a realisation that art of the people, by the people, for the people had come to us. It came to this New World in the old historic way. From the seed sown in the Orient, through Greece, through Italy from Byzantium, wafted ever westward, its timid flowering from our Atlantic seaboard had been carried a thousand miles inland to find its first full eclosion; not as a single growth, but as the triple flower of architecture, painting, and sculpture.[32]

There were even those who held that the New World was not merely becoming the equal of the Old World in the arts but was actually superseding it.[33] Taken all together, the technological, architectural, and artistic marvels of the White City seemed to confirm the most extravagant boasts of *Triumphant Democracy*. It was not entirely unreasonable, then, to suppose that Carnegie's efforts in Pittsburgh would provide additional confirmation.

The Institute's art gallery was given a distinguished part to play in Carnegie's experiment in cultural uplift, one that, like the part played by the Palace of Fine Arts at the World's Columbian Exposition, would promote both local and national goals: it was to help spiritualize the local populace and encourage "the development and maintenance of the coming school of national American art." This latter goal was to be achieved by the creation of a "chronological collection," beginning in 1896, that would receive the finest works produced each year by American artists. Carnegie hoped that someday they would "strive to have one of their productions selected as the best of its year, and placed in the historical collection of this gallery, as today they strive to be admitted to the Luxembourg, and through the Chantrey Bequest, to the British National Gallery." And he intimated that this day was not likely to be remote.[34]

Carnegie's initial plans for the chronological collection, formulated in 1895, made no specific mention of an annual exhibition; but such an exhibition — which would serve to supply the collection just as the Paris Salons supplied the Luxembourg and the Royal Academy exhibitions supplied the Chantrey Bequest — was a logical corollary of his design and obviously in keeping with his desire to make Pittsburgh the artistic arbiter of the nation. He did, in fact, express a preference that the collection be selected from works exhibited in the gallery, and on at least one occasion he likened the proposed collection to the Salon, which he had described in *Triumphant Democracy* as "the highest art tribunal in the world."[35] According to William Nimick Frew, president of the Institute and Carnegie's friend and advisor, "something as nice as a salon in Paris" was what the philanthropist wished to give Pittsburgh. In 1898, when the annual exhibition was well established, Carnegie unambiguously declared his intentions for it: "What the opening of the Salon is for France, the Academy for Britain, we now expect to make for this continent the opening of the exhibition which you are to celebrate today."[36]

Although the idea of creating an American Salon in Pittsburgh may have been Carnegie's, the idea of an annual exhibition was not. A poll conducted by the *Pittsburgh Dispatch* in December 1894, shortly after it became public that Carnegie intended to endow his gallery with $50,000 a year, revealed that virtually all the leading local artists favored using part of the endowment to subsidize an annual or semiannual exhibition, which would offer prizes generous enough to secure the best work of the best-known artists. Most artists envisioned a series of exclusively American exhibitions on the lines of those held by the National Academy of Design and the Pennsylvania Academy of Fine Arts; however, the sculptor William Spriestersbach proposed an exhibition of international scope to be juried by an international committee.[37]

These suggestions probably influenced the plans for the new gallery, for Carnegie was sensitive to local opinion and organized the Institute's administration in such a way as to ensure that it would be taken into consideration. He appointed a board of trustees composed of the city's most prominent business and professional men to govern the affairs of the Institute. The board, in turn, appointed eight of its members to serve on the Fine Arts Committee, which controlled the gallery. This committee enjoyed almost perfect autonomy: the only specific requirement that Carnegie imposed was the formation of the chronological collection; apart from that, the committee members were free to conduct their affairs as they saw fit.[38]

The artists interviewed by the *Pittsburgh Dispatch* in 1894 were unanimous that the new gallery should be managed by experienced artists, critics, and connoisseurs, but Carnegie strongly disagreed. Experts, he told Frew, were too narrow-minded: "for this reason, painters of the day ridiculed Millet as vulgar; the musicians of the day, Wagner as insane; writers of the day, Shakespeare as bombastic. The future is to laugh at many pictures which experts are extolling today, and art-amateurs are buying to be in the fashion, and at many books which are supposed to have the elements of enduring fame." He felt that his endowment would be better administered by "men of affairs" who, though they might seek advice from experts, would not be influenced by professional rivalries and allegiances to particular schools of art. He also wanted the committee to include members recruited "directly from the people," because "unless the institution be kept in touch with the masses, and therefore popular, it cannot be widely useful."[39] This was a matter of deep concern to Carnegie. In his 1895 dedication speech, he deplored "the cant of art" and the fact that "each petty school calls aloud that it has the truth, the whole truth and nothing but the truth." But, he continued,

> No school can embrace the whole, since art is universal, and the judgement of the masses of the people is finally to prove the truest test of the supreme in art, as it admittedly is in literature. Let us hope that the pictures exhibited here from time to time will be of all schools, and reach both extremes — the highest critic and the humblest citizen . . . and attract not only the few but the many.[40]

Here again is an echo of Arnold, who in *Culture and Anarchy* had warned against those who would "try to indoctrinate the masses with the set of ideas and judgements constituting the creed of their own profession or party." This, Arnold maintained, was not true culture, for culture does not try to win adherents to a particular sect, but "seeks to do away with classes and sects; to make the best that has been thought and known in the world current everywhere."[41]

Although Carnegie did not personally appoint the members of the Fine Arts Committee, the fact that they were selected from the board of trustees ensured that most of them would be men of affairs. Only two artists — Alfred Bryan Wall and Joseph Ryan Woodwell — served on the board, and Woodwell was as much a businessman as an artist, being the proprietor of a successful hardware store. From 1896 to 1901 the remaining six seats on the committee were filled by leading business and professional men: Henry Clay Frick and William McConway were industrialists; William Nimick Frew was an oilman; David Thompson Watson and James Murdock Clark were lawyers; John Grier Holmes was a banker; Edward Manning Bigelow was a civil engineer and Pittsburgh's director of Public Works; and John Caldwell, the committee's chairman, was the treasurer of the Westinghouse Airbrake Company. Obviously, none of the members were drawn "directly from the people," but several had risen from lowly origins. Caldwell and McConway, for example, had both emigrated from Ireland as children; Clark had begun life as a farm boy. Carnegie — who liked to portray himself as "one who was himself a wage earner, and who has the good of that class greatly at heart" — doubtless considered their proletarian credentials as valid as his own, and sufficient to keep the gallery in touch with the masses.[42]

The committee, however, was by no means as devoid of expertise as Carnegie had envisioned, even ignoring its two bona fide artists. Frew owned a small but choice collection of paintings; Caldwell owned a larger collection of paintings, as well as a collection of etchings, rich in Rembrandts and Whistlers, reputed to be one of the finest in the country. D. T. Watson was also a noted connoisseur: "He can instinctively tell a Corot, or a Daubigny; a Bonheur or Schreyer, a Turner or Reynolds," wrote a local reporter in 1899, "so adept has he become by reason of his many years of picture purchasing and art culture."[43] Frick had been collecting since the early 1870s, when he was described, in a report to a Pittsburgh banker to whom he had applied for a loan, as "a little too enthusiastic about pictures, but not enough to hurt."[44] In the 1890s Frick had not yet begun to acquire old masters; his tastes, like those of the other collectors on the committee, were solidly contemporary, Francophile, and middle-of-the-road. Caldwell occasionally bought a modern American painting, and Watson had several examples of the late eighteenth- and early nineteenth-century English school, but their collections were dominated by Barbizon and Barbizon-influenced European landscapes, with an admixture of such admired academics as Jean-Léon Gérôme, Rosa Bonheur, Adolphe Bouguereau, and Jean-Jacques Henner. The same French plein-airist taste inspired the work of J. R. Woodwell and A. B. Wall. Woodwell, whose studio Frick loved to visit on Sunday afternoons to chat about art, had studied painting at Barbizon for several years in the 1860s. Wall specialized in scenes of shepherds and their flocks that strongly recall the work of the popular Barbizon-inspired Dutch painter Anton Mauve (figures 2, 3).[45]

One position in the gallery's administration that absolutely required professional expertise was that of the director of fine arts. The director would manage its day-to-day business, treat personally with artists, critics, dealers, and collectors, and be in the eyes of the world the most visible exponent of the new enterprise. A nationally known artist or critic would have been the logical choice for this position—and there is little doubt Carnegie could have found one had he set his mind to it—but, true to the principle of local control, the man selected was a native Pittsburgher, John Wesley Beatty (figure 4). Born in 1851, Beatty was the son of a Pittsburgh grocer. Although he began his career in art as a silver engraver in the 1870s, his interests and aspirations extended far beyond the merely decorative, and he spent much of his spare time sketching and painting, often in the company of another hopeful young artist, John White Alexander. From 1876 to 1878 he studied at the Royal Bavarian Academy in Munich, which at the time was extremely popular with American art students. There he met William Merritt Chase, John Twachtman, Frank Duveneck, and several others who were to become major figures in American art, and he renewed his friendship with Alexander. After returning to Pittsburgh, he resumed his old craft of silver engraving, contributed occasional illustrations to both local and national magazines, and established a small but sound reputation for himself as a skillful painter and etcher of farm scenes that invariably included horses (figure 5). He taught at the Pittsburgh School of Design for Women and in 1887 founded a small art school with George Hetzel, the city's leading landscape painter (figure 6).[46]

Beatty's association with Carnegie began in 1890, when Carnegie asked the Pittsburgh Art Society to organize a loan exhibition for the opening of the Carnegie Free Library in Pittsburgh's sister city of Allegheny (now Pittsburgh's North Side). Most of the work fell to Beatty, who had served as the society's secretary and treasurer from its founding in 1886. By the fall of 1894, the trustees of the Carnegie Institute were discussing the possibility of a similar, but larger, exhibition to mark its opening the following year, and one of them, the wealthy collector Henry K. Porter, began a correspondence with Beatty on the subject. Beatty was enthusiastic: "Count on me for anything I can do," he wrote, "even to the helping to raise the money." Porter was quite willing to count on him; in fact, he took it for granted that Beatty, as secretary of the Art Society, would perform the same task he had undertaken in 1890. The trustees,

Porter told Beatty on 17 October 1894, were not prepared to make an immediate decision regarding the loan exhibition, but, he added, "I do not believe that you would be anticipating their action unduly in entering upon any preliminary correspondence that might be of value to be started at a very early day."[47] The exhibition, Carnegie's second effort at spreading the Gospel of Art, was a success, and Beatty was appointed to the directorship in March 1896. By all accounts, he was Carnegie's personal nominee for the position, and the board of trustees voted unanimously in his favor.[48]

It is clear from contemporary descriptions of Beatty that his character was such as to inspire trust and respect in Carnegie and his fellow businessmen. W. B. Morris, a writer for the *Pittsburgh Press*, described him as one of those rare men "in whom business instincts and artistic talent are combined":

> At a glance, one would never take Mr. Beatty for an artist. He somehow lacks the manner one has become accustomed to expect in a member of the craft. A satisfied businessman is the impression one gets. His eyes are quick and piercing, his bearing alert, and his conversation brisk and to the point. There's no idle questioning, no vaporings or long discussions, the sentences mean something, and there are no more of them than the subject demands. The man must have his moments of quiet, dreamy temperament, however, for his work is of a quiet, poetical nature; but at the galleries this temperament is set aside. It's business there; nothing more.

Another local journalist summed up Beatty's character more succinctly: "John Wesley Beatty never will call to mind a sunset on the seashore or nymphs sporting by the fountain's brink."[49]

As Morris pointed out, however, Beatty *was* an artist, and a very talented and knowledgeable one at that. He told Morris that he delighted in intimate discussions about art "with the men who do the things, and who speak of subtle meanings and qualities incomprehensible to the average observer."[50] Beatty was able to hold his own in such discussions, and his artistic discernment, coupled with an affable and diplomatic character, enabled him to win the confidence and esteem of artists. That he was not himself widely known as an artist was probably more of a help than a hindrance: an artist of wide reputation might have enhanced the prestige of the Institute in its early years, but he might also have brought with him professional loyalties and enmities that would have impaired the universality Carnegie hoped to achieve. From the beginning, Beatty was identified, not with any particular school of art, but with the Carnegie Art Gallery, and his tastes were both catholic and progressive.

Beatty's taste in art is relevant to an understanding of the character of the exhibitions held under his directorship. Although subject to the authority of the Fine Arts Committee, and after 1897 to the authority of three foreign advisory committees and an elected jury as well, his power and influence were enormous. It was Beatty who visited the major art centers of Europe and America to solicit the participation of artists, who compiled the lists of invitees and prospective jurors, who recruited members for the foreign committees. He could, at the very least, make it difficult for any artist he disliked to exhibit at Pittsburgh. The absence of Modernism in the later exhibitions organized by Beatty might easily give the impression that his influence was strongly conservative.

This impression is strengthened by reading *The Relation of Art to Nature*, Beatty's fullest exposition of his aesthetic creed. Published in 1922, the year he retired, this work sets forth his conviction "that the art of the painter and sculptor is imitative, not creative; that the great masterpieces of art which have withstood the test of time rest firmly upon the supreme expression of character and beauty as these qualities are revealed in man and nature; that it is the mission of art to reveal and make plain these rare and lovely qualities."[51] Beatty dismissed as a popular misconception the idea of the artist as an inspired creator of beauty: art is *never* superior to nature, and the artist's whole talent lies in his ability to perceive the beauties of nature and faithfully reproduce them. Both personal expression and technique receive short shrift in Beatty's philosophy, the former as a minor element that inevitably arises from the artist's choice of subject and presentation, the latter as merely the "obvious and superficial aspect" of a work of art. As one might expect, Beatty took a dim view of Modernism: in 1913, the year of the Armory Show, he brushed aside "this so-called school of art" as a "passing fad," unworthy of serious consideration; and in 1924, the year of his death, he charged the Modern movement with charlatanism, sensationalism, vulgarity, and incompetence.[52]

Beatty published no aesthetic manifestos in the 1890s, but it is apparent from scattered statements that then, as in the 1920s, truth and beauty were the foundations of his creed.[53] However, the same views that stamped him as a diehard conservative in the 1920s appeared progressive in the artistic climate of the 1890s — not, indeed, ahead of their time, but certainly up-to-the-minute. Modernism lay in the near but unforeseeable future: the Fauves would not burst upon the world until the Salon d'Automne of 1905; Picasso would not paint *Les Demoiselles d'Avignon* until 1907; the pioneering works of Van Gogh, Gauguin, and Cézanne were unknown to all but a small group of avant-gardists. For most art-conscious people in America and Europe, the cutting edge of modern painting was still Impressionism. Beatty's taste enthusiastically embraced not only Impressionism, which he praised for exemplifying in art the truthful, scientific spirit of the age, but also the controversial, unflinching Realism of Thomas Eakins, the Tonalism of Whistler, and the Symbolism of the Munich Secession and Giovanni Segantini. He was very much in agreement with the proponents of "art for art's sake," arguing that language was the proper medium for ideas and stories, and that art should represent "beauty for beauty's sake alone."[54] Compared to a genuine conservative of the period such as Kenyon Cox (who deplored all nineteenth-century Realism as the mindless, literal transcription of nature, and who advocated a wholesale retreat to Renaissance and Baroque traditions), Beatty appears to be almost radical in his views.[55]

To his businesslike demeanor and skills and his broad knowledge and appreciation of art, Beatty added another great virtue: he shared Carnegie's vision. "The influence of the collection of paintings which will doubtless be assembled in the Carnegie Gallery," he wrote in 1895, "will spread and widen until it permeates the entire community. . . . Our children and their posterity will receive a rich inheritance not easily dissipated, because it will become a part of the fibre of every man and woman, and therefore of the whole community. This makes the dedication of this art building an inspiration to our people."[56] He also believed that the gallery's influence would be more than local, that it would help make Pittsburgh an important art center: "The gallery will reach pretentious proportions, there is no doubt about that," he told reporters on New Year's Day 1896.

> Pittsburgh's location is conducive to the success of such a project. I think it has been amply demonstrated that the art galleries of the United States will not hug the seashore. There was a time when the biggest collections were in New York and Philadelphia, but that is past. See what was at Chicago during the world's fair. Chicago, being

so near the center of population, more people viewed those paintings than if they had been in New York. In like manner, Pittsburgh is the center of a large number of cities east of the Rocky Mountains.[57]

Having provided the new gallery with funds and long-range goals and having secured the services of men capable of running it, Carnegie was, for the most part, content to sit back and await results. Occasionally, he offered suggestions, and these suggestions had the force of commands. "Now what is the use in waiting for me to be there?" John Caldwell once asked Beatty, who had wanted to postpone a committee meeting that Caldwell was unable to attend. "What can we do but *approve* the suggestion or action of AC and his friends?"[58] Such occasions, however, were few. Similarly, the Fine Arts Committee rarely interfered with Beatty's management, though they had the authority to do so. As the years passed, Beatty would find himself in quiet, but growing, opposition to Carnegie and the committee on the fundamental question of whether the annual exhibitions were the best way, or even a good way, to build the permanent collection. But relations between the various parties remained harmonious. Their mission—to bring "sweetness and light" to Pittsburgh and the nation—was clear to them, and they were confident of achieving it.

# 2

# The First Exhibitions
# 1895–1896

## The Loan Exhibition of 1895

IN OCTOBER 1894 John Beatty told H. K. Porter that the loan exhibition proposed for the following year should "emphasize the national importance of the founding of this superb gallery, with its magnificent endowment, and I cannot but think that we ought to strike as high a key as possible. For the time being we will have the attention of the nation and the art world, and all future efforts on behalf of art in Pittsburg will be made with comparative ease if the opening exhibition make the right impression." This was an accurate prediction of the significance of the 1895 loan exhibition, which was, in effect, the first of the Carnegie art gallery's great annual exhibitions, even though the official first annual exhibition did not take place until November 1896. In Beatty's own opinion, the fact that the former was a historical loan exhibition and the latter a competitive exhibition featuring the recent work of living artists was an "essential difference" that permitted "no comparison to be instituted between them," but apart from the competitive aspect the differences were more of degree than of kind.[1]

The later exhibitions were always to some extent loan exhibitions: necessarily so, because many well-known artists (such as John Singer Sargent and Dwight W. Tryon) painted only commissioned works or sold their paintings almost immediately upon completion. The historical element also persisted: in 1896, for example, works were shown by George Inness (died 1894), Jean Meissonier (died 1891), Alphonse de Neuville (died 1885), Narcisse Diaz (died 1876), and Charles-François Daubigny (died 1878). Nor was the 1895 exhibition purely historical. Most of the 325 paintings were less than fifty years old, and at least two-thirds of them were by living artists. A fifth of them were very recent indeed, Beatty having invited a large number of American artists to send their work directly to the Art Society's hanging committee. "It is particularly desired," read the circular letter sent on 8 July 1895, "that all works be new, and in no case should any work be older in date of exhibition than the Spring exhibitions of 1895." Although it was nowhere mentioned in the circular, the hanging committee — composed of Beatty, A. B. Wall, Martin Leisser, and John Caldwell — acted as a jury of acceptance, thus strengthening the resemblance of the loan collection to the subsequent competitive exhibitions. Artists assumed as a matter of course that an invitation meant automatic acceptance of any work they chose to send. This was substantially true for the major painters whom Beatty personally invited, but not for the minor painters who wrote asking for circulars and whom Beatty was happy to oblige. Between seventy-five and eighty pictures, many the hopeful contributions of such nonentities as Linford R. Beck of Philadelphia and Elizabeth Washburn Brainerd of Boston, were rejected.[2]

Although Porter had urged Beatty to begin the preliminary correspondence in October 1894, there was little that Beatty could do toward organizing the loan exhibition until it had been formally approved. This did not happen until June 1895, which meant that he had less than five months to prepare everything for the opening on 5 November 1895. It is not surprising, considering the limited time at his disposal, that he spent the summer and early autumn of 1895 in a flurry of letter writing and hurried trips to New York, Boston, Philadelphia, and Chicago. Artists had to be encouraged to send; private collections had to be viewed and their owners persuaded to lend particular paintings.

Fortunately, Beatty could rely upon the good offices of some of the country's foremost artists and collectors. In Boston, I. M. Gaugengigl and Edmund Tarbell represented Pittsburgh's interests to their fellow artists. In New York, the noted muralist and figure painter Walter Shirlaw (whom Beatty had known at Munich) and the artist and critic William Coffin acted on Beatty's behalf. Also in New York, John White Alexander — who was motivated to help as much by friendship as by more abstract concerns — proved to be an invaluable ally. He had lived in Paris since 1891 and was well established in artistic circles there; his influence, especially with the large body of expatriate American artists, was considerable, and he was eager to use it to ensure the success of the exhibition. Alexander took upon himself the task of corresponding with the expatriates, personally and repeatedly urging them to contribute. He also made all the necessary arrangements with foreign shipping agents, received the works when they arrived in New York on 2 October 1895, and saw that they were sent to Pittsburgh together with the New York works. He even offered to come to Pittsburgh to help hang the exhibition—an offer that Beatty would have done well to accept, in view of the criticisms later leveled against the Art Society's hanging committee.[3]

In his dealings with artists, Beatty encountered problems in 1895 that would continue to beset subsequent exhibitions. Many artists, he found, were difficult to reach in July, August, and September, the very months in which most of the preparations for a fall exhibition had to be made. Some painters went to the country to work or to escape the discomfort of the pre–air conditioning urban summer; others traveled abroad. The result, as Coffin pointed out in September 1895 after Beatty sent him a long list of New York artists who had failed to respond, was that letters received in the summer were usually neglected until September. This same annoying difficulty was encountered among European artists and continued until 1908, when the obvious solution was adopted of holding the exhibitions in the spring.[4]

Another problem arose from the demand for new work. In part, this was a consequence of the fall exhibition date: unless he was a thoroughgoing pleinairist, an artist might have little more than sketches to show for his summer's work. Also, some artists were reluctant to send their newest works to major exhibitions, preferring to be represented by pictures of established merit or by ones that had remained in their studios for several years and undergone many revisions. Alexander understood this and took the liberty of not sending Beatty's circular to those who he knew would dislike its conditions. "The part about having new work would make Whistler tear his hair," he told Beatty. "He never exhibits a new work and a good picture unproven with age." Also, many artists, especially the most successful ones, rarely had new work available; it was sold on or before completion and immediately passed into private hands. Even when this was not the case, artists knew they stood a better chance of selling their work through a private dealer, who would use all his salesman's skills on their behalf, than through a large, noncommercial public exhibition. A case in point is that of the prominent figure painter George DeForest Brush. He declined Beatty's invitation initially on the grounds that he had been away all summer and had nothing ready to send. Pressed further, he admitted that he would have something finished soon but could not send it because he had to hold it for private sale. It was a pity, he said, that so much of his work could not be seen by the public, and he wished that "public-spirited people" would remedy the situation by buying his paintings and donating them to galleries. This problem was aggravated in the 1896 and 1897 exhibitions by a rule that allowed only previously unexhibited works owned by the artist to compete for honors.[5]

However, in the context of a loan exhibition, these were minor difficulties. If a particularly desired artist failed to contribute, his work could be supplied by private owners, and for the most part Beatty found the private owners cooperative. There were, of course, exceptions: Mrs. George Vanderbilt curtly informed Beatty through her secretary that she "never lends"; John D. Rockefeller deeply regretted that he was unable to oblige his friend Carnegie, citing his family's "unfortunate experiences" with lending pictures in the past.[6] But these exceptions were rare. As one might expect, Pittsburghers such as Frick, Caldwell, Porter, Colonel J. M. Schoonmaker, Charles Lockhart, and Charles Donnelly responded enthusiastically. Overall, 157 works, nearly half the paintings in the exhibition, were from local collections, which demonstrated to the nation (as their owners no doubt intended) that Pittsburgh businessmen, as discerning and generous patrons of culture, were second to none. In Philadelphia, B. W. Elkins agreed to lend and also introduced Beatty to other collectors of that city, including John G. Johnson, C. F. Haseltine, and Frank Thomson. In New York, Thomas B. Clarke, one of the foremost patrons of American art, contributed, as did his fellow New Yorkers William T. Evans, Samuel P. Avery Jr., and William S. Hawk. In Chicago, Charles L. Hutchinson, president of the Art Institute, looked after the interests of the 1895 loan exhibition. Hutchinson approved of what Carnegie was trying to do for Pittsburgh, so similar to his own efforts in Chicago, and exerted his considerable influence to promote it, securing valuable loans from Martin Ryerson, Cyrus McCormick, and James W. Ellsworth. Beatty expressed his gratitude to him with a characteristically graceful and diplomatic gesture: "You evidently discovered my weakness during your short stay in Chicago," wrote Hutchinson on 30 August 1895,

"I confess it is a love of flowers, and I was pleased to find the beautiful roses upon my desk this morning."[7]

The loan exhibition, together with the Institute as a whole, opened on Tuesday, 5 November 1895. As Beatty had predicted, the eyes of the art world were on Pittsburgh: a large contingent of East Coast art critics arrived in town on a special car at half past seven in the morning. In the afternoon, several hours before the exhibition opened, carriages conveyed them to the Institute's new Florentine Renaissance–inspired building (figure 7) on the edge of Schenley Park in the city's still mostly un-developed Oakland section.[8] This building, the visible emblem of Pittsburgh's cultural ambitions, was praised several years later by an English critic as "without doubt . . . one of the finest of the many noble buildings in the United States, and vastly superior to our 'pepperbox' National Gallery or the Rijksmuseum in Amsterdam . . . it holds its own well with the chaste beauty of the building of the Louvre." After entering the building, the critics walked down a long pilastered corridor, decorated with copies of the Parthenon frieze, and ascended a broad branching staircase to the suite of three galleries on the second floor (figure 8). "Whatever else there may be said about Mr. Carnegie's gift to the City of Pittsburg," wrote Arthur Hoeber of the *New York Times*, "and there is but little fault to find, the art galleries in the new library are splendid rooms, high as to ceiling, spacious and well-lighted" (figure 9).[9]

Whatever the merits of the gallery, however, the success of the ex-hibition depended primarily on the paintings hung in tiers upon the traditionally dull red walls. The visiting critics were uniformly pleased. Interviewed at their hotel, W. L. Fraser, art director of the *Century Maga-zine*, said that they were all "agreed that the collection, excepting only the exhibition held seven or eight years ago in the interest of the Bar-tholdi Statue of Liberty, is the finest collection of paintings ever gathered in America." John V. Sears, a Philadelphia critic, told the same reporter, "It is the first large collection I ever saw in my life without any bad pictures in it. I have not thus far found a single weak point in the line. While I do not so fully appreciate the impressionists as many others do, nevertheless you have here the strongest possible representation of that school."[10]

It was the strong representation of Impressionism and other contem-porary schools that most impressed the critics. In their reviews, they ignored the few pre–nineteenth-century works: the Constable and Gainsborough landscapes and the Rembrandt portrait, loaned by James W. Ellsworth of Chicago, which, specially draped and lighted, held the place of honor. Instead they focused on the most recent work. Hoeber, for example, admired the excellent selection of current American art: "All of the various schools are to be seen," he declared; and he singled out Winslow Homer, the recently deceased George Inness (especially well represented with eight canvases), and "the startling Impressionism" of Childe Hassam, Julian Alden Weir, John Twachtman, and other native followers of the movement. He also admired the predominantly French foreign works but observed that many of these were familiar from loan exhibitions held during the past twenty years. It was obviously the new paintings obtained directly from the artists that most caught his eye — so much so that he mistakenly declared that the collection consisted primarily of these works. Another major critic, Alfred Trumble of the *Collector,* was similarly drawn to the exhibition's most up-to-date aspects and particularly liked the grouping of the American Impressionists in a single small gallery "where their good qualities may be studied without the derogatory comparison stronger pictures would exercise upon their faults." He found the exhibition as a whole "of rare and indeed astonishing quality, considering the brief time permitted for its formation," and he commended Beatty's efforts.[11]

There was universal praise for Carnegie's cultural philanthropy. The *New York Journal* hailed Carnegie as an exemplar of

> the true communism under which the rich man regards himself as a trustee for society. In the inevitable redistribution of accumulated wealth the communistic principal finds its highest expression, and the process is doubly beneficial to mankind when it is performed intelligently, voluntarily, and in ways that secure the greatest good to the greatest number.

The national press wished Carnegie's experiment well and was confident of its success. For example, a reviewer for the *Philadelphia Record* wrote, "This worthy magnanimity is proper encouragement to the new-born art center of the western metropolis of the Commonwealth, which will do much in the future to regain for Pennsylvania that leadership in later American art that she possessed in the earlier art of the nation."[12] Frank Weitenkampf's glowing review in the *Art Interchange* centered on his conviction that Pittsburgh's new gallery "may and probably will give impetus to art in that city." He briefly sketched the existing state of the arts in Pittsburgh: there were a few professional artists, a few dealers, an Art Students League modeled after New York's, a school of design, and "despite the absorbing interest of its manufacturing interests, which overshadow everything else," some fine collectors. There was nothing remarkable in any of this, yet it was enough to provide fertile ground:

> Given these factors, may we not hope that the enthusiasm awakened by Mr. Carnegie's gift and its attendant results will bear fruit in the form of a gradual improvement in taste? . . . And especially may the spirit of grace and beauty enter into the daily life, into homes and public places, into the industries and objects of everyday use, so that the thousands engaged in soul-destroying toil may be warmed by the ray of refinement breaking through the murky fog of utilitarianism that overhangs the city.[13]

The local press quoted the out-of-town reviews frequently and at length and added its own words of praise. The most extensive local review appeared, without a byline, in the *Pittsburgh Dispatch* for 5 November 1895. Much of it consisted of lofty superlatives and a tedious enumeration of the works on exhibit, but it also included a lengthy and optimistic consideration of the new gallery's significance for Pittsburgh. As yet, the reviewer observed, no elaborate plan had been developed for the gallery, but the best plan would be to hold an annual exhibition of contemporary art, from which the most outstanding works would be purchased for the permanent collection. American artists would come to "look to the Pittsburg gallery as the quarters in which the highest stimulus will come for their efforts," and the slow growth of the permanent collection would serve to educate the public gradually: "In place of trying to grasp the various phases of art that bewilder at first sight of a large collection, the community can have the better experience of growing up with its gallery, and developing taste and capacity for capable criticism as the gallery grows." Much of this is similar to the ideas Carnegie would set forth in his dedication speech later that same day, but unlike Carnegie, the reviewer emphasized the commercial rather than the spiritual benefits that the gallery could be expected to produce. France, he pointed out, was famous for its beautiful manufactures because the French government had cultivated its citizens' taste for art through public collections and exhibitions;

the Carnegie art gallery could do the same for Pittsburgh. He predicted that under its influence art schools would be founded "upon a better scale than any we have had heretofore. From these in turn will come a struggle for best art results in the numerous industrial products of Pittsburg, from structural iron to glass, with a benefit at every stage for our business interests." In an essay written for the 1895 catalogue, Beatty also stressed the beneficial influence of art upon industry, but more practically he believed that the influence would flow, not from exhibitions of painting, but from a separate collection of industrial art.[14]

Amid the chorus of general praise there were a few sour notes. Both critics and artists felt that the hanging committee had not done its work particularly well. Some of the adverse criticism was purely aesthetic — brightly colored paintings had been placed next to somber ones, for example, making the former appear lurid and the latter dull — but the most serious complaint was that the work of many prominent painters had been "skied," that is, hung in the uppermost row of pictures, nearest the ceiling, instead of "on the line" at eye level. Arthur Hoeber observed:

> With American painters, the committee has had, it is quite evident, a struggle. The hanging has been a happy-go-lucky affair, with astonishing results. For example, a dainty, exquisite little portrait by Thomas W. Dewing, is hung so high as to be absolutely lost, and yet it may be doubted if there is anything here better in its way than this. Per contra, a wretched, colorless, and thoroughly amateurish effort, "A Gray Evening," by quite an unknown, is flaunted on the line. And these are only instances. A dozen good men are skied, with pictures that deserved well of the committee.[15]

Nineteenth-century artists were extremely sensitive to where their work appeared in the rows of paintings in which exhibitions of that time were customarily hung, and the established leaders of the profession regarded the choice positions on the line as their due. To give one of these positions to "quite an unknown" (who in this instance was Joseph Woodwell, a member of the hanging committee) while denying it to such a well-known painter as Dewing was an insult, whether intended or not, and one that John White Alexander, had he assisted the committee, would have avoided instinctively. The fault obviously lay in the committee's inexperience, but several artists proved unforgiving. Dewing refused to participate in the following year's exhibition, "in view of the fact that last year, when I sent one of my most important and latest works in response to your invitation, the picture was placed so high upon the wall that it was almost invisible." The eminent landscape painter Henry W. Ranger initially declined to send for the same reason. He had to live from the sale of six paintings a year, he explained, and he could not afford to have any of them poorly hung. He added that there had been "practically no sales in Pittsburgh."[16]

Indeed, there were no sales at all from the 1895 loan exhibition. This would not have posed a problem had the exhibition consisted solely of works lent by collectors, but many American artists had sent unpurchased works in the hope of selling them. Moreover, the language of the invitation had been calculated to raise their hopes: "This event is of the utmost importance to American art, as Mr. Carnegie not only makes a gift of the building, which has already cost between Eight and Nine Hundred Thousand Dollars; but he also promises to endow the gallery with One Million Dollars, the purpose being to found a representative collection of Art works." It was easy to assume from this that works for the permanent collection would be bought from the loan exhibition. Actually, the endowment had not yet been made, and no funds were available for this purpose. Ranger was not the only artist to express dissatisfaction. According to Alexander, the expatriate community was thoroughly incensed. In April 1896 he wrote from Paris that there was "the divel to pay over here because Pittsburgh did not buy all the pictures in the last Exhibition, and the men swear they will never send again — but — we shall see." Although Alexander was inclined to treat the matter lightly, his message to Beatty was clear: if future exhibitions at Pittsburgh did not offer a prospect of sales, artists would not participate.[17]

The 1895 loan exhibition also marked the beginning of the Institute's generally bad relations with local artists. An established member of the Pittsburgh artistic community, H. S. Stevenson, had received an invitation and had painted three landscapes expressly for the exhibition, only to discover on opening day that they had been rejected. Furious, he demanded an explanation from William Nimick Frew, who replied that he had nothing to do with the committee's actions and asked Stevenson to keep quiet about the matter until the dedication ceremonies had concluded and Carnegie had left town. Stevenson then called on Joseph Woodwell and hotly accused him of being partner to a conspiracy to drive him out of the city. The next day, following Carnegie's departure, Stevenson and his friends took their complaints to the press. Stevenson was a talented artist, they said, who regularly exhibited at the National Academy of Design. The landscapes in question had been praised as "masterpieces" by "reliable" (but unidentified) "art critics," and their rejection could be explained only by the personal enmity of a clique led by Beatty and Woodwell and apparently composed of most or all of the members of the hanging committee. The committee, they pointed out, had served its own interests very well indeed: its members had exhibited their own work, and even the work of Woodwell's daughter Johanna, who was not strictly speaking a professional.[18]

An interview with Woodwell published in the *Pittsburgh Press* at first appeared to give color to these assertions. He was quoted as saying that Stevenson was a first-class artist, that the rejected landscapes were very good, and that there was "a little unfriendly feeling between Mr. Stevenson and Mr. Beatty." However, Woodwell subsequently denied having made several of the statements attributed to him in the *Pittsburgh Press:* he had *not* said that there were hard feelings between Stevenson and Beatty, nor that Stevenson was a first-class artist whose rejected paintings were equal to others that had been accepted. Although he refrained from saying flat out that, in his view, Stevenson's work was inferior stuff, the implication was obvious, and when it was pointed out that Stevenson had shown at the National Academy, he blandly observed: "Our standard is higher than that of the National Academy." Woodwell also denied the charges of conspiracy and favoritism, noting that two of his own works had been rejected and that he had abstained from voting on his daughter's entry. Beatty refused to become involved in the controversy. When reporters attempted to speak to him at his Wilkinsburg home, they were told politely but firmly that Mr. Beatty, exhausted from his recent labors, had gone to bed.[19] Several months later he offered to propose Stevenson for membership on the Fine Arts Committee — a conciliatory gesture that suggests neither Beatty nor the committee harbored any deep enmity — but Stevenson coldly declined the offer.[20]

On the whole, the reaction of both critics and artists to the exhibition was encouraging. The public whom the collection was intended to enlighten also responded favorably. Attendance was estimated at 500,000 (an exceptional figure, considering that Pittsburgh's population in 1900 was only 321,616), and a reporter who visited the exhibition on the last Sunday overheard many expressions of regret that it could not be extended beyond its 4 December closing date.[21] Carnegie and his trustees moved quickly to follow up their initial success. On 30 December 1895, the gallery was formally endowed with one million dollars' worth of 5 percent bonds, securing it a yearly income of $50,000; on 15 March 1896, the Department of Fine Arts was created, with Beatty as its director; and on 15 April 1896, the trustees voted to hold another exhibition.

## The First Annual Exhibition, 1896

On 17 April 1896, William Nimick Frew received the following communication from Andrew Carnegie:

> Dear Sir: The City of Pittsburg has been so generous this year in providing for the library that Mrs. Carnegie and I feel that we should like to do something to testify our appreciation. Therefore, in addition to the $50,000 per year we send you the sum of $8,000 to be used by the trustees for paying $5,000 for the best picture and $3,000 for the second (the pictures to be adjudged worthy of the prizes), and to be placed in the Chronological Collection, under the provisions of Article III, section 5 of your bylaws. We look forward to the first exhibition with deepest interest, and not without hope that it will still further enhance the surprising record of the Carnegie art galleries.[22]

Three days later, Frew announced that the first annual exhibition, featuring the finest recent work of American and European artists, would open on Tuesday, 3 November 1896. The Fine Arts Committee would award purchase prizes of $5,000 and $3,000 to the two best works painted by American artists in 1896 and first exhibited at the Carnegie art gallery. In addition, the gallery planned to make all its purchases for the year from the exhibition, a course of action intended to benefit foreign as well as domestic painters.[23] The opening date was later changed to 5 November to avoid conflicting with the presidential election scheduled for 3 November, and additional incentives were offered in the form of first-, second-, and third-class medals to be awarded irrespective of nationality. In making the announcement, Frew took the opportunity to describe in glowing terms the blessings that the new competitive exhibition would bestow upon the city and the nation. Pittsburgh would become the American Paris, "the radiating center of an artistic atmosphere which will permeate the country." On a more mundane level, the influx of visitors would benefit the city's hotels, restaurants, and other businesses and would advertise to the world Pittsburgh's fine points, including "opportunities for investment of capital."[24]

The announcements — both of the million-dollar endowment and of the exhibition — were well covered by the national press and unleashed a flood of inquiries from art dealers, collectors, and artists. The dealers and collectors, ranging from the salesman for the National Academy of Design to a seventy-two-year-old California evangelist who owned a number of landscapes by obscure painters, hoped that an art gallery needing to build a permanent collection would prove a ready market.[25] The artists, including both established professionals and hopeful amateurs, were primarily interested in the upcoming exhibition. Artists are always interested in opportunities to sell their work, of course, but in 1896 they were especially interested. As the *New York Times* observed in an article publicizing the exhibition, America was just beginning to recover from the economic slump following the panic of 1893, and recent sales of American art had been "veritable slaughters." A new source of revenue was welcome, and for the very best artists, the purchase prizes were extraordinarily attractive. According to the *New York Times*, equally generous prizes had been offered elsewhere — for example, the $5,000 Elkins prize for the best American painting at the Pennsylvania Academy — but by private persons who reserved the right to place the pictures in their private collections. Winners of the Carnegie prizes, on the other hand, were assured of public display in the only "Chronological Collection" in the country.[26]

Beginning in late May, circulars were sent to the leading artists of America and Europe, inviting them to send their most recent work to Pittsburgh at the expense of the Carnegie Institute. Circulars and entry forms were also sent to any artist, no matter how obscure, who asked for them — though in this case the artist himself had to pay for shipment. Beatty was not content to organize the exhibition by post, however. On 16 April 1896, the day following the trustees' approval of the plan for a fall exhibition, he began a tour of the major eastern cities in order to meet with artists there and personally solicit their contributions. From New York, where his efforts met with "abundant success," he left for Europe to secure the cooperation of the foreign and expatriate American painters. He spent two months abroad, and his itinerary included extended stays in London, Paris, and Munich.[27]

Beatty was a stranger to European art circles, but the cooperation of several friendly American expatriates made his task easier. Frank D. Millet, a leading muralist and historical genre painter who divided his time between England and America, helped smooth his path in London by sending a letter of introduction to John Singer Sargent. "I am certain J.S.S. will make it pleasant for you," he assured Beatty. Beatty's friend Thomas Shields Clarke, a former Pittsburgh artist pursuing a successful career in New York, provided an introduction to another prominent expatriate in England, Edwin Austin Abbey, whose carefully researched drawings and paintings of Shakespearean subjects were immensely popular on both sides of the Atlantic and who had just been elected an associate member of the Royal Academy. Abbey at once took a deep interest in the Pittsburgh exhibition, although he frankly (and as events would prove, rightly) disapproved of several of its features. The Fine Arts Committee, he objected, lacked sufficient prestige to act as a jury of award: "I do not see," he wrote to Beatty on 31 May, "how an artist of reputation could possibly submit his work for 'prizes' to be awarded by a committee not one of whom is an artist of whose ability and position he has any knowledge." He also thought that to offer medals unaccompanied by cash prizes was a mistake: "Nobody wants medals in these days, unless they are very rare things indeed, and awarded by a particularly distinguished body of one's own profession." A few days later, he expressed similar views less diplomatically to his brother:

> I had a man from Pittsburgh, the manager of the Carnegie Gallery, a day or two ago. They seem to be going to award medals there, although I fail to see the real value of a medal awarded to a painter by half a dozen ironfounders. They call buying an artist's picture "awarding" him a prize. I have just awarded a prize of five shillings to a blacksmith who did a little job for me.

Despite his reservations, Abbey offered Beatty his assistance and a warm invitation to visit his home in Gloucestershire. Abbey, Millet, and Sargent would later serve on the exhibition's London advisory committee.[28]

In Paris, the recognized art capital of the world, Beatty had an excellent agent and advisor in the person of John White Alexander, who was thoroughly at home in Paris. He knew many of the artists intimately, and his own reputation meant that he could deal with the greatest of them as an equal. In July, he wrote casually, for example, of having "raked over"

Giovanni Boldini, Europe's most fashionable portrait painter, in order to secure his promise to send something good to Pittsburgh. During the summer of 1896, Alexander was busy raking over and, as he put it, "shaking up" his fellow artists on Beatty's behalf. He also secured loans of particularly desirable canvases from private dealers, worked closely with the shipping agents, and attended to a host of prosaic details. "But I want you to understand," he told Beatty on 3 September, "that anything of this kind that I do is for you personally, so nothing need be said to the board." To his other virtues, Alexander added a hard-headed practical sense that led him to disregard his own preferences, which favored elegant idealization over realism, for the good of the exhibition. On one occasion, he informed Beatty that he had persuaded the dealer Georges Petit to lend a historical costume piece by Ferdinand Roybet. Although he described it on 14 September as being "of a style that I sincerely hate," he felt that Roybet was too popular to be omitted: "The Roybet, I am afraid, will be one of the successes of your show and I may be the means of fastening on your gallery a vile piece of realism, but I have done what seems best in spite of my artistic judgment."[29]

Alexander performed another valuable service by candidly telling Beatty what the artists were saying privately about the Pittsburgh exhibition. In 1896, the talk of the studios was not uniformly encouraging. There was a reluctance to compete on the part of many expatriates, Alexander observed. They refused to send, or they sent only works that were ineligible for prizes. This, apparently, had nothing to do with the anger that he had mentioned in April over the lack of sales from the loan exhibition. He never alluded to it in his later correspondence, and the promise of prizes and purchases must have done much to dispel it. Instead, he noted "a firmly rooted conviction over here that no American who lives abroad will ever get the prize," based on a widespread belief that no expatriate had received an American money prize before. This conviction was forcibly expressed by George Hitchcock, an internationally famed painter of Dutch genre subjects. Although willing to contribute to the exhibition "in order that I may do my best for art in my native land," he felt that he was thereby placing himself in a false position. "Of course I hope the jury may see their way to giving me one of the many medals," he wrote to Beatty, "but since it will be composed of my own countrymen and since I have the misfortune to dwell on the wrong side of the ocean, I tell you frankly that I do not expect either a medal or fair play; I speak from many sad experiences." Hitchcock failed to win a prize, but his close associate, Gari Melchers, did—a move that might have placated the expatriate community, as no doubt it was intended to do, had difficulties not arisen over the eligibility of Melchers's entry.[30]

According to Alexander, there was also a general suspicion that, in order to save money, the Fine Arts Committee would not award a purchase prize to a painting whose stated price was less than the prize itself. Why should the committee pay $5,000 or $3,000 for a work when, by refusing it a prize, it might be had for $800 or $1,000? As only the most celebrated painters could command prices equal to the prizes, it was thought that artists of lesser renown would compete in vain. Alexander tried to dispel this idea, but many artists were disposed to await the results of the first exhibition. In view of this suspicion, which was widely held on both sides of the Atlantic, it is curious that Beatty did not publicly deny it until 29 November, several weeks after the exhibition had opened and only a few days before the prizewinners were announced. He may have been unable to do so earlier—the committee had actually considered adopting the suspected policy, and the decision against it probably was not made until a late date.[31]

Alexander's reports of discontent among the expatriates were trustworthy and deserved to be taken seriously. The same cannot be said of the highly publicized report of a more virulent discontent among New York artists. This appeared in the *New York Journal* for Monday, 2 November 1896, and was immediately reprinted in the *Pittsburgh Dispatch* and the *Pittsburgh Leader*. The unidentified writer claimed that many New York artists—also unidentified—were furious with the management of the Carnegie art galleries because it had failed to appoint a special New York jury and refused to cover the costs of shipping and insurance for any but a few foreign artists and "American favorites." Moreover, the Pittsburgh committee did not include a single well-known artist and had already revealed its incompetence in the hanging of the 1895 loan exhibition. The writer predicted that Carnegie, "who is now posing as a patron of painting and sculpture," would be disappointed by the turnout of New Yorkers: many had been prepared to send their work but were now asking to have their names withdrawn from the catalogue. Carnegie would have done better to build his gallery in New York, "where his encouragement of American art would have met with the appreciation it deserves." Beatty and the Fine Arts Committee flatly denied that there was any truth to this report. Beatty dismissed it as a "sensational story" concocted by "someone who evidently has an axe to grind"; John Caldwell observed that there was a full representation of New York artists on the gallery's walls, and that none had withdrawn their pictures. Only artists of recognized merit, he said, had been invited to exhibit and were entitled to send at the Institute's expense; the complaints were obviously inspired by producers of "truck," whose contributions had not been solicited.[32]

The evidence supports Beatty and Caldwell. Although the Department of Fine Arts' correspondence files contain a good many angry letters, there are none from New York artists demanding to have their names dropped from the 1896 catalogue. As Caldwell pointed out, New York was very well represented in the exhibition. Forty-two of its artists participated, as opposed to only seven from Boston and five from Philadelphia, and this number included most of the first rank, including William M. Chase, John La Farge, John Twachtman, Kenyon Cox, D. W. Tryon, H. W. Ranger, J. Alden Weir, Childe Hassam, Robert Blum, Walter Shirlaw, and others. Having been invited to send their work at the Institute's expense, they had nothing to complain about on the grounds cited by the *New York Journal*.

This is not to say that there were no complaints at all, however. The New York shipping agents, W. S. Budworth and Son, told Beatty in mid-October that they were being hounded by several artists whose names were not on the invitation list, but who insisted that they had been invited and were entitled to have their paintings shipped free of charge. One of these, John Twachtman, had been accidentally omitted from the list, and Beatty quickly wired Budworth to correct the oversight. The others—Nathan N. Bickford, George B. Waldo, Jenny Taylor, Anthony Berger, William Walton, C. Warren Eaton, and Harry Roseland—were told that, as uninvited artists, they were welcome to submit their work to the jury at their own expense. Berger, Bickford, and Walton did so; Berger and Bickford were accepted. Roseland submitted only once, in 1905, and both his entries were rejected. Only Eaton, whom Budworth recommended to Beatty as "one of our best and most artistic landscape painters" was subsequently listed, in 1897, and became a regular contributor to the exhibitions. With the exception of Twachtman, each of the artists mentioned by Budworth had an ax to grind on 2 November 1896, and it is likely that one of them was responsible for the article in the *New York Journal*. In Paris, Alexander was similarly plagued by minor artists who claimed to have been invited but who were unable to show him their invitations. "I am becoming a master of bouncing," he told Beatty.[33]

Difficulties notwithstanding, by 1 November 1896, Beatty had assembled a collection he could be proud of. Some artists, he confessed, had sent "comparatively mediocre" works, a circumstance he attributed to the limited time they had been given to prepare, but he declared that on the whole the Pittsburgh exhibition would "equal, if not surpass, the exhibitions of the Paris Salon and those of London."[34] He ensured a high standard by eking out the artists' contributions with loans, though in doing so he compromised the exhibition's avowed purpose. According to a note in the catalogue, these loans were needed to represent several important artists who, owing to time constraints, had been unable to send. It is obvious, however, that deceased artists like Inness, Meissonier, Daubigny, and Diaz (who had been dead for twenty years) could not have contributed had they been given all the time in the world to prepare. Other loans, although representative of living artists, had been painted years earlier, such as Dagnan-Bouveret's *Madonna of the Rose*, lent by Thomas Shields Clarke, which was eleven years old in 1896. As a critic for the *Art Interchange* was quick to point out, these works were clearly included "to add interest . . . though why, in an exhibition that was to be mainly representative of the art of 1896, these should have been admitted, is not quite clear."[35]

Whereas most of the loans in the 1895 exhibition had come from private owners (almost half of them Pittsburghers), the majority of the lenders in 1896 were dealers. Pittsburgh's collectors had already displayed their finest jewels in two loan exhibitions, and borrowing from the major dealers of Europe and America allowed the local audience to see pictures they had never seen before. Durand-Ruel supplied Monet's *Ravine of the Creuse, Ice Floes at Vethouil, Red Poppies,* and *Palms of Bordighera;* Degas's *Repetition of the Dance;* Puvis de Chavannes's *Charity* and *Shepherd's Song;* and a *Bather* by the leading Swedish painter Anders Zorn. Arthur Tooth and Son of London sent Meissonier's *1806* and Dagnan-Bouveret's *Brittany Peasant.* George Petit of Paris provided works by Roybet and Henner. Boussod Valadon and Company, also of Paris, loaned Burne-Jones's *The Merciful Knight* and Alphonse de Neuville's *The Ambuscade.* Among the New York dealers, M. Knoedler contributed a Roman genre piece by Lawrence Alma-Tadema; H. Wunderlich loaned Whistler's *Arrangement in Black: Portrait of Señor Pablo de Sarasate;* and L. Crist Delmonico loaned

Fantin-Latour's *The Toilet*, which had appeared in that year's Salon de Champs-Elysées. Henry Clay Frick was the most generous of the private collectors, loaning Gérôme's *Sculpturae Vitam Insuflat Pictura*, George Inness's *Spirit of the Night*, George Frederick Watts's *Little Red Riding Hood*, Frank Millet's *How the Gossip Grew*, and works of Diaz, Daubigny, and Henner. Other important loans came from Alexander Reid of Glasgow, industrialist Charles Lang Freer of Detroit, Samuel P. Avery of New York, and John Johnson of Philadelphia.[36]

Sixty-three paintings, a fifth of the total collection, had appeared at the St. Louis Exposition from early September to mid-October. An exhibition of art had been part of St. Louis's annual Interstate Fair since 1884, but in 1895, to the astonishment of eastern reviewers, this became "the most advanced art exhibition of the year in the country," due to the efforts of its director, Charles M. Kurtz, a New York art critic. Kurtz's background included the directorship of the art department of the Southern Exposition at Louisville, Kentucky, and the position of assistant chief in the World's Columbian Exposition's fine arts department, and he had personally selected a massive collection of more than six hundred American and European paintings notable for including recent works of the leading French Impressionists and Munich Secessionists and for introducing the American public to the poetic naturalism of the Glasgow School. The St. Louis exhibition was quickly acclaimed by critics and artists, particularly by artists because more works were sold there than at any other American exhibition: over 12 percent of the pictures up for sale were sold in 1895; over 10 percent in 1896.[37]

John White Alexander had advised Beatty in April to work in concert with Kurtz, so that foreign and expatriate artists might conveniently send to both exhibitions.[38] Kurtz was agreeable to the plan, which, apart from its convenience for the artists, allowed Pittsburgh and St. Louis to share shipping expenses and removed the necessity of having to compete for the same pictures. For Pittsburgh, there was the added advantage of an alliance with an established, successful exhibition. Artists unwilling to send to the as yet unproved Carnegie annual had no qualms about sending to St. Louis, and it was a fairly simple matter to persuade them to have their works sent on to Pittsburgh. The Munich painters, for example, had been unresponsive to Beatty's requests to send works directly to Pittsburgh; according to the local shipping agent, they were resolved to await the results of the first exhibition.[39] Of the twenty-four German paintings shown at Pittsburgh in 1896, all but one—a portrait by Franz von Lenbach loaned by its owner—first appeared at St. Louis. Similarly, the Glasgow School would have been wholly unrepresented had it not been for the thirty-seven canvases sent on from St. Louis. Six of these had become loans by the time they reached Pittsburgh, having been bought by the St. Louis Museum of Fine Arts, Kurtz, and others.[40]

However, in his passion to secure a fully representative collection, Beatty accepted more works than the gallery could hold without overcrowding. In total, 312 paintings were catalogued, in contrast to an average of 260 paintings in each of the six subsequent annuals, which were held in the same space. The 1896 figure was not exceeded until 1904 when, due to construction work to expand the Institute, 324 works were hung in temporary galleries. Although critics praised the 1896 hanging—there were only two rows of paintings, and no upper row over large works (figure 10)—this "Carnegie generosity in giving them room," as one reviewer called it, was achieved only by the unsatisfactory expedient of holding many pictures in reserve and substituting them for others later in the exhibition.[41] This made the published catalogue a theoretical rather than a practical document, for all the works listed could never have been viewed at the same time. Although the number withheld was estimated to be as low as eighteen or twenty, the Carnegie art gallery's own list of acceptances and rejections reveals that the surprisingly high figure of ninety-two, cited in an unfriendly review in the *Philadelphia Item*, was correct. Sixty-eight of these were entered under the category "Paintings Accepted and Not Hung" and twenty-four under "Pictures Rejected—Held Subject to Further Action by the Committee." Despite their "rejected" status, most of these latter works were included in the catalogue and hung.[42]

Further complicating this untidy situation, Beatty had, in May, agreed to forward twenty-six paintings to the winter exhibition of the Pennsylvania Academy of Fine Arts, scheduled to open on 23 December 1896. This arrangement offered many of the same advantages as the one with St. Louis: convenience for the artist, shared shipping expenses, and an alliance with an established exhibition, in this case one of America's oldest and most distinguished. Had the Fine Arts Committee adhered to its original intention of closing the exhibition on 12 December 1896, no problems would have arisen. However, shortly before the opening, the committee decided to change the closing date to 1 January 1897, which meant that the paintings destined for Philadelphia could not stay the full term. Despite Beatty's entreaties, director of the Pennsylvania Academy Harrison Morris remained adamant—the plans had been made months earlier, the artists clearly intended to appear at both exhibitions, and the pictures had to be sent to Philadelphia on 12 December as agreed. The problem might have been minimized had the works in question been hung in the first week of November and then replaced by withheld works in mid-December, but this was not consistently done. The correspondence with Morris reveals that some of these paintings had not yet been hung on 21 November and so could not have appeared in the exhibition for more than three of its eight weeks.[43]

The changeable nature of the hanging did not endear Pittsburgh to the artists. The Fine Arts Committee had not publicized its intention to withhold paintings; consequently many artists wondered what had become of works that they believed had been accepted, and they sent Beatty anxious inquiries. When the facts became known, it was widely assumed that the pictures first hung constituted a "preferred exhibition," and that those withheld had been adjudged inferior.[44] The quality of the latter supports the committee's claim that some of the choicest entries had been reserved to add freshness to the exhibition later, but many artists remained skeptical and took offense at the apparent slight. The most detailed statement of their objections came from Frederick Freer, a nationally known Chicago-based painter who, on learning that his entry was in storage, demanded that it be sent at once to the Boston Art Club. "When an artist sends one of his works to an exhibition," he told Beatty, "he expects it to stay through the full term. . . . I do not relish having my picture hidden away to be used at a supplementary hanging." This practice, he pointed out, might lead prospective buyers to believe that an unhung work had been rejected, and, as the major reviews were generally published in the early days of an exhibition, it denied artists a chance to receive critical attention.[45]

The press reaction varied. J. N. Fort, a critic for the *Philadelphia Item*, devoted an entire article to the withheld paintings. "It will be quite a surprise to such men as E. L. Weeks, Abbott Thayer, Thomas Eakins, John La Farge, Elihu Vedder, Benjamin-Constant, etc. to find that they are not represented in the exhibition," he wrote. "It is a shame and an outrage to solicit their compositions and then treat them in this fashion." During a visit to Pittsburgh he had spoken to Beatty about the problem and, to no avail, had suggested putting up temporary screens in the galleries to expand the available space. The *Art Interchange*'s "Observer" felt that a more judicious arrangement would have easily allowed all the pictures to be shown and predicted that the "inexperience and incapacity" of the gallery's management would impair the success of future exhibitions: "Being treated in this manner once, many artists will refuse to send their work to Pittsburgh a second time."[46]

This prediction turned out to be unduly bleak. However, several artists did indeed hesitate to send in 1897 until they had received assurances that their work, if accepted, would be hung for the full period. Kenyon Cox refused to have anything to do with the exhibition, either as a prospective juror or as a contributor: "[Y]ou can hardly be surprised to hear that the conduct of the authorities in inviting pictures and then not exhibiting them, and in failing to notify the artists of their action until the matter had become public through the press, has had the effect of inclining some of us to have no further dealings with the Carnegie Art Galleries."[47]

Despite his condemnation of the hanging, Fort conceded that the overall quality of the exhibition was high, and in this the majority of critics agreed with him. Few reviews were published outside Pittsburgh (fewer, certainly, than the exhibition's self-purported significance would have warranted), but most of them were favorable. The *New York Times* praised the exhibition as "most excellent," having "such a number of contributions by famous artists as to take on the aspect of a first-class loan exhibit . . . the richness of which is bewildering." The reviewer for *Harper's Weekly* declared the Pittsburgh exhibition to be "a fine showing," distinguished by its highly progressive character. Its representation of the most progressive American artists — such as Winslow Homer, Cecilia Beaux, Arthur Davies, John White Alexander, William Chase, and Gari Melchers — was in his opinion especially thorough. Among the foreigners, he felt that too many concessions had been made to popular conservative painters like Meissonier (whose *1806*, he predicted, would be "the rallying point for the crowd"), but he commended the inclusion of the Glasgow School and cited as a novelty the representative gathering of modern English pictures. The *Philadelphia Inquirer* described the exhibition as "a little Salon with all — or nearly all — of the trash left out." The *Chicago Evening Post* praised the exhibition for its "modernity and its universality" and saw in it the beginning of "an epoch in American Art."

The only unfavorable out-of-town review beside Fort's appeared in the *Art Interchange*. Although he admired the hanging and the well-lighted galleries, the reviewer wrote that the pictures "created something of a disappointment in the minds of those who had expected to see a notable display of the works of American painters whom it was especially intended to benefit. Mr. Carnegie's notable intentions have miscarried through the inexperience and incapacity of those entrusted with their carrying out."[48]

Local reviewers were uncritical for the most part. They took the excellence of the exhibition for granted and concerned themselves with pointing out to their readers the most important pictures, the criterion for importance being the fame of the artist rather than the quality of the work as determined by the reviewer's critical judgment. Although this was hardly criticism of the highest order, it at least served an educational purpose, telling uninformed Pittsburghers who the leading contemporary painters were. Because the French school was the most famous, the French entries received the lion's share of attention. It was agreed that Meissonier's *1806* was "the masterpiece of the collection," followed closely by Dagnan-Bouveret's *Madonna of the Rose* (figure 11), which was praised as "exquisitely beautiful" and "so vivid . . . that other pictures near it are unnoticed except by the artist who examines minutely into everything." Most of the Frenchmen singled out were well established and conservative (Gérôme, Henner, Tony Robert-Fleury, Jean-Paul Laurens, and the like) but several well-known Impressionist painters (Monet, Raffaëlli, and "the remarkable Degas") were also cited. Boldini's *Woman in Black* was considered doubly alluring, for it was not only the work of a famous artist but also a famous painting in its own right, "so often reproduced," remarked the reviewer for the *Pittsburgh Leader*, "that a description of it would be unnecessary." The reviewers' attitude is seen most clearly in their treatment of Aime Morot's dramatic bullfighting scene, *Toro Colante*. For them, its intrinsic merits were less significant than the fact that Morot was the son-in-law of the celebrated Gérôme, who had pronounced it to be the artist's best work.

The most frequently mentioned English works were Alma-Tadema's *Tibullus in Delos*, Burne-Jones's *The Merciful Knight*, William Quiller Orchardson's *Master Baby*, and Luke Fildes's sketch for *The Widower*. Alma-Tadema and Orchardson were both pillars of the Royal Academy, while Burne-Jones was a famed eccentric, few of whose original works had ever been seen in America (and none at all in Pittsburgh). Although Fildes's twenty-year-old oil sketch could hardly have been one of the more impressive works in the exhibition, he was probably better known to the average Pittsburgher than any other English artist. He had scored a phenomenal popular success at the Royal Academy in 1891 with *The Doctor*, a sentimental genre scene of a country doctor keeping vigil over a poor fisherman's sick child, and the photogravure of this work had rapidly become a fixture of British and American drawing rooms. Over a million copies were sold in the United States alone during its heyday.

The much talked about Glasgow School was recommended to the reader's attention, especially *Lady in Brown* (figure 12) by its most famous exponent, John Lavery. Among the Americans, Whistler, Homer, Alexander, and Beaux were the names most frequently mentioned. Whistler, like Burne-Jones, was touted as a celebrated eccentric genius; his portrait of the Spanish composer and violin virtuoso Pablo de Sarasate (figure 13) was already a famous picture, well known through engravings. Winslow Homer had recently come to the forefront of American art, and the reviewers predicted (accurately, as it turned out) that his entry, *The Wreck* (figure 14), would win a prize. Cecilia Beaux, too, had recently become a name to conjure with, and one of her entries, *The Dreamer* (figure 15), had drawn rave reviews at the previous spring's Salon de Champs-Elysées. Interest in John White Alexander was due as much to his Pittsburgh origins as to his standing as an artist: he was the hometown boy who had risen to international fame, and the exhibition afforded a rare opportunity to view his work.[49]

An exception to the foregoing type of review was a somewhat irritable-sounding article by W. G. Kaufmann, an occasional critic for the *Pittsburgh Dispatch*. Kaufmann had strong reservations about the quality of the exhibition. Like the critic for the *Art Interchange*, he found the representation of American art both incomplete and disappointing. Among the major artists whose works were absent, he cited Edwin H. Blashfield, Thomas Dewing, Frederick Bridgman, Will H. Low, R. Swain Gifford, Frederic Remington, Frederick Freer, and J. Carroll Beckwith. Perhaps, he suggested, these and other artists had been unaware of the exhibition or had not had enough time to prepare for it. In his comments on the American paintings exhibited, Kaufmann revealed an intense dislike for the same progressive tendencies that *Harper's Weekly* had praised. He expected artists to tell stories, to depict human life (Henry Mosler, a narrative genre painter of solid but scarcely exalted reputation, was his favorite among the Americans), and he had little more than contempt for art that elicited a purely aesthetic response. He dismissed John White Alexander's four entries as mere "studies of effect," and Edmund Tarbell's as mere "arrangements." Robert Reid's impressionistic *Moonrise* was, in his opinion, an unfinished work "chiefly noteworthy for its impertinence," and John Twachtman's *Snow Storm* was an abomination, impossible to take seriously. "Why," he asked, "is this a picture of a snowstorm any more than it may be a picture partially covered up with a coat of whitewash?" Even Homer's *The Wreck* failed to satisfy him. The composition was splendid, he granted, but was spoiled by "an atmospheric effect that is rather weird and peculiar to the point of being unnatural." Kaufmann concluded that the Americans in general were unworthy of their fame. He was much better disposed to what *Harper's Weekly* called "the popular element" among the foreigners: Meissonier and Alma-Tadema were excellent, Dagnan-Bouveret "truly wonderful," and Luke Fildes "one of the sincerest painters of human emotions now living." Kaufmann especially recommended Orchardson's *Master Baby* to the attention of American art students, because the artist dealt with "ideas" rather than with mere formal qualities. Predictably, he dismissed Jean-François Raffaëlli's Impressionist *Notre Dame, Paris*, as "another one of those singular productions which for some reason or another have come into high favor within the last few years."[50]

Probably most Pittsburghers would have agreed with Kaufmann's judgments. They had until recently few opportunities to see the latest developments in art, and their own painters tended to work in styles that had been current twenty or thirty years earlier. Recognizing this situation, two local writers tried to help their readers come to terms with the more progressive works in the exhibition. One — identified only as "L. M." — contributed an article to the *Pittsburgh Dispatch* on "Manet and His School," in which he pointed out that Impressionism, although it had at first shocked people in France and America, was now generally accepted. However, recognizing that there were still people who had trouble with it, L. M. quoted for their benefit an extract from the writings of George Moore, which explained Impressionism in terms of optical properties, and instructed viewers to stand at a distance from the paintings sufficient to blend the colors.[51]

John Angus MacKay, writing for the *Pittsburgh Times*, offered his readers much the same advice, but from a different perspective. Unlike L. M., MacKay was not a wholehearted convert to the new art; his basic viewpoint was similar to Kaufmann's. He entitled his article "Twenty Freak Pictures," spoke of "glaring oddities," "garish color," "crazy quilt brushwork," and observed that the Glasgow School was "tainted with eccentricity." He described Twachtman's *Snow Storm* as "something that looks like an obliteration, if that has an appearance," and roundly declared that there was "nothing in the picture worth anything. It is mere trickery to be looked at and laughed over." But, for the most part, MacKay made an honest attempt to find something of value in each of the "freaks," and in general he succeeded. "There is something good in all of them," he wrote, "and something new to be learned." His comments on Childe Hassam's entry are typical: "Childe Hassam in 'Spring' has another seemingly patchy picture in which there is a very yellow cart and a strangely blue boy. The faces are just blotches of color and the brushwork seems to be something akin to stippling. Yet the effect of sunlight seen under heavy foliage with the glare in the background is cleverly accomplished." In each of these works (excepting the Twachtman) MacKay discovered that a particular effect of nature had been precisely captured, which, if it did not altogether excuse the artist's eccentricity, at least helped to redeem it.[52]

In 1896 the press emerged as a valuable ally in the effort to educate and refine the masses, and to transform Pittsburgh into a leading art center. The Institute's own efforts were restricted to the gallery itself. Admission was free, and the hours of opening were made as convenient as possible for workingmen: from ten in the morning to ten at night, Monday through Saturday, and from two to six on Sunday afternoon. It was also decided to open the exhibition from two to six o'clock on Thanksgiving Day. This decision, according to a report in the *Pittsburgh Times*, produced exactly the intended effect. The attendance for that day, approximately eighteen thousand people, was the largest of the season, and the crowd, judging from the absence of fashionable attire, was largely composed of "small tradesmen, shopkeepers, mechanics, millmen and laborers," who, because of the long hours demanded by their work, had had no previous opportunity to view the exhibition.[53]

But merely looking at pictures could do little to educate the viewer about art. One way of doing this, at least for a small segment of the public, was to encourage organized visits by art schools and by secondary school art classes. During the 1895 loan exhibition, Beatty had suggested that local art schools should replace their afternoon sessions with visits to the galleries, but his advice had been ignored.[54] In 1896, such field trips became common, and there were even visits from public schools in which art formed no special part of the curriculum. Although the gallery did not offer guided tours of the exhibition, Beatty, eager to cooperate, volunteered to accompany school groups on request whenever his schedule permitted. The Fine Arts Committee members discussed using "capable lecturers" on certain days to explain the merits of the paintings to the public, but they made no arrangements to do so.[55]

The catalogue played another part in the attempt to educate the public. The small, handsome, hardbound volume (figure 16) was far more elaborate than its 1895 predecessor — indeed, quite fancy compared with other late nineteenth-century catalogues, although it was a far cry from the scholarly exhibition catalogues of today. The checklist of works was expanded with short biographical notes on each artist, giving their place of residence, place of birth, and principal honors won (figure 17). Photographs of many of the artists were included, a novel feature applauded by the directors of the St. Louis Exhibition and the Pennsylvania Academy.[56] Its utility in enhancing the public's understanding and appreciation of art would appear to have been negligible, however, beyond personalizing the artists to some extent. Cecilia Beaux assumed this was the purpose and refused to allow her photograph to be used. "I have no doubt the book will be attractive and I should be in good company," she wrote, "but I have made a great effort thus far to keep my personality out of my more or less public life, and do not feel as if I could make this exception."[57]

More relevant features of the catalogue were twenty-five black-and-white photographs of paintings in the exhibition; a detailed description of the gallery's reproductions of ancient sculptures; and, more useful to would-be students, a long list of books about painting, complete with call numbers, in the Carnegie Library. This list did not deal exclusively, or even chiefly, with contemporary art; instead, it was a grab bag of general histories, encyclopedias of art, biographies, gallery guides, and collections of reproductions and criticism. A more complete list could be consulted at the library's reference desk. Although the catalogue cost eleven cents a copy to produce, it was sold for ten cents a copy in order to make it as widely affordable as possible. This was a reasonable price, but by no means extraordinarily cheap: it would have cost a laborer in one of Carnegie's mills a full hour's wages.[58]

Arthur Burgoyne, a writer of humorous topical verse for the *Pittsburgh Leader,* doubted both the utility of the catalogue and the likelihood of educating average Pittsburghers in the fine points of art. "Folks neither skilled nor presuming," he wrote, would attempt to "follow the catalogue's lead," but

> the acme of popular pleasure,
> Unmarred by a drawback or hitch,
> Is to view each pictorial treasure,
> And not know t'other from which.[59]

Burgoyne's view, however, did not represent that of the local press as a whole, which regarded the art gallery's social and civic mission with the utmost seriousness or, at least, found in it an attractive hook upon which to hang its coverage of the exhibition. The optimistic predictions about Pittsburgh's future as an art center that were made on the occasion of the 1895 loan exhibition were repeated in 1896, and there was greater attention paid to the public's response. Monday papers usually published short accounts of Sunday crowds at the gallery, and from time to time reporters were sent to make more detailed observations of the crowds' size, composition, and behavior.

These observations were not always in agreement. A reporter for the *Pittsburgh Post*, for example, declared that a "taste for the beautiful" had become a fad pervading all levels of society. He described the Sunday crowds as enormous (from fifteen to eighteen thousand people), largely composed of working-class families who had "come to improve themselves." This improvement was especially noticeable in the younger visitors, who unlike their elders had the advantage of a common school education: they became "art students as soon as they cast their eyes on the pictures." But a reporter for the *Pittsburgh Dispatch* estimated the number of Sunday visitors at only six thousand and observed that the working-class families were much more interested in the mounted orangutans and medieval armor at the museum than in the paintings in the gallery. Reporters agreed nevertheless that the exhibition was thronged, and that every rank of society could be found there.[60]

One newspaper, the *Pittsburgh Times*, not content to point out the highlights of the exhibition or to make observations on the number and character of the gallery-goers, hit upon a plan to further the Institute's goals and boost its own circulation as well. On 10 November 1896 the paper announced to its readers that it was offering $500 to the person who could most accurately guess which paintings would receive which awards at the first Carnegie annual. Contestants were allowed to submit as many entries as they wished, provided they used the entry blanks printed daily in the *Pittsburgh Times* and its sister paper, the *Pittsburgh News*. "The *Times* has always been a leader in the promotion of intelligence and the cultivation of taste," declared the editor. "As a family newspaper it believes it can do nothing better for the families into which it is daily received as a welcome visitor than to inspire in every member as much as possible a love and taste for everything that is elevating and that has a tendency to cultivate higher and nobler aspirations." The contest was intended to serve this high purpose: it would give people an additional incentive to attend the exhibition and would "bring about a more critical and careful examination on the part of all . . . and thus aid in carrying out more fully the beneficent design of the founders and promoters of this institution."[61]

The gallery gave the contest its fullest cooperation. The day after the announcement, Beatty and William Nimick Frew publicly declared their support, the latter praising the *Pittsburgh Times* for its public spirit. The Fine Arts Committee met the following day to discuss ways to assist the *Pittsburgh Times*, and within a week all the unhung competitors had been brought out of storage and all competing works identified with cards marked "PM" (competing for cash prize and medal) or "M" (competing for medal only).[62] As it would have been impossible to hold the contest without the gallery's cooperation, the *Pittsburgh Times* must have secured promises of assistance before making the announcement; there is, however, no reason to believe that the Fine Arts Committee was secretly sponsoring the contest, as J. N. Fort charged in the *Philadelphia Item*. The *Pittsburgh Times* flatly denied the charge and denounced Fort as a "fool" and a "liar."[63]

During the run of the contest and for several days after, the *Pittsburgh Times* publicized the exhibition in a series of daily articles. On 10 November 1896 they reprinted the complete catalogue, on 21 November they published the list of recommended art books, and there were frequent lists of works in competition and works hung and unhung. Their reporters kept an eye out for notable visitors, including Andrew Carnegie, the celebrated comedian Joseph Jefferson, the son of the Paris dealer Durand-Ruel, and William Merritt Chase, and were quick to record their words of praise.[64] The *Pittsburgh Times* had a special fondness for remarks that praised the Pittsburgh exhibition at the expense of the National Academy of Design's fall exhibition. A New York businessman, described as "officially connected" with the National Academy, told a reporter that the older institution was having trouble maintaining standards in 1896 because Pittsburgh had secured all the best paintings. The wife of an unidentified member of the Fine Arts Committee reported that there were "less than half-a-dozen great painters" represented at that year's National Academy show, most of the exhibitors being "society amateurs, unknown to the art world," and that she had seen only three people besides herself when she visited the galleries.[65]

The greatest concern of the *Pittsburgh Times* was to demonstrate that the contest was having its intended effect on the public. It constantly emphasized the size of the crowds in the galleries and cited the testimony of visitors who had been attracted by the hope of winning $500, especially when this testimony provided evidence of heightened aesthetic sensibilities. We read of the elderly man who had never much cared for painting, but, having decided to enter the contest for lack of anything better to do, had discovered "more love for art in my soul than I ever realized before"; of the woman who, after five visits to the galleries, claimed she could see effects she hadn't noticed before; of the fifteen-year-old boy who read art books in the library every day after school in order to make more informed guesses, and who was beginning to think that he might like to be an artist himself. The *Pittsburgh Times* believed that its goal of bringing about "a more critical and careful examination" of the exhibition by the public was being realized, and a member of the Fine Arts Committee, who had expected the contest to do little beyond increasing attendance, agreed: "My idea was that many people would come in, look at the paintings and guess at random; without attempting to get at the fine points of the paintings. I am very glad to say that I see very little of that kind of work." The public's response to the pictures, he observed, was intuitive and untrained, but also earnest and often perceptive.[66]

The announcement of the contest's winners on 15 December 1896 was something of an anticlimax. Of the 5,486 entries submitted, not one had listed more than two winning pictures in the proper order. The prize money was therefore split among the twenty-eight best entries, each contestant receiving $17.86 apiece. This, though not an inconsiderable sum in 1896, was a far cry from the much-touted $500.[67]

The prizewinners at the first annual exhibition had been announced eleven days earlier, on the afternoon of Friday, 4 December 1896.[68] The first prize, worth $5,000, went to Winslow Homer's *The Wreck*; the second prize, worth $3,000, went to Gari Melchers's *The Shipbuilder* (figure 18). John Lavery's *Lady in Brown* won the gold medal; Jean-François Raffaëlli's *Notre Dame, Paris,* the silver medal; and Cecilia Beaux's *Ernesta,* the bronze medal. The medal, designed by the Tiffany Glass and Decorating Company, bore on its face (figure 19a) an allegorical head of "America" wearing a stylized American eagle headdress, and the inscription *honos alit artes* (honor feeds the arts). On its reverse (figure 19b) appeared female personifications of Victory and Industry in classical garb, jointly holding the Torch of Enlightenment over a wreath encircling the artist's name and the title of the prizewinning picture.[69]

In future exhibitions the announcement of prizewinners always concluded the opening day ceremonies; in 1896, however, it was delayed until the middle of the exhibition, and no definite date appears to have been decided upon until shortly before the event itself. On 5 November, Beatty professed himself totally in the dark concerning the Fine Arts Committee's intentions, and as late as 29 November, it was known only that the prizes would be awarded sometime before 1 January 1897.[70] The delay and uncertainty may have been a deliberate ploy designed to build suspense, or it may equally have betokened a cautious attitude on the part of the committee, a determination not to make the awards until committee members had tested the critical waters and had assured themselves that the awards would be well received.

It was important to the committee members to avoid controversy in this matter, for, as Edwin Abbey had predicted on 31 May, there was a widespread feeling that a jury composed of businessmen and minor artists was unfit to sit in judgment on the world's greatest living painters. Shortly after the exhibition opened, the *Pittsburgh Leader* reported that a great many New York artists were hostile toward the "business man's jury," and that their sentiments were shared by many Pittsburgh artists. "Who ever heard of putting business men on a jury of selection for so important an exhibition as this one?" said an unnamed local artist. "It is customary in the great annual exhibits of the Paris salon for the artists to make up the jury from among themselves, and only the acknowledged masters are ever chosen." Why, he wondered, should artists risk the insult of having their work rejected by amateurs?[71] The excellence of the exhibition did nothing to mollify hostility toward the jury. The *New York Sun* thought well of the paintings but devoted the greater part of a short review to criticizing the Fine Arts Committee:

It would naturally be supposed that the Art Committee or the trustees would hasten to call upon competent judges to make the awards, but these excellent gentlemen have no such intention. Not all of their time is taken up in manufacturing iron and looking after their bonds and real estate, so they will make the awards themselves. They have a couple of artists of local reputation among them, and that is considered sufficient. The awards are not made yet, but it is worth while to point out that they will not have the value they might have. It is not the money that makes the honor; the value of a prize is measured by the critical standing of the members of the jury.[72]

This was precisely the point that Abbey had made. Following the announcement of the awards, "an admirer of art" told the *Pittsburgh Leader* that, owing to the character of the jury, the art world would probably not be at all pleased with them. A jury of businessmen, he said, was "a thing without precedent in the annals of modern art," and it would be

> an extraordinarily fortunate outcome of the dangerous experiment if the judgment of these practical and successful men of affairs, absolutely amateurs in art or even less, should tally with the judgment of the best artists and art critics in Europe and America, men whose whole lives have been devoted to the training of their minds and hands to perceive and reproduce the beautiful.[73]

The "admirer of art" was to be disappointed in his expectations.

In the matter of aesthetic judgment, the Fine Arts Committee had done its work well, and there were few adverse comments from artists, critics, or the general public. The winners were all painters of considerable stature, and their entries were all recognized as their best work. Homer's *The Wreck* had been a great favorite from the beginning of the exhibition. Most critics had described it in some detail, and several had considered it likely to take first prize. The public agreed: of the 5,496 entries in the *Pittsburgh Times* contest, 562 gave it first place and 1,456 gave it some place, making it by a wide margin the most popular painting in the exhibition. Melchers's *The Shipbuilder* ranked just below *The Wreck* in popularity, receiving 247 votes for first place, 319 for second place, and 740 votes in all. Lavery's *Lady in Brown* and Beaux's *Ernesta* were also favorites, although critics and public generally agreed that Beaux's *The Dreamer*, though ineligible to compete, was the better work. The only surprise was Raffaëlli's *Notre Dame, Paris*, which had won no special mention from the critics and, according to the *Pittsburgh Times*, had been almost entirely overlooked by the public. But it did not provoke controversy.[74]

Locally, there was some quibbling over whether Lavery deserved a higher place than Beaux, and a feeling that Alexander, as a native Pittsburgher, should have received something. Out-of-town newspapers and magazines simply published the awards without comment. The only negative criticism came from the *Art Interchange*'s "Observer," who, in the midst of castigating the Fine Arts Committee for its failure to hang all the paintings, remarked "it is difficult to understand or feel . . . satisfaction over the three medals; and it looks very much as if the matter had been decided wholly by one man on the committee." The "Observer" did not, however, give specific reasons for his dissatisfaction, and he had no quarrel with the awards made to Homer and Melchers, both of which, he conceded, reflected "credit on the taste of the committee."[75]

Committee members had until the middle of December to congratulate themselves on having proved detractors wrong; then they discovered that they had made a serious error in awarding the prizes. The bad news came in a note from John White Alexander to Beatty: "I have just come across this," he wrote ("this" being a clipping from the Paris edition of the *New York Herald* about the $3,000 award to Melchers), "and am sure it is wrong, and will make trouble as it was exhibited here last salon — when you were here. A number of the men here did not send because they had nothing new. Won't you write me at once a letter that will show that the telegram is wrong?" But the telegram sent to the *New York Herald* was right, and the Fine Arts Committee had violated its own condition that only works that had not been previously exhibited were eligible to compete. Melchers freely admitted to having made a mistake: he had given the circular only a cursory reading, had assumed that the restriction applied only to works previously exhibited in the United States, and so had failed to note on his entry blank that *The Shipbuilder* was ineligible for a prize. He pointed out that it had appeared on the line at the Champs-de-Mars Salon and had been well publicized, so obviously he had not intended to deceive the committee. By this, he clearly implied that they ought to have been aware of a major painting by a major American artist conspicuously displayed at a major exhibition (an exhibition, moreover, that Beatty had attended). Alexander's "when you were here" makes the same implication. Understandably, the committee did not hurry to publicize the error but waited until mid-January, when the board of trustees formally rescinded Melchers's prize.[76]

Beatty's behavior toward Alexander reveals his embarrassment. Except for a short and unsatisfactory note, he wrote nothing to Alexander for weeks on end. In a letter dated 27 January 1897, Alexander upbraided him for his silence, chided him for not being a good friend, and complained of having been placed in an awkward position: "Aside from my own mortification as regards my native city," he wrote, "I am not very comfortably situated over here." The error made in awarding a prize to Melchers, though "difficult to understand," was not the only problem. Alexander was being "besieged by the men who sent to know why not a single picture has been bought. All the men are furious and say that the money to be spent was simply a blind. . . . All swear they will never send again — I do all I can but that is not much."[77] It was the aftermath of the 1895 loan exhibition all over again: the artists had expected to sell their work, and once more they had been disappointed.

It was not true that no pictures had been bought. *The Wreck* had been acquired by virtue of its being awarded the first prize. The Carnegie art gallery also paid $5,000 for Whistler's *Arrangement in Black: Portrait of Señor Pablo de Sarasate*, thus becoming the first public gallery in America to own a painting by the country's most famous expatriate. Alexander may well have played a part in persuading the Fine Arts Committee to make the purchase. During a brief visit in the middle of November, he had devoted the better part of an interview with the *Pittsburgh Dispatch* to urging Pittsburgh to acquire one of the Whistlers in the exhibition, stressing that Whistler was underrepresented in American public collections. The decision to buy *Sarasate* was made well before the purchases were announced on 15 December, for when Charles Lang Freer telegraphed from New York on 5 December to ask if he might acquire it for his private collection he learned that the gallery had already bought it. Freer was America's foremost collector of Whistler, and his interest underlined the prestige of the gallery's latest acquisition, as did a remark made by Harrison Morris, director of the Pennsylvania Academy: "The Academy was envious of one thing, and that was the possession by Pittsburg of the Whistler painting."[78]

Two other paintings, John Lavery's *Bridge at Grez* and Humphreys Johnston's *Moonlight: Pointe de Beg-Meil, Finistere*, were purchased from the first annual exhibition. The purchase of the Humphreys Johnston work was an unexpected triumph for the artist, an American expatriate living in Paris. Alexander had shown Beatty one of his works at the Champs-de-Mars Salon, but Beatty had disliked it and decided not to invite Johnston to send to Pittsburgh. A few months later Alexander was surprised to get a letter from Johnston saying that in the end Beatty had invited him but had neglected to send a circular and entry form. Alexander assumed that Beatty had changed his mind, but he became suspicious when the Paris shippers asked if it was all right to accept his pictures since Johnston's name was not on their list. Alexander said yes, because Johnston was a friend, but he doubted Johnston's story and wrote to Beatty about the matter. Afraid that he had made a mistake, Alexander assured Beatty that Johnston's work would be "a feature of your exhibition — for the color almost makes up for the lack of drawing." The Fine Arts Committee obviously agreed, for it accepted all four of his entries (including the *Portrait of the Artist's Mother* that Beatty had disliked at Paris) and bought one of them. In the correspondence it is unclear whether Johnston had in fact lied his way into the exhibition, but one of his letters, written during a visit to Pittsburgh to see the exhibition, refers to a conversation with Beatty "in which all the disagreeables came first and the pleasant things afterwards," which suggests that Beatty had taken him to task for his deception before complimenting his work and informing him of the purchase.[79]

Excluding *The Wreck*, which was paid for from a special prize fund donated by Carnegie, the Fine Arts Committee bought only three paintings from the first annual exhibition, worth a total of $6,400 ($5,000 for the Whistler, $1,000 for the Lavery, and $400 for the Johnston). In his annual report, Beatty pointed out that this was a very small number of purchases and explained that there had been some doubt about how much money would be available for purchases after the expenses of the exhibition and of the gallery in general had been met.[80] The artists' disappointment arose largely from, or was at least aggravated by, a basic misunderstanding: they believed that $50,000, a sum sufficient to buy dozens of pictures, was to be spent for works of art. This belief was confidently set forth by Jean-François Raffaëlli in a letter to Carnegie: $50,000 were available for purchases, he said, yet to his amazement his *Notre-Dame, Paris*, though worthy of a medal, had not been bought; indeed only a single European painting, the Lavery, had been acquired. European artists would regard the exhibition as "a veritable swindle," he declared, and would refuse to send, "thus destroying your generous and noble idea."[81]

In fact, the gallery's entire endowment was $50,000, and the sum available for purchases was only between $10,000 and $15,000, but the artists were hardly at fault for not realizing this. They had gleaned their information from the press, and the press reports had been misleading, even inaccurate. For example, the *New York Times* stated on 2 January 1896 that the $50,000 endowment was "for the use of the trustees in the purchase of works of art" and repeated this assertion on 26 April.[82] Perhaps the artists would have been less disgruntled had there been a large number of sales to private parties. But unfortunately, there were none. The fact that many of the artists had just exhibited at the St. Louis Exposition, which had an excellent sales record, must have made Pittsburgh's failure in this regard all the more striking.

Raffaëlli was not the only prominent artist in Europe to take offense at the management of the Carnegie art galleries, nor was the lack of sales the only ground for complaint. The latter days of the exhibition brought a spate of complaints on various issues. Alexander Harrison, an internationally famed expatriate marine painter, wrote from Pont Aven that he was "far from content" with his experience of the Pittsburgh exhibition and would not contribute again. Nor did he until 1901, a year after his election to the jury had effected a reconciliation. He did not state the reasons for his discontent, but no sales, no honors, and the fact that one of his entries, *The Red Twilight*, had not been hung until Thanksgiving Day are the likeliest explanations. Another leading expatriate, the genre painter George Hitchcock, was annoyed that three of his honors had been omitted from the short biography in the catalogue. By mid-January he had whipped himself into a fury, charging Beatty with "unfair and malicious intentions" and threatening to denounce the exhibition to his fellow artists, to the press, and to Andrew Carnegie himself, unless he received an immediate apology. Beatty succeeded in placating him; by mid-February Hitchcock was apologizing to Beatty for the incident and inviting him to visit him in Holland. Alfred Roll, a pillar of the more progressive wing of the French art establishment known for his depiction of peasant and working-class life, was angry that one of his two entries, *Nude in Open Air*, had been rejected; Giovanni Boldini was furious that one of his paintings, *Portrait of Princess P.*, had been hung above the line. "I thank you, sir," he wrote in an ironic vein, "for your *kind reception of my works, assuring you that never again shall I trouble you to receive them a second time.*" Roll did not exhibit in Pittsburgh again until 1900; Boldini did not exhibit again until 1899.[83]

Beatty failed to see that Boldini had cause for complaint, but Alexander took Boldini's part. "You say he should not be angry as he had one on the line and a small one above," wrote Alexander after several futile attempts to persuade Boldini to send to the 1897 exhibition, "but that is just the point—his worst picture is usually so much better than others that he thinks it should always be in a good place. The merits of a picture should decide its place—and not the feeling that everyone should have a chance."[84] However, merit was not entirely the point. The great men of Europe, including those Americans who had earned distinction abroad, were jealous of their prerogatives, and when they deigned to exhibit their work, they expected it to be hung on the line as a matter of course. For a committee of provincial American businessmen to hang it above the line, to reject it, or to withhold it from exhibition even temporarily were grave offenses. In denying Boldini and the others their prerogatives, the Fine Arts Committee may have acted through ignorance, but such behavior was implicit in Carnegie's desire to have his gallery managed by "men of affairs" who would exercise their own judgments without regard to received opinion and established reputations. To sky a Boldini and reject a Roll was to display precisely the sort of independence that Carnegie wanted.

In his annual report for 1896, Beatty wrote glowingly of the first annual exhibition:

> That the first annual exhibition exerted a powerful influence in the cultivation of love for the true and beautiful is beyond question. In addition, it has given to the Fine Arts Department a definite place in the estimation of people everywhere, as an exponent of a high standard in the field of art. The Carnegie Art Galleries have become favorably known throughout this country and Europe.[85]

Beatty certainly had reason to congratulate himself. Pittsburgh, hitherto a city of little consequence in the arts, had successfully mounted what many considered to be the year's finest display of contemporary painting. Yet, as he was well aware, there had also been problems, and problems of such a nature as to alienate the artists upon whose goodwill the future of the enterprise depended. Even as he wrote, a revised plan of organization — designed to meet the artists' objections — was being discussed. On 22 January 1897, the tentative outlines of a new scheme were made public, and by the end of March a completely different plan had evolved and been adopted, one that won the almost universal approval of artists and critics and was to remain in force until Beatty's retirement in 1922.

# Illustrations

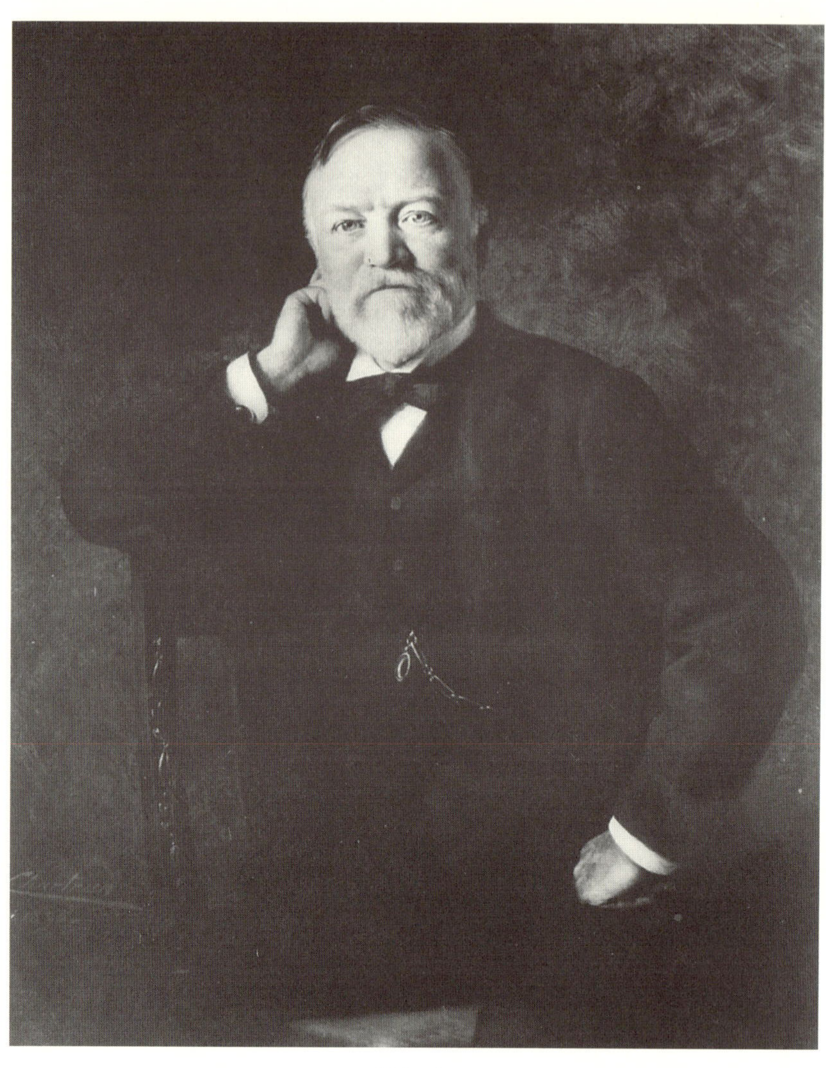



Theobald Chartran, *Portrait of Andrew Carnegie*, 1895.
Oil on canvas, 46 x 35 in.
Carnegie Museum of Art, Pittsburgh; gift of Henry Clay Frick, 96.5.
*Photo*: Pittsburgh Photographic Library, Carnegie Library of Pittsburgh.

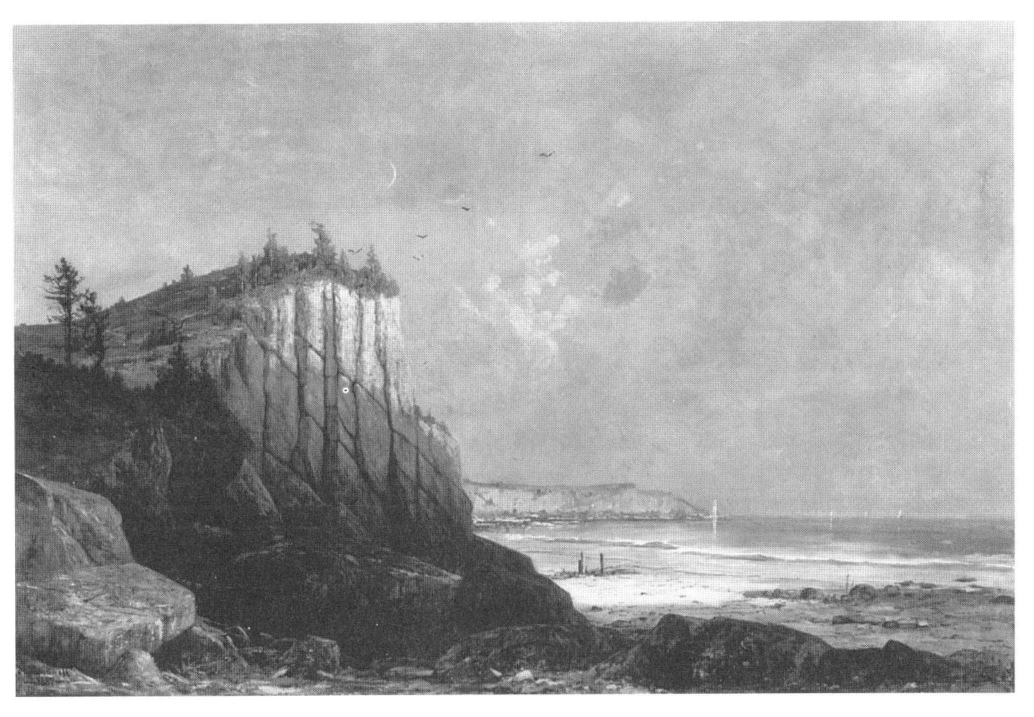



Joseph Ryan Woodwell, *Seascape, Magnolia, Massachusetts*, 1880.
Oil on canvas, 40 x 60 in.
Westmoreland Museum of Art, Greensburg, Pennsylvania;
Mary Marchand Woods Memorial, 86.201.

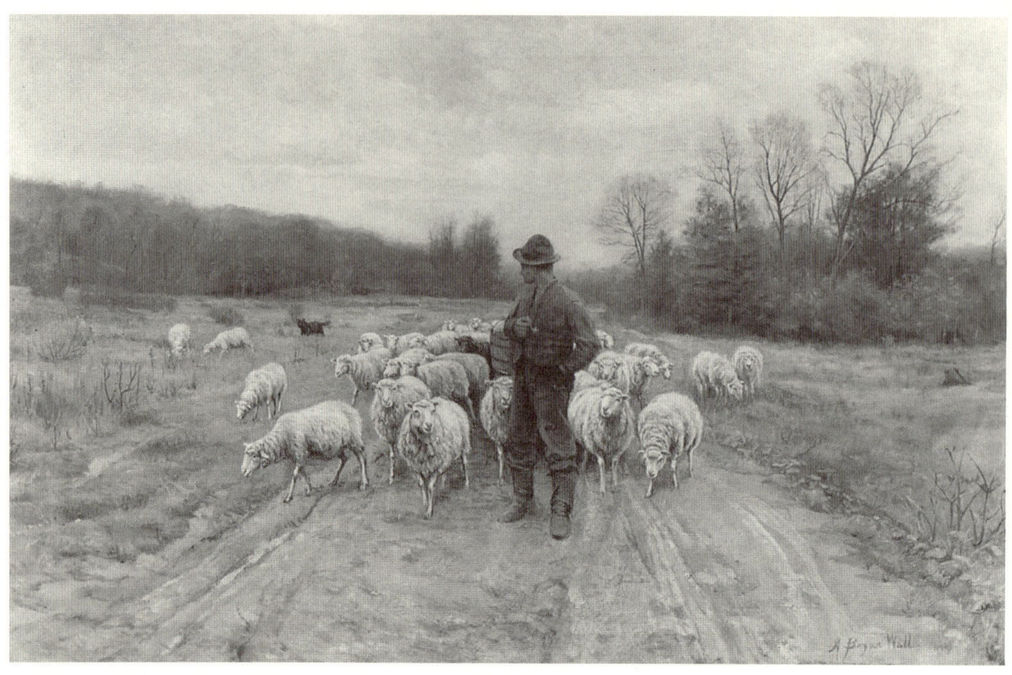

FIG. 3.
Alfred Bryan Wall, *Shepherd and His Flock*, ca. 1900.
Oil on canvas, 19½ x 29½ in.
Westmoreland Museum of Art, Greensburg, Pennsylvania;
gift of Mr. and Mrs. John Barclay Jr., 59.57.

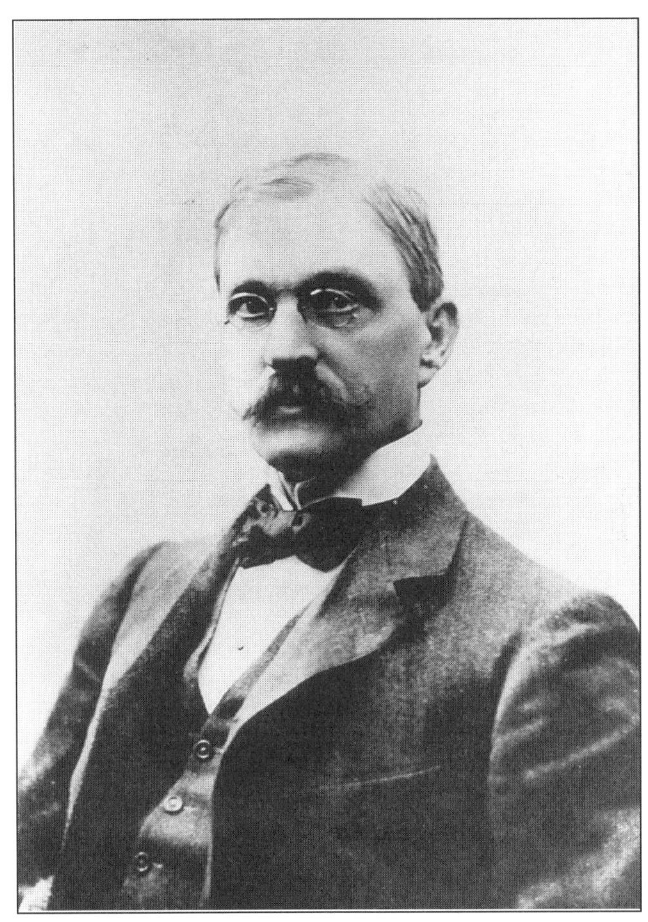

FIG. 4.
John Wesley Beatty, ca. 1900.
From *Annals of Old Wilkinsburg and Vicinity*,
ed. Elizabeth M. Davison and Ellen B. McKee (Wilkinsburg, Pa., 1940), facing p. 534.
*Photo:* Pittsburgh Photographic Library, Carnegie Library of Pittsburgh.

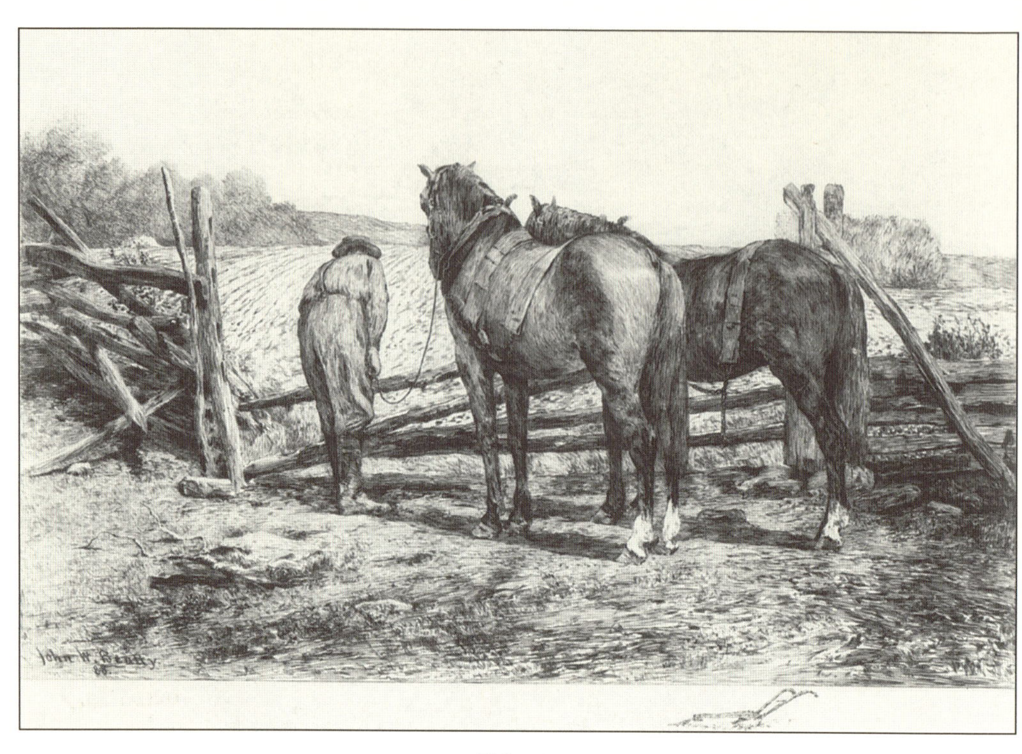

FIG. 5.
John Wesley Beatty, *Farmer with Team of Plow Horses*, 1888.
Etching, 13 x 19½ in.
Westmoreland Museum of Art, Greensburg, Pennsylvania;
gift of James T. Donohoe, 82.92.

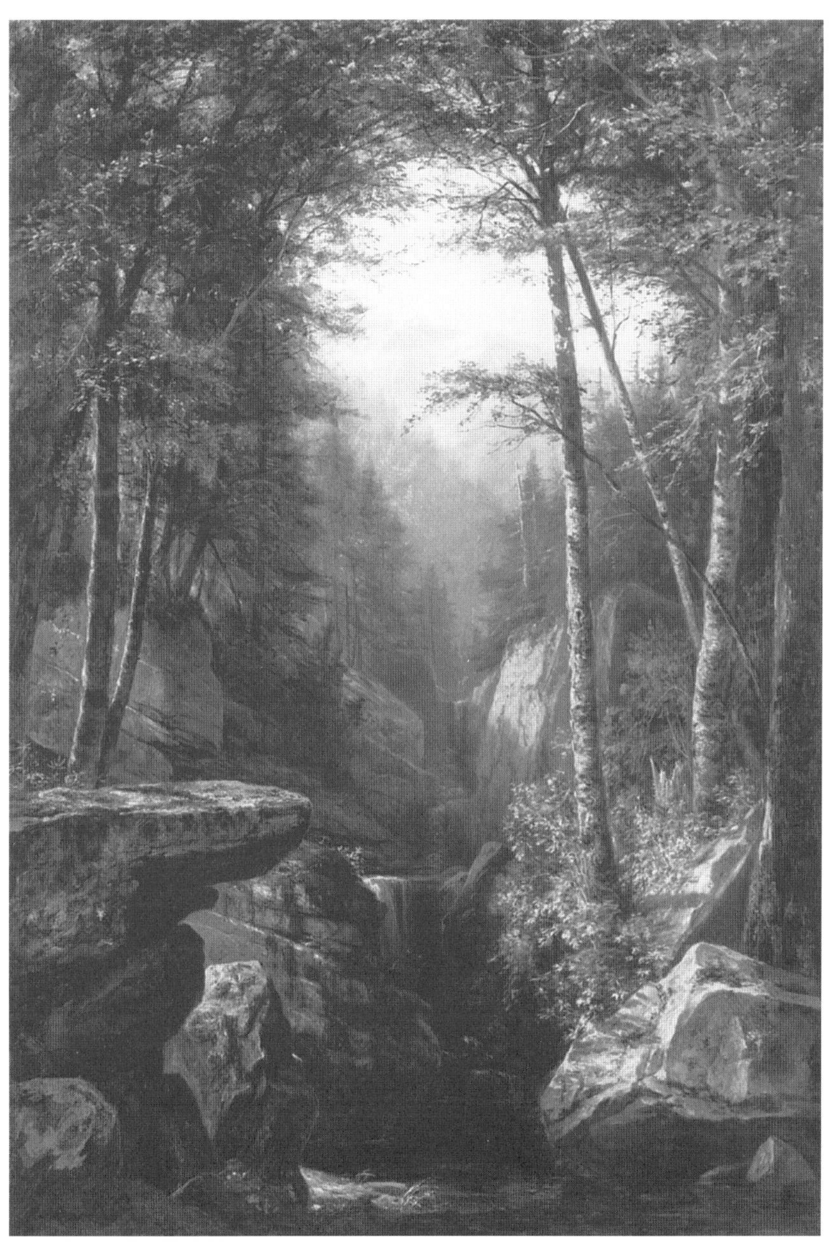

FIG. 6.
George Hetzel, *Rocky Gorge*, 1869.
Oil on canvas, 42 x 29 in.
Westmoreland Museum of Art, Greensburg, Pennsylvania;
Director's Discretionary Fund, 80.33.

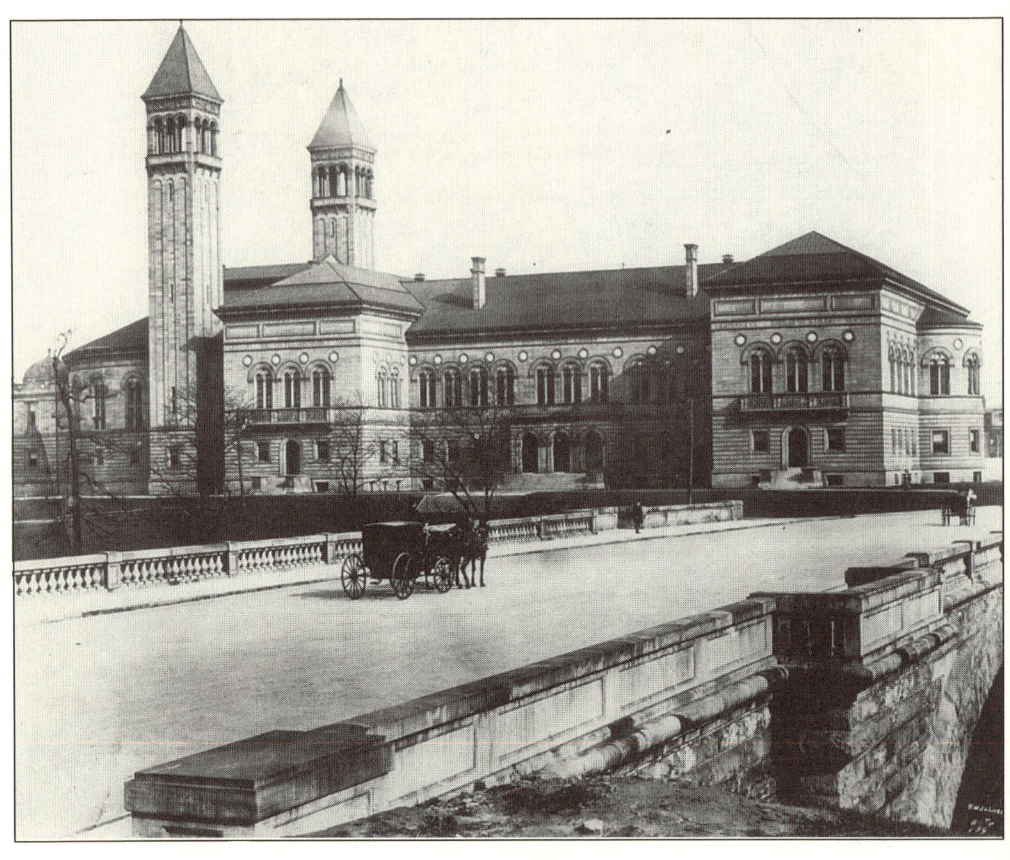

FIG. 7.
View of the Carnegie Institute, Pittsburgh, in 1899.
Photo: Pittsburgh Photographic Library, Carnegie Library of Pittsburgh.

The art galleries occupied the second floor of the wing immediately
to the right of the bell towers.

FIG. 8. (OPPOSITE)
The second floor plan of the Carnegie Institute, Pittsburgh,
as it appeared in the 1890s.
Photo: Pittsburgh Photographic Library, Carnegie Library of Pittsburgh.

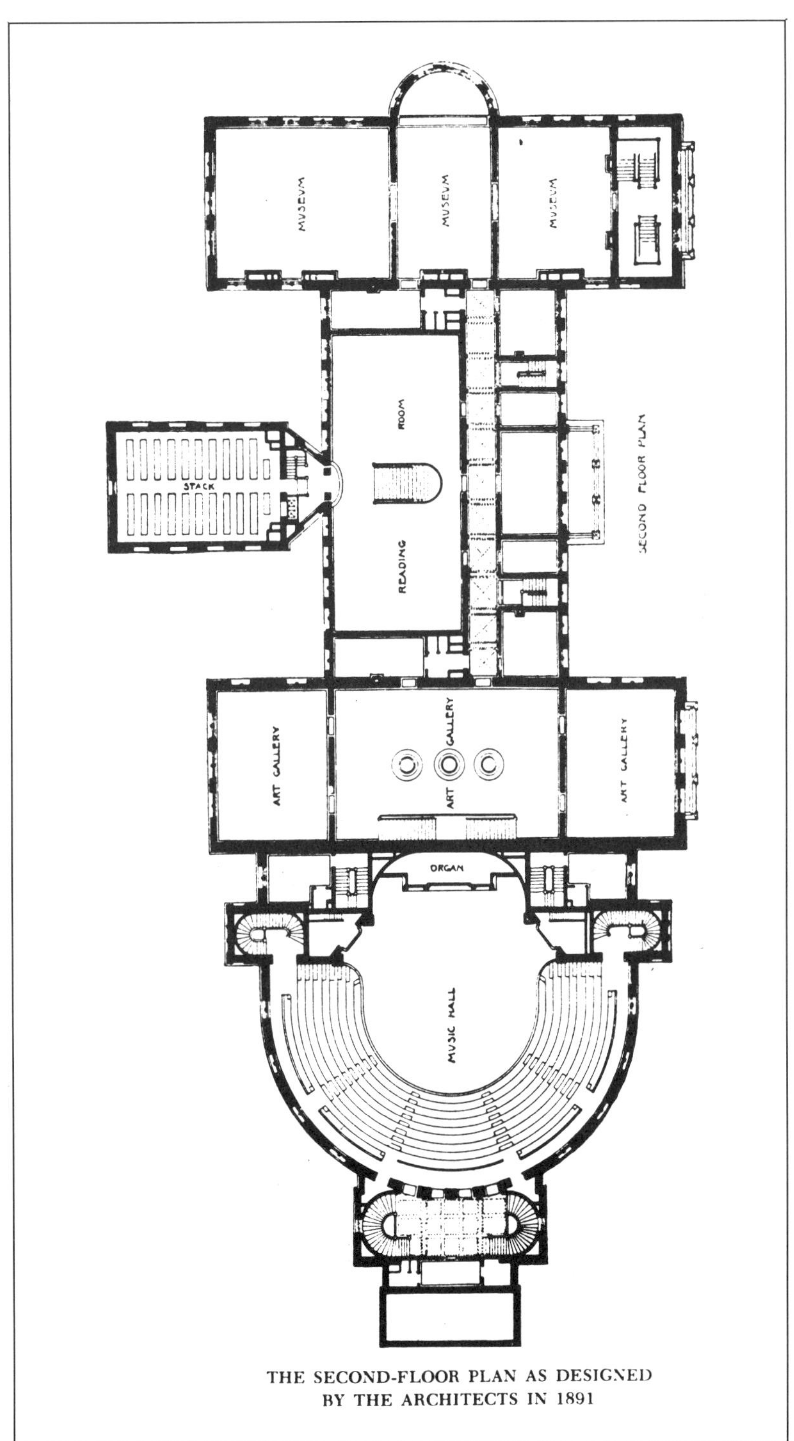


THE SECOND-FLOOR PLAN AS DESIGNED
BY THE ARCHITECTS IN 1891

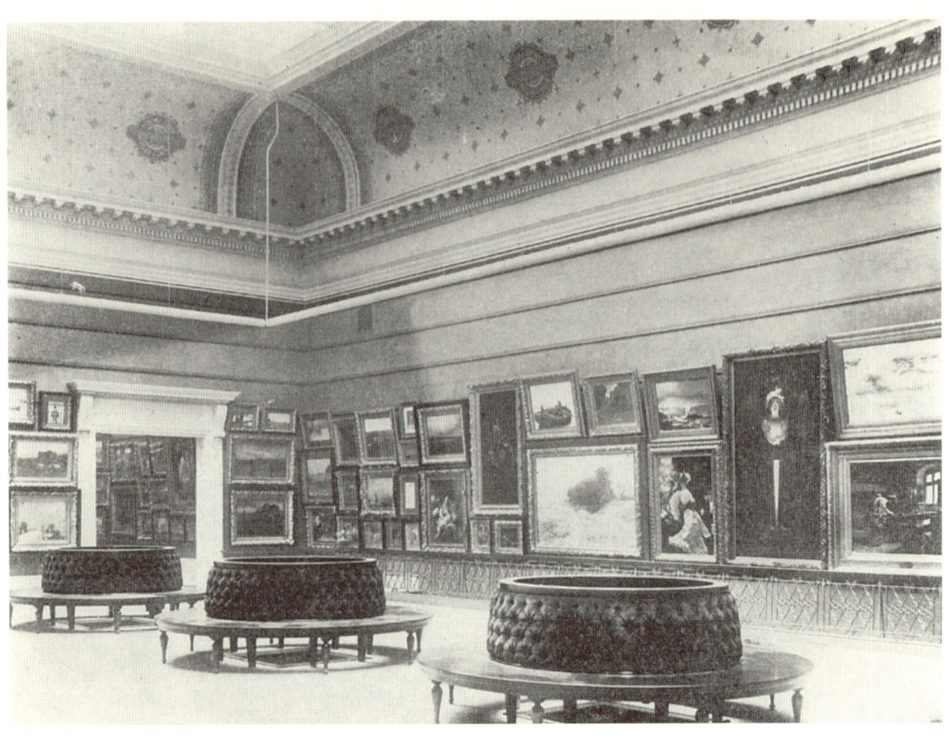



View of the Main Gallery during the 1895 loan exhibition.
From the *Pittsburgh Bulletin*, 30 November 1895, 4.
*Photo*: Pittsburgh Photographic Library, Carnegie Library of Pittsburgh.

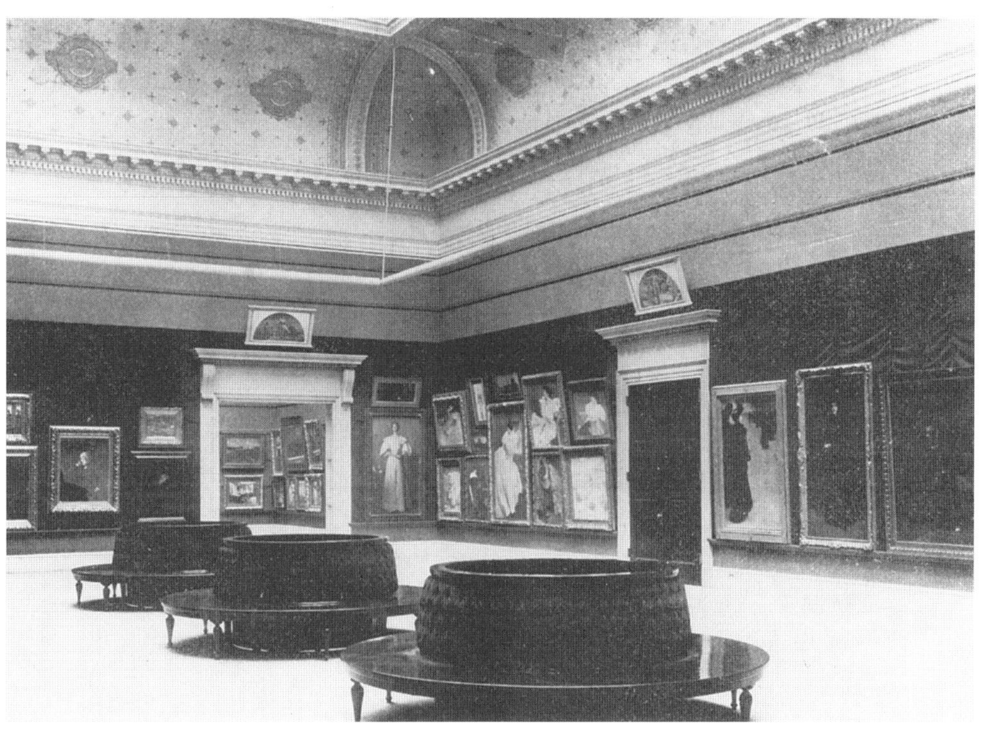



View of the Main Gallery during the 1896 annual exhibition.
From the *Pittsburgh Bulletin*, 14 November 1896, 4.
*Photo*: Pittsburgh Photographic Library, Carnegie Library of Pittsburgh.

Note that the walls have been partially covered with red fabric.

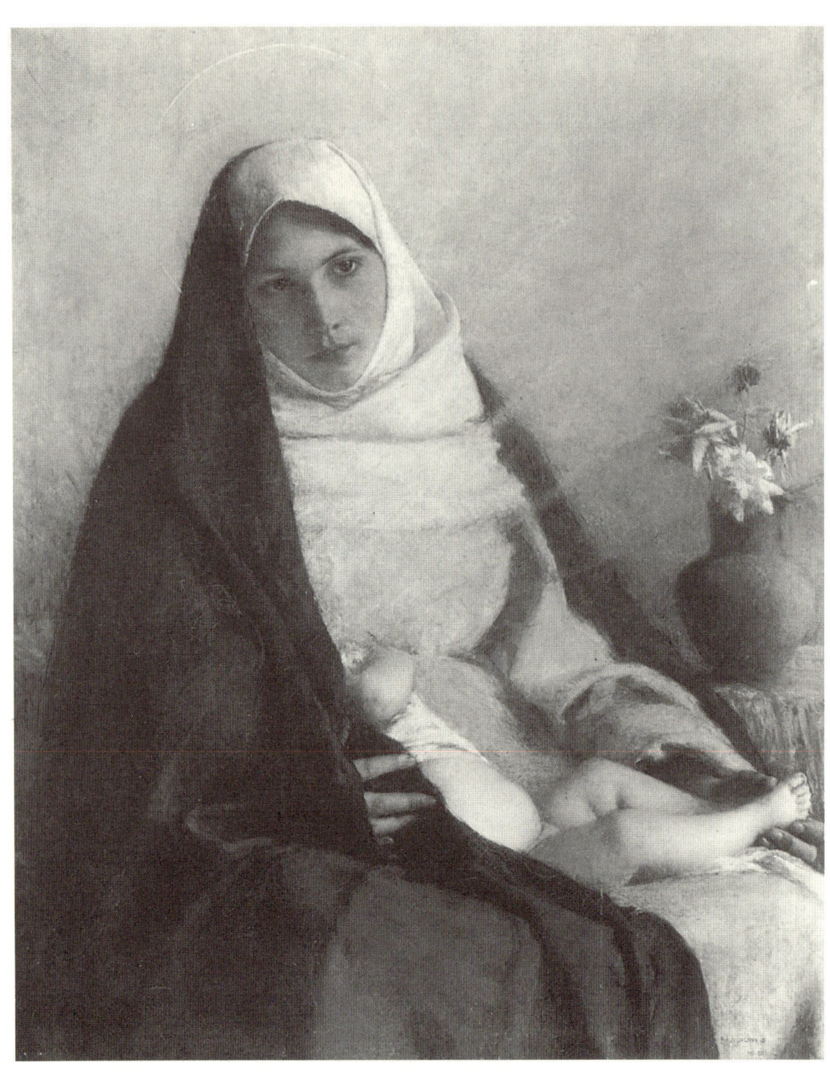

FIG. 11.
Pascal Adolphe Jean Dagnan-Bouveret, *Madonna of the Rose*, 1885.
Oil on canvas, 33¾ x 27 in.
Metropolitan Museum of Art, New York;
Wolfe Fund, 1906, 06.1233.2.

72

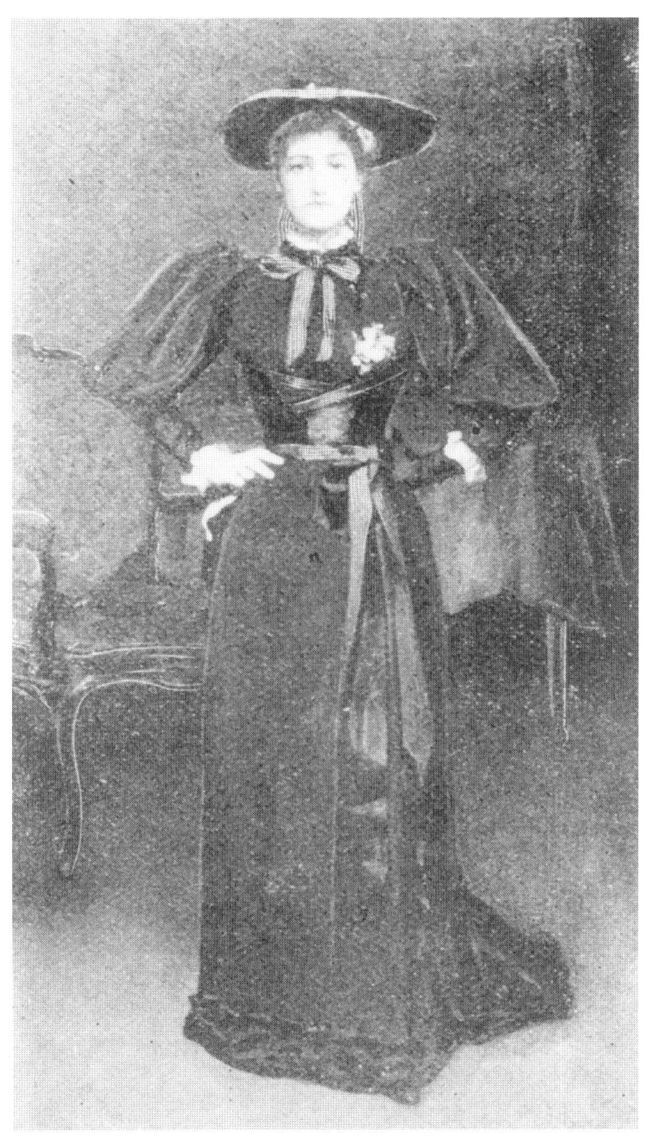

FIG. 12.
John Lavery, *Lady in Brown*, 1895.
From the 1896 catalogue.

73

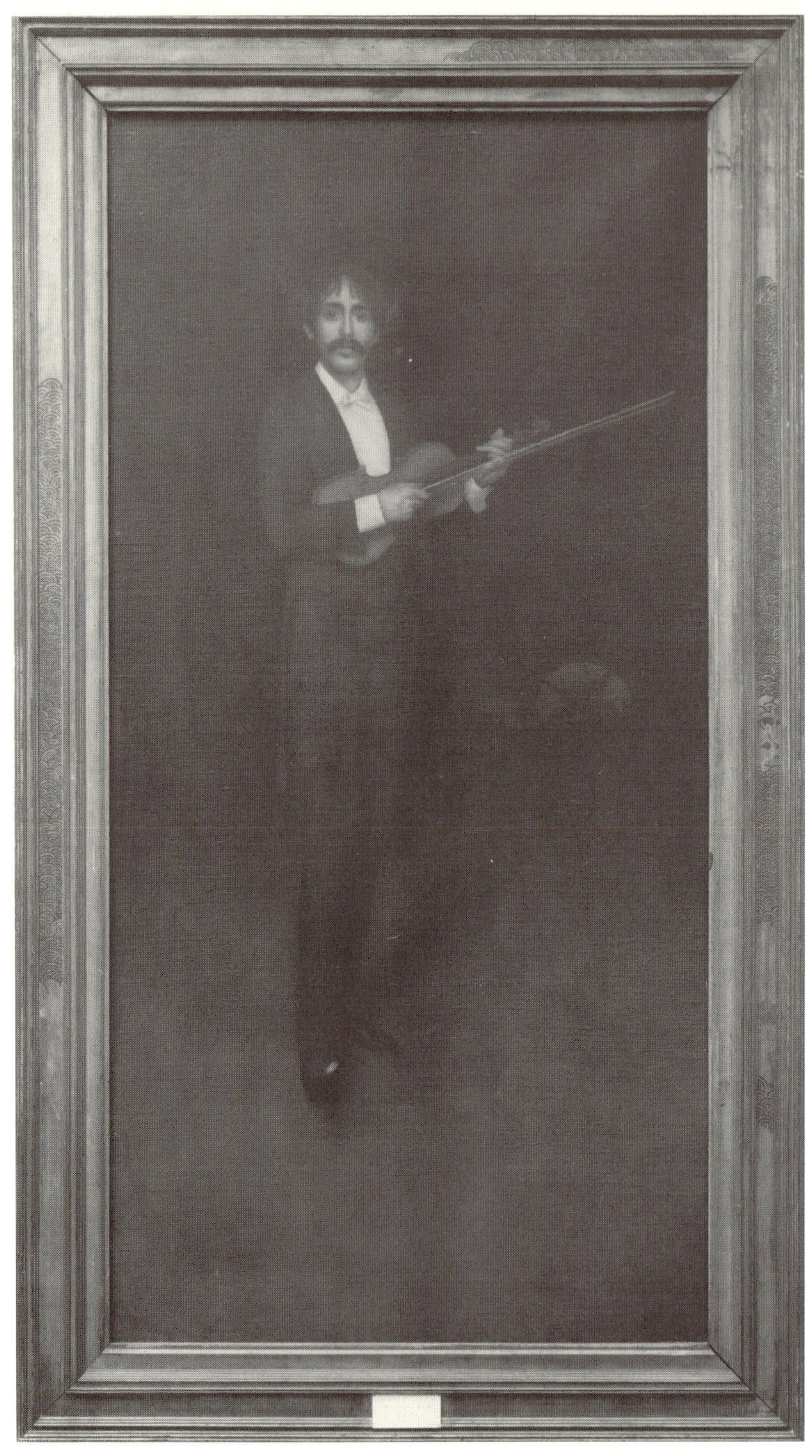

74

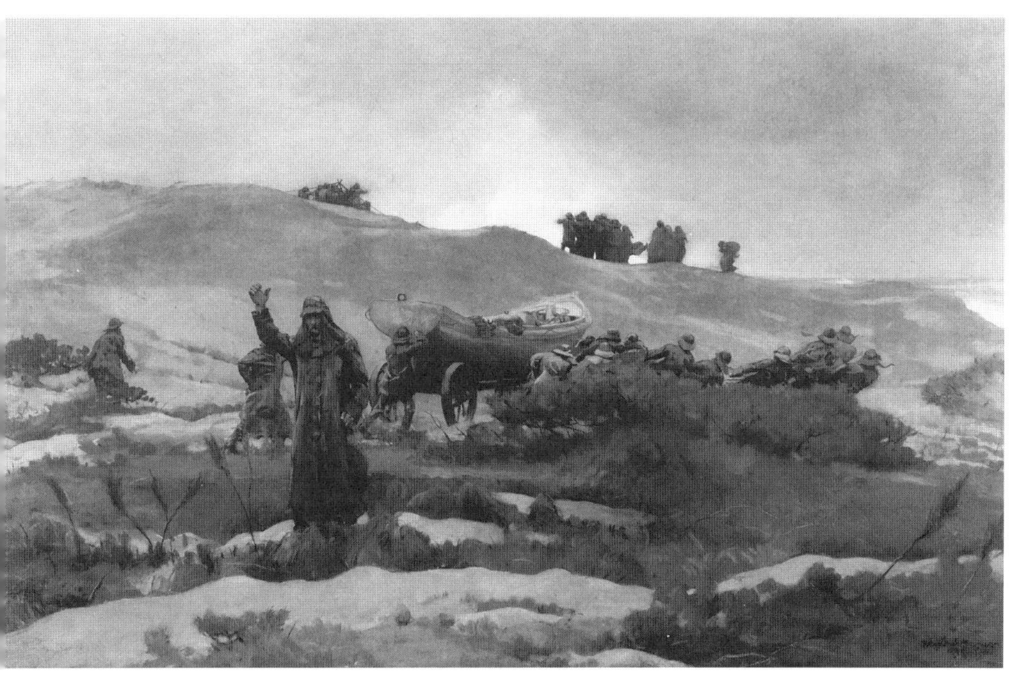

FIG. 14.
Winslow Homer, *The Wreck*, 1896.
Oil on canvas, 30 x 48 in.
Carnegie Museum of Art, Pittsburgh, 96.1.

FIG. 13. *(OPPOSITE)*
James McNeill Whistler,
*Arrangement in Black: Portrait of Señor Pablo de Sarasate*, 1884.
Oil on canvas, 85 ½ x 44 in.
Carnegie Museum of Art, Pittsburgh, 96.2.

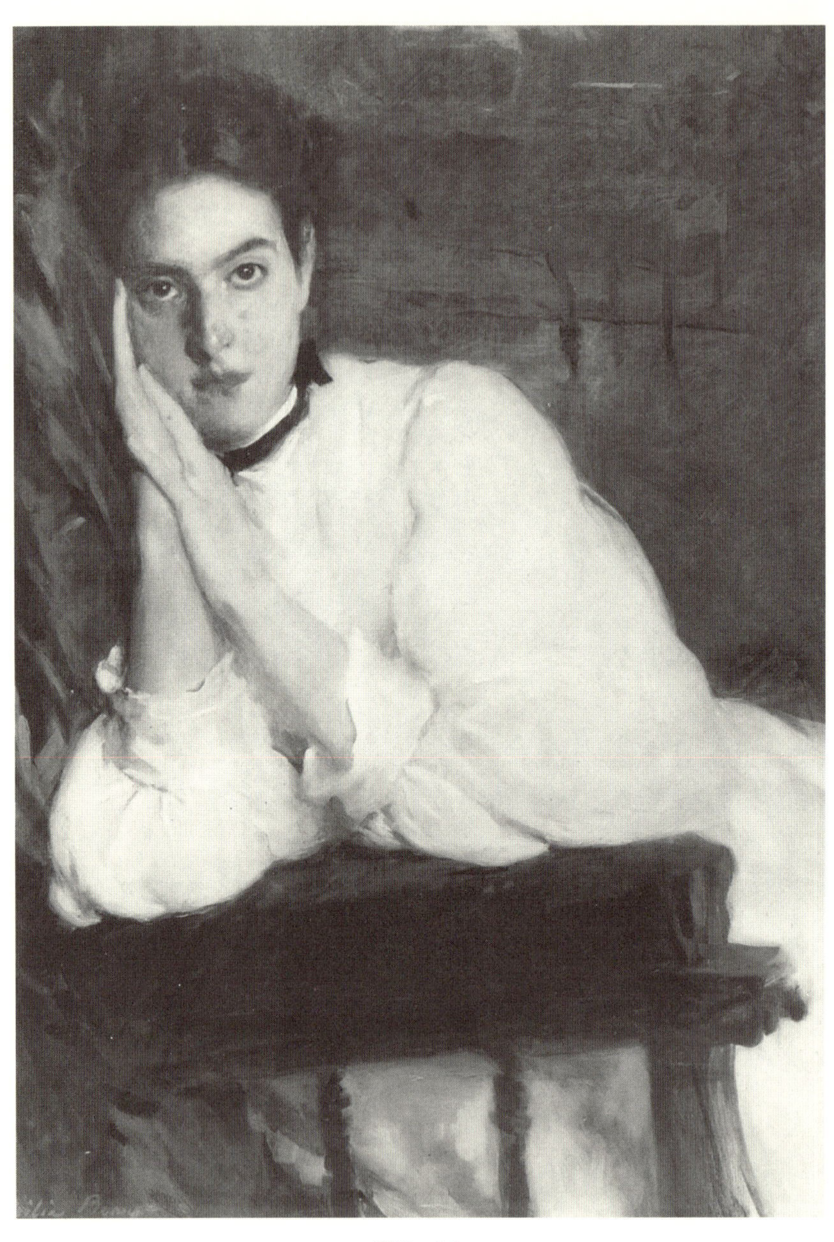

FIG. 15.
Cecilia Beaux, *The Dreamer*, 1894.
Oil on canvas, 33 x 25 in.
The Butler Institute of American Art, Youngstown, Ohio.

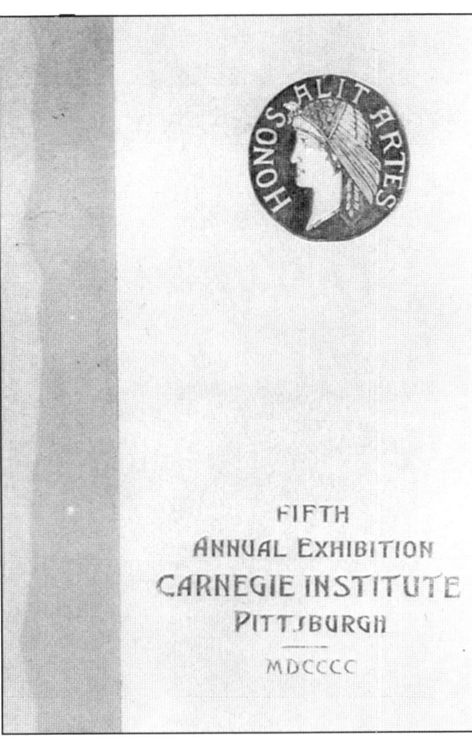


FIG. 16. (*LEFT*)
Front cover of the 1900 catalogue. This is an unusually well-preserved example of the cover design first used in 1896. The title, date, and medallion logo are stamped in gold on cream-colored paper.

FIG. 17. (*BELOW*)
Two pages from the 1896 catalogue.

**Blenner,** Carle J., New York.
22—Portrait of Miss K. G.
23—The Poem.

**Blum,** Robert, New York.
24—Cherry Blossoms.

**Boldini,** Jean, Paris, France; born Italy. Grand Prize, 1889; Legion of Honor, 1889; Officer St. Michael; Commander Italian Crown; First Medal, Berlin, Munich, New York, Chicago, Boston.
25—Woman in Black.

26—Portrait of Princess P.
27—A Piano Duet.

**Boston,** Joseph H., Brooklyn, N. Y.

**Boughton,** Geo. H., R. A., London, England; N. A.; born Norwich, England.
28—On a Highland River (Glen Afric).
29—The Gardener's Daughter.

**Brangwyn,** Frank, London, England; born Bruges, France. Medals—Paris, 1891, 3d Class, Champs Elysees; Chicago World's Fair.
30—Venice.

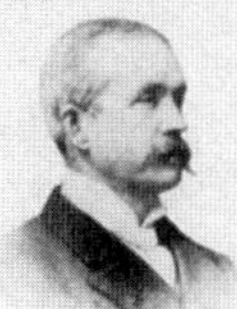
George H. Boughton.

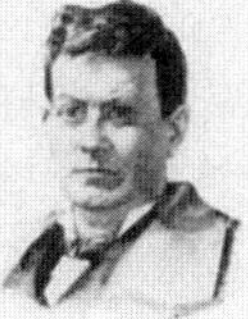
Frank Brangwyn.

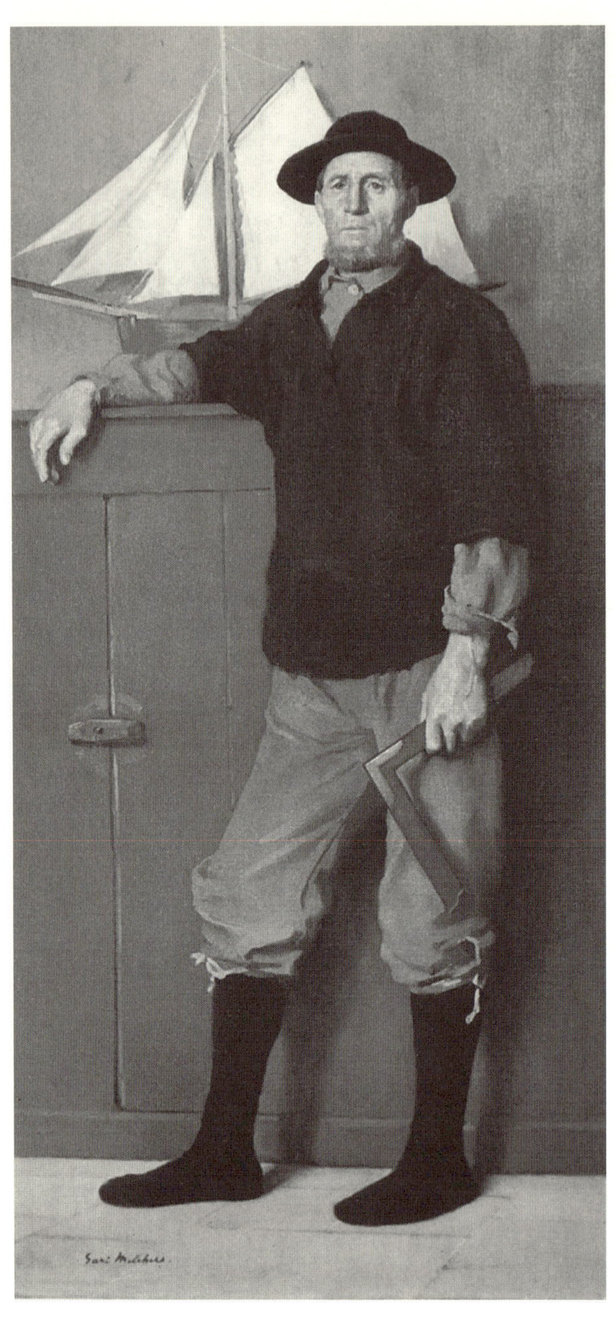



FIG. 18.
Gari Melchers, *The Shipbuilder*, 1896.
Oil on canvas, 80 x 39 in.
Gemäldgalerie Neue Meister, Dresden, 1061 (2530).

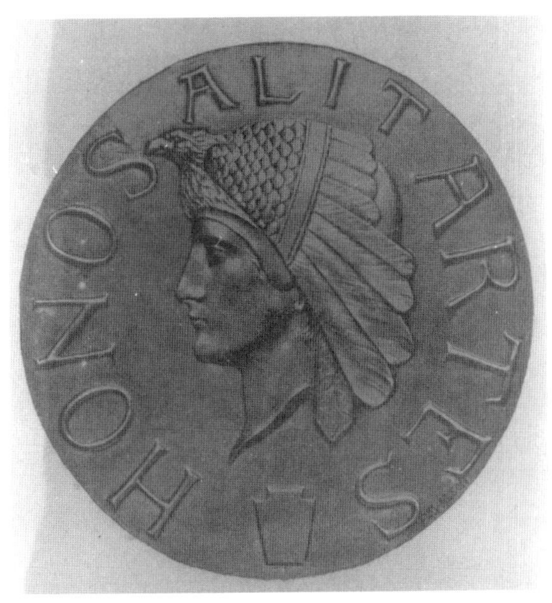


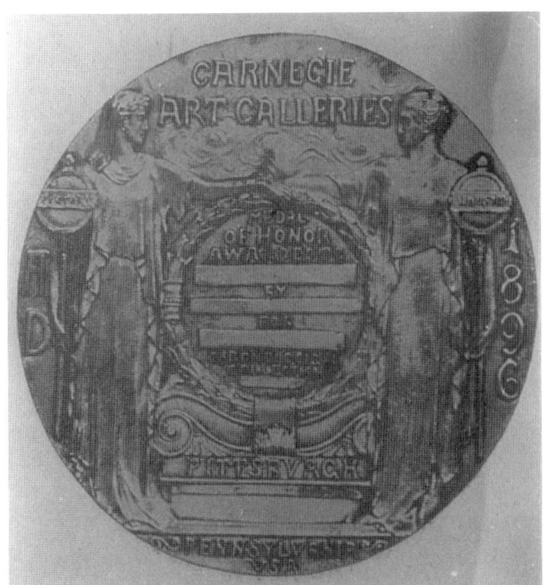


FIG. 19.
Medal of Honor designed in 1896
by the Tiffany Glass and Decorating Company,
New York, for the Carnegie Art Galleries:
(a) obverse (top), (b) reverse (bottom).
From the 1900 catalogue.

79

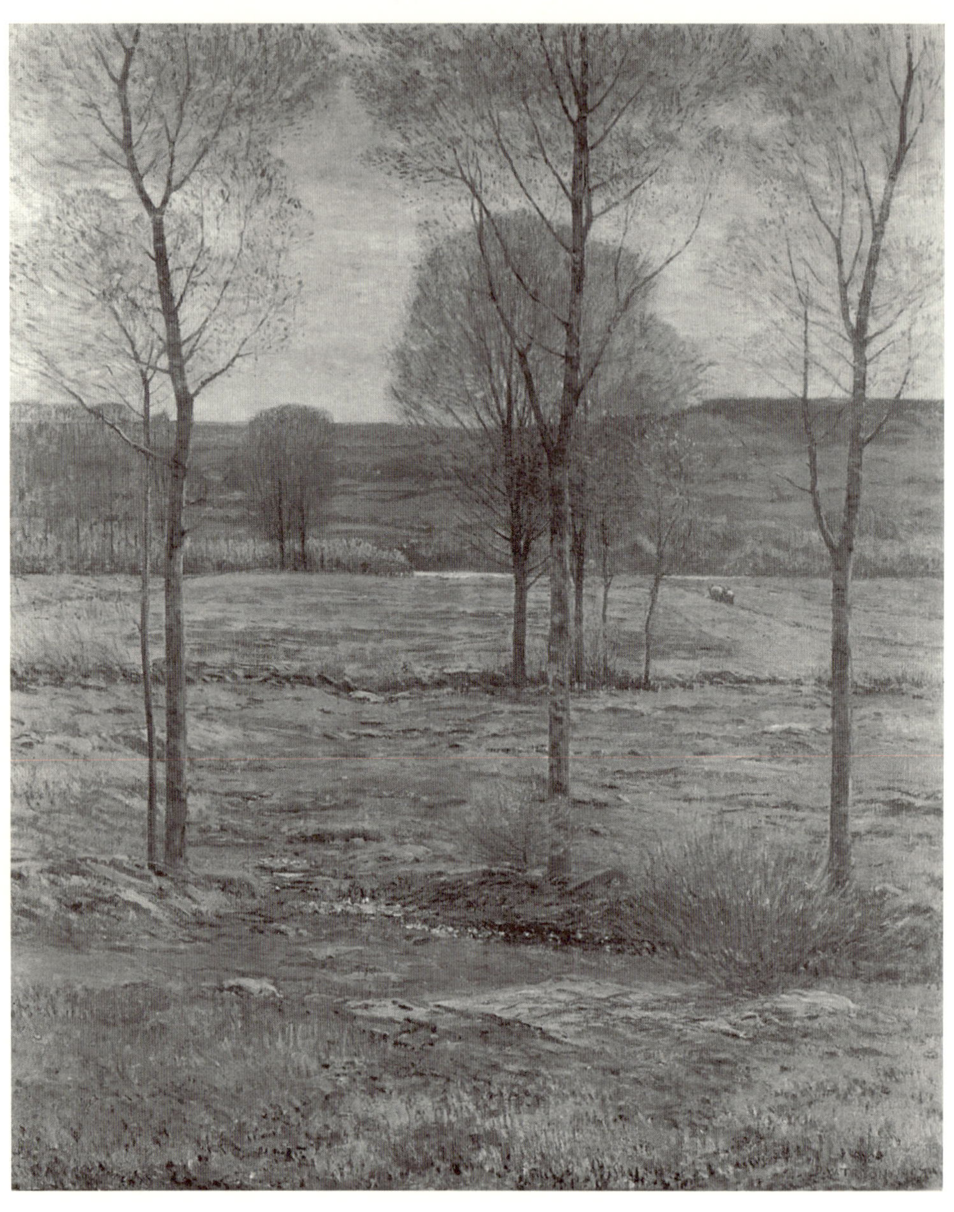


FIG. 20.
Dwight William Tryon, *Springtime (Early Spring in New England)*, 1897.
Oil on canvas, 70⅔ x 57⅞ in.
Courtesy of the Freer Gallery of Art, Smithsonian Institution, Washington, D.C., 06.77.

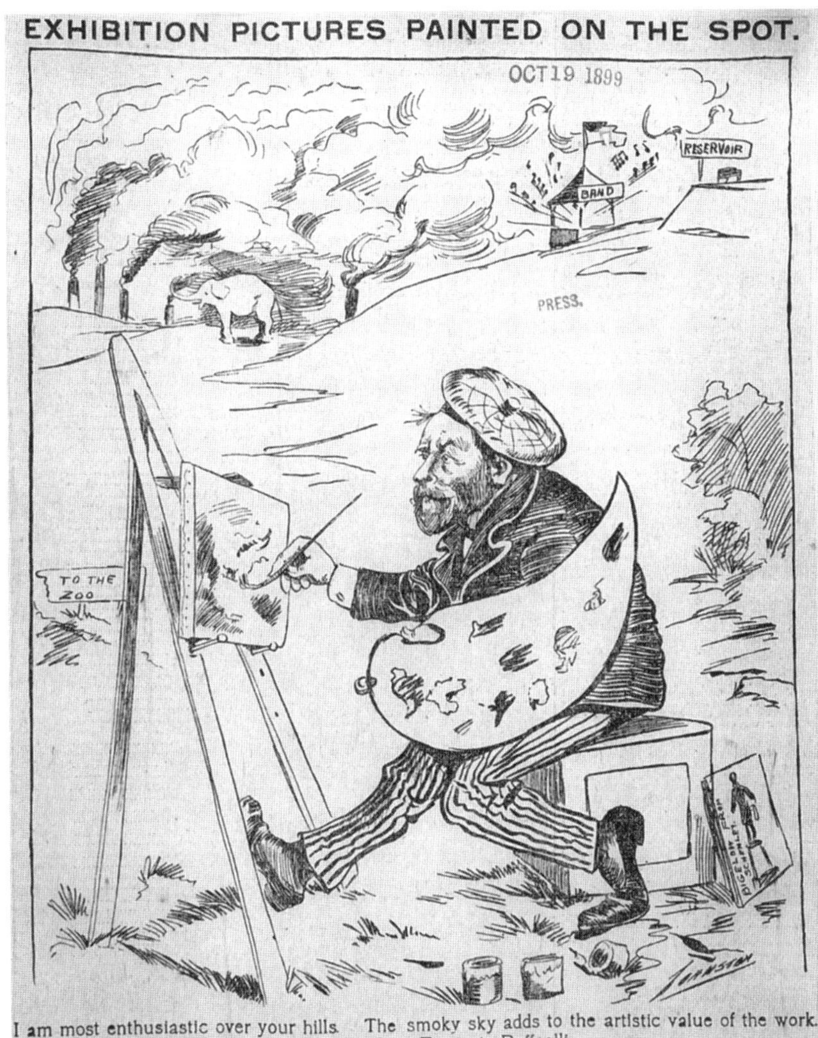


FIG. 21.
"Johnston the Cartoonist," *Exhibition Pictures Painted on the Spot*.
From the *Pittsburgh Press*, 19 Oct. 1899.
*Photo:* Pittsburgh Photographic Library, Carnegie Library of Pittsburgh.

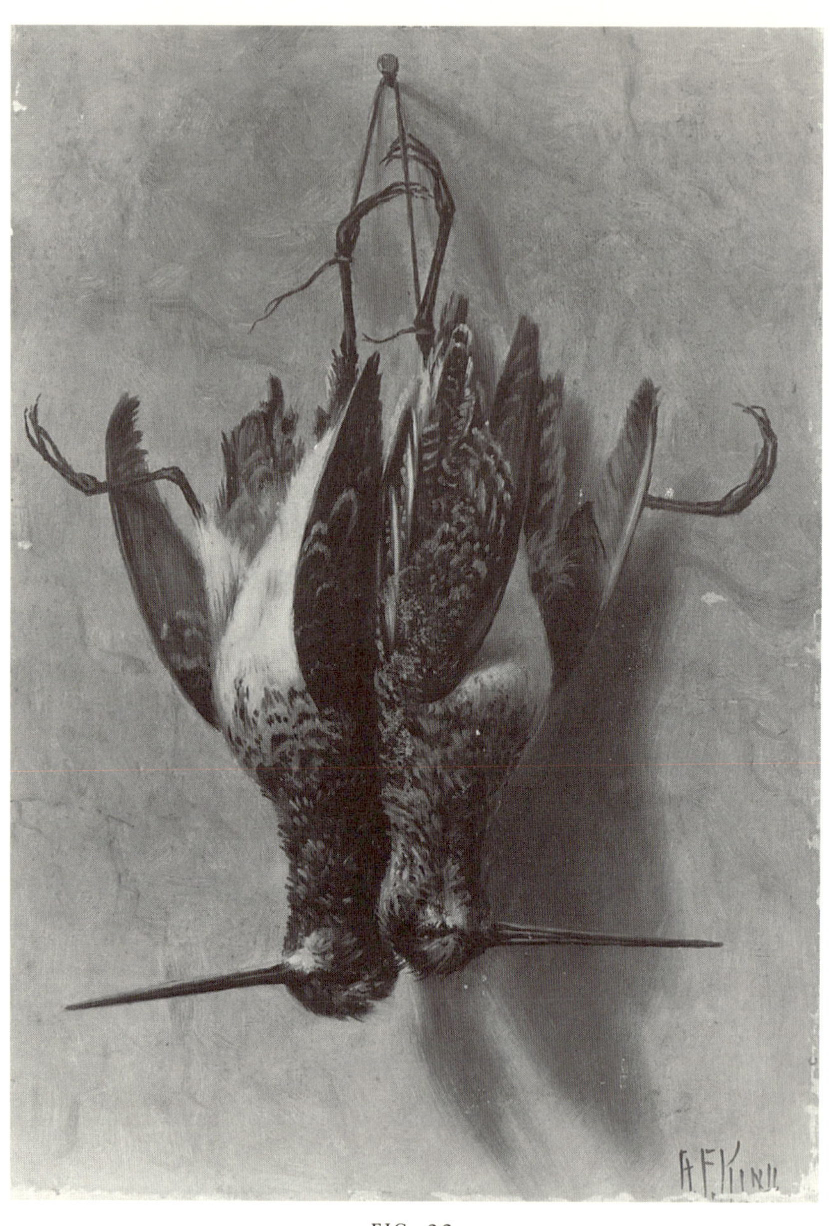



FIG. 22.
Albert F. King, *Woodcocks Hanging from a Nail*, ca. 1925.
Oil on canvas, 14 x 10 in.
Westmoreland Museum of Art, Greensburg, Pennsylvania;
gift of Mr. and Mrs. Paul G. Sailer, 82.99.

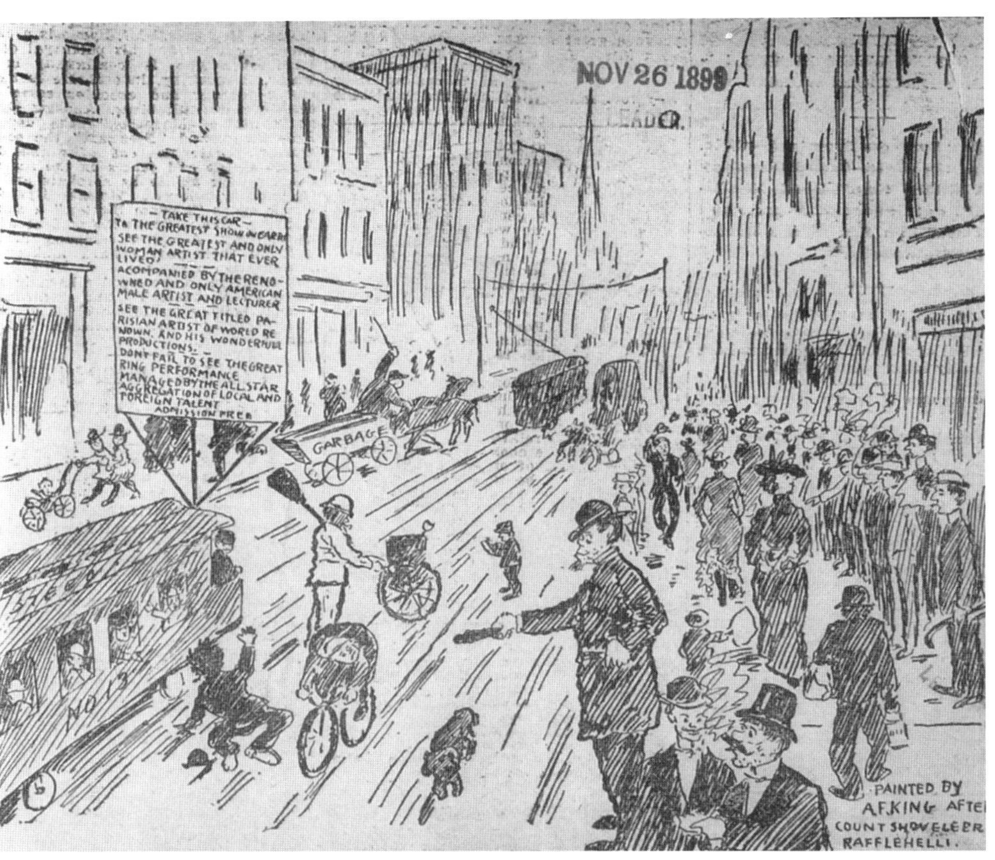


FIG. 23.

Drawing after A. F. King's parody of Impressionism.
From the *Pittsburgh Leader*, 26 Nov. 1899.
*Photo:* Pittsburgh Photographic Library, Carnegie Library of Pittsburgh.

"The greatest and only woman artist that ever lived" referred to on the oversized
streetcar sign was Cecilia Beaux; "the renowned and only American male artist
and lecturer" was William Merritt Chase; "the greatest titled Parisian
artist of world renown" was Jean-François Raffaëlli.

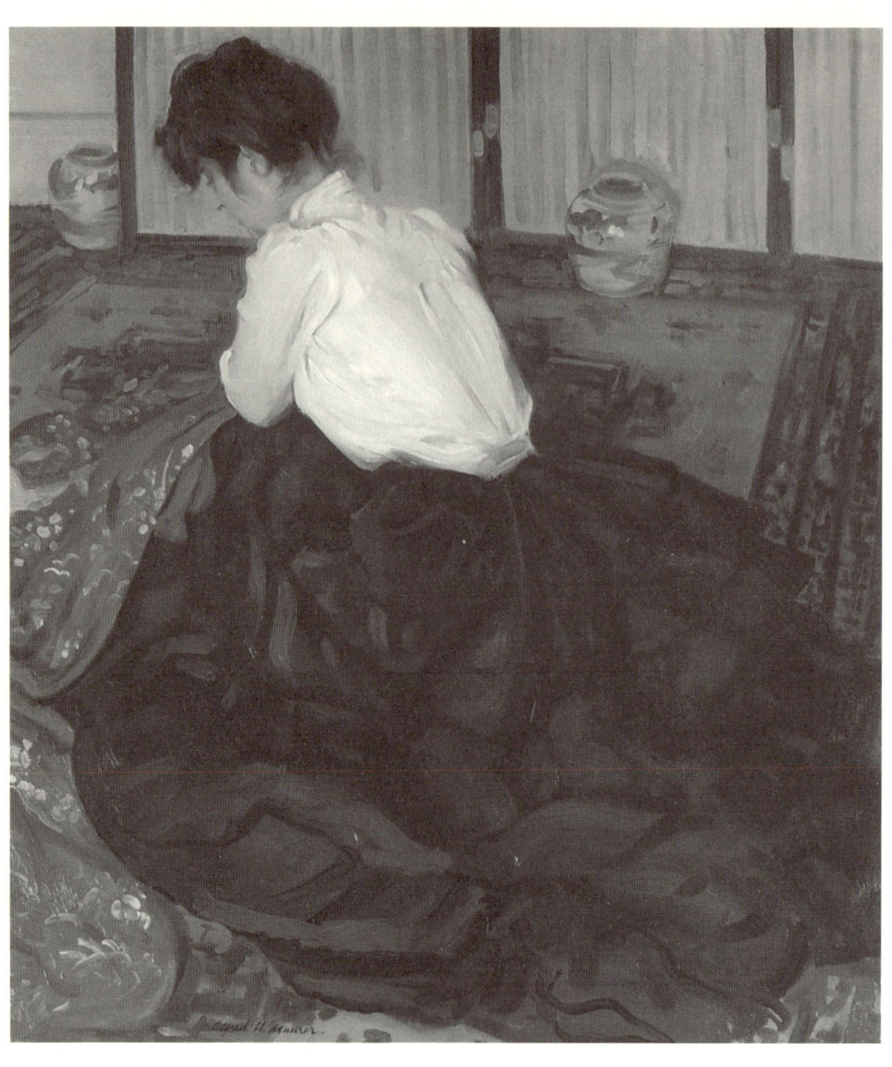

FIG. 24.
Alfred H. Maurer, *An Arrangement*, 1901.
Oil on cardboard, 36 x 31⅞ in.
Collection of the Whitney Museum of American Art, New York;
gift of Mr. and Mrs. Hudson D. Walker, 50.13.

84

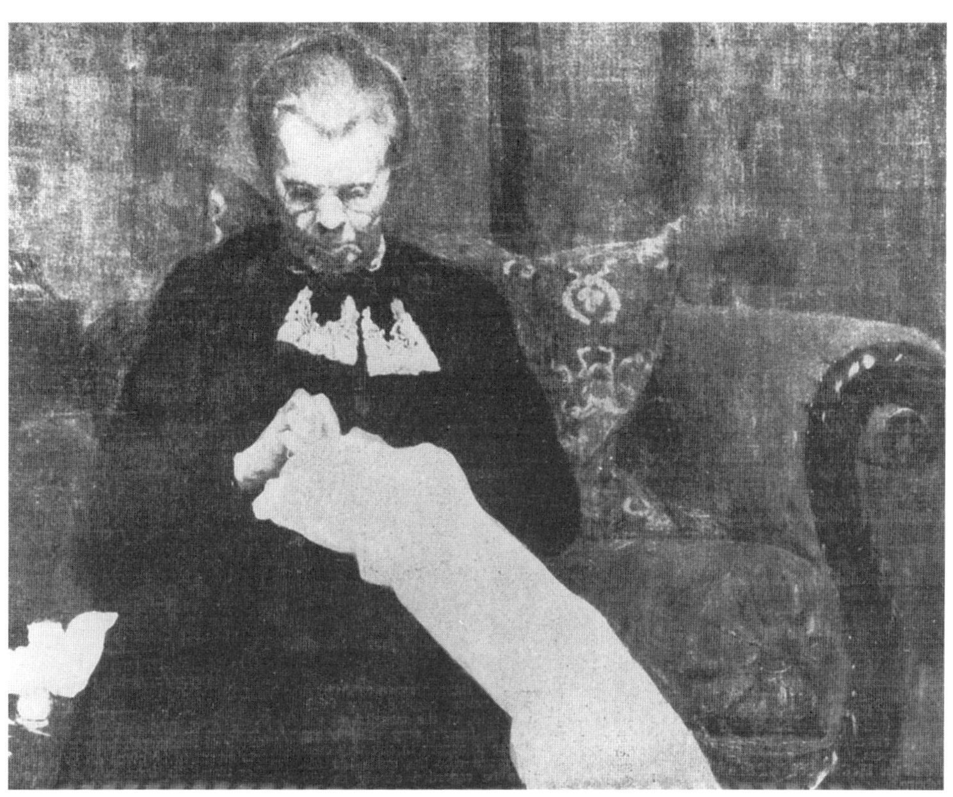



Elizabeth Wetherall Ahrens, *Sewing—A Portrait*, ca. 1901.
From the *Pittsburgh Index*, 9 Nov. 1901, 7.
*Photo:* Pittsburgh Photographic Library, Carnegie Library of Pittsburgh.

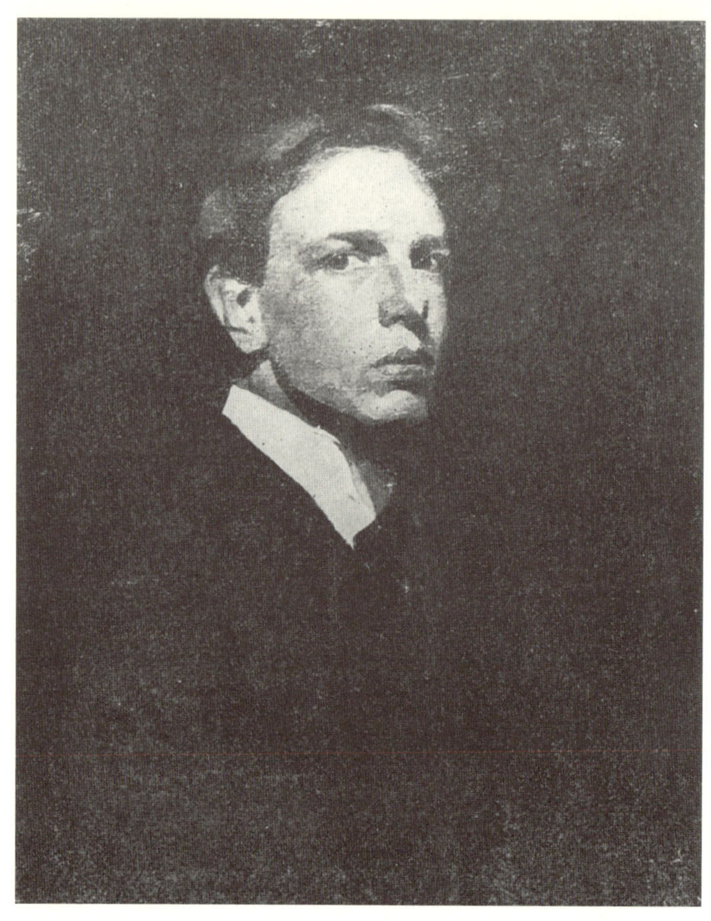



FIG. 27. (*OPPOSITE*)
John White Alexander, *A Woman in Rose*, ca. 1901.
Oil on canvas, 40 x 22 ½ in.
Carnegie Museum of Art, Pittsburgh, 01.2.

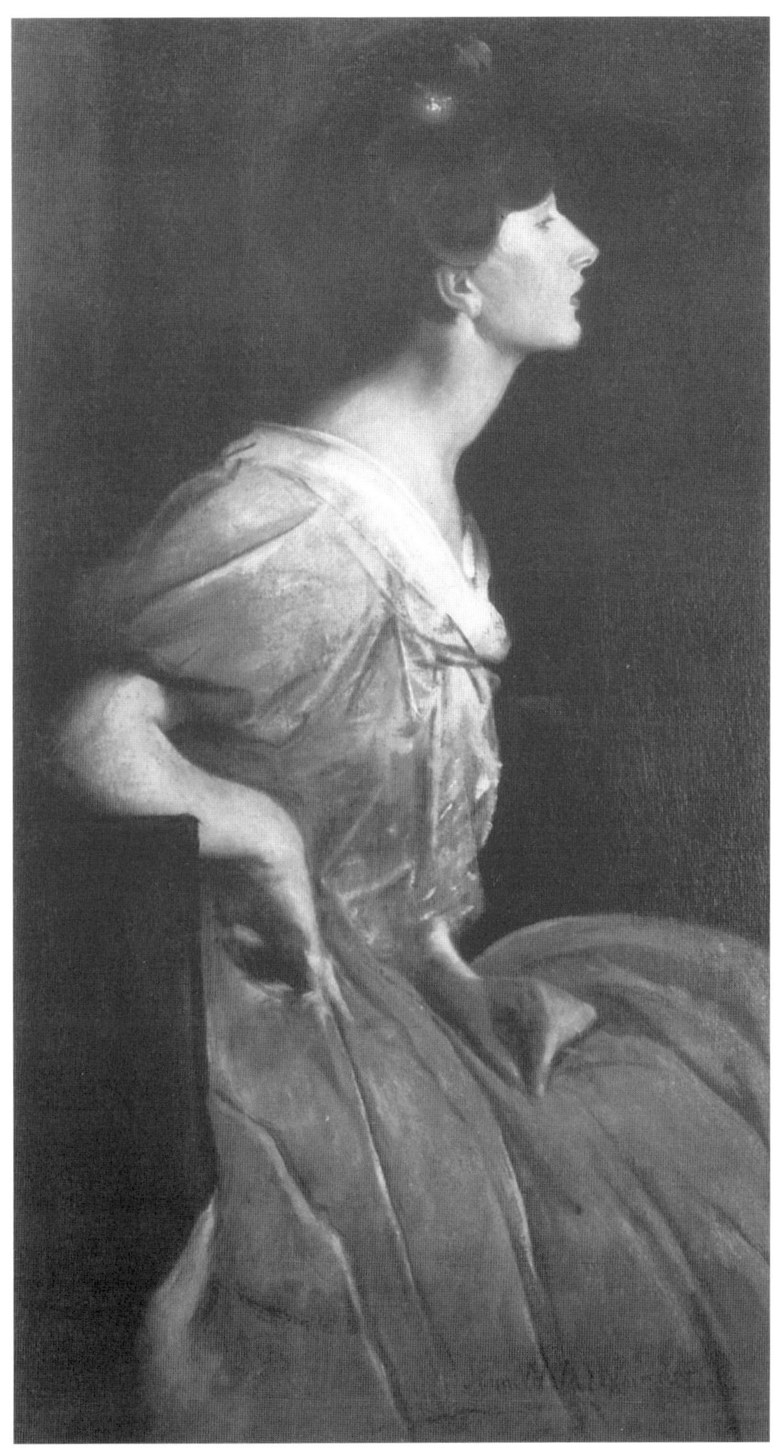

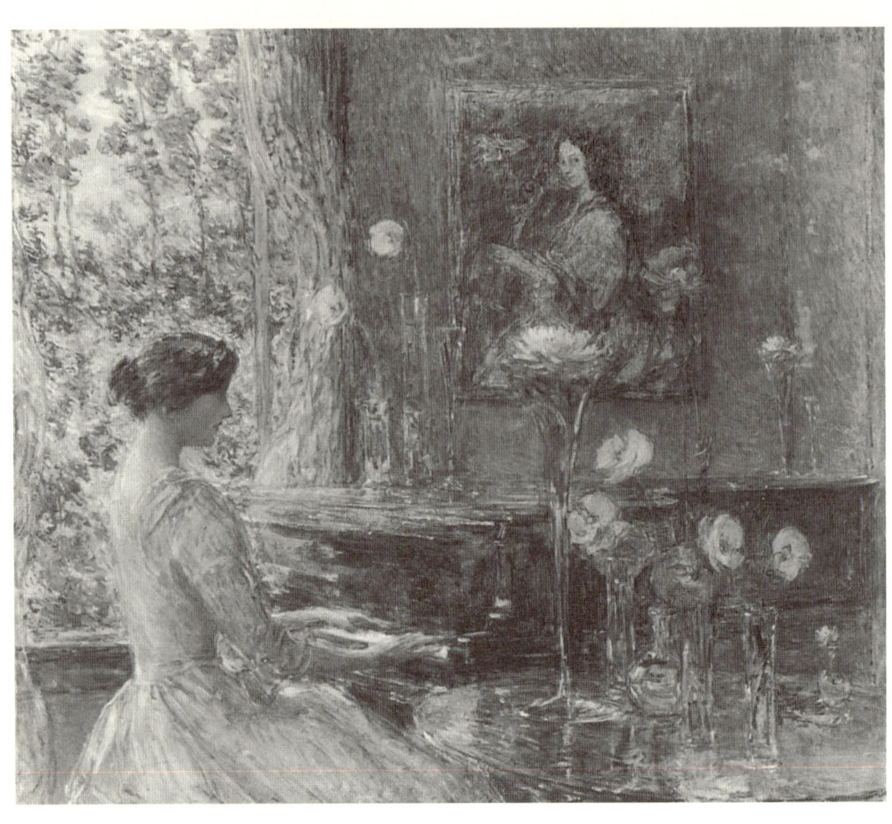

FIG. 28.
Childe Hassam, *Improvisation*, 1899.
Oil on canvas, 30 x 33 in.
National Museum of American Art, Smithsonian Institution, Washington, D.C.,
gift of John Gellatly, 1929.

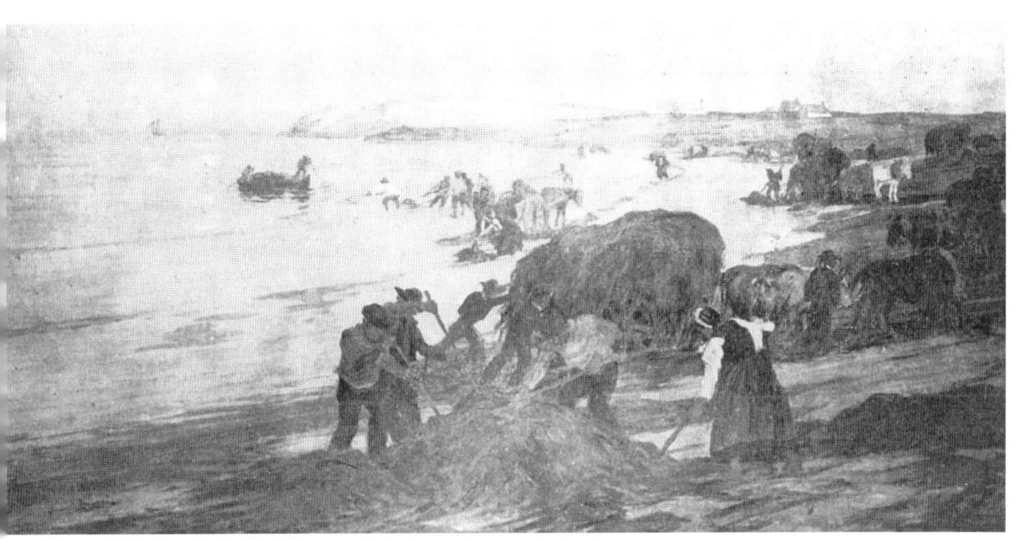

FIG. 29.
André Dauchez, *The Kelp Gatherers*, ca. 1900.
From the *Pittsburgh Bulletin*, 3 Nov. 1900, front cover.
*Photo*: Pittsburgh Photographic Library, Carnegie Library of Pittsburgh.

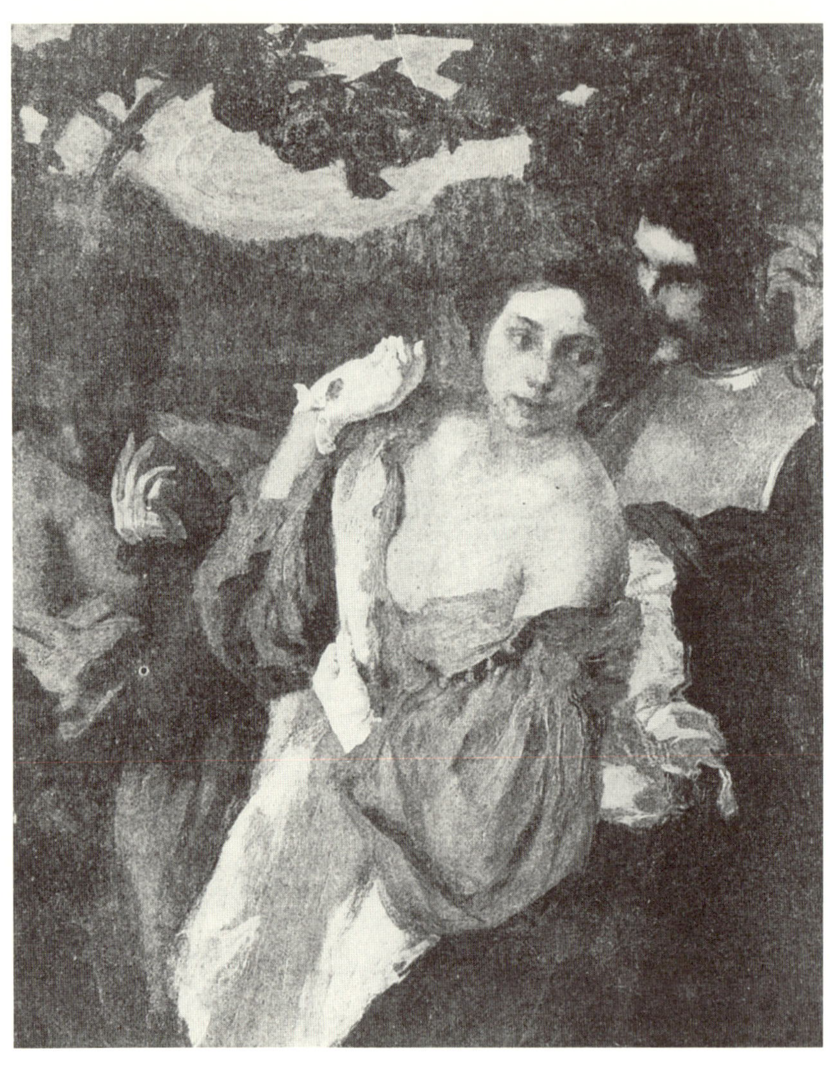

FIG. 30.
Edmond Aman-Jean, *Comedy*, ca. 1901.
From the *Pittsburgh Index*, 9 Nov. 1901, 5.
*Photo*: Pittsburgh Photographic Library, Carnegie Library of Pittsburgh.

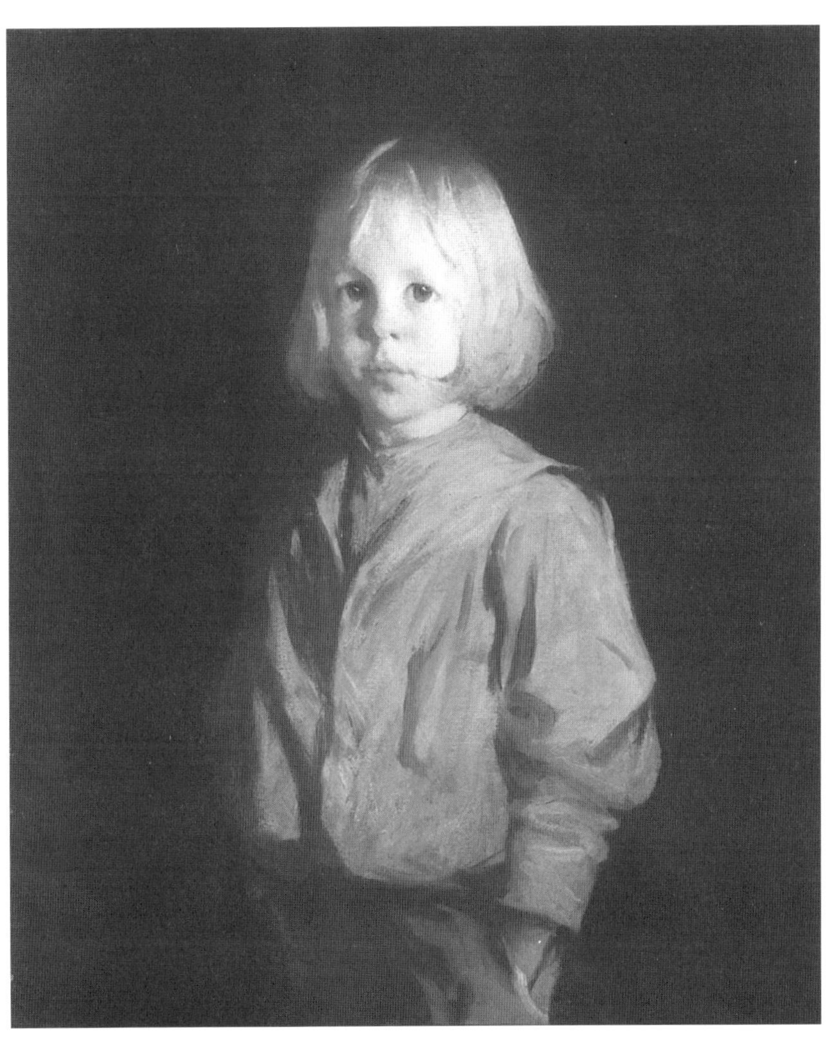

FIG. 31.
Frank W. Benson, *Portrait of a Boy,* 1896.
Oil on canvas, 30 x 26½ in.
Carnegie Museum of Art, Pittsburgh, 97.5.

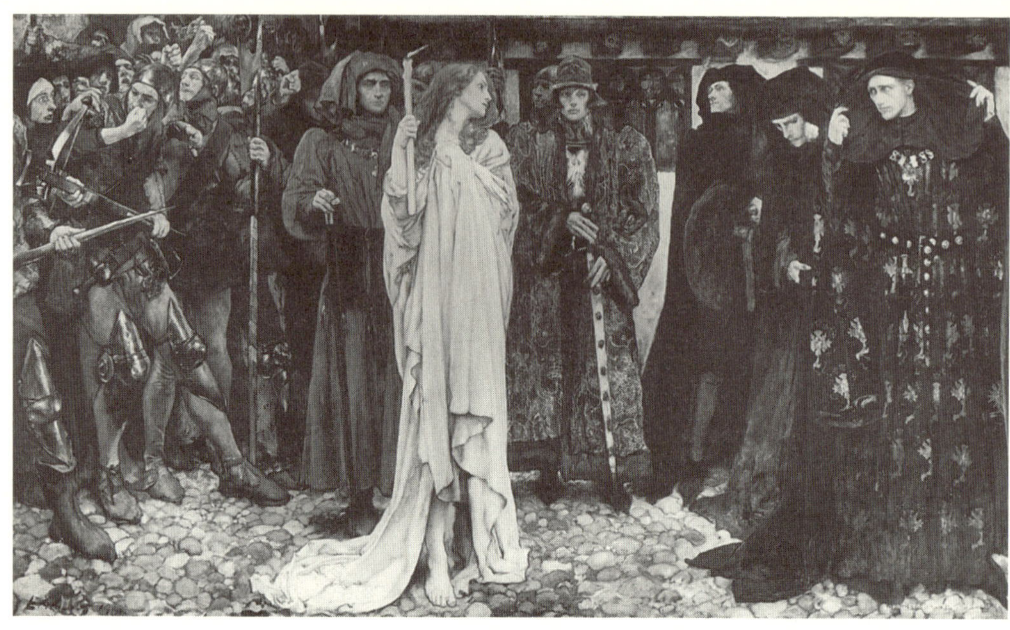

FIG. 32.
Edwin Austin Abbey, *The Penance of Eleanor, Duchess of Gloucester*, 1900.
Oil on canvas, 49 x 85 in.
Carnegie Museum of Art, Pittsburgh, 02.1.

FIG. 33. *(OPPOSITE)*
James Jebusa Shannon, *Miss Kitty*, 1897.
Oil on canvas, 66 x 40 in.
Carnegie Museum of Art, Pittsburgh, 97.4.

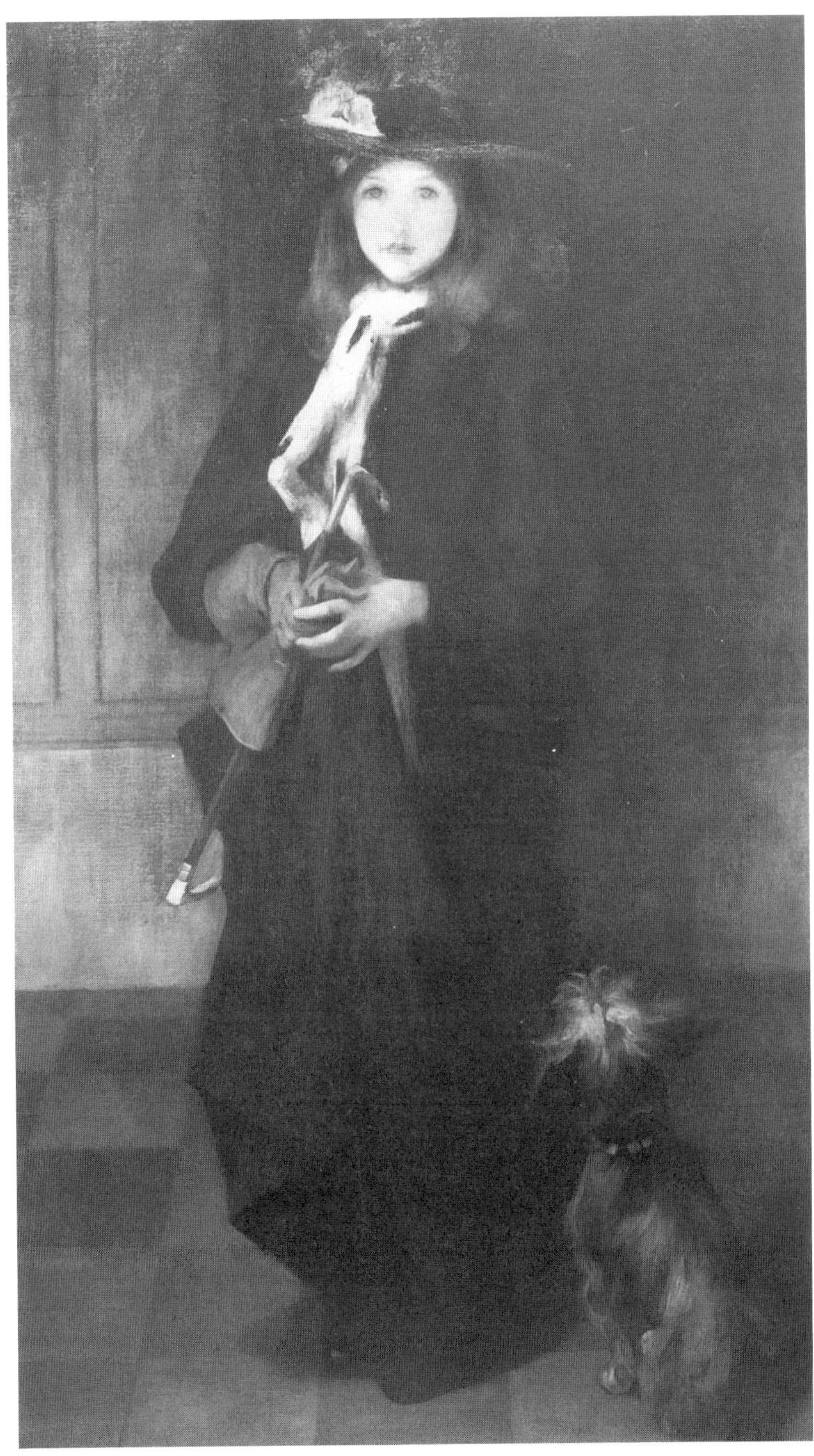

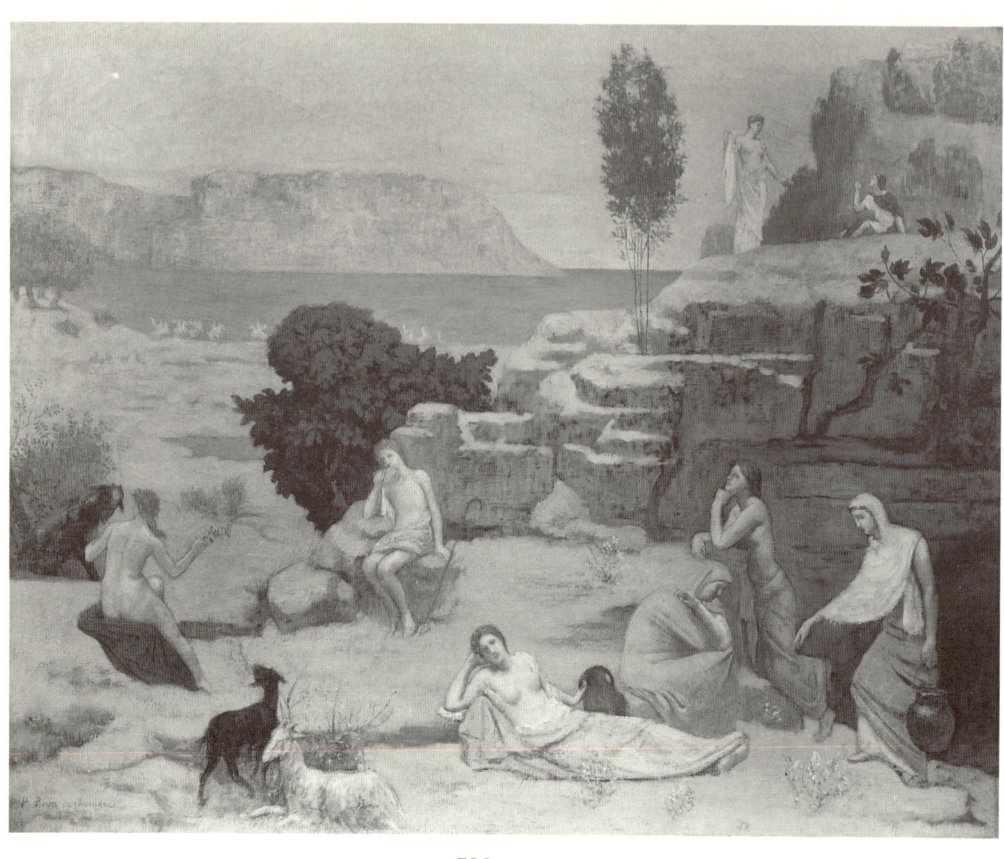



FIG. 34.
Pierre-Cécile Puvis de Chavannes, *A Vision of Antiquity — School of Form*,
ca. 1887–1889.
Oil on canvas, 41 ¼ x 52 in.
Carnegie Museum of Art, Pittsburgh, 97.3.

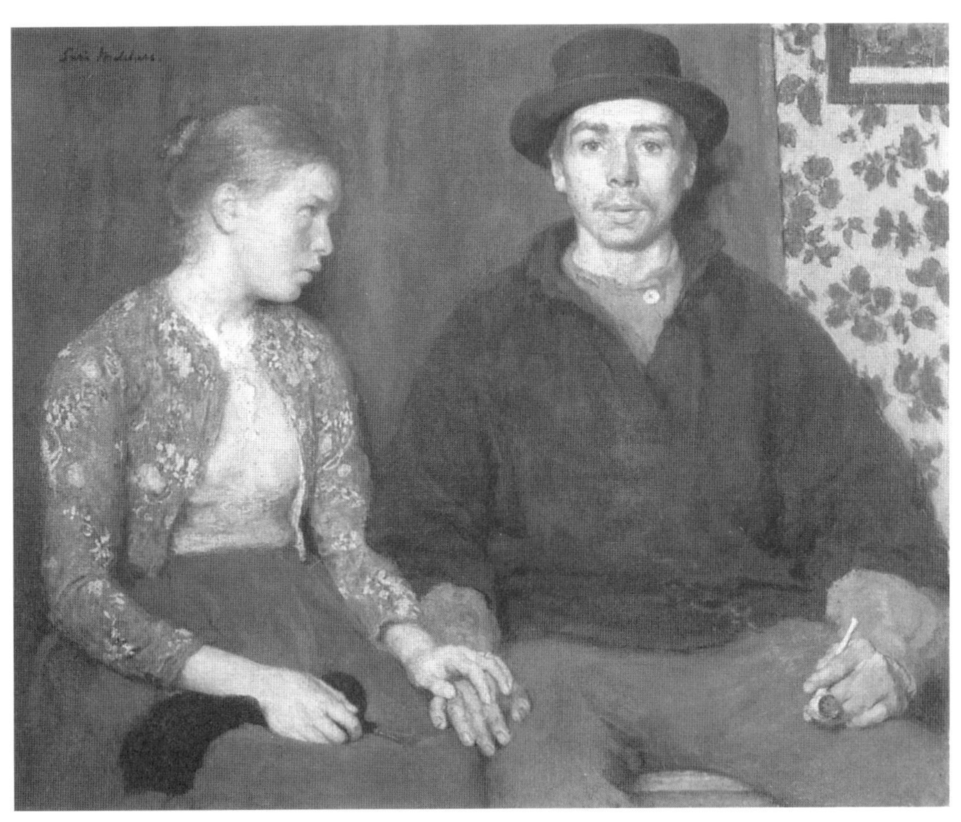



FIG. 35.
Gari Melchers, *A Sailor and His Sweetheart*, ca. 1898.
Oil on canvas, 33¼ x 41 in.
Courtesy of the Freer Gallery of Art, Smithsonian Institution, Washington, D.C., 13.10.

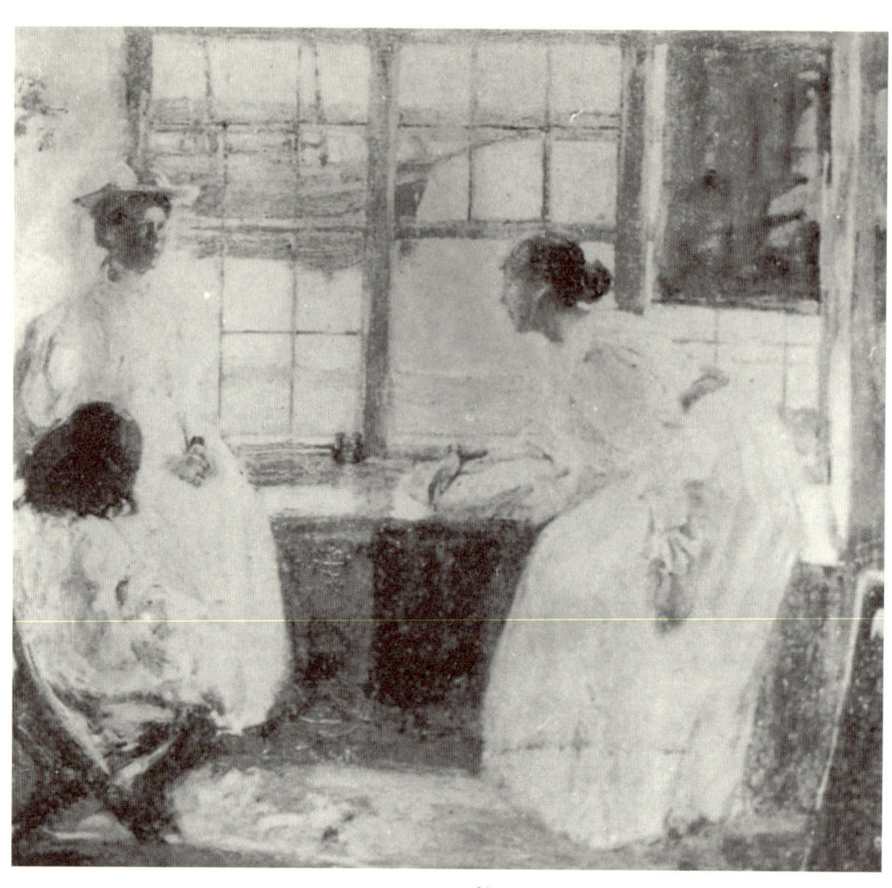



Alexander Roche, *The Window Seat*, ca. 1898.
Oil on canvas, 31 x 31 ½ in.
From the 1898 catalogue;
formerly in the collection of the Carnegie Museum of Art, Pittsburgh.

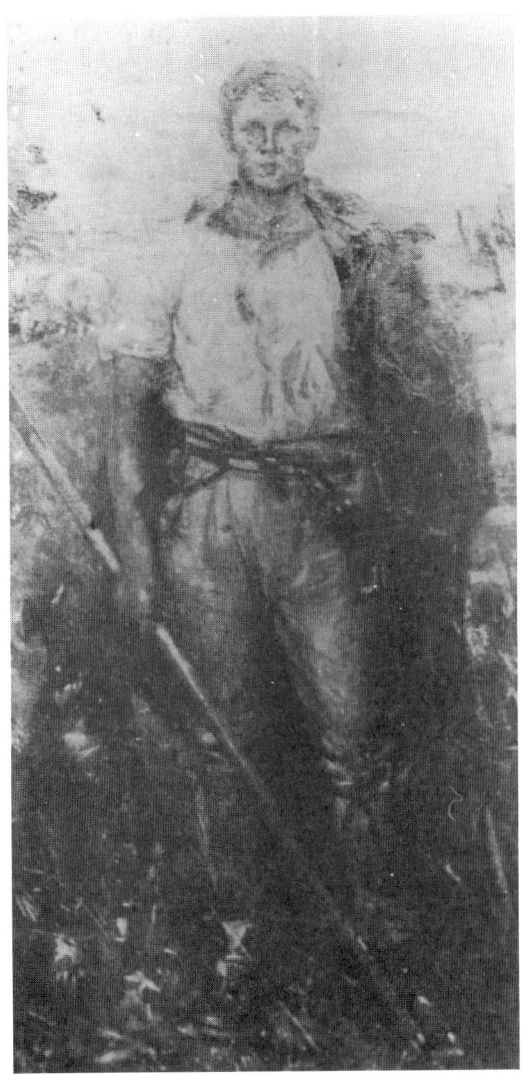

FIG. 37.
Edward Arthur Walton, *The Shepherd*, ca. 1898.
Oil on canvas, 77½ x 39 in.
From the 1898 catalogue;
formerly in the collection of the Carnegie Museum of Art, Pittsburgh.

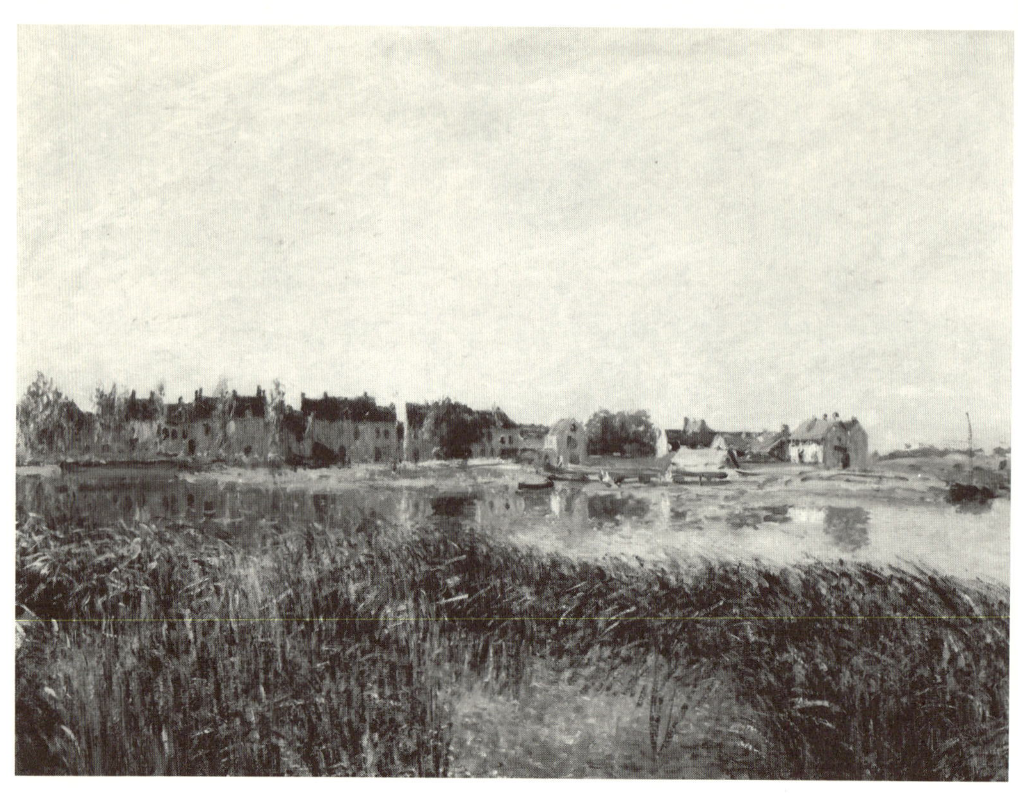

FIG. 38.
Alfred Sisley, *Village on the Shore of the Marne*, ca. 1890s.
Oil on canvas 22 x 30 in.
Carnegie Museum of Art, Pittsburgh, 99.7.


FIG. 39. (*OPPOSITE*)
Jules Bastien-LePage, *Paysanne*, ca. 1880.
Oil on canvas, 71 x 29 in.
Carnegie Museum of Art, Pittsburgh, 98.4.

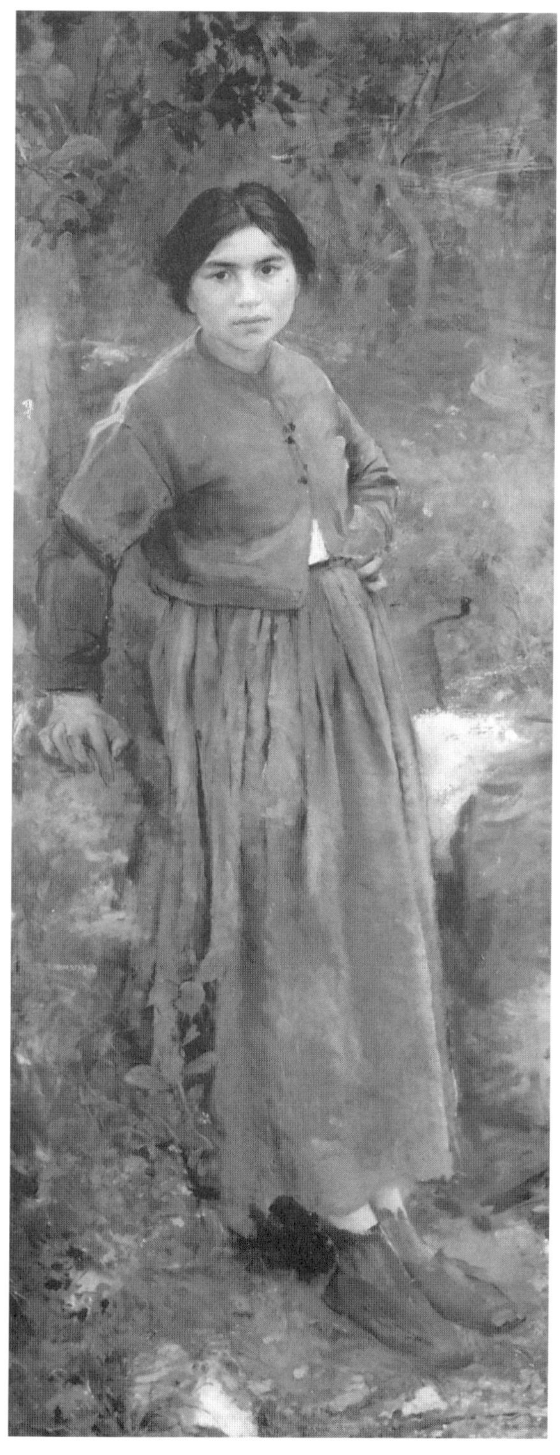

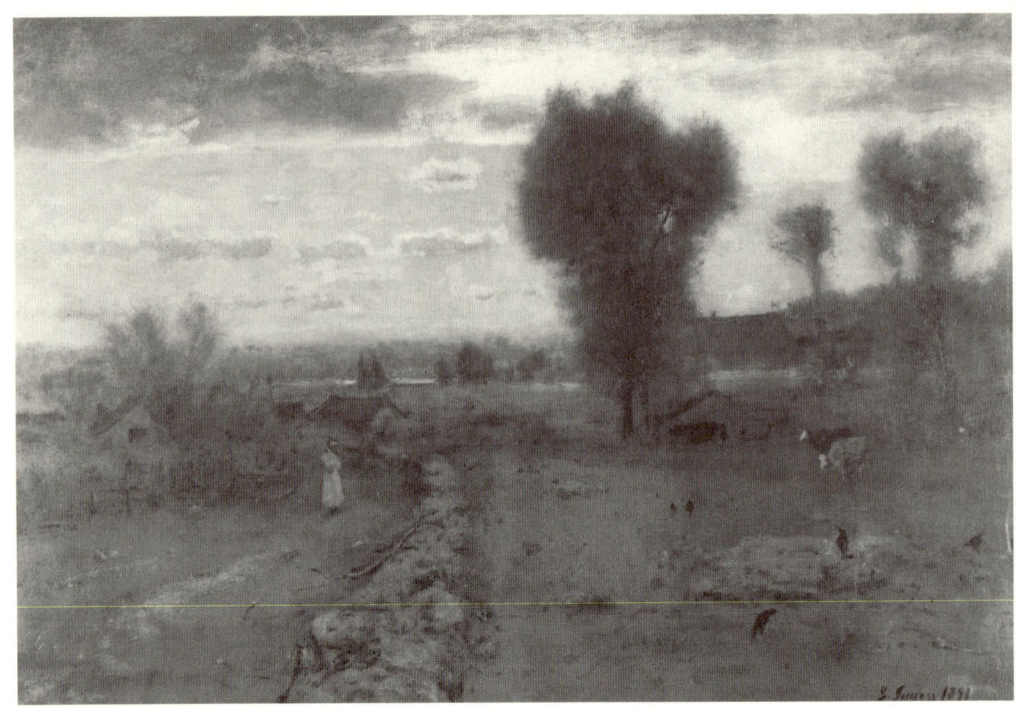



FIG. 40.
George Inness, *The Clouded Sun*, 1891.
Oil on canvas, 30⅛ x 45¼ in.
Carnegie Museum of Art, Pittsburgh, 99.9.

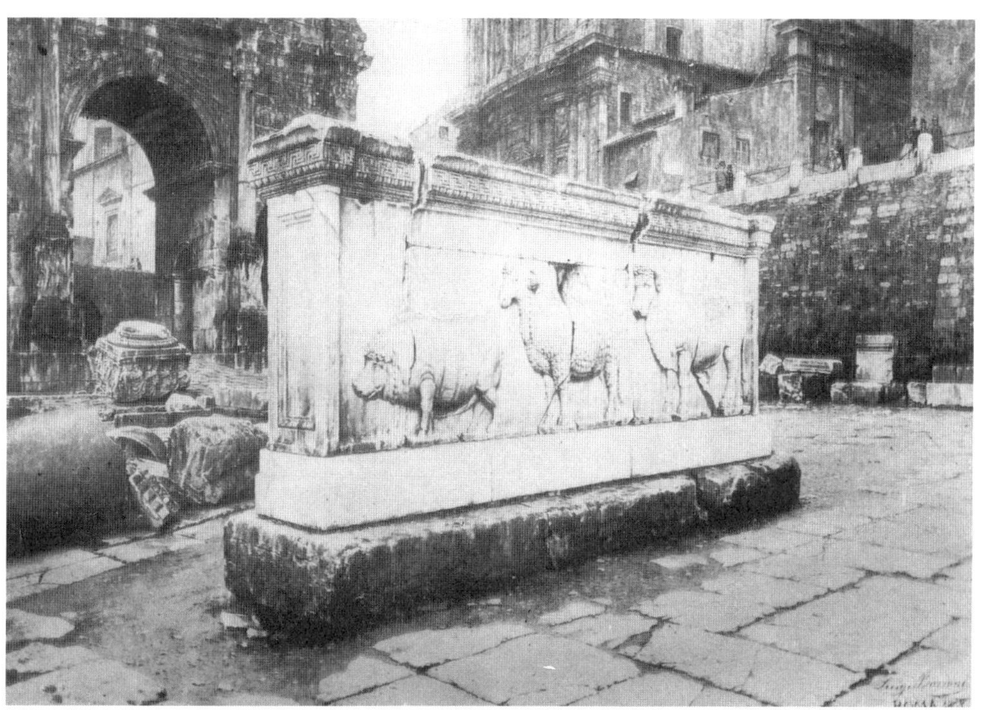

FIG. 41.
Luigi Bazzani, *The Anaglyph of Trajan in the Roman Forum*, 1897.
Oil on canvas, 30 x 40 in.
From the *Pittsburgh Bulletin*, 27 Jan. 1900, 6;
formerly in the collection of the Carnegie Museum of Art, Pittsburgh.
*Photo*: Pittsburgh Photographic Library, Carnegie Library of Pittsburgh.

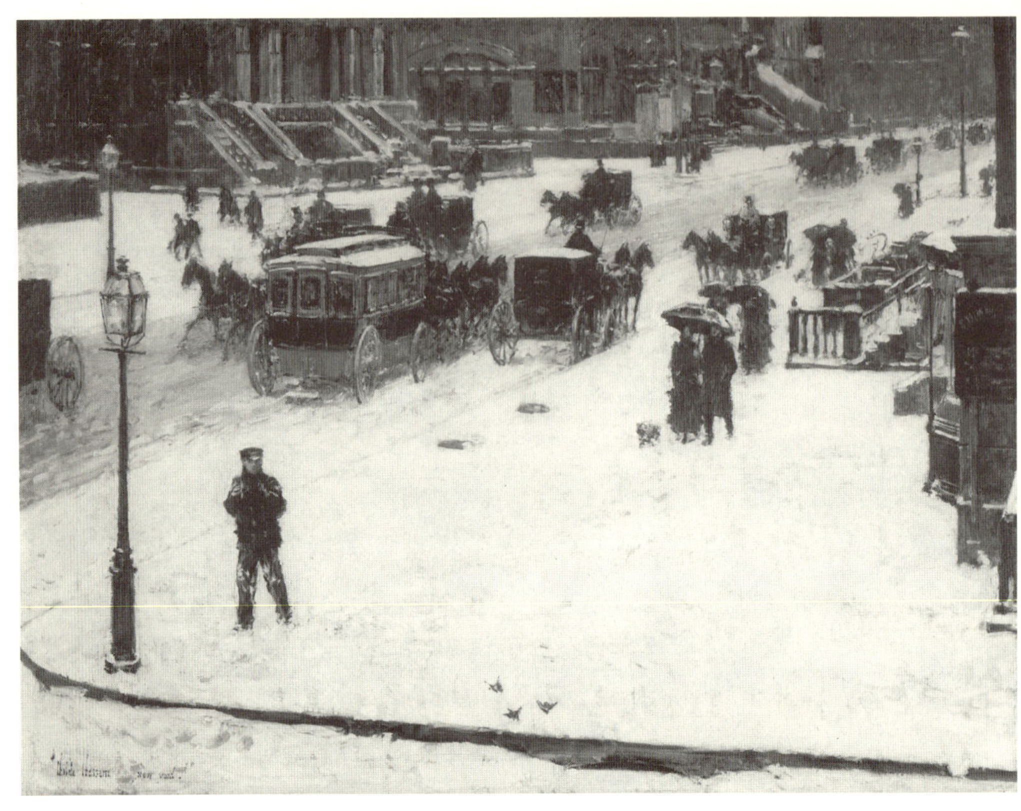



FIG. 42.
Childe Hassam, *Fifth Avenue in Winter*, 1892.
Oil on canvas, 21⅝ x 28 in.
Carnegie Museum of Art, Pittsburgh, 00.2.

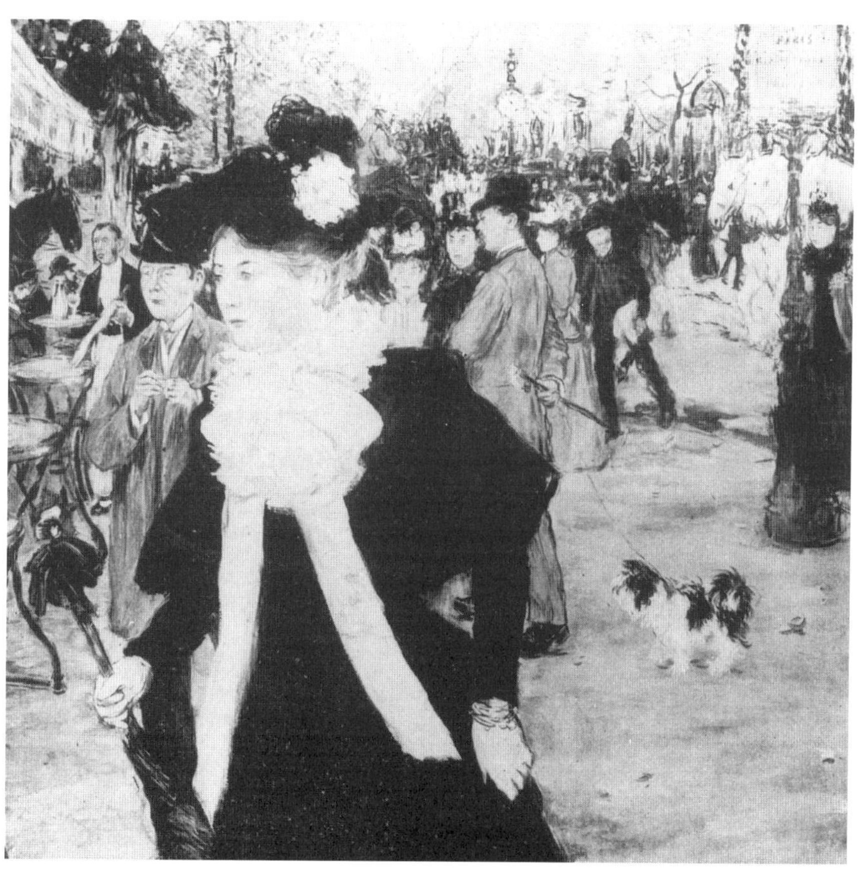



FIG. 43.
Jean-François Raffaëlli, *Boulevard des Italiens, Paris*, ca. 1899.
Oil on canvas, 47 x 52 in.
From the *Pittsburgh Bulletin*, 3 Feb. 1900, 6;
formerly in the collection of the Carnegie Museum of Art, Pittsburgh.
*Photo*: Pittsburgh Photographic Library, Carnegie Museum of Pittsburgh.

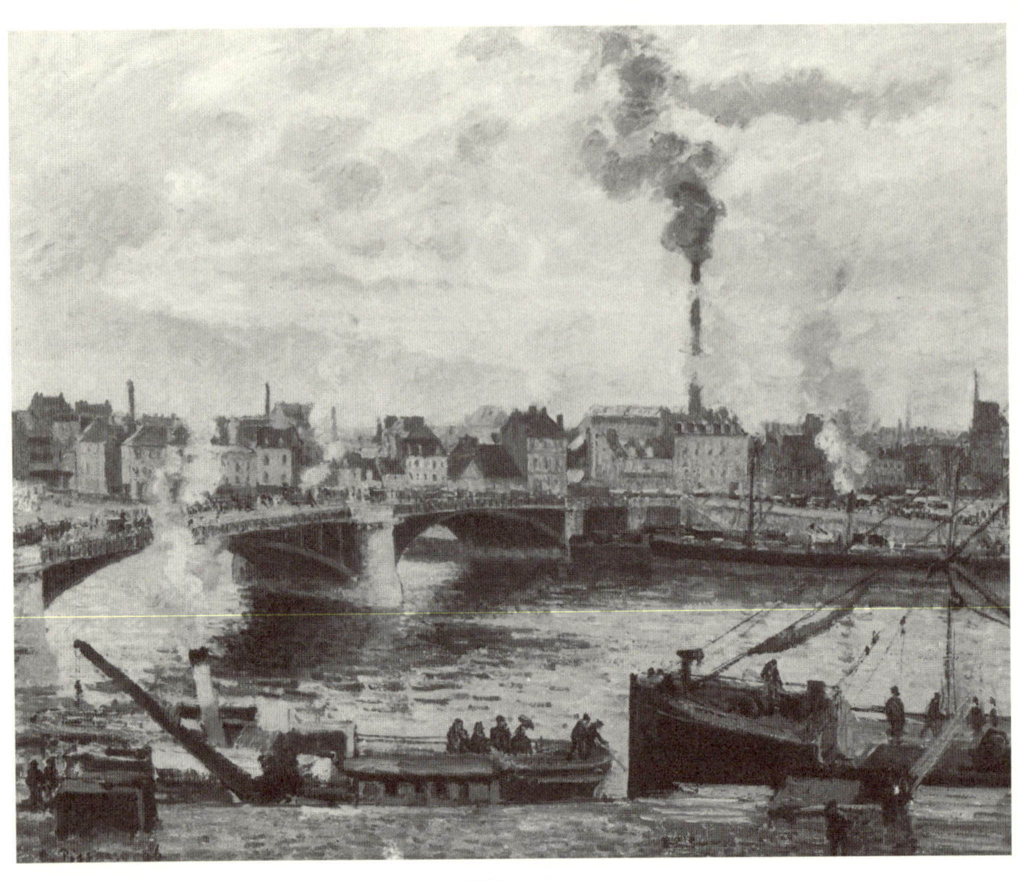

FIG. 44.
Camille Pissarro, *The Great Bridge at Rouen*, 1896.
Oil on canvas, 29¼ x 36¼ in.
Carnegie Museum of Art, Pittsburgh, 00.9.

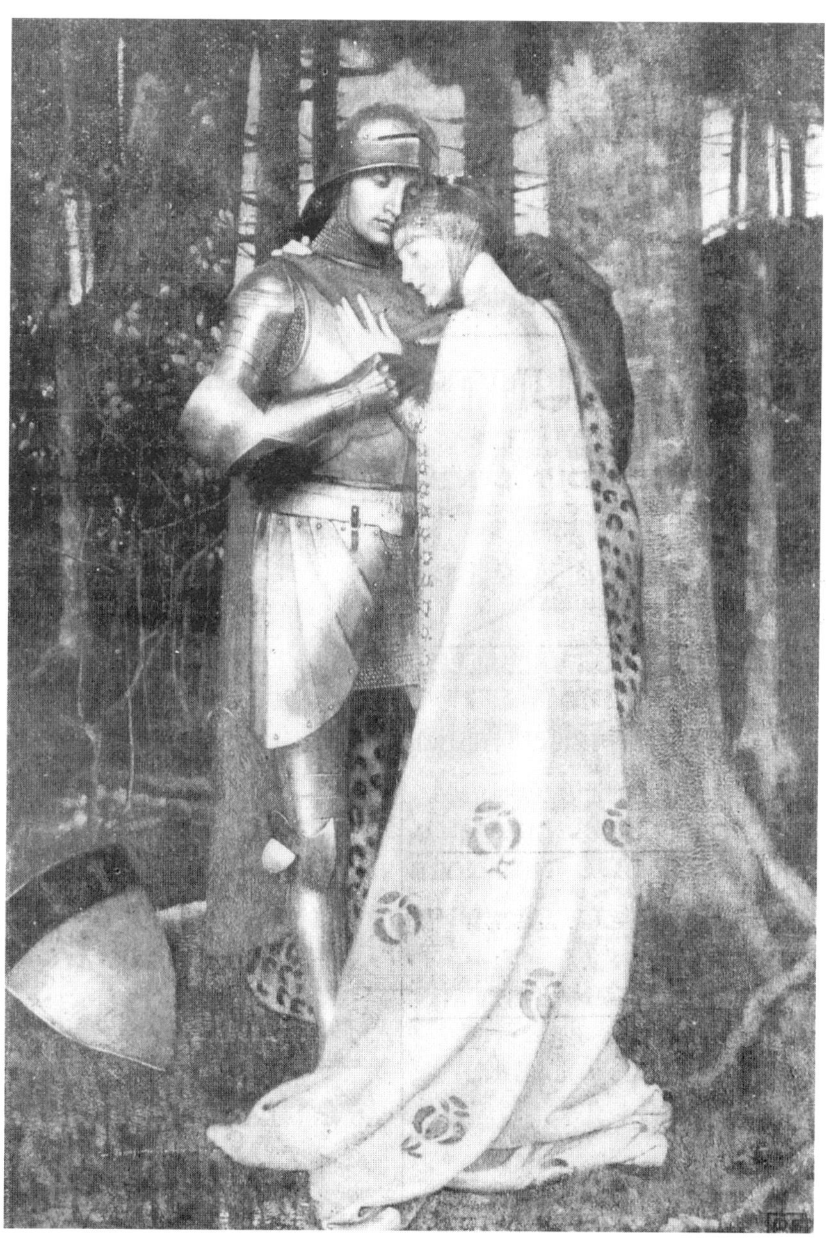

FIG. 45.
Marianne Preindlsberger Stokes, *Aucassin and Nicolette*, ca. 1900.
Oil on canvas, 49 x 32 in.
From the *Pittsburgh Bulletin*, 19 Jan. 1901, front cover;
formerly in the collection of the Carnegie Museum of Art, Pittsburgh.
*Photo:* Pittsburgh Photographic Library, Carnegie Library of Pittsburgh.

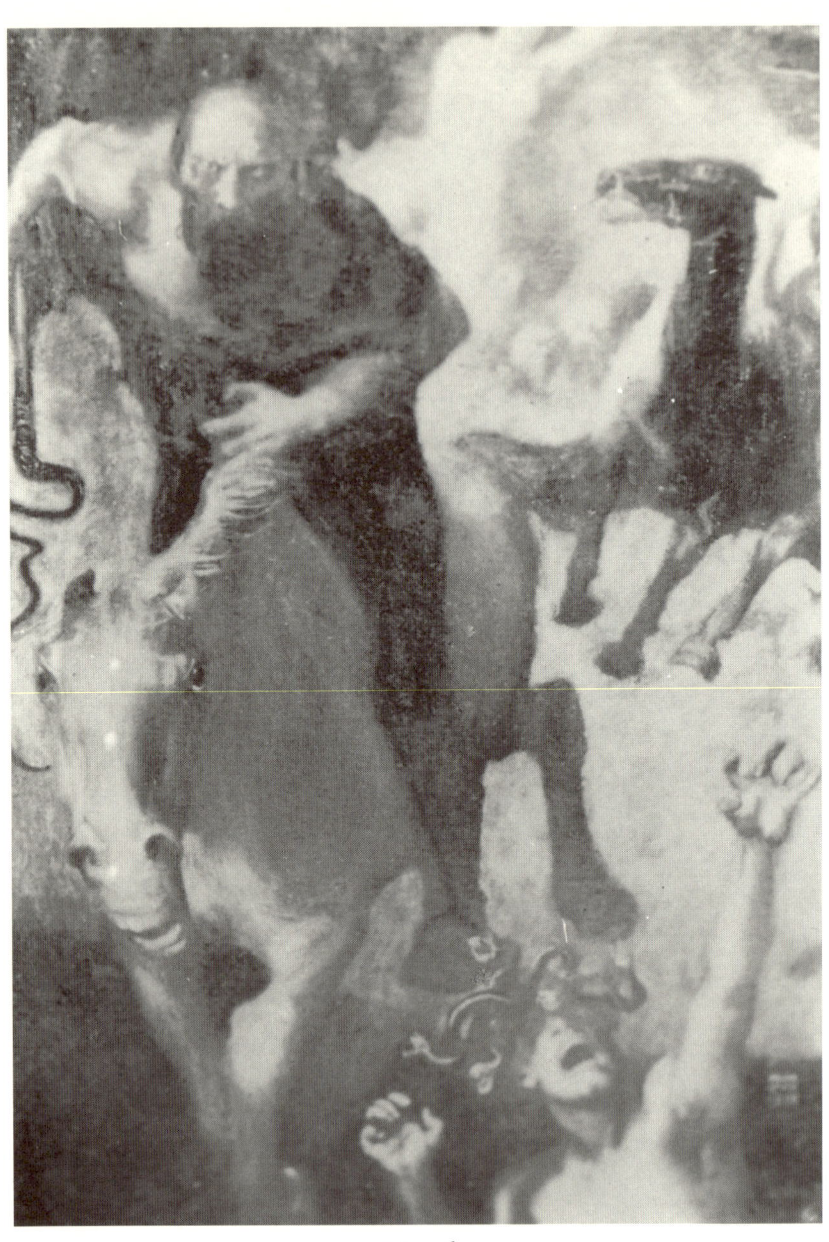

FIG. 46.
Franz Stuck, *The Wild Chase*, 1899.
Oil on canvas, 38 x 26½ in.
From the 1900 catalogue;
formerly in the collection of the Carnegie Museum of Art, Pittsburgh.

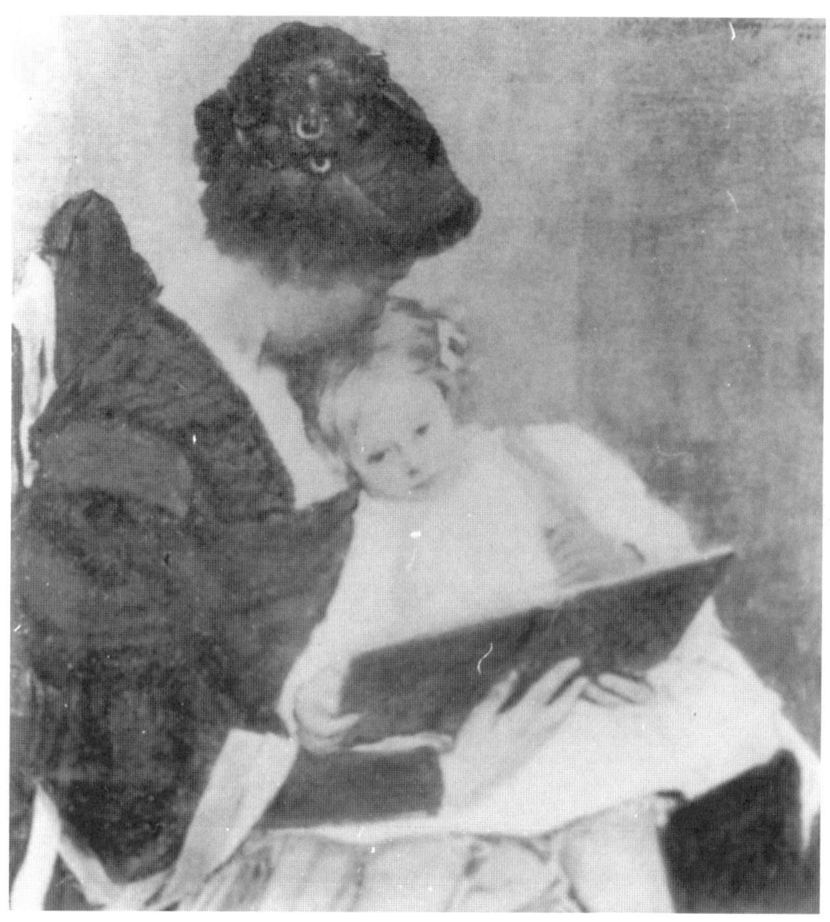

FIG. 47.
Sergeant Kendall, *The End of the Day*, ca. 1900.
From the 1900 catalogue.

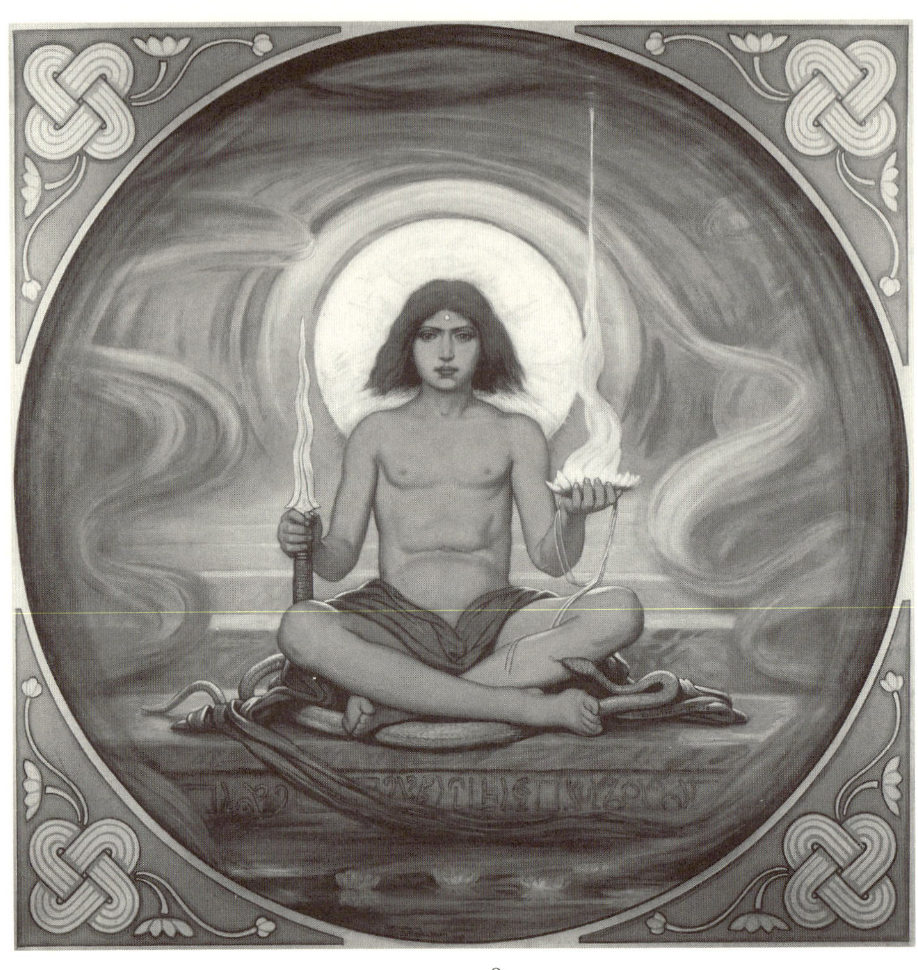



FIG. 48.
Elihu Vedder, *The Keeper of the Threshold*, 1897–1898.
Oil on canvas, 51 ¾ x 51 ¾ in.
Carnegie Museum of Art, Pittsburgh, 01.1.

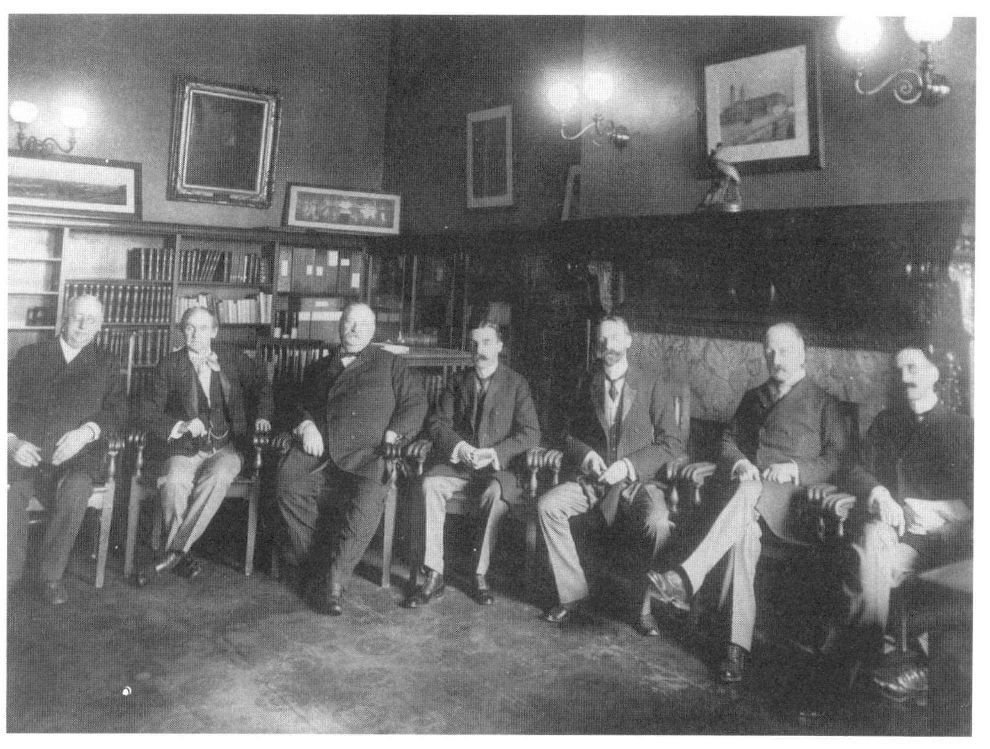



Founder's Day speakers, 7 November 1901.
From the left to right, the speakers are the Rev. Thomas N. Boyle, the comedian Joseph
Jefferson, former president Grover Cleveland, William Nimick Frew, John White
Alexander (juror), Robert W. Allen (juror), Samuel Harden Church
(secretary of the board of trustees).
*Photo:* Pittsburgh Photographic Library, Carnegie Library of Pittsburgh.

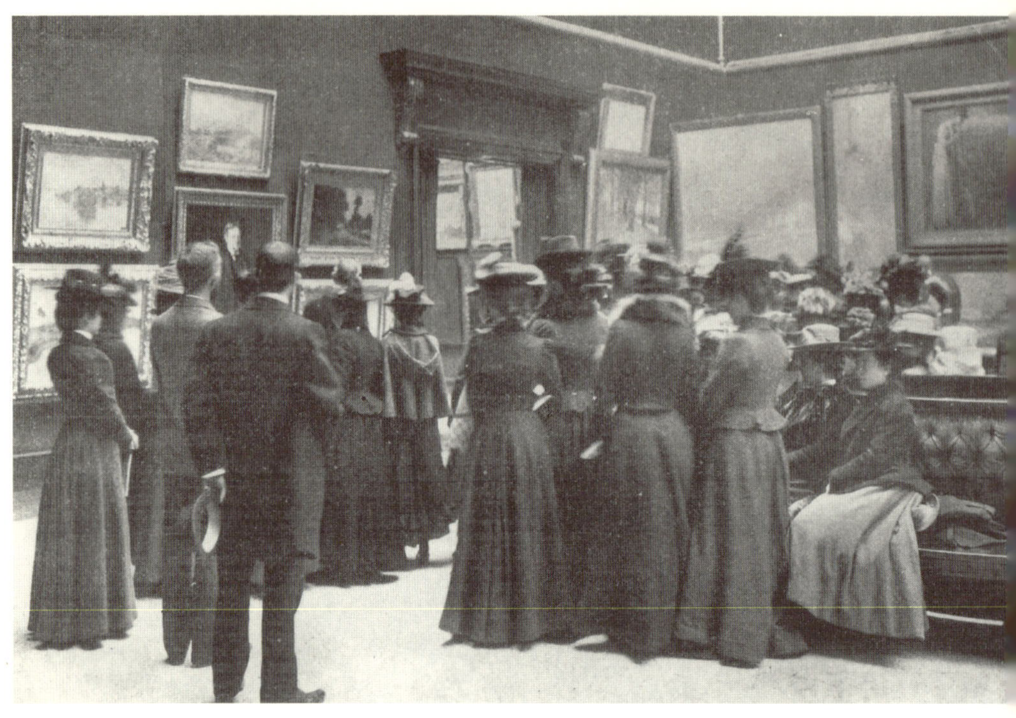

FIG. 50.

John Beatty giving a tour of the annual exhibition to high school
seniors in November 1900.

From the *Pittsburgh Bulletin*, 24 Nov. 1900, 5.

*Photo*: Pittsburgh Photographic Library, Carnegie Library of Pittsburgh.

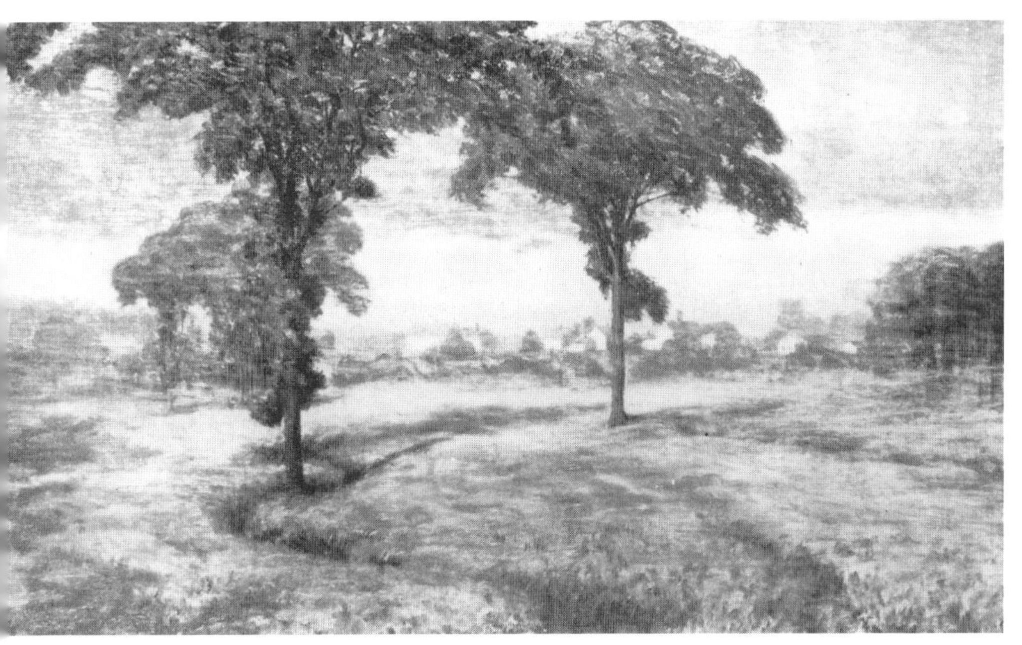


FIG. 51.
Ben Foster, *Misty Moonlight Night*, ca. 1900.
From the *Pittsburgh Bulletin*, 3 Nov. 1900, front cover.
*Photo:* Pittsburgh Photographic Library, Carnegie Library of Pittsburgh.

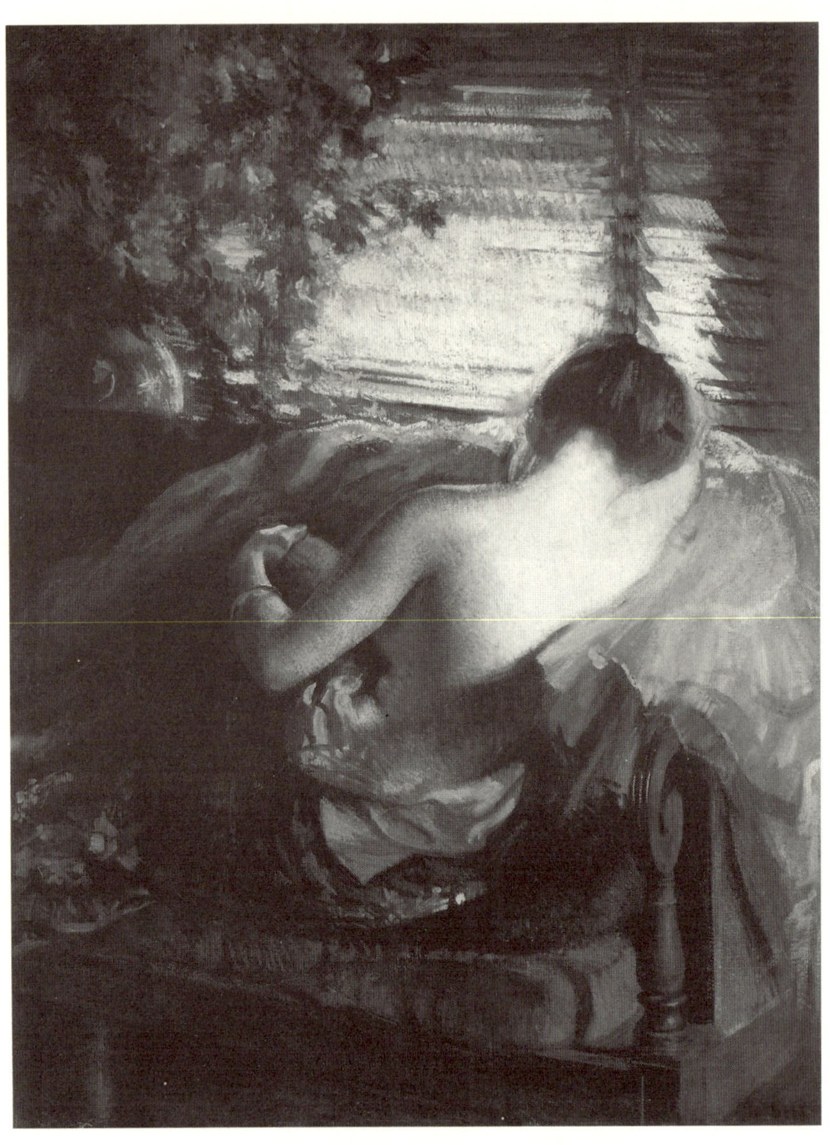

FIG. 52.
Edmund Tarbell, *The Venetian Blind*, 1901.
Oil on canvas, 51½ x 37 2.3 in.
Worcester Art Museum, Worcester, Massachusetts;
museum purchase, 1904.63.

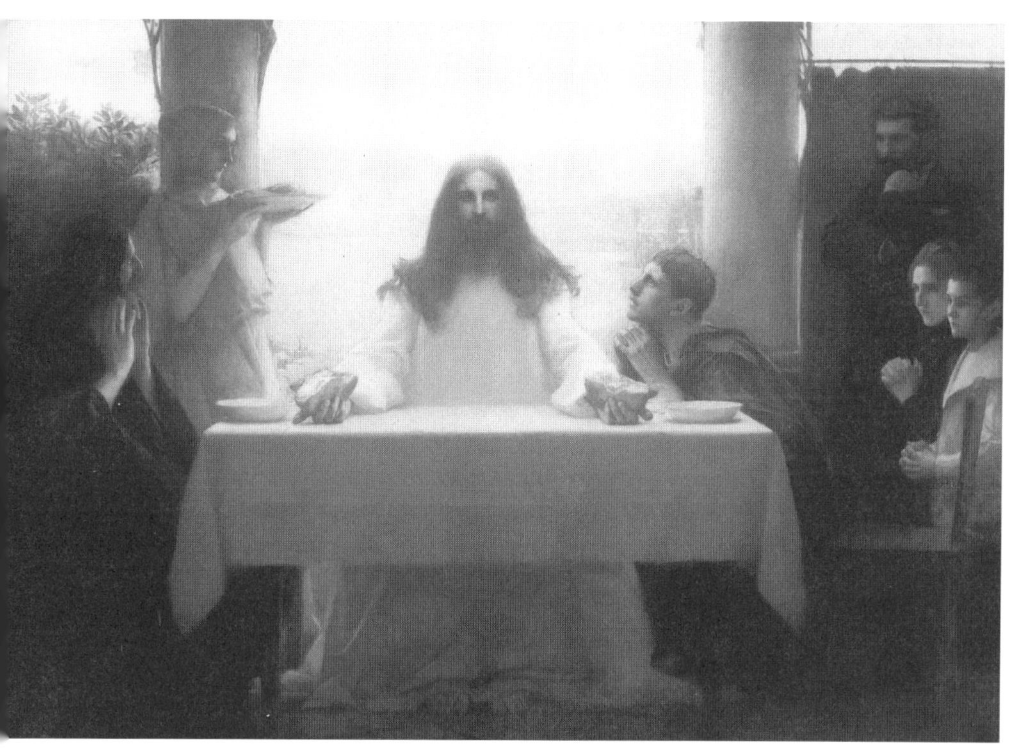


FIG. 53.
Pascal Adolphe Jean Dagnan-Bouveret,
*Christ and the Disciples at Emmaus*, ca. 1896–1897.
Oil on canvas, 78 x 110½ in.
Carnegie Museum of Art, Pittsburgh;
gift of Henry Clay Frick, 98.5.

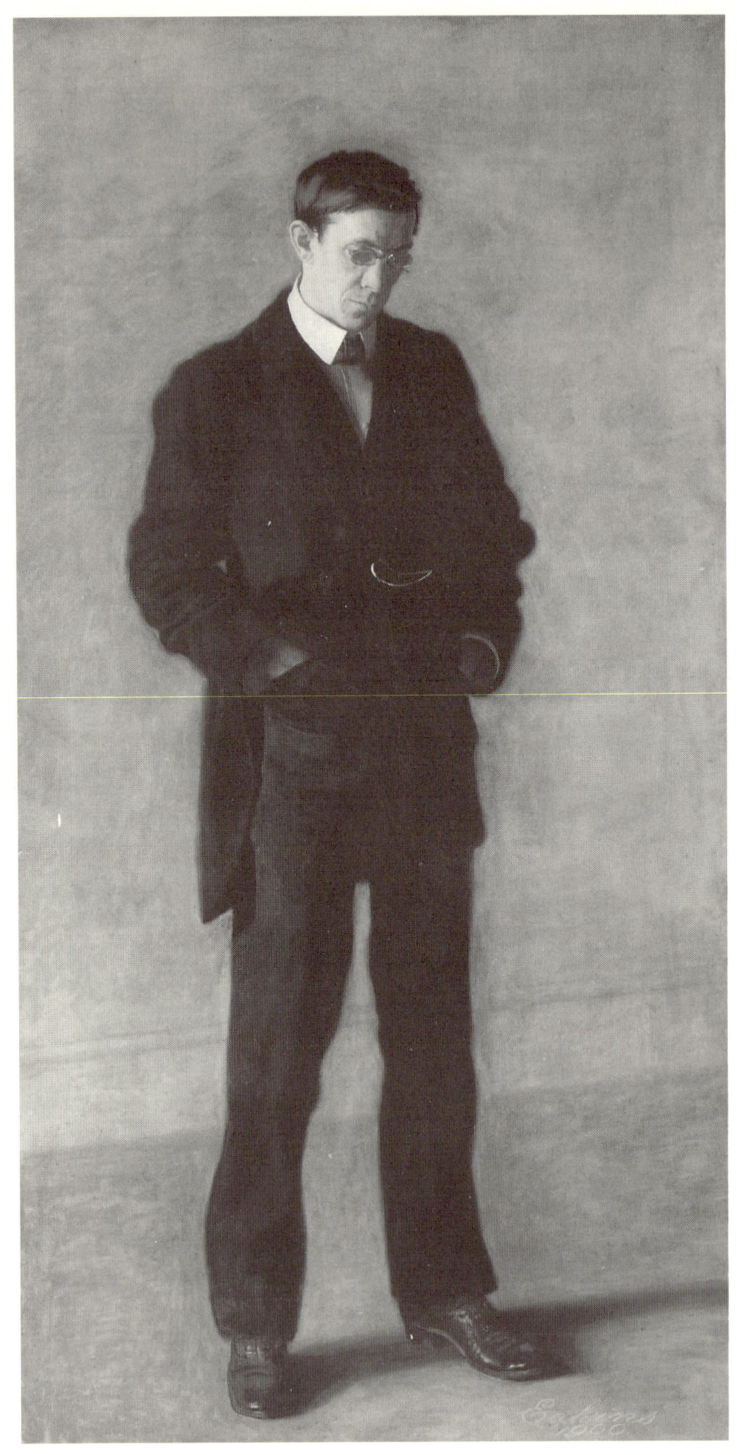

114

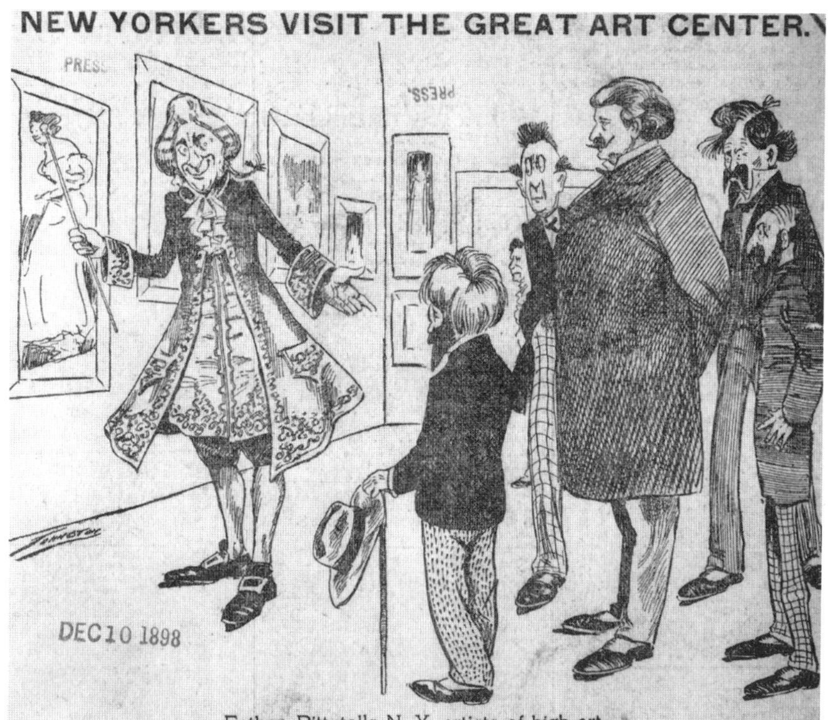


FIG. 55.
"Johnston the Cartoonist," *New Yorkers Visit the Great Art Center.*
From the *Pittsburgh Press*, 10 Dec. 1898.
*Photo:* Pittsburgh Photographic Library, Carnegie Library of Pittsburgh.

FIG. 54. *(OPPOSITE)*
Thomas Eakins, *The Thinker: Portrait of Louis N. Kenton,* 1900.
Oil on canvas, 82 x 42 in.
Metropolitan Museum of Art, New York;
Kennedy Fund, 1917, 17.172.

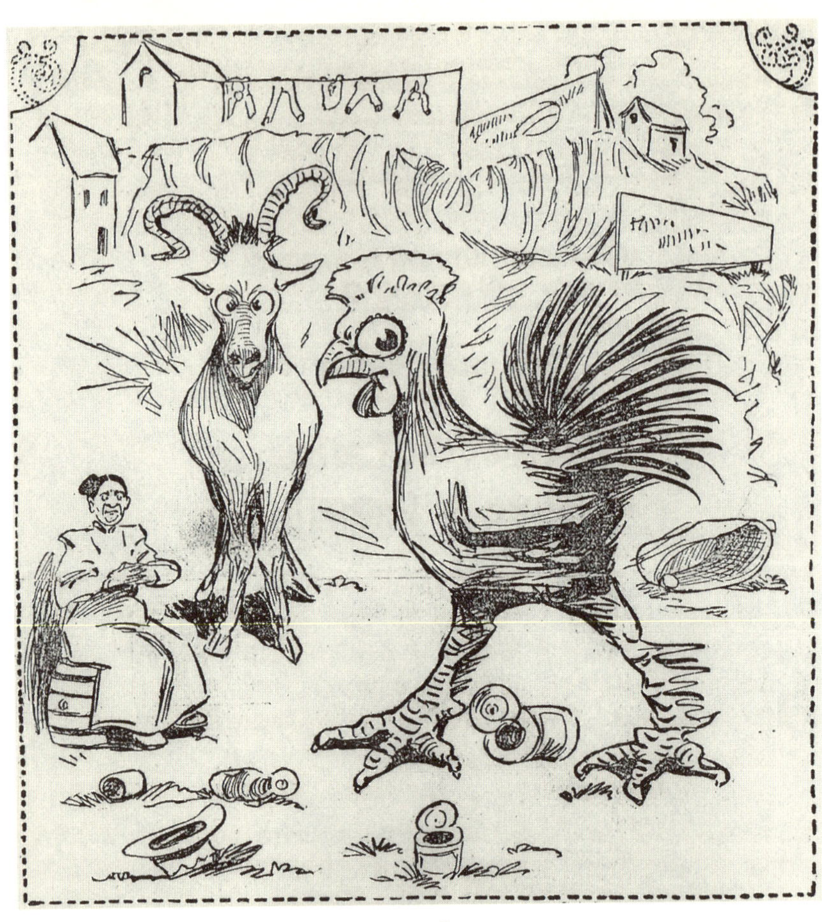

FIG. 56.
"Johnston the Cartoonist,"
caricature of Raffaëlli's painting of Pittsburgh's Soho district.
From the *Pittsburgh Press*, 10 Dec. 1899.
*Photo:* Pittsburgh Photographic Library, Carnegie Library of Pittsburgh.


FIG. 57. (*OPPOSITE*)
Cecilia Beaux, *Mother and Daughter*, 1898.
Oil on canvas, 83 x 44 in.
Courtesy of the Pennsylvania Academy of Fine Arts, Philadelphia;
gift of Frances C. Griscom.

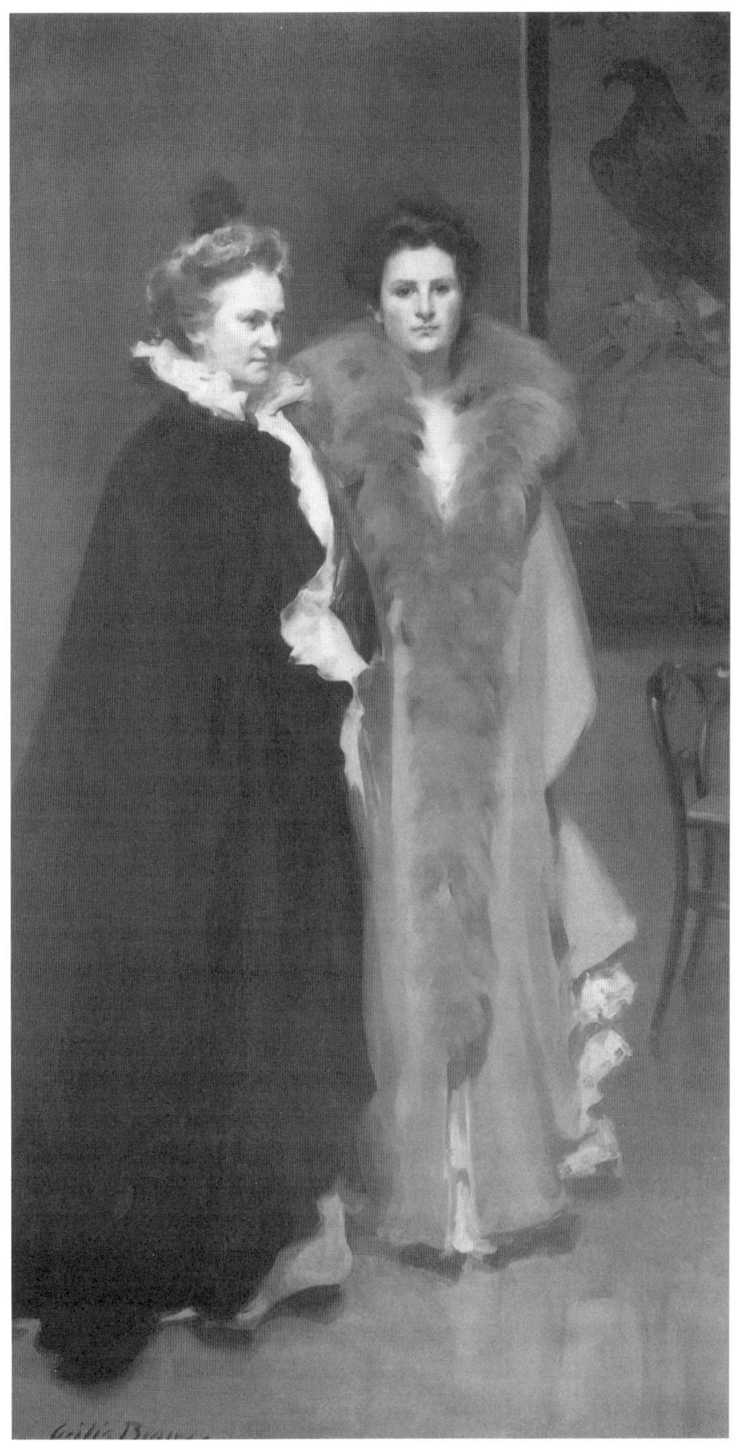

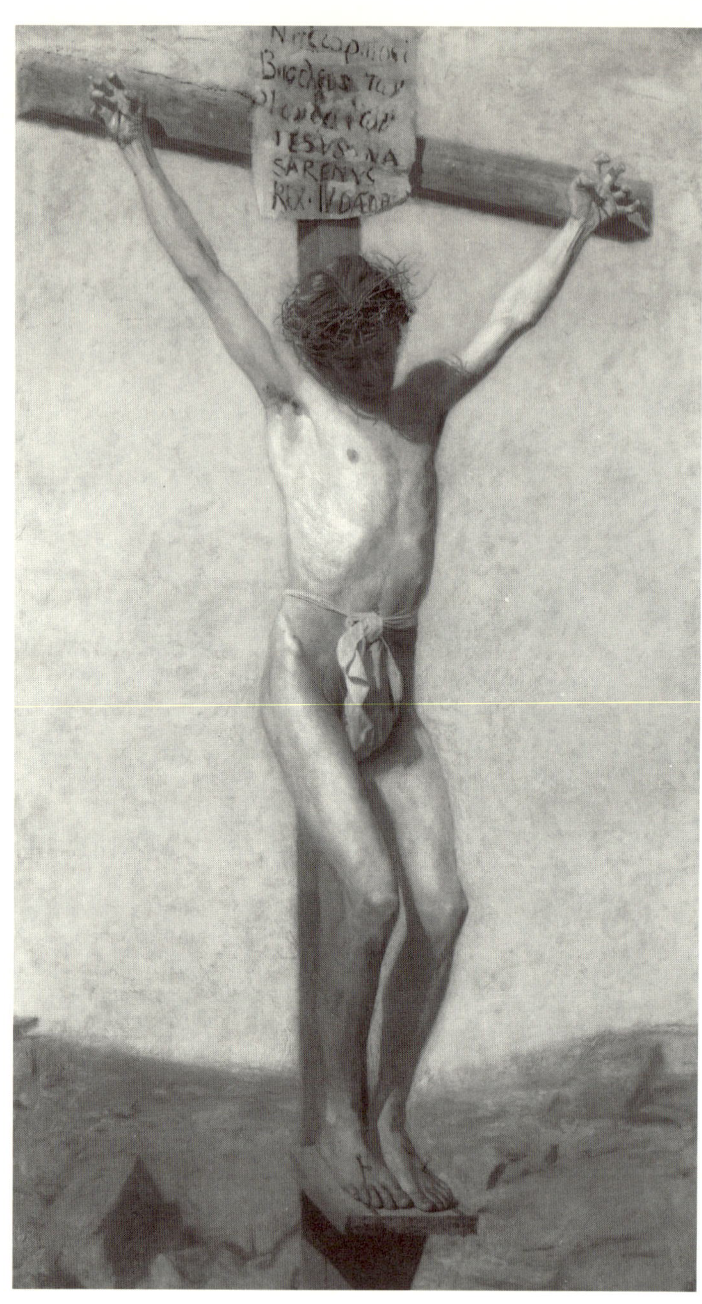


FIG. 58.
Thomas Eakins, *The Crucifixion*, 1880.
Oil on canvas, 96 x 54 in.
Philadelphia Museum of Art;
gift of Mrs. Thomas Eakins and Miss Mary Adeline Williams, '29–184–24.

118

❧ 3 ❧

# The Exhibition and
# the Artists

## An Original and Democratic Plan

THE PURPOSE of the 1897 reforms was to eliminate the odious "business man's jury" and replace it with a jury that would command the respect and confidence of the art world. The Fine Arts Committee never stated this explicitly and preferred to speak of enhancing the value of the exhibition and making Pittsburgh a great art center, but the unveiling of a new plan only a few days after the error in awarding a prize to Gari Melchers was made public allowed obvious conclusions to be drawn. According to the *Pittsburgh Times*, the Melchers incident was alone responsible for the proposed changes; the *Pittsburgh Leader*, however, regarded the changes as a tacit confession of general inadequacy by the Fine Arts Committee:

> The leaving of the selection of paintings to a jury of business men this year raised such a commotion among artists and art lovers throughout the whole country, and brought forth such unfavorable criticism of this policy, that the committee has acknowledged the fright they have had ever since they discovered their inability to control the opinions of artists and set aside the canons of art.

An unidentified artist (who may have been motivated by personal or professional animosities) bluntly declared, "It is an admission of incompetence."[1]

The initial impetus to reform may have come from Andrew Carnegie

119

himself. The earliest recorded suggestions for a new plan, undated but filed with the correspondence for late 1896, were submitted by his associate Howard Russell Butler, an artist and the president of both the Fine Arts Federation of New York and the Carnegie Music Hall Company. It is unlikely that Butler would have sent these suggestions without first discussing them with Carnegie, and he well may have sent them at Carnegie's behest. Of all the plans proposed, it is the one that least departs from Carnegie's original intention of having his galleries administered by men of affairs. Under Butler's plan, the awards would be made by a jury of ten artists (five from New York and one each from Boston, Philadelphia, Pittsburgh, Cincinnati, and Chicago), to be chosen by the Fine Arts Federation of New York and sent to Pittsburgh at the expense of the Carnegie Institute. The Fine Arts Committee, however, would continue to select the paintings, hang them, and determine purchases. Butler also suggested altering the system of awards: instead of two large purchase prizes and three medals, there would be just three awards, worth $2,000, $1,000, and $500, and the prizewinners would retain ownership of their work.[2]

The plan unveiled by the Fine Arts Committee on 22 January 1897 was far more radical, in that it virtually eliminated the committee's role in the exhibition. Selection, hanging, the awarding of prizes, and even the purchase of works for the gallery were all to be handled by a jury of "distinguished art critics and recognized connoisseurs." Artists were explicitly excluded from serving on the jury, presumably on the grounds that they would be too biased and self-interested.[3] This was the extent of the plan, the committee apparently having decided to see how it was received in its general outlines before filling in the details.

Andrew Carnegie gave the plan his full approval and promised to use his influence to persuade leading connoisseurs to serve on the jury. No doubt he had recognized at last that an inexpert jury, whatever its advantages in theory, was anathema to the art world and would prevent the success of the exhibition. In most quarters, however, the jury of connoisseurs raised little enthusiasm. Although the *New York Times* agreed that it was best to exclude artists, who might be "oversensitive," it doubted that connoisseurs were sufficiently knowledgeable about art. Art critics would have a far better knowledge, but the paper dismissed the idea of having critics on the jury as "somewhat preposterous" and proposed instead a jury made up of the presidents of the leading American academies of art. The

*Pittsburgh Leader* implicitly condemned the plan by quoting at length "one of Pittsburgh's most prominent artists," who argued (not surprisingly) that the best judges of paintings were painters. The jury, this artist maintained, should be composed of artists whose reputations were exalted enough to lift them above professional jealousies. He added darkly that if this course was not followed, "all Pittsburgh's credit will be lost with the artists of the United States and Europe, and our fall exhibit, which could become such a glorious affair, will become a mere farce."[4]

By the end of March, a final revised plan had been developed, and it had been adopted by the board of trustees. Under this plan, control of the exhibition passed largely to a jury of ten artists, elected annually by the votes of all invited contributors. The chairman of the Fine Arts Committee served as the eleventh juror; however, his role was limited to casting the deciding vote in the event of a tie. The rules specified that eight of the ten elected jurors were to be American artists living in the United States, and that no more than three could be from the same city; the two remaining jurors were to be foreign nationals or American expatriates. The jury's duties were to accept or reject works submitted in the United States, award the prizes, and recommend where paintings should be hung relative to the coveted line. In order to save the trouble and expense of shipping unwanted works to Pittsburgh, the Fine Arts Committee proposed the establishment of juries of admission, termed "foreign advisory committees," in London, Paris, and Munich, the members of which were to be the most prestigious artists whom Beatty could induce to serve on it.

The conditions of eligibility and the system of prizes were also altered. In order to compete, a painting still had to be owned by the artist and previously unexhibited, but it no longer had to have been completed within the current year: provided it was no more than three years old, it would be considered eligible. The purchase prizes for the two best American works were eliminated, and cash prizes were attached to the medals. The gold medal carried a prize of $1,500; the silver, a prize of $1,000; and the bronze, a prize of $500. They were to be awarded without regard to nationality, and no artist could win the same prize twice. These were not purchase prizes: a winning artist retained full ownership of his picture, limited only by the condition that the Fine Arts Committee had a sixty-day option from the opening of the exhibition to buy it at the artist's original valuation. Whereas the old system had required an annual expenditure of $8,000 for prizes, the new system required only $3,000, which thus allowed the committee greater flexibility in managing its budget. With the exception of the newly established honorable mention category, the new plan also eliminated the awarding of medals without money—a practice that, as Edwin Austin Abbey had pointed out in May 1896, was generally unpopular with artists.[5]

The new jury was suggested, at least in its broad outlines, by Andrew Carnegie at a conference held in early 1897 at the home of Henry Clay Frick. As usual, Carnegie preferred to remain in the background, and his role in formulating the plan was not revealed until 1899, when Beatty briefly mentioned it in a newspaper interview. Years later, in a speech delivered at the Institute's 1914 Founder's Day celebrations, Carnegie finally stepped forward, with a slight show of modesty, to claim credit:

> One strong reason for [the exhibition's] growth in popularity among painters is found in the system by which it chooses the international jury. I remember painters generally criticized the prize-awards of the judges. Why, it is the very nature of a man when he doesn't get a prize to complain of the judgement of the judges. I think it was my suggestion, but, as the Scotch say, I will not assert it pos-i-teeve-ly! I suggested that the best way to overcome this was to require the painters themselves to select a jury from among the greatest names in the world, from all countries, their expenses to be paid to Pittsburgh and return, including, of course, their bills here. This happy solution was instantly adopted, and is now the permanent policy of the Institute. Not one of my Trustees is on the jury—the painters themselves choose its members. And when these painters, after seeing Pittsburgh, come back to New York, they say, "How wonderful it was!"

Although both Carnegie and Beatty describe Carnegie's idea as a "suggestion," it doubtless had the force of a command. The exact date of the meeting at Frick's house is unknown, but John Caldwell's remark to Beatty that the committee had no choice "but [to] *approve* the suggestion or action of AC and his friends," written on 25 February 1897, may very well refer to the outcome of this meeting.[6]

The new plan did not represent a full retreat from Carnegie's earlier decision to exclude experts from the management of his gallery: the Fine Arts Committee still had complete control of purchases, so the gallery, considered as a permanent collection of paintings, still remained in the hands of businessmen. But, at the insistence of artists, the businessmen's jury had to go, and Carnegie made a virtue of necessity by replacing it with a jury more in accord with his conviction that art was a supremely republican institution. In *Triumphant Democracy* he had written:

> In art, the source of that which gives the finer touches to human life, all is republican; there is no trace of hereditary privileges within its bounds; it is as free, as unstained of these injustices as the American Republic itself. . . . What claims from birth have Liszt, Rubenstein, Gluck, or the Scotch laddies from their heather hills, the sons of shepherds and tradesmen, the Millaises, Orchardsons, Petties, Hunters and Blacks, but from the republicanism of art? Our rulers these, in art, by virtue of the universal suffrage of their fellows.

His new jury system was in effect a translation of the republican metaphor into a practical reality. The annual exhibition was henceforth to be conducted along the lines of a representative democracy. In 1907, speaking at the dedication of the newly expanded Institute, Carnegie explicitly connected the jury system with the ideas set forth in *Triumphant Democracy*. With considerable relish, he told the story of how the 1898 jury had assigned a position in the uppermost row to Edouard Detaille's *Examining the Prisoners*. Questioned as to the propriety of skying the work of one of France's great masters, the jury replied, "We can't help that; we don't regard names here, but art. It would have been the same if it had been painted by Rembrandt." Commenting on this anecdote, Carnegie said, "I congratulate Pittsburgh upon this exhibition of triumphant democracy. Pedigree does not count in the Pittsburgh institute, and the manner in which we elect our jury is thoroughly democratic." Detaille did not, of course, owe his fame to "hereditary privileges," but to have given him a place on the line simply because he was famous and had received the highest honors that France could bestow, rather than because the particular work deserved it, would have been a form of privilege in Carnegie's eyes, and therefore undemocratic.[7]

Both inside and outside the Institute, the jury system was described as "original and democratic."[8] It was not, in fact, an original system at all, but a logical consequence of Carnegie's desire to create the American equivalent of the Paris Salon. Nearly seventy years before, in September 1830, French artists had vainly petitioned the French king Louis Philippe for the right to elect the jury of the Salon. The unjuried 1848 Salon was hung by an elected committee; the jury for the 1849 Salon was wholly elected; and the jury of admissions for the 1850 Salon was elected by a vote of all previous exhibitors, while the jury of award was partly elected and partly appointed by the minister of the interior. In 1880, following a period of thirty years in which the method of jury selection varied with almost every Salon, the Académie des Beaux-Arts turned the exhibition over to the Société des Artistes Français, whose membership was open to all previous exhibitors and whose juries were wholly elected by its members. When the Société Nationale des Beaux-Arts split from the Société des Artistes Français in 1890 and established its own Salon (the Salon de Champs-Elysées), it retained this method of selecting its jury. Although Pittsburgh gave the vote to invited artists instead of to previous exhibitors, this amounted in practice to the same thing, for an uninvited artist whose work had once been accepted was normally placed on the invitation list. An elected jury was not even a novelty in an American context, having been one of the liberal practices adopted by the Society of American Artists when it seceded from the National Academy of Design in 1877.[9]

Moreover, the system was only imperfectly democratic. The international jury, for which all invited contributors were entitled to vote, acted as a jury of admissions solely for works submitted in America. Artists living in Europe had to send their work to the foreign advisory committees appointed by the Fine Arts Committee; thus, they had no voice in determining who would accept or reject their submissions. The democratic selection of the international jury itself was apt to be compromised if an insufficient number of candidates appeared on the ballot. In 1901, the American landscape painter Walter L. Palmer condemned the jury system as "pretentious and entirely abortive" on this account. There were twenty-three candidates in 1901 for the eight American jury positions, an apparently ample number. Sixteen of them were New Yorkers, however, and contributors were forbidden to vote for more than three jurors from any one city. Assuming the voter chose three from New York, this left only seven candidates for the remaining five positions, and two of these, Palmer complained, were Pittsburghers unknown to the larger world of art. Write-in votes were permitted, but he dismissed these as a waste of effort; he told Beatty that he would be surprised if a single unlisted artist was elected or if at least four of the five nationally known non–New Yorkers were *not* elected. The results of the election, he concluded, were for a large part foreordained. Palmer's prediction was fairly close to the mark: all of the five prominent non–New Yorkers (Thomas Eakins, Robert Vonnoh, Winslow Homer, Frank Benson, and Frederick Freer) were elected, together with two New Yorkers (John White Alexander, John La Farge) and one Pittsburgher, Clarence Johns, who doubtless owed his election more to the feeling that it would be nice to have a local artist on the Pittsburgh jury than to his modest reputation as an animal painter. Beatty admitted both the justice of Palmer's criticisms and his inability to find an alternative. There should indeed be more names on the ballot, he conceded, but it was difficult to persuade artists to offer themselves as candidates. Indeed, the records show that each year Beatty asked virtually every American artist of note to appear on the ballot, and had all of them consented the list would have been at least two or three times larger than it was.[10]

The jury system was, on the whole, well accepted. The *New York Times* found it "well considered" and "judiciously planned," declaring that "the awards made by a body thus created will have a peculiar and unusually high value among artists." The New York dealer William Macbeth called it "a stroke of genius." With few exceptions, the artists whom the plan was intended to please pronounced themselves satisfied. In early 1898, following the first exhibition under the new plan, Beatty sent a typewritten questionnaire to a number of leading artists in an effort to learn how they felt about the system. Their reactions ranged from unreserved praise to qualified approval. Frederick Freer of Chicago believed the plan could not be improved; John White Alexander held the same view and added that it appeared to be giving "general satisfaction" in Paris. Frank Benson of Boston, who had served on the 1897 jury, attributed the high quality of the exhibition to the new system, and predicted that it would inspire confidence in the artists. Three expatriates, Edwin Austin Abbey, Walter Gay, and Edwin Lord Weeks, liked the method of selecting the jury, but not the division into eight jurors from the United States and two from abroad. This was understandable, considering their own status as "foreigners." Abbey felt that there should be no geographical criteria whatsoever: "A good artist is a good artist whether he be born in Europe or as an American citizen," he wrote, overlooking the fact that the distinction between American and foreign jurors was based on residence, not citizenship. Edwin Lord Weeks, an American citizen working in Paris, served as a foreign juror in 1897, as did Alexander Harrison in 1900. Weeks's own view was that the number of European jurors should be proportionate to the number of Europeans in the exhibition, or that they should be allowed to cast more votes. He also would have preferred a "composite jury," partly appointed by the Fine Arts Committee, to a wholly elected one. This, he argued, would enable the committee to "equalize the neglect of any school that might be outvoted by the followers of any passing fad or fashion." Walter Gay, another American working in Paris, also wanted more Europeans on the jury, but these, he thought, should be American expatriates like himself. He advocated excluding foreign nationals entirely. In 1899 George Hitchcock cited the minority status of Europeans on the jury as one of the chief complaints made about Pittsburgh abroad.[11]

Although the democratically elected jury pleased most of the artists, the democratic rule that required everyone to submit to it, regardless of his standing in the profession, was unsatisfactory to some. This was not an innovative rule, having been previously adopted by the Society of American Artists, but it was far from being standard practice. Most exhibitions had an *hors concours* or exempt category, which allowed certain artists to contribute whatever they chose without the approval of an admissions jury. It was an honor, and one that the great men of the time regarded as their due. An aversion to submitting to the foreign advisory committees was particularly widespread in Europe (the lack of an exempt category was another major grievance cited by Hitchcock in 1899) and was exacerbated by the mistaken assumption that an invitation to contribute was an invitation to bypass the committees. However, the leading proponent of an *hors concours* category was the American landscapist Henry Ward Ranger, who from 1896 to 1900 regularly lectured Beatty on the subject. His views are summed up in his letter of 24 May 1899, in which he agreed to contribute and serve on the jury, if elected, but added:

> I think it a poor system, except for young men who are still uncertain — in that case a jury is meaningful. In the case of men who have arrived and are doing consistent work it is a mistake. I should feel guilty of an impertinence in judging a great number of men — for instance, why should it rest with me to say what Mr. Whistler, or Swan or Thaulow, etc. should care to send? Of course, there should be no question, but why should there be a chance of raising one?

As if to prove his point, the question was raised about his own work in 1899, and one of his two submissions was rejected. Deeply offended, he did not send to Pittsburgh again until 1907.[12]

The only works admitted *hors concours* to the Carnegie annuals were those of jurors and foreign advisors, who were not permitted to compete for prizes, and specially requested loans, which were subject to review by the Fine Arts Committee. Exempting the jurors was a measure obviously designed to spare them the embarrassment of having to judge one another's work. However, one juror, Frank Benson, said it would not embarrass him in the least, and he opposed allowing anyone to bypass the jury: "Such things lead to slackness," he wrote, "and every year it admits poor pictures to the Salon and other exhibitions." Perhaps Beatty held the same opinion, for the *hors concours* category for jurors and advisors was established only on 4 August 1897, well after the jury plan and the foreign committees had been formed. He certainly shared Benson's dislike of the category: when William McConway, a member of the Fine Arts Committee, suggested having one in order to overcome the artists' objections, Beatty contemptuously described it as "a pit."[13]

Most of the artists whom Beatty questioned also disagreed with the eligibility requirements, the general sentiment being that prizes should go to the best pictures, whether painted within a three-year time limit or not, whether owned by the artist or not. These rules, it should be noted, did not prevent ineligible works from being shown in Pittsburgh; it only excluded them from competition. The Fine Arts Committee remained adamant about the three-year limit but dropped the ownership requirement in the summer of 1898.

Beatty's difficulties with D. W. Tryon illustrate the problems that this rule created. No exhibition purporting to represent the cream of American art could possibly have been considered complete without one of Tryon's atmospheric, somewhat stylized landscapes; and if that exhibition had the further aim of awarding prizes to the best contemporary work, it was necessary for Tryon, like all first-rate artists, to compete. Beatty realized this and badgered Tryon to send during the spring and summer of 1897. Tryon explained that all his work was sold upon completion, or even before; he therefore had nothing eligible to send and never would, unless he refused to sell his work. When Beatty defended the rule on the grounds that it prevented dealers from vying for the awards, Tryon countered that, as the awards went directly to the artists, it hardly mattered where the pictures came from. The rule, he said, only made sense when purchase prizes were being offered, which was no longer the case in Pittsburgh. His most telling point was that the rule undermined the quality of the exhibition: the best pictures were likely to find buyers, and if these were excluded, only unsold, inferior works would be left to compete.[14]

Tryon repeated his objections in 1898, and these were seconded by the New York dealer Roland Knoedler, who, because Alexander was unavailable that year, offered to stir up the French artists on Beatty's behalf. He had little success, however, and the reason, he reported, was that "the greater part of artists of talent rarely have unsold or free things in their studio." The rule was obviously too inconvenient to be retained. Upon learning in early September 1898 that the rule had been dropped, Tryon sent his *Early Spring in New England* (figure 20), owned by Charles L. Freer of Detroit. It won the first prize.[15]

There were surprisingly few objections to the rule excluding previously exhibited works from the competition, even though, like the rule excluding sold works, it was inconvenient for the artists. "I cannot understand the clause in your prospectus which reads, '*not heretofore exhibited,*'" complained Robert Minor, a New York landscape painter:

> If it means that the paintings must be virtually painted *for your institution* to be eligible for prizes, I cannot see how any artist of repute can afford to enter a picture — worthy and serious — and spend his time and his opportunities on such an inducement, and I cannot see how the fact of a picture having been exhibited in New York, Boston, or Philadelphia is any the less worthy or valuable when it gets to Pittsburgh.

Charles Sprague Pearce made much the same objection in his response to Beatty's 1898 questionnaire, arguing that the rule would prevent the best works from competing for honors. Yet it is clear from the exhibition records that most artists did in fact paint pictures expressly for the Carnegie galleries, or at least withheld pictures from exhibition until they had been sent to Pittsburgh. From 1897 to 1901, less than a quarter of the works exhibited were ineligible to compete, and these included not only previously exhibited works but also works by jurors and advisors, loans, works that had arrived too late for consideration, and works that artists did not wish to place in competition. Previously exhibited paintings may well have constituted an even smaller proportion of total submissions: of the 509 works that the jury considered in 1901 (the first year for which accurate figures are available), only 66, slightly more than one-eighth, were ineligible for honors.[16]

According to the November 1899 *International Studio*, the rule did indeed result in the submission of inferior work:

> It is no doubt an expensive transaction to get such juries together, and we sometimes wonder if the game is worth the candle. Do our New York artists, for instance, appreciate the trouble the Carnegie management takes to ensure a creditable exhibition? If a canvass were made among our artists, how many would confess to having prepared an important work for this year's Carnegie Exhibition? Would ten per cent? Is it not true that our painters send either some old picture that has been battered around at other exhibitions for twenty years, or hurriedly dash off a hastily considered composition and send it half-done to Pittsburgh?

Nevertheless, the rule was indispensable to furthering Pittsburgh's ambitions. Without it, many artists would have been tempted to enter previous prizewinners (why risk something new and untested when one has a certified masterpiece at hand?) and the Carnegie annual would have become little more than a provincial echo of the long-established East Coast and European exhibitions. It also helped to keep the exhibition fresh—an important consideration, for, as Harrison Morris of the Pennsylvania Academy reminded Beatty, "The newspaper man is apt to slur an exhibition if he sees too many familiar faces in it."[17]

Despite the *International Studio*'s comment about twenty-year-old paintings, a critic for *Brush and Pencil* commended the Carnegie annuals for, "an absence of many of the pictorial tramps that have gone the rounds of exhibitions in former years." It is significant that this remark was made in 1900, the year of the fifth great Universal Exposition at Paris. Beatty had feared that artists would send their best recent work to Paris, leaving nothing for Pittsburgh; he had even contemplated canceling the 1900 exhibition. However, both Alexander and John B. Cauldwell, director of the American fine arts exhibit at the exposition, assured him that there would be no difficulty: artists were allowed to submit anything painted after 1889, no matter how frequently exhibited, and most would send the best of their old works, that is, the very works excluded from competition at Pittsburgh. As it turned out, the "pictorial tramps" flocked to Paris that year, and Beatty had all the new work he wanted.[18]

With the exception of the ownership rule, the plan developed in 1897 remained in force unchanged until 1922 and was largely responsible for the success of the exhibition. The key features in this success were the money prizes and the jury system. Although the prizes were smaller than in 1896, there were more of them and they were still substantial. The prizes were, according to Alexander, the chief topic when the Pittsburgh exhibition was discussed abroad: "Painters as a class need money," he observed, " — they *sometimes* eat."[19] The jury system conferred prestige on the prizes, and on the exhibition as a whole, making the occasion a yearly gathering of ten of the world's most celebrated artists. The new system enhanced the prestige of the exhibitors as well, in that to have one's work hung at the Carnegie Institute signified the approval of the leading members of one's profession. It also added to the prestige of the jurors themselves, in that election to the jury was a tribute from one's fellow artists.

The Fine Arts Committee made every effort to ensure that the jurors enjoyed their stay in Pittsburgh. The committee paid their expenses (providing the foreign jurors an inexpensive trip to America) and treated them like visiting dignitaries. The jurors were greeted at the railway station by a delegation of committee members; they were honored at a round of chrysanthemum-smothered banquets and receptions, were interviewed by the press, and were shown the sights of the city. The red carpet treatment began for foreign jurors as they disembarked in New York, for Beatty always arranged for someone to welcome and entertain them on the Institute's behalf.

Serving on the jury was as much a social as a professional experience, and one of the chief attractions was the opportunity afforded artists to rub elbows with their most distinguished colleagues. It was often an occasion for renewing old acquaintances — as in 1899, when the English painter William Stott of Oldham discovered to his delight that he had studied in London and Paris with all but one of his fellow jurors. It was also an occasion for making new acquaintances — as in 1897, when Winslow Homer served on the jury. In the 1890s Homer was regarded as a mysterious figure, an eccentric and reclusive genius who rarely stirred from the fishing village of Prouts Neck, Maine, and who took virtually no interest in exhibitions. Although his work was widely acclaimed, he himself was so little known that Frank Duveneck, who also served on the 1897 jury, spent several hours talking to him on the train to Pittsburgh without realizing who he was. Another juror, Cecilia Beaux, had a similar experience — following a guided tour of the city, she asked Beatty to identify the "mysterious stranger" with whom she had shared a carriage. "Why," replied Beatty, "Winslow Homer, of course."[20] By consenting to serve on the jury, Homer excited the curiosity of the art world and endorsed the Carnegie annual's claim to possess a unique distinction among American exhibitions.

Homer was unusual in that he did not enjoy his jury service. He felt that he owed it to the Institute in exchange for the prize he had received in 1896 — "a most tremendous and unprecedented honor and distinction," he called it — and was by all accounts extremely conscientious in performing his official duties, but he was anxious to get through them as quickly as possible and return to Prouts Neck. The efforts of the Fine Arts Committee to entertain the jurors merely annoyed and frustrated him. He flatly refused to join an excursion to view Carnegie's steelworks in Homestead: "Mr. Beatty," he protested, "I came here to work, and if we go to Homestead it will delay us, and I want to get home as soon as I can, for if I am late, my father will be anxious about me." To Cecilia Beaux he offered the excuse that he had planted nine stands of corn to use as models, and he needed to get back to them.[21]

Although these excuses ring false by virtue of their inconsistency, Homer's feelings are obvious: he was uneasy in Pittsburgh and wanted to leave. For the next three years he refused Beatty's invitation to appear on the ballot, and he announced in 1901, "I will never serve on another Jury, having been retired at the age of 65 years" (as if he had ever served on more than one jury, anyway). Beatty, however, persuaded him to relent, and in 1901 Homer proved to be a somewhat more sociable juror than he had been four years earlier. He arrived in Pittsburgh several days before the jury was scheduled to convene, "for the express purpose of viewing the attractions of the city," and spoke to a reporter to the extent of telling him that he liked the low tones of the western Pennsylvania landscape.[22]

Most jurors enjoyed their stay in Pittsburgh, and the more extroverted took to the role of visiting celebrity with great enthusiasm. The year 1899 was a particularly good one for outgoing jurors. William Stott of Oldham put himself forward as an apostle of Anglo-American unity, a cause dear to the heart of Andrew Carnegie, who advocated the political unification of Britain and America. Stott was only too happy to give interviews and after-dinner speeches, in which he described the United States as "all so typically English" and roundly declared that Americans and Britons shared "the same spirit, the same progress, the same sentiment, the same blood."[23] William Merrit Chase lectured the Art Students League and reviewed the students' work at the request of Mrs. Henry Kirke Porter, wife of one of the Institute's trustees and a founding member of Chase's Shinnecock summer art school. He agreed to perform this service once a month for a year and timed his second visit to coincide with the Founder's Day celebration, where he delivered a controversial speech urging Pittsburghers to invest in art.[24]

Both Stott and Chase, however, were thrown into the shade by the consummate showmanship of Jean-François Raffaëlli. Raffaëlli remained in Pittsburgh for the better part of a month, during which he kept himself continually in the public eye. Unlike his countryman Edmond Aman-Jean, who served on the jury in 1901, he was fluent in English and was eager to talk at length to anyone who would listen. His hosts could always count on him for an impromptu after-dinner speech, and any reporter who called on him at the Hotel Schenley was sure to be rewarded with an interview. Indeed, he was so agreeable to the press that he wrote an article for the *Pittsburgh Dispatch* praising the paintings in the exhibition. Not to be outdone by Chase, Raffaëlli delivered two addresses to the Art Students League and three to the Twentieth Century Club, and he also spoke at the Founder's Day celebration about internationalism in art. The conclusion of this speech gives a good idea of his effusive and dramatic style: "There is only one art in the world, as there is only one God [applause]. There is only one art, as there is only one ideal among civilized people. There is only one art, as there is only one brain in a head, as there is only one heart in a body, as there is only one soul in every one of us [applause]."[25]

Raffaëlli confirmed reports that he was an enthusiastic Americanophile by frequently extolling American liberty, American art, American landscape, and American women. He announced that he wanted to paint "a typical American girl" and hoped he would find a suitable model in Pittsburgh. After inspecting several candidates, he expressed doubts about Pittsburgh women being typically American but assuaged local pride by declaring them "very beautiful."[26]

He also announced a desire to paint the American landscape and commended Pittsburgh as an excellent subject for the painter. During the last two weeks of October he was frequently seen at various locations about town, sketching and painting in a carriage fitted as an informal studio.[27] Pittsburghers were flattered, but puzzled: the rural landscape of western Pennsylvania, so often depicted by local artists, was unquestionably picturesque, but it was hard for them to see the aesthetic merits of the dirty, industrial city. The press lampooned Raffaëlli's intentions in cartoons that showed him seated at his easel before a scene of belching smokestacks (figure 21). Arthur Burgoyne of the *Pittsburgh Leader* wrote some humorous verses in the same spirit:

> His art, of course, he'll first invoke
> To reproduce great clouds of smoke,
> The kind which, to his great distress,
> The smoke inspector can't suppress.
> And then he'll work in overhead
> The sun, a dingy ball of red,
> Which tries in vain these autumn days
> To pierce the dull and muddy haze.

Burgoyne suggested, too, that Raffaëlli might want to paint the slums of the Soho district, site of the city dump. When it became apparent that Burgoyne's verses were close to the truth—Raffaëlli mentioned that the smoky sky added "to the artistic value of the work," and he was indeed seen sketching in Soho—the Fine Arts Committee endeavored to turn the artist's attention to the East End residential district, which was considered the prettiest part of town. Their efforts were only partly successful. Of the two Pittsburgh scenes that Raffaëlli hung at that year's exhibition, one was a view from the entrance of the Carnegie Institute's Music Hall, showing cows grazing on what is now the lawn of the University of Pittsburgh's Cathedral of Learning. This was the much desired East End scene. The other, however, portrayed "the Soho dump on a foggy morning." Having observed the reactions of Pittsburgh's leading citizens on Press View Night, a writer for the *Pittsburgh Dispatch* commented that it was "a very clever picture, but one calculated to annoy Pittsburghers who have any love for the beauties of their city."[28]

From the Institute's point of view, a few offended Pittsburghers were a fair price to pay for a happy Raffaëlli. A contented juror was an asset to the exhibition: he could be counted on to speak well of it to other artists and to contribute his own best work in the future. The British marine painter Robert Allan, for example, told all his friends how well he had been treated during his 1901 jury service, and he informed Beatty that, as a result, they were eager to send to Pittsburgh. Alexander Harrison — who in 1897 had pronounced himself dissatisfied with Pittsburgh and had resolved never to send there again — praised the exhibition extravagantly when he served as a juror in 1900 and contributed regularly for the next twenty-three years.[29]

Both Edwin Lord Weeks and the Franco-Norwegian landscapist Fritz Thaulow, who served in 1897 and 1898, respectively, published flattering appraisals of the exhibition. Thaulow's, which appeared in the weekly art magazine *The Criterion,* was the more lavish, extolling everything from the light in the galleries to the picturesque aspects of the steel mills at night and predicting Pittsburgh's imminent emergence as the art center of America. Weeks's article, published in *Harper's Weekly,* took a more moderate, objective stance, merely claiming that Pittsburgh had joined the ranks of the nation's older, better established art centers. Weeks's intentions were nevertheless purely promotional: "If our Pittsburgh friends do not find it enthusiastic enough in tone," he wrote to Beatty, "they must remember that it should not sound like a 'boom' or an advertisement paid by the line — as in that case it would do no good."[30]

For several artists (John M. Swan, Fritz Thaulow, John Lavery, and Raffaëlli), serving on the jury was a prelude to serving on the foreign advisory committees. The appointments of Swan, Thaulow, and Raffaëlli continued the amicable relations they had formed with the Institute during their jury service. Lavery's appointment, however, was an attempt to repair a falling-out with the artist. Far from having enjoyed his jury service in 1898, Lavery felt that it had been a waste of time. In order to spend twenty-four hours in Pittsburgh, he complained to Beatty, he had to give up five weeks of valuable time; as a result, "I find it difficult to express a fair opinion of your exhibition to my fellow artists this side of the Atlantic." Yet this difficulty did not prevent him from expressing an opinion, fair or not. By March 1899, according to George Hitchcock, Lavery had become "most outspoken" and was telling his fellow artists he had "been bluffed and generally made to look foolish."

This would not do: if a contented juror could help the exhibition, a discontented juror could damage it. In July 1899, Beatty offered Lavery a seat on the London advisory committee, believing, perhaps, that Lavery's animosity was directed more toward the committee than toward the jury system. The London advisory committee had rejected one of his entries for the 1898 exhibition, and Lavery was convinced that the committee was biased against him (all its members, with the exception of Frank Millet, belonged to the Royal Academy, whereas Lavery was the co-founder and vice president of the antiacademic International Society of Sculptors, Painters, and Gravers). Jurors, of course, were exempt from foreign committee action, but when the London committee met, the foreign jurors were to be Fritz Thaulow and the English painter Frank Brangwyn. Lavery replaced Brangwyn only at the last minute, when Brangwyn's wife fell ill. This allowed him to exhibit his rejected painting but did nothing to change his opinion of the committee. Appointing Lavery was a move nicely calculated to turn foe into friend, in that it diluted the committee's Royal Academic bias, removed Lavery from its jurisdiction, and obligated him to speak for, not against, the exhibition. Apparently it worked, for he accepted the appointment and made no further trouble. In his autobiography, written many years later, he had nothing but praise for the Pittsburgh exhibition, describing it as "an inestimable service to both painters and public" and "the best annual collection of contemporary art that an international jury with unlimited means at its disposal could select."[31]

While the jurors' social activities were well chronicled by the press, their official duties were conducted in the utmost secrecy, and there is no record of the discussions, deliberations, and dissensions that took place behind the locked doors of the gallery. It was obviously in the best interests of the jurors to dissolve their individual identities in the corporate identity of the jury as a whole, thereby avoiding friction with the artists whose work they had to judge; and each of them scrupulously observed a code of silence in matters relating to the jury's decisions. We know, for example, that Winslow Homer required hourly infusions of alcoholic beverage, but we do not know which works he voted to accept or to reject. An interview given by Jean-François Raffaëlli in 1899 purporting to betray the jury's secrets disclosed nothing more than that some very good American paintings had been chosen for that year's exhibition. In that same year the *Pittsburgh News* published a highly circumstantial account of an incident supposed to have occurred during the jurying of the 1897 exhibition. According to the pseudonymous "Patricio," an English juror, whom he called "Madder Brown," glanced at a picture as it was being unpacked and told the workman, "You needn't trouble about that daub. Put it back in the case." When Beatty learned of this, he "felt the perspiration break out on his brow" and showed the juror the signature on the painting: it was the illustrious painter Rosa Bonheur. There was indeed an Englishman, John M. Swan, on the 1897 jury and a Rosa Bonheur in the exhibition, but the story is improbable. No juror had the power to single-handedly reject a work, nor was any juror permitted to see the signature on a work until the entire jury had passed on it.[32]

The jury procedure was a simple and straightforward affair. At ten o'clock in the morning, the ten elected jurors assembled in the galleries, where they were welcomed by Beatty, president of the board of trustees William Nimick Frew, and chairman of the Fine Arts Committee John Caldwell. Following short addresses by Frew and Beatty, in which they urged the jurors to exercise the utmost discrimination in regard to quality and impartiality in regard to schools and artists, the jurors seated themselves in a panel about fifteen feet away from a large table draped in gray fabric. The wall behind the table and the floor around it were covered with the same fabric. The first order of business was to pass on those works that had not been submitted to the foreign advisory committees, a category that included most of the American pictures. These were brought forward, one by one, and placed on the table. Caldwell called out the title of each painting as it was presented to the jury, but he did not identify the artist and politely refused to do so if asked. If a painting got six or more votes it was accepted; if it got four or fewer, it was rejected. A painting that received five votes in its favor was set aside for reconsideration, and if the second vote resulted in another tie, John Caldwell, acting as president of the jury, cast the deciding vote.

Each accepted American and foreign work was then assigned a number from one to three, to indicate whether it was to be hung on the line (1), in the second row (2), or the third row (3). This was done by the method of voting described above. Quality was the sole consideration in determining a picture's position; the task of arranging the works aesthetically fell entirely to the hanging committee. When all the paintings had received their positions, those assigned to the line were hung on the gallery walls, and the prizewinners selected from among them. Working from ten in the morning to five in the afternoon, with a long break for lunch and shorter breaks for refreshment at a bar set up in the gallery, the jurors usually managed to complete their task in three days. Considering that several hundred works had to be juried, there can have been little prolonged discussion about the merits of individual paintings.[33]

The taste of the jury can be characterized as thoroughly mainstream, but mildly progressive. It may seem inaccurate to speak of "the jury" when there were five different juries from 1897 to 1901; but in fact, one jury was very much like another. Frank Benson had warned Beatty in 1898 that the new jury system might "in the course of years result in giving you substantially the same jury," and his fears proved well founded.[34] In theory, as many as forty American artists could have served on the five juries; in practice, only twenty-four were elected and only twenty-two served. Benson himself served on three juries, as did William M. Chase, Robert W. Vonnoh, and Thomas Eakins. Frederick Freer served on four in succession. Each of these men served on later juries. Chase, elected eleven times between 1897 and 1914, was the most popular juror, followed closely by Charles H. Davis (nine juries) and John White Alexander (eight juries). Eleven artists served only once during the five-year period under consideration, but this figure includes Cecilia Beaux, who was elected in 1898 and 1899 but was unable to serve; E. H. Blashfield, who was unable to serve in 1898; John LaFarge, who had to withdraw in 1901 because of illness; and Alexander, who was unavailable until he returned to America in 1901. Indeed, all but four of the eleven served on juries after 1901. This lack of diversity is hardly surprising—only the most prominent artists were elected, and the roster of prominent artists remained more or less the same for years at a time.

Nor is it surprising, in view of the prominence of the jurors and of many of the artists who elected them, that the taste shown in the Carnegie annuals belonged to the progressive mainstream. In the 1890s the Modernist demand for constant innovation had not yet asserted itself. Artists built their reputations upon the skill and originality they brought to an existing style, rather than to the creation of a radically new style, and it took many years for innovators to win acceptance. As Henry Ward Ranger remarked to Beatty in 1900, the jury represented "the average taste and intelligence of several hundred painters"; therefore, it represented a compromise between conservative and radical sympathies and was inevitably firmly in the mainstream. But whereas successful artists could not be ahead of the current fashion, they had to be in it; their work had to be perceived as up-to-date rather than behind the times. As the jurors were leading exponents of the latest accepted style, they tended to favor the progressive over the *retardataire*. Comparing the first exhibition juried by artists to its predecessor (juried by the Fine Arts Committee), a reviewer for the *International Studio* felt that the artists were inclined to be a bit too trendy. "This year's canvases," he wrote, "seem to be painter's pictures, which, should the art of today change in character as it has in the last ten years, would be decidedly out of fashion in the decade to come."[35]

It is plain to a twentieth-century eye that the fashion espoused by the jurors might be called Painterly Naturalism, comprising the Barbizon School and Impressionism together with their various derivatives and hybrids, such as Tonalism, Stimmungslandschaft, the Hague School, the Glasgow School, and the art of the New English Art Club. As anyone who studies late nineteenth-century painting soon discovers, the boundaries between the various categories were vague and fluid, by no means clear to the artists and critics of the day. The term *Painterly Naturalism* therefore has the advantage of recognizing their common features and avoiding hairsplitting distinctions. In all its manifestations, this style aimed at giving an accurate transcript of carefully observed reality. Sometimes, as in the purest Impressionism, the emphasis was primarily on the rendering of optical facts; often, especially where the Barbizon influence predominated, the artist additionally sought to convey the mood and sentiment evoked by the subject, without, however, resorting to any but the most subdued narrative and dramatic devices.

Nowadays we reckon such artists as Gauguin, Cézanne, and the Nabis among the major figures of the 1890s and are apt to regard their absence from the early Carnegie annuals as a sign of conservatism. But there is no reason to believe that their pictures were deliberately excluded or that an opportunity to exclude them even arose. The proto-Modernists never submitted to the foreign advisory committees, nor does the Institute's correspondence mention them. It would appear that Beatty and the jurors were unaware of them. Although Americans were deeply interested in European — and especially French — art, their interest tended to focus on the most prestigious artists and exhibitions; the most radical innovations known to them were those to be seen at the Salon of the Société Nationale des Beaux-Arts, whose policies were more liberal than those of the older Société des Artistes Français but by no means avant-gardist.

I shall discuss the critical reception of the Carnegie annuals in the next chapter, but here suffice it to say that the most innovative art known to American critics in the late 1890s was Impressionism. Some still disapproved, and to them the Carnegie jurors appeared extremely, even excessively, progressive. The 1899 jury, for example, does not strike us today as a hotbed of radicalism, but that was how it appeared to a writer for the *Pittsburgh Dispatch:* "Raffaëlli and Brangwyn are extremists," he informed his readers, "Lockwood and Vonnoh are theorists, and all the others, with the possible exception of one or two, have given evidence of strong individual tendencies not wholly acceptable to all students of art." As the artists named are currently regarded as rather muted and impure Impressionists, it is hard for us to appreciate the writer's point of view. In 1901 a reviewer for the *New York Mail and Express Illustrated Saturday Magazine* (probably the paper's regular art critic, Samuel Swift) observed that Pittsburgh's juries were "generally composed of men well in the van of progress" and pervaded by "latter day art thought."[36]

The most conservative art of the day—the art of the French academic tradition, with its taste for historical and mythological subjects and its emphasis on the nude, and the similar art of such British academics as Leighton, Poynter, and Waterhouse—was rarely to be seen at the Carnegie annuals, so rarely, indeed, that when a painting by the English academician Herbert James Draper was hung in 1901, Samuel Swift urged exhibition-goers to study it carefully in order to get an idea of what the Royal Academy was like. "They need only to multiply it mentally by a thousand, and then, except for a few paintings of real worth, fancy themselves walking about the handsome London galleries surrounded by well-dressed admirers of the art that tells stories on canvas." Anna Lea Merritt—whose *Love Locked Out* (in which a nude Eros vainly struggles to open the door of a tomb) was a star of the 1890 Royal Academy—blamed Pittsburgh's rejection of her *Fame and Youth* in 1899 on Impressionist jurors determined to exact revenge for their long exclusion from major exhibitions. George Boughton, an American expatriate known for depictions of American colonial history, expressed himself more mildly than Merritt, perhaps because his work had never been rejected. He told Beatty that although he was willing to contribute, he saw no point in doing so, because he felt out of touch with the "prevailing culture of the moment" and therefore could hardly expect to do well in Pittsburgh.[37]

Older American artists who had come to prominence in the heyday of the Hudson River School came to feel no less unfashionable and unwelcome. In 1897 Martin Johnson Heade sent two flower paintings at his own expense and had both rejected. In 1901 Beatty flatly told M. Knoedler and Company not to bother shipping an enormous landscape that the once illustrious Albert Bierstadt wanted to contribute. R. Swain Gifford consented to appear on the list of prospective jurors in 1899 but predicted that he would not be elected until the "Impressionistic period" had passed and American art had become more conservative. It apparently never occurred him that Impressionism, which was still going strong when he died in 1905, would itself come to be seen as conservative.[38]

Also among those who fared ill at the hands of the elected juries were the artists of Pittsburgh. In 1896, when the Fine Arts Committee juried the exhibition, twenty-one local painters had been accepted; in 1897 this number dropped to four and did not increase substantially thereafter. The resentment felt by many is easily understood: Pittsburgh had captured the attention of the international art world, but Pittsburgh's own artists were unable to share in the newfound glory. Year after year they submitted their work; year after year most of them were rejected. In 1898 they attempted to improve their chances by sending as many as four works apiece, but to no avail. In 1900 their hopes were raised by the election to the jury of a local landscapist, Eugene A. Poole, only to be dashed again, and there was no improvement when another local painter, Clarence Johns, was elected in 1901.[39]

The Pittsburgh Artists Association, formed on 1 March 1897, became a major vehicle for their discontent. The motives for its founding are unclear: according to one member, its purpose was to protect local artists from the incompetence of the "business man's jury," but this same jury had shown itself unusually generous toward them. Perhaps they were dissatisfied with even their relatively strong representation in the 1896 exhibition; perhaps they had heard rumors of the new plan being prepared at that time and realized that a jury of internationally renowned artists would be less sympathetic toward them than the Fine Arts Committee had been. Whatever the initial motives, the Pittsburgh Artists Association was opposed to the Carnegie Institute, and within a few years the elected juries' rejection of local art was being given as the principal reason for the association's existence. Although Beatty (who, in his usual spirit of diplomacy, had become a member) repeatedly invited the Pittsburgh Artists Association to exhibit in the Carnegie galleries, the local artists invariably turned him down. "They feel that they have been rather shabbily treated and discriminated against in the past," explained a reporter for the

*Pittsburgh Leader* in 1901, "and as long as they cannot exhibit their work in the regular exhibition, they do not care to take a kind of second place by holding a separate local salon in the same place." However, hostility toward the Institute was not enough to make a success of the organization, and it had passed out of existence by 1910, the year the Associated Artists of Pittsburgh was founded. The Associated Artists established cordial relations with the Institute, and to this day holds its annual exhibitions in the galleries of the Carnegie Museum of Art.[40]

It is difficult to find any merit in the charge that local artists were discriminated against. H. S. Stevenson, who had stirred up so much trouble during the 1895 exhibition, claimed in 1901 that "several years ago all the Pittsburgh artists except two or three were excluded from the exhibition, and those who were admitted tried to cut off the heads of the others."[41] He presumably meant that in 1897 two of the accepted artists—Joseph R. Woodwell and A. Bryan Wall—used their influence as members of the Fine Arts Committee to have other local artists rejected. But how? In 1897 the power to accept and reject belonged to the jury, who would have had no reason to gratify the professional animosities of Woodwell and Wall, assuming that such animosities existed. Nor could they have done so had they wanted: all works were presented anonymously, and the jurors are unlikely to have been familiar enough with particular Pittsburgh artists to identify them on the basis of their styles. Only one member of the Fine Arts Committee, John Caldwell, had a voice on the jury, and his role was limited to reading out the titles of pictures and casting the deciding vote to break ties. Even if he had decided to conspire with Woodwell and Wall, he could have done nothing apart from rejecting those works upon which the jury was evenly divided. Are we to assume that the jury was equally divided upon all but a few of the local submissions? Considering the large number of rejections, it is far more likely that the division was usually unequal, with the majority of jurors voting against the local artists for the excellent reason that their paintings were not up to the exhibition's standards.

The problem confronting Pittsburgh artists was that the Carnegie annuals were not, except in a purely geographic sense, local exhibitions. Their avowed aim was to create a new art center by exposing Pittsburghers to the best contemporary art of the Western world, not to the best art of their fellow Pittsburghers. Indeed, the desire of Carnegie and his associates to turn their native city into an art center implied that it did not yet possess the caliber of artists necessary to make it one. When local artists submitted their work to the jury, they were in effect pitting themselves against the leading artists of Europe and America, and in most cases they were unequal to the contest.[42] The "business man's jury" of 1896, whatever its defects, had given them the advantage of local sentiment, but they lost this advantage with the introduction of the elected jury. The last trace of localism disappeared from the Carnegie annuals in 1897 — had they been held in Indianapolis or Buffalo, their character would not have been altered in the least.

Moreover, Pittsburgh's older, more established painters were out of sympathy with the jurors' taste. The most frequently exhibited Pittsburghers — A. Bryan Wall, Joseph R. Woodwell and his daughter Johanna Hailman, Anna Woodward, Christian Walter — were also among the most progressive. Indeed, Walter was described in 1900 as a struggling young Impressionist, one of "a Bohemian aggregation of artists" whose elder colleagues ridiculed them as "faddists" and treated them "with something not unlike contempt."[43]

Judging by the published opinions of A. F. King, a leading painter of portraits and still lifes (figure 22), this may well have been an accurate description of the attitude of many local artists. Interviewed in November 1899, King declared that the Carnegie exhibitions consisted almost entirely of inferior paintings, and that Pittsburghers were "getting tired of the abominable specimens set up before them as a high order of art." The worst abominations, in his view, were those inspired by "the prevailing craze of Impressionism," which he predicted would soon die out because of its falseness to nature. As for the non-Impressionist works, most of them were "done very slovenly — without care or patience — and are necessarily not correct in either drawing or coloring." King charged the artists with trying to take advantage of Pittsburgh: "They think," he said, "that they can send a lot of hastily gotten-up canvases and dispose of them here to a lot of yahoos who will rush to buy any old thing that has their name attached to it." Words, however, were insufficient to express his wrath, so he painted a parody of what he took to be the Impressionist style, featuring weird colors, false perspective, and childish drawing, signed it "Rafflehelli," and put it on display at a downtown art store (figure 23). According to the sympathetic reporter who interviewed King, "thousands of art lovers rejoiced that so palpable a hit had been made at a school of modern painting that is regarded as perverted and holding a distorted mirror up to nature."[44]

Despite King's belief that the Carnegie annual existed solely to provide a forum for famous artists, regardless of the quality of their work, the jurors were never reluctant to admit obscure artists like Christian Walter. Although well-known painters were always in the majority, in keeping with the expressed aim of showing Pittsburgh the best contemporary art, every exhibition included a scattering of unknowns whose pictures measured up to the jury's standards. The exhibition of 1901 demonstrated that even the highest honors were not beyond their reach. In that year Alfred Maurer, later to become one of America's first modernists, won the first prize for *An Arrangement* (figure 24), a Whistleresque study of a woman in a white shirtwaist crouching on a rug before a Japanese screen. Maurer had won a prize at New York's Salmagundi Club in 1900, but he was still little known in the world of art. The second prize went to another unknown, Elizabeth Ahrens of Philadelphia, for her *Sewing—A Portrait* (figure 25). Ahrens was astonished by the honor: the Pan-American Exposition had rejected the painting just a few months earlier, and she had sent it to Pittsburgh at her own expense "more out of curiosity than anything else, to see what the jury would do with it." Perhaps the greatest surprise of 1901 was the appearance on the line of two portraits (figure 26) by a Pittsburgh native, George Carspecken. Two pictures on the line was an unusual distinction for any but the most eminent artist; in Carspecken's case it was doubly unusual because the artist was only seventeen years old. Critics both local and national agreed that the distinction was well deserved; they praised Carspecken's bold decisive manner and predicted great things for one who showed so much promise early in life.[45]

Carspecken also had the distinction of being Andrew Carnegie's only artistic protégé. "Are you rich men doing anything for this fellow?" Andrew Carnegie asked his trustees when Carspecken's work was pointed out to him. "Now, some person ought to look after that young man," he declared. "Some of the great artists of the day ought to take him in hand. He might become foolish and get a big head, and then his work would come to naught." By January 1902 Carnegie had decided that he himself was the person to look after Carspecken; accordingly, he sent the budding genius to Paris and paid for him to study there. Carspecken seemed to profit from his study abroad, but ill health forced him to return to America in 1904. The following year, while staying with relatives in Burlington, Iowa, he suffered an attack of vertigo and fell down a flight of stairs to his death. The 1905 jury unsentimentally rejected his posthumous entry.[46]

Owing to the secrecy that shrouded the juries' deliberations, it is impossible to confirm or deny rumors that the Fine Arts Committee had an unwritten policy against exhibiting nudes and that it occasionally subverted the jurors' decisions regarding such works. In 1895 Carnegie pronounced himself strongly opposed to nudity in copies of classical sculpture, and he made it clear that he did not favor its appearance anywhere in his galleries, at least until the Pittsburgh audience had become sophisticated enough not to be offended by it. "Remember my words in speech," he wired Frew. "We should begin to gently lead people upward. I hope nothing in gallery or hall will ever give offense to the simplest man or woman. Draping is used everywhere in Britain except in London. If we are to work genuine good we must bend and keep in touch with the masses. Am very clear indeed on this question."[47] Were Carnegie's wishes respected? and if so, to what extent? It is possible that Alfred Roll's *Nude in Open Air* was rejected for this reason in 1896, when the Fine Arts Committee had full control over the exhibition; but it would have been difficult to make the elected juries toe that particular line, and dangerous to the exhibition's reputation for fairness to overrule them.

Suspicion attaches most strongly to the 1897 exhibition. On 7 October 1897, one of the jurors, Frank Benson, commended Joseph De Camp's *Magdalen* to Beatty as "a fine thing" and urged him to accept it, although the deadline for submissions had passed. Beatty consented. But in December De Camp learned that the painting, which he described as "the nude with red hair," had not been hung at Pittsburgh but had instead been sent to Cincinnati, where he had asked to have it forwarded after the exhibition. Surprised and angry, he told Beatty that he knew for certain that the painting had been accepted: both Benson and his fellow juror Edmund Tarbell had assured him "that the picture was received by the jury with acclaim, and that it was there ready to be hung when they left." "If you lack the courage to hang a nude," he added, "or feel yourself at liberty to modify the action of the jury by disposing of contributions at your convenience, the craft at large will, I am sure, be glad to know it." In 1898 the Cincinnati artist J. H. Sharp gave a substantially different version: two jurors, he said (he named only one, Frank Duveneck) told him that his own submission, De Camp's, and several others had been withheld from the jury because of nudity. "In New York last spring I heard something similar about nudes, and rather took it for granted that nudes were not desired (you know what some people in the West are like)." Beatty replied that pictures were never prevented from going to the jury, and the records state that both De Camp's and Sharp's paintings were examined and rejected. But records can be altered, and the accounts of De Camp and Sharp suggest, despite their inconsistencies, that something improper had occurred. It is conceivable — though not provable — that the Fine Arts Committee, members of which had charge of the hanging, acted behind Beatty's back to enforce Carnegie's wishes. That a rather full-bodied nude, Renoir's *Seated Bather,* appeared at the same exhibition would not disprove this suspicion, for it had been loaned at Beatty's own request and could not have been withheld without his knowledge; it does, however, excuse Beatty himself from the charge of provincial prudery. In any event, no further rumors of this kind plagued succeeding exhibitions, and in 1901 Edmund Tarbell's nude study (albeit a fairly chaste one), *The Venetian Blind* (figure 52), won third prize. The nude was never conspicuous in the early years of the Carnegie galleries, but this was probably due less to a dislike of it than to a dislike of the academic art that had traditionally made it a principal subject.[48]

## The Foreign Advisory Committees

The Carnegie Institute's boast of having achieved a perfectly democratic jury system must be taken with a grain of salt. For artists working in the United States, the system was indeed democratic (provided they were contributors); for those working in Europe, it was not. The former group submitted directly to the elected jury; the latter had to submit to the foreign advisory committees, which were juries in all but name and completely undemocratic. They could not assign positions or award honors, but their powers of acceptance and rejection were as absolute as those of the juries that met in Pittsburgh. In its circulars and announcements, the Institute tended to obscure their true functions. As Charles Sprague Pearce, a member of the Paris committee, pointed out, the term *advisory committee* did not make it clear that it was a jury, and the statement that it was empowered to accept works did not make it clear that it was also empowered to reject them. The reason for this lack of candor may have been a circumstance that Pearce mentioned: many European artists sent to exhibitions only when personally invited and refused to submit to juries.[49] Had the Institute been more open from the start, it might have avoided the unpleasantness that arose when artists realized that an invitation to submit to Pittsburgh was in fact an invitation to submit to a jury of admission.

Foreign advisory committees were set up in London, Paris, and Munich during Beatty's trip abroad in the late spring and early summer of 1897. Serving on the London advisory committee were Edwin Austin Abbey, Lawrence Alma-Tadema, John Singer Sargent, William Quiller Orchardson, George H. Boughton, Luke Fildes, Francis D. Millet, and J. J. Shannon. Five of the eight members — Abbey, Sargent, Boughton, Millet, and Shannon — were expatriate Americans. The members of the Paris committee were Pierre Puvis de Chavannes, James McNeill Whistler, P.A.J. Dagnan-Bouveret, John White Alexander, J.-J. Benjamin-Constant, Walter Gay, Léon Lhermitte, Charles Sprague Pearce, and Mary Cassatt. Five of the nine — Whistler, Alexander, Gay, Pearce, and Cassatt — were expatriates. The Munich committee had five members, of whom three (Carl Marr, Orrin Peck, and J. Frank Currier) were Americans and two (Ludwig Löfftz and Franz Stuck) were Germans. In securing a slight majority of Americans, Beatty may have been addressing the concerns of expatriate artists who, as he learned in 1896, felt they were being treated unfairly in American exhibitions. This may even have been a reason for making the committees appointive rather than elective, for a poll of foreign contributors would probably not have resulted in so many American advisors. Another factor, certainly, was the greater willingness of American artists abroad to promote the success of an American exhibition. In this there was an element of homesickness: "I do not believe anyone who is not in exile can know the depth of his interest in the concerns of his native land," wrote Abbey to Beatty in December 1897.[50] The most active members of the committees were invariably the expatriates.

The composition of each committee changed with the passage of time. In Paris, Puvis de Chavannes died in 1898 and was replaced in the following year by the landscape and history painter Jean Cazin. Fritz Thaulow also joined the committee in 1899, and Jean-François Raffaëlli was added in 1901 after the death of Cazin. John M. Swan joined the London committee in 1898, John Lavery and E. A. Walton in 1899, whereas Frank Millet, feeling that he had "served long enough," resigned in 1901.[51] J. Frank Currier returned to America in 1898 and was replaced on the Munich committee by another expatriate, Toby Rosenthal, in 1899; Orrin Peck returned to America in 1901 and was not replaced. Swan, Lavery, Thaulow, and Raffaëlli had all served on the Pittsburgh jury prior to their appointments, and Walton had won an honorable mention in the 1898 exhibition.

Paris, the art capital of the Western world, appropriately had the largest and most prestigious committee. All its members, with the sole exception of Benjamin-Constant, were associated with the liberal Société Nationale des Beaux-Arts, and the paintings that the committee approved and forwarded to Pittsburgh reflected the progressive taste of that organization's salon. This bias was so pronounced that in 1901 Charles Sprague Pearce suggested a policy of giving the members of the more conservative Société des Artistes Français equal representation with those of the Société Nationale in order to avoid alienating important artists connected with the older salon.[52]

Caution must be exercised in attributing the decisions of the Paris advisory committee to the influence of particular members. Gabriel Weisberg, for example, has correctly observed that the type of Naturalism associated with Dagnan-Bouveret was well represented at Pittsburgh, but he errs in implying that this was due to Dagnan-Bouveret's presence on the Paris committee.[53] In point of fact, Dagnan-Bouveret never attended a single meeting of the committee nor judged a single submission. Similarly, it would be tempting to ascribe to Mary Cassatt the favor shown to Impressionism, were it not that she, like Dagnan-Bouveret, was an advisor in name only and never participated in the committee's deliberations. Beatty, who frequently borrowed Impressionist works from Durand-Ruel and once tried in vain to persuade Camille Pissarro to place himself in nomination for the Pittsburgh jury, was unquestionably more influential in this regard.[54]

The impressive list of Paris advisors that prefaced every Carnegie annual catalogue was little more than a fiction: of the nine members appointed in 1897, four (Cassatt, Dagnan-Bouveret, Puvis de Chavannes, and Whistler) utterly neglected their duties, and three (Alexander, Benjamin-Constant, and Lhermitte) performed theirs on only two occasions. Gay and Pearce were the most reliable, the former missing one meeting and the latter none. Alexander assured Beatty that four members were sufficient to discharge the committee's business, and this number was usually attained, but in 1899 only one member, Pearce, appeared on the appointed day. Unable to reschedule the meeting and unwilling to assume sole responsibility, he gave the submissions what must have been an extremely cursory examination, then told the shipping agents that all were good and should be sent to Pittsburgh at once.[55]

Beatty had realized from the start that not every artist appointed to the committee would be an active participant, but he accepted this in the hope that their names would enhance the prestige of the exhibition. "It is not probable," he told the Fine Arts Committee in July 1897,

> that Puvis de Chavannes will be able to take an active part in the work of the committee this year, because of a serious illness which will prevent him from undertaking any active work for some time, but it seemed desirable to have him connected with the committee on account of his position as the President of the National Society of Fine Arts of France, and also because of his great reputation as a painter.

Similarly, Mary Cassatt, who abominated juries and refused to take part in them, allowed her name to appear among the foreign advisors on the understanding that she was never to serve.[56]

After several years, however, Beatty was so disappointed by the consistently low level of participation that he asked the faithful Pearce to suggest some means of remedying it. Pearce's response was a virtual admission that nothing could be done. The best course, he said, would be for Beatty to draw up a list of paintings that he wanted from the two salons and other exhibitions. The committee would invite the artists to submit these paintings, which could then be shipped to Pittsburgh without being passed on by the advisors.[57] Beatty did not implement this suggestion, and it is easy to see why. It would have meant forgoing his preference for previously unexhibited work. It would also have meant barring uninvited contributions, unless he was prepared to accept any work that anyone chose to deposit with the shipping agents, or to empower the Pittsburgh jury to pass on foreign submissions. In any event, the Paris committee would have effectively ceased to function as a jury of admissions.

Perhaps that would have pleased many of the Paris advisors. The excuse usually given for their absence was that they were out of town during the early part of September; yet those who did attend managed without difficulty to visit Paris for the few hours needed to transact the committee's business. Another common excuse was that of being too busy; yet the meetings were short and, having been scheduled weeks in advance, could surely claim to be considered prior engagements. There appears to have been a positive disinclination to attend, and a complaint by Pearce throws some light on this. The great difficulty with absences, he wrote in 1901, was that the responsibility for the committee's actions fell on only a few members instead of on the entire committee: too many members, when reproached for a controversial decision, said, "I wasn't there," thereby avoiding their share of the blame.[58] This suggests that many members stayed away in order to preserve amicable relations with their fellow artists and to avoid becoming embroiled in quarrels.

Their caution — or cowardice — was understandable, for Beatty's correspondence reveals that French artists did not take rejection lightly. The year 1901 was particularly rich in outraged letters, as an unusually large number of works had been rejected. Joseph Saint-Germier, who had made two submissions of which one had been turned down, wrote that he would willingly submit to the judgment of "painters of worth," but "I do not recognize the right of the jury whom the shipping agent named to judge me." Had he known that he would have to pass before a jury, "and especially that one," he would have sent nothing. Apparently the rejection of one work was of greater significance to him than the acceptance of another. The husband of Virginie Demont-Breton, daughter of the celebrated Jules Breton, was indignant at the insult to his wife's reputation. "Refused! Who ever heard of such a thing!" he exclaimed, and he demanded to be told why. The shipping agent, he said, had refused to name the committee members responsible; "so it's an anonymous jury, how bizarre!" (One can imagine the angry scene that convinced the shippers it would be prudent to conceal the identities of the Paris advisors.) Henri Martin and Paul Dannoye both argued that, having been invited, they should have been exempt from the admissions process; Dannoye regarded the committee's actions as "quite extraordinary, to say the least" and, like M. Demont, insisted on knowing the culprits' names. The situation was very much as Pearce had expected when he complained to Beatty of his fellow advisors' frequent absences:

> I fear our proceedings this year will bring forth a very considerable amount of discontent, as the number of refused comprises one member of the Institute of France, one member of the delegation of the

> Société Nationale, and three or four members of the jury of the old
> Salon, to say nothing of the many men of established reputations.

He emphasized the importance of pleasing the leading artists lest they use their authority to damage the Pittsburgh exhibition.[59]

The problem was that French artists who had made names for themselves expected to exhibit whatever works they pleased and resented having to submit to juries of admission. To them, as Pearce explained to Beatty in 1898, an invitation to exhibit customarily meant complete exemption from the admissions process; indeed, many artists of exalted stature accepted personal invitations only and refused to have anything to do with juries. By using the word "invitation" and by disguising the admissions jury under the term "advisory committee," Beatty created a misunderstanding that led to anger and indignation once the truth came out. The Paris advisors were themselves initially uncertain about how to handle these invitations. According to Alexander, the question of whether they had the right to reject invited works was debated at the 1897 meeting of the committee, and it was decided in the negative, even though some were "very poor," and one by Henri Martin was "almost an insult." Until 1901, the committee remained reluctant to turn down any artist who had received an invitation.[60]

Dissatisfaction with the advisory committee was undoubtedly an important reason that many French artists sent only minor works whose acceptance or rejection would not affect their reputations. Some failed to send at all. Every year Beatty announced on his return from Europe that he had secured a large number of major French paintings for the upcoming exhibition; every year he received letters from the Paris shipping agent telling him that large numbers of French painters had declined to submit or had ignored their invitations. Between this lack of participation on the part of the artists and the committee's reluctance to weed out inferior work, the quality of the French contribution noticeably declined after 1896. Walter Gay told Beatty in 1898 that sixty-four pictures had been passed, "and between us, they were a pretty bad lot. I almost wish they had been really bad, and then we would have refused them. As it is, they were only tolerably bad, the kind that fills most exhibitions. It is a pity that the Pittsburgh exhibition could not keep up in the way it began, for it had a very good 'send off' in the first year." In 1899 A. F. King was pleased to note in his diatribe against the exhibition that the leading artists of Paris sent "only light studies" to Pittsburgh, and this observation was confirmed the following year by a far more sympathetic commentator, Anna Woodward, one of the few local artists to be hung in the Carnegie galleries. Jean-Jacques Henner, she wrote in her report on the Paris salons, sent only studies of "red-haired girls with deathly green faces and haunting eyes," quite unlike the misty, allegorical nudes for which he was famed; Virginie Demont-Breton sent "tight little studies done in her student days" that hardly justified her reputation as the greatest living woman painter in France; Tony Robert-Fleury sent small ideal heads, which he told Woodward were merely entertaining experiments done at odd times as diversions from his serious work. And, she added, many artists sent nothing. In 1899 William Nimick Frew admitted to the press that "heretofore we have been compelled to receive and hang a number of paintings from the other side which were really unworthy a place on the walls of the galleries." His assurances that this was no longer a problem may be doubted, for this was the year when the Paris shipper told Beatty that he had reaped only a "meagre crop," and Pearce, left to perform the committee's work alone, threw up his hands in despair and had the entire lot sent to Pittsburgh.[61]

That the French contribution was no worse than it was — and critics did not find it notably bad as a whole — was largely due to the efforts of John White Alexander. Although not particularly dutiful about attending committee meetings, he was in all other respects the most active of the advisors, constantly urging his fellow artists to accept Beatty's invitations, and badgering them to submit their paintings on time. It is a testimony to his influence that two of the prizewinners of 1899 — André Dauchez's *Boats*, which took third prize, and Lucien Simon's *Portraits*, which won an honorable mention — had originally been promised to other institutions and were sent to Pittsburgh only as personal favors to him. He sometimes performed services of a less conventional sort, as in 1898 when he got out of bed at four in the morning to rush off to Dieppe and spend a day reassuring Fritz Thaulow, who was "really scared to death at the prospect of crossing the ocean" to serve on the Pittsburgh jury. Alexander scheduled his annual visits to America to coincide with the exhibition and was always eager to sing its praises to the press in the most effusive terms. He was also quick to defend it against its detractors. Upon hearing, for example, that a minor New York artist named George Torrey was spreading nasty stories about the Fine Arts Committee, claiming that from motives of personal spite it had rejected his pictures without so much as unpacking and looking at them, Alexander promptly confronted the man, called him a liar to his face, and challenged him to prove his assertions. "If he can prove what he says," Alexander told Beatty, "I will get him a written apology from you as the director and each and all of the art committee." Torrey did not accept the challenge, and no apologies were required.[62]

Alexander had said in 1896 that his activities on behalf of the exhibition were done solely out of affection for Beatty, and his motives appear to have remained unchanged during the succeeding years. Certainly, he did not profit financially from his association with the Carnegie Institute, and he felt no great love for the Fine Arts Committee, which, despite his and Beatty's frequent urgings, refused year after year to acquire one of his paintings for the permanent collection. In 1900, after yet another attempt failed he wrote, "I won't go over the old story — it was a bitter pill to me but I have put it out of my mind entirely — and I never expect to have a picture in the gallery of my native town." At last, in 1901, the committee purchased his small *A Woman in Rose* (figure 27), and the chairman, John Caldwell, expressed an intention of exchanging it for a larger work at some future date and paying Alexander the difference in price. This plan was never carried out, but Alexander received a far more generous reward four years later in the form of a commission to paint a huge mural program, *The Crowning of Labor*, for the Institute's newly expanded quarters.[63]

The policy of rejecting invited artists was no more acceptable to the British than to the French. "It is like inviting a man to dinner and turning him away by the butler," wrote Mark Fisher in 1898, after one of his two submissions had failed to pass the London advisors. In that same year Alfred East (who was to serve on the jury in 1909) flatly refused to submit on the grounds that the policy "does not commend itself to any artist of standing"; John McClure Hamilton had "strong words" with a member of the committee; George Sauter (who was to win the second prize in 1909) predicted dire consequences: "The rejection of invited pictures appears to me a monstrous insult to every law of hospitality and to every feeling for right and justice, and if this state of things continues it will inevitably degrade your institution, started though it was with all fair and honest intention." At least one of the advisors, the American expatriate Frank Millet, was inclined to agree with Sauter, though he expressed himself less dramatically. He attributed the inferior quantity and quality of submissions in 1899 to the "deterrent effect" of the policy and declared, "It is impossible to get together anything like a representative collection under your present system." The artists, he said, preferred to send their work to Birmingham, Manchester, and other provincial galleries, whose invitations allowed them to bypass the juries of admission.[64]

The problem was, if anything, worse in Britain than in France, for the character of the London committee differed considerably from the committee in Paris. Absenteeism occurred from time to time but never became an issue; the London advisors were on the whole dutiful, conscientious, and thoroughly intent on maintaining the highest possible standards. Whereas the Paris committee shrank from rejecting the work of an established artist, the London committee appears to have had an unwritten rule that when an artist submitted two or more paintings, only one would be accepted. This did nothing to sweeten the tempers of the artists, and it must have frequently tried the equanimity of Beatty himself, in that many of the works rejected were ones he had seen during his annual visit to London and specifically requested for Pittsburgh. Even when the advisors were informed of his wishes, they remained immovable. When one of H. H. La Thangue's three submissions for 1897 was turned down (he was lucky to have had two accepted), the London shipper wrote:

> We are all quite aware that you stated that you particularly wanted these three of Mr. La Thangue's, but you did not instruct us that we were *not* to submit them to the Committee, and they were of course submitted with the rest. I read to the Committee the wish expressed in your letter that you wanted them very particularly, but unfortunately the Committee did not like this picture.

Although the shipper took the liberty of sending it to Pittsburgh, Beatty held to his policy of never interfering with the actions of jurors or advisors and did not hang it.[65]

The London advisory committee was, like English art itself, somewhat conservative. When the decision was made to appoint foreign advisors in 1897, Beatty immediately got in touch with Edwin Austin Abbey, a leading light of the Royal Academy, who in turn consulted Edward Poynter, president of that institution. Beatty conferred with both Abbey and Poynter during his visit to England that year, and although Poynter declined to serve as an advisor (he offered the press of public duties as an excuse, but Beatty surmised that he did not want to "antagonize members of the Society which he represents officially"), the committee bore strongly the impress of the Royal Academy. This was recognized by the British artists and was resented by those whose works failed to pass the committee. The sentiments of these men were forcefully expressed by H. Muhrman:

> The Royal Academy with its brilliant and infallible judgement has never shown me any mercy, but I did not expect a committee composed of its members would carry on the same old game outside its walls, or I should not have submitted *anything* of mine to their tender mercies and to this renewed insult. As long as the committee is composed of this charming Academy clique, I will not send pictures — you can bet your bottom dollar that I shall not give them a *second* opportunity to refuse my work.[66]

The committee was not, however, as conservative as it might have been. The Victorian classicism of Poynter lacked a spokesman and did not appear in Pittsburgh. The nearest approach to it among the London advisors was the Roman genre painting of Alma-Tadema, which tended to be more intimate and less idealized than the work of Poynter. Abbey, Millet, and Boughton were devoted to historical and literary subjects, full of narrative content but handled with a relatively high degree of realism; Fildes was a sometimes sentimental social realist; Orchardson was a skilled delineator of the private life of high society; Sargent was attracted to Impressionism; and Shannon, despite being an associate of the Royal Academy, was a cofounder of the antiacademic New English Art Club. With the appointments of Lavery and Walton, the committee acquired two members who were wholly unconnected with the Royal Academy; their loyalties lay instead with the liberal International Society of Sculptors, Painters, and Gravers. Nevertheless, many of the progressive Francophile artists associated with the New English Art Club — men like Frederick Brown, Philip Wilson Steer, William Rothenstein, and Charles Conder — ignored Beatty's repeated invitations to contribute to the Pittsburgh exhibition. Brown finally explained their position in 1901: "Briefly, it may be said that we decline to subject our works to a jury in London who are out of sympathy with us, least of all to a jury in which any members of the Royal Academy have any voice."[67]

Unlike the Paris and London committees, the Munich committee was never subject to angry complaints about the bias of its members or the injustice of rejecting invited artists. Absenteeism did occur—for example, Carl Marr was the only advisor to inspect the submissions in 1900—but it never became a serious problem; the number of German artists invited was so small that, even if all had submitted, a single advisor could have inspected them in less than an hour. Nevertheless, Munich was a great disappointment to Beatty. Every year he hoped to get about fifteen pictures from that quarter; every year he received about half that number, sometimes fewer, together with a letter from the committee lamenting the meagerness of Munich's contribution. The Symbolist Franz Stuck, himself a member of the committee, was the only German of the first rank to send to Pittsburgh with any regularity. Beatty dearly wanted to exhibit the works of Munich's leading masters Wilhelm Leibl and Franz von Lenbach, but Leibl died in 1900 without having contributed, and Lenbach led Beatty and his advisors on a wild-goose chase.

Lenbach first promised to contribute in 1899, but then he reneged on the promise. In the spring of 1900, Beatty wrote to him, asking to see him personally, and added, "My personal admiration for your work is so great that I desire to give a number of people the pleasure I myself have enjoyed." Lenbach was agreeable, and the meeting (to which Beatty was accompanied by Toby Rosenthal, one of the advisors) concluded with the great man promising to select a painting to be sent to Pittsburgh. A week later, after Beatty had left Munich, Rosenthal visited Lenbach, who said that he had not yet made his selection but would do so within a few days. A few days passed, and Lenbach once more put off his decision, promising to write when it had been made. At last, as Carl Marr explained, "Lenbach declined point blank: details and explanations are superfluous: I know Lenbach pretty well, and his doings in this direction do not surprise me." The following year Beatty urged Marr to "*do your utmost*" to secure a work from Lenbach, but to no avail. The other established artists of Munich were no more accommodating. "I can assure you it is uphill work to try to get Munich artists to contribute to your exhibition," said Rosenthal after a typically fruitless round of visits to the major studios.[68]

According to Marr, the German painters regarded Pittsburgh as a faraway and unimportant city; they preferred to show their work at continental exhibitions. Another reason for their disinclination to participate, mentioned by Marr and stressed by Rosenthal, was that many pictures sent to Pittsburgh were returned to Munich in a damaged condition.

Instances of damage are inevitable even today in the transportation of works of art over long distances, and reports from London, Paris, and several American cities reveal that the problem was not an uncommon one; but it appears to have been particularly severe in Munich, or at least to have bulked larger in the minds of the artists there. It might have made a difference had the possibility of remunerative sales in Pittsburgh offset the risk of damage, but this was not the case. "There is something wrong with your organisation," wrote Rosenthal in 1900, "there are too many complaints and rumours afloat, and the artists do not consider their works safe in the charge of the Carnegie exhibition. Cases like Bartels, Dill, Becker, etc. are not apt to encourage the artists. Besides, those that have exhibited say that to expose their works to severe damage without either hope of *compensation, nor sale*, was asking too much of them." He noted that Lenbach was aware of this problem, so it undoubtedly was one of the explanations for his refusal to send that Marr dismissed as superfluous.[69]

The difficulty of securing contributions from Munich was, in Marr's view, insurmountable under the foreign advisory system. The best solution, he suggested in 1900, would be to put everything into the hands of the Munich Secession, an antiacademic organization founded in 1892 to promote the more avant-garde Realist, Impressionist, and Symbolist tendencies in German art. He had obviously discussed the matter with Stuck, the president of the Secession, for he presented a list of specific conditions under which the organization would consent to provide its services: the advisory committee would have to be abolished; only Munich artists belonging to the Secession would be allowed to exhibit; their works would be hung separately from the rest of the exhibition, in their own room or rooms, and clearly identified as Secessionist. Marr admitted that the Munich contribution would be one-sided under this plan but pointed out that most of the men whom Beatty invited were Secessionists anyway (though not Lenbach) and that the Secession, feeling its reputation at stake, would make every effort to secure a respectable number of pictures.[70] Although Beatty did not accept what was clearly an informal offer by the Secession itself, he adopted a similar plan in 1903, when he restricted the invitations and awards to American artists residing in America and substituted a traveling exhibition of 137 works by members of the International Society of Sculptors, Painters, and Gravers for the entire foreign contribution.

## Sales and Purchases

In November 1895, a "gentleman identified with art" told the New York correspondent of the *Pittsburgh Dispatch* that the newly opened Carnegie Institute would unquestionably become a major market:

> It will afford the artists of New York a new and profitable field for exhibiting their works . . . for undoubtedly the Pittsburgh Gallery will come to the fore as one of the important annual or semi-annual displays of contemporaneous American paintings, and its presence in the midst of so wealthy a community cannot but be followed by many sales which would not be likely to occur without so good an opportunity to effect them.[71]

Unfortunately, this prediction did not come true. Five years later, as we have seen, the Munich artists were dissatisfied with Pittsburgh's sales record, and according to the American expatriate Frederick Bridgman, the French were no better pleased. "We certainly like to have our pictures sold," he said, "it becomes discouraging otherwise." Two years earlier, after sending some flattering press clippings to the Paris Society of American Painters in an attempt to encourage its members to contribute, Beatty was told by its secretary that although the clippings were interesting, "a detailed list of the sales that have been made would have been more so, and would doubtless have a stronger influence on the desires of the painters in regard to taking part in your next exhibition." Several months later, Will H. Low, who had served on the first international jury, informed him that the New York artists thoroughly agreed with their colleagues abroad:

> Not speaking for myself alone, but reflecting the general feeling here, the future success of your exhibition will be greatly helped by a more generous patronage of the exhibiting artists. With the great wealth of Pittsburgh, independent of your generous endowment, it is possible to create conditions such as which a painter could not afford to abstain from sending to your annual exhibition.

When, in a letter to the Anglo-American artist Anna Lea Merritt, Beatty defended the poor sales record on the grounds that it was not the purpose of the exhibition to secure the best market, she replied bluntly that such a market was precisely what the artists needed.[72] The honor of participating in a small, select exhibition and assisting in the noble effort to spiritualize a materialistic people apparently did not outweigh the necessity of earning a living. If sending pictures to Pittsburgh did not pay the bills, so much the worse for Pittsburgh.

Beatty was, of course, fully aware of the importance of sales to the success of the exhibition. In an 1896 press statement he expressed the hope that the purchase of several additional pictures by the Fine Arts Committee would "call attention to the fact that the works now on exhibition may be bought from the painters. Nothing exerts a more stimulating influence upon contributors to an annual exhibition than the announcement of a reasonable number of purchases." The *Pittsburgh Post* was quick to second Beatty's remarks, pointing out in an editorial that the more affluent portion of the community could perform no better service than to buy from the exhibition.[73] Persuasion, however, was futile: when the exhibition closed in January, there had been no private sales at all to announce.

The problem was serious enough to require the intervention of Andrew Carnegie himself. In 1897 he appointed a special committee to buy paintings for him from that year's exhibition. The names of the persons composing the committee were never recorded or released to the press — indeed, the very existence of the committee was not publicized — but considering its somewhat clandestine nature, it is safe to assume that it was recruited from the Fine Arts Committee and included Beatty. The works selected and purchased were:

> Frank Bramley, *Sleep*
> Frank Brangwyn, *The Sweetmeat Seller*
> Ludwig Dill, *Landscape*
> Ben Foster, *A Misty Moonlight*
> Walter Gay, *The Sewing School*
> J. W. Hamilton, *A Scottish Farm*
> Wilton Lockwood, *The Violinist*
> Emile Menard, *Autumn*
> Julius Olsson, *The Golden Isle*
> Willbur A. Reaser, *Mother and Daughter*
> Alexander Roche, *Peggy*
> J. H. Twachtman, *Last Touch of Sun*
> George Wetherbee, *A River Bank*[74]

The paintings were of high quality: one, Lockwood's *Violinist*, received an honorable mention; six (Bramley, Brangwyn, Foster, Hamilton, Menard, Olsson) were considered for honors. Carnegie was abroad during the entire run of the exhibition and so was unable to express a preference for specific works, but the committee clearly kept his tastes in mind. Except for the paintings of Dill and Menard, the selections were either American (Foster, Gay, Lockwood, Reaser, Twachtman) or British (Bramley, Brangwyn, Hamilton, Olsson, Roche, Wetherbee), reflecting Carnegie's self-consciously British-American identity. Most were solidly realistic landscape and genre pieces, and the more extreme forms of Impressionism were avoided. Although Carnegie tended to be atypically modest in his pronouncements on art, never criticizing particular schools or trends, some idea of his response to Impressionism may be gathered from his comments on Childe Hassam's *Improvisation* (figure 28), exhibited in 1899. According to a reporter for the *Pittsburgh News*, "he said he was sorry, but it did not impress him that the girl was capable of playing anything classical. Her appearance rather suggested a ditty or a ragtime melody."[75]

Carnegie's purchases allowed the Fine Arts Committee to announce that thirteen paintings had been privately sold from the second annual exhibition, thereby creating the impression that the Pittsburgh exhibition was developing into a profitable art market. It can hardly be doubted that they intended to create such an impression, for they concealed not only the existence of the special committee but also the identity of the purchaser and the fact that there had been only one. Their method of publicizing these sales is exemplified by a press release that appeared in a number of local newspapers on 28 January 1899. It boasts of sixteen paintings sold in 1897 — proving that the annual exhibition was "not only a treat for the public, but a good thing in a financial way for the artists" — and then lists the paintings by title and artist without mentioning who purchased them, or distinguishing between the thirteen bought by Carnegie and the three bought by the Fine Arts Committee for the permanent collection. On the basis of this and other press releases, one might have assumed that rich Pittsburghers had at last awakened to their duty to promote the exhibition; in reality, the only sales made in 1897 were to Carnegie and the Department of Fine Arts. Even the artists involved in these transactions were somewhat confused about their exact nature: they knew that Carnegie had bought their works but believed that he had bought them for the permanent collection. Ecstatic over the sale of his *A Misty Moonlight,* Ben Foster wrote a letter of effusive thanks to Henry Clay Frick, at that time a member of the Fine Arts Committee, in which he praised Carnegie for having "chosen the best and wisest means of encouraging artists, in purchasing their work and placing it on permanent exhibition, instead of secluding it in his own private gallery for his own and his friends' enjoyment." Willbur Reaser made the same assumption and did not learn until 1901, when he asked Beatty to lend his *Mother and Daughter* to the Pan-American Exposition at Buffalo, that the picture was one of those that had been bought through the special committee, and had been sent, after remaining in the Pittsburgh galleries for about a year, to Skibo, Carnegie's newly refurbished residence in Scotland.[76]

Carnegie bought several paintings each year from 1898 to 1901; thereafter, he never purchased more than a single work from a particular exhibition, and in some years bought nothing. After 1897 he dispensed with the services of the special committee and made his selections in person, but this does not mean he failed to take advantage of the expertise available to him. Sometime in November 1899, Beatty sent a letter to Carnegie giving him an estimate of several pictures in which Carnegie had expressed an interest. Gérôme's *Diana,* he wrote, was one of the artist's best; René Billotte's *Moonrise on the Canal, St. Denis,* was a fine example of "one of the strong modern painters"; Charles Proctor's *Grandpa* was good enough to have been considered for an award; J. H. Sharp's *Spotted Bird that Sings (Crow Indian Girl)* and William Howe's *A Day at Home — Brandywine Courtyard* were of fairly high quality, though not first-rate. Carnegie bought all these works except the Billotte. He no doubt consulted Beatty and the members of the Fine Arts Committee on other occasions, but their advice must have been given verbally and no record of it has been preserved.[77]

Carnegie's purchases appear to have been dictated as much by his philanthropic purposes as his aesthetic inclinations. A major object of the exhibition was to encourage American art, and Carnegie bought mostly the work of American artists, followed closely by British artists. He personally selected only a single French painting, Gérôme's *Diana,* no doubt because he felt that French art was in no need of special encouragement. Another important object was to turn Pittsburgh into a leading art center; accordingly, he made a point of buying the work of local artists. In 1898 he bought a painting by Johanna Woodwell Hailman; in 1900, after praising the local contribution to the exhibition, he bought Christian Walter's *Dusk;* in 1901 three of his five purchases were by Pittsburghers. One of these was the much talked about portrait by the ill-fated George Carspecken; another was a landscape by the late George Hetzel; and the third was A. Bryan Wall's *Twilight,* which Carnegie presented to former First Lady Frances Folsom Cleveland, who had admired it during a tour of the galleries.[78]

Beginning in 1898 there was a slight but definite improvement in the sales record; that is, a few paintings were sold each year to private patrons other than Carnegie. Seven pictures were sold in 1898: two by Fritz Thaulow, who had served on that year's jury and had won the second prize in 1897; *The Looking Glass,* by that year's third-prize winner, Alexander Roche; John F. Weir's *Roses,* one of the two winners of an honorable mention; the *Tigers Drinking,* of the English painter John M. Swan, who had been a juror the year before; and works by R. Macauley Stevenson and Pietro Frangiacomo. The names of the buyers were neither divulged to the press nor preserved in the records, raising the suspicion that certain members of the Fine Arts Committee, or persons closely connected to Carnegie, were attempting to inflate the sales figures as Carnegie himself had done the previous year. In 1899 Lawrence C. Phipps, a nephew of Carnegie's old associate Henry Phipps and a partner in the Carnegie Steel Company, emerged as a major patron of the exhibition, purchasing *The Huts* by third-prize winner André Dauchez, *A Night in Venice* by Bartholomeo Bezzi, and *Proud Maisie* by Alexander Roche (thus making the Scotsman, with four sales to his credit since 1897, the most purchased artist of the early Internationals). The Pittsburgh Club acquired *The Corso, Rome,* by the Italian painter Gustave Bacarisas; and works by Walter Crane, Louis Paul Dessar, and local artist Olive P. Black were bought by unidentified parties, bringing the total of private sales to seven.

The following year, 1900, was a relatively good one for sales. Lawrence Phipps bought landscape paintings by the Scottish artist Grosvenor Thomas and the American George H. Bogert; Willis F. McCook, a local attorney, bought the first-prize winner, André Dauchez's *The Kelp Gatherers* (figure 29), and one of the honorable mentions, W. Elmer Schofield's *Twilight.* Benjamin Thaw, of the prominent Pittsburgh family, bought one of A. Bryan Wall's perennial sheep scenes, and a Mr. J. W. Painter of McKeesport, a nearby industrial town, acquired a landscape by the local artist Eugene Poole, who had served on the jury that year. Mr. Stevenson of the Sharon (Pennsylvania) Steel Company, and Mr. Stephenson of Scranton shared a taste for the Glasgow School, the former purchasing John Downie's *The Flax Carder — Dutch Interior*, the latter James Hamilton's *The Banks of the River Eye*. Not all of the purchasers were Pennsylvanians: J. B. Butler, General Manager of the Brier Hill Iron and Coal Company in Youngstown, Ohio, bought a picture of a Sioux Indian chief by his fellow Ohioan J. H. Sharp; an unidentified "resident of Cleveland" bought Ferdinand-Jan Monchanblon's *Valley of the Saône*; Charles F. Grey of Evanston, Illinois, bought *Misty Sunlight* by H. H. Gallison of Boston. Eleven paintings were sold in all. In 1901 the number of sales dropped to nine. The records are incomplete, and most of the buyers are unidentified, but we know that a work by one of the jurors, Edmond Aman-Jean's *Comedy* (figure 30), was acquired for Chauncey J. Blair, one of the eminent Chicago Blairs, through the agency of another juror, Robert W. Vonnoh, and that Mrs. William Thaw purchased *A Rose* by John White Alexander. The remaining seven works sold were by American artists: William Verplanck Birney, George Beechert, Robert David Gauley, Birge Harrison, Walter Gay (who was lucky enough to sell two), and a local artist, Hugh Newell.[79]

From 1896 to 1901 the total number of sales for a single year, including those to Carnegie and the Department of Fine Arts, never exceeded eighteen, and it was usually fewer. As an average of 260 works appeared in each exhibition, an artist's chances of making a sale were remote. In 1896 the veteran landscapist George Hetzel, voicing a complaint often heard from artists in America's culturally ambitious "western" cities, doubted that local talent would derive much benefit from the Carnegie galleries. Wealthy Pittsburghers, he said, preferred to go to New York and Europe for their paintings, just as they did for their carpets and wallpapers.[80] This preference apparently held true even when the paintings of New York and Europe were brought to their doorsteps.

Where gentle persuasion and example failed, direct exhortation proved no more successful. At the 1899 Founder's Day ceremonies, attended by the city's leading citizens, William Merritt Chase delivered an address entitled "The Utility of Art." His audience no doubt expected to hear the customary platitudes about art refining the character and elevating the soul; instead, the body of the speech was devoted to urging them to buy the paintings on display in the galleries. Art, he said, was an excellent investment in terms of both money and prestige: in his opinion, many prominent New Yorkers owed their positions in society solely to having invested in art. Chase's attempt at a sales pitch was not well received. According to an account in the *Pittsburgh Dispatch*, the audience's response was "mildly deprecating," and the observation that some of the most exalted figures of the American plutocracy had nothing more to recommend them than the pictures on their walls produced a "shocked silence." It certainly did not produce a sudden surge of sales.[81]

None of this is to say, however, that the annual exhibitions did not have a positive effect on the art market in Pittsburgh. In December 1896, the *Pittsburgh Leader* reported that local art dealers were enjoying a boom in their Christmas trade, unparalleled in previous years. Indeed, business was still brisk on December 26, so much so that the dealers were "rushed to death" and could hardly spare a moment to talk to the reporter. The *Pittsburgh Leader* did not connect this phenomenon to the current exhibition in Oakland, then in its second month, but by October 1899 a "representative of the leading art stores on Wood Street" was referring to "the usual rush consequent upon the opening of the Carnegie galleries" and was attributing the considerable patronage by men earning only moderate salaries to the educational influence of the exhibitions. "More than one canvas was sold here last week as a result of a visit to the Carnegie Gallery," declared a writer for the *Pittsburgh Dispatch* on 12 November 1899, "and both artists and dealers admit that the general trend of interest in the pictures exhibited in the gallery is beneficial for the business end of local art."[82] Pittsburghers were willing to buy paintings, but they either could not or would not pay for major works by major artists. Ironically, the local artists who tried and failed to get into the yearly exhibition may have benefited more from it than the famous men with whom they vainly sought to compete.

The single largest purchaser from the Carnegie annuals was the Department of Fine Arts, which acquired paintings from each year's exhibition in order to build a permanent collection. Beatty never doubted for a moment that the permanent collection should be the department's primary object, and that it should take precedence over the more highly publicized annual exhibition. "This, after all, is our more important work," he reminded Carnegie in 1899. The following year, speaking to reporters just before he sailed to Europe, he unambiguously declared his priorities: "The founding of great permanent collections representing the fine arts is, in my opinion, much more important than the work connected with the merely temporary or annual exhibitions."[83]

By the time Beatty made this assertion, he had learned from experience that the annual exhibition, although theoretically subservient to the permanent collection, could be conducted only at the expense of the latter, since the sum required to mount it frequently exceeded the sum available for acquisitions. In his report for the year ending 31 March 1898, during which $13,834.63 had been spent on the exhibition and $15,638.50 on purchases, he calmly observed: "As was anticipated from the beginning, the use of the fund necessary to prosecute this important work has retarded progress in the direction of the establishment of permanent art collections." During the following year, $12,121.25 was spent on the exhibition, $17,602.24 on purchases, and Beatty held his peace. But when $11,799.28 was spent on the exhibition and only $9,216.02 on purchases, he made his dissatisfaction clear to the trustees:

> The total amount expended for these seven works was comparatively small, being only $9,216.02, but no materially greater amount can be expended by the Department in any one year for permanent acquisitions while it is the desire of the Trustees that international exhibitions be continued. The largest item of annual expense is that imposed by the annual exhibition. It is true, the success of the annual exhibitions has been very great and the attendance almost phenomenal, but each dollar expended for an annual or temporary exhibition is a distinct loss to the more important work of founding permanent collections of paintings, statuary, and other works of art.[84]

Beatty frequently reiterated this complaint during his long tenure as director of fine arts, but he never succeeded in persuading Carnegie and the trustees to either give up the exhibition or provide more money for purchases. In his final annual report, submitted 1 July 1922, he pointed out that from 1896 to 1921 an average of only $16,010.88 had been available for each year's acquisitions, owing to the expense of the annual exhibition, and he recommended, not for the first time, that the trustees establish a larger purchasing fund: "I have not done all that I hoped to do for the Institute," he wrote, "because the limited amount placed at the disposal of the committee for each year prevented this."[85]

Expense was doubtless among the factors that led to the Fine Arts

Committee's quiet abandonment of the chronological collection, Carnegie's projected "historical record of what was considered by a commission in this early day of the world's history the best that the United States year after year produced." Under the constitution and bylaws of the board of trustees, the Fine Arts Committee had to submit to the trustees at least two American paintings a year for this collection. If the trustees failed to approve the submissions by a two-thirds majority, or if the committee was unable to secure pictures worthy of submission, two more works painted in the same year could be presented at a later date. Preferably, these works should have been exhibited at the Carnegie galleries, but to ensure the desired quality the committee was permitted to select from any source. Once a painting had been approved for the collection, it was to be hung in the galleries with the year of its execution prominently displayed.[86]

The chronological collection would have automatically grown from year to year had the plan of the first annual exhibition — under which the only cash prizes were purchase prizes for the two best works by American artists — been followed. However, the revisions of 1897 and 1898 made such an automatic growth impossible. From 1897 on, there was no guarantee that the top prizewinners would be American, nor that they would be available for purchase. The chronological collection grew (if that is the word for it) by fits and starts. On 5 December 1896, John Caldwell presented two paintings, Winslow Homer's *The Wreck* and Gari Melchers's *The Shipbuilder*. Both were approved, but the award to Melchers was later rescinded when it was discovered that his picture had been previously exhibited. On 10 April 1898, Caldwell moved to submit a work to represent 1897 in the collection, but less than two-thirds of the trustees were present at the meeting, so his motion was not put to a vote. The work is not identified in the minutes, and no paintings were subsequently submitted for 1897. In fact, nothing more was done about the chronological collection until 18 April 1900, when the trustees accepted Frank Benson's *Portrait of a Boy* (figure 31) to fill the position for 1896 vacated by Melchers, and Dwight Tryon's *May* to fill one of the positions for 1899. The Benson portrait had been bought over two years before from the 1897 exhibition, and Tryon's *May* had been bought from the artist in March 1899 as a substitute for his *Early Spring in New England*, which had won the first prize in 1898 but had been unavailable for sale; therefore, the trustees were merely approving their designation for the collection, not their purchase. Two years later, on 16 April 1902, Edwin Austin Abbey's

*The Penance of Eleanor, Duchess of Gloucester* (figure 32) was submitted and approved to represent 1900. It had been purchased from the 1901 exhibition for $9,000, completely exhausting the funds for that year. The chronological collection never materialized beyond these four pictures.[87]

In a memorandum written sometime between 1919 and 1921, Beatty briefly explained why the chronological collection had been abandoned:

> This question was frequently discussed by the Committee, but the difficulty of securing the two pictures qualified for their superior excellence to represent the American Art of the year seemed to the members of the Committee so difficult (if not impossible), that action by the committee was deferred from time to time until the plan became inoperative. Each time the question came up, the Committee faced the fact that many of the finer works were constantly going from eastern studios and exhibitions direct to the Metropolitan Museum, the Corcoran Art Gallery, the Smithsonian Institution and other art institutions, as well as to private collections, without our having an opportunity to see them.

This was certainly one reason, but surely not the only one. Given the funds at its command, the Fine Arts Committee could not buy from dealers, artists' studios, private owners, or other exhibitions without reducing its purchases from its own annual exhibitions, and that was the last thing it wanted to do. Beatty pointed out in 1900 that the committee's policy was to buy only from the annual exhibition, and although this was not altogether true — Tryon's *May*, H. W. Ranger's *An East River Idyll*, Elihu Vedder's *The Keeper of the Threshold*, George Inness's *The Clouded Sun*, and John White Alexander's *A Woman in Rose*, were exceptions — it was adhered to with a fair degree of fidelity.[88]

In addition, works of the quality and stature required for the chronological collection were usually the most expensive works, as in the case of Abbey's *The Penance of Eleanor, Duchess of Gloucester*. The acquisition of one or two such works a year would have severely limited the number of purchases from each exhibition, and the Fine Arts Committee wanted to be able to advertise the largest number of purchases possible. Finally, one suspects that Beatty and the more sophisticated committee members regarded the whole idea as naive and pointless. The most astute critic would have hesitated to select the two "best" paintings from the vast yearly production of American artists, and the Fine Arts Committee, still smarting at being described as a "business man's jury" in 1896, could hardly have done so with any assurance. The historical record would have been served well enough by simply purchasing good American pictures from the annual exhibitions. Perhaps they believed that the chronological collection was a mere passing enthusiasm of Carnegie's, in which it would have been imprudent to invest too much money and effort. If so, they were wise, for Carnegie never mentioned it after 1896 and allowed it to die a quiet natural death.

Whereas Carnegie had conceived of the permanent collection as primarily a record of American art, Beatty and the Fine Arts Committee wanted it to encompass the entire range of contemporary art, both American and European. American painting was well represented but made up less then half the works (thirteen out of thirty-two) acquired from 1897 to 1901. In 1896 they bought three American paintings and one British; in 1897, freed from the necessity of awarding large purchase prizes to American artists, they began to pursue a more cosmopolitan policy. Two of that year's purchases were American: Frank Benson's *Portrait of a Boy* and Douglas Volk's *Puritan Mother and Child*. Five were foreign: J. J. Shannon's *Miss Kitty* (figure 33), which took the first prize; Fritz Thaulow's *Arques at Ancourt — Evening*, which won the second prize; Martin Rico's *San Trovaso, Venice*; Puvis de Chavannes's *A Vision of Antiquity — School of Form* (figure 34), a modestly scaled but thoroughly characteristic specimen of its creator's modernized classicism; and Charles Jacque's *In the Sheepfold*, representing the still popular Barbizon School. Jacque had been dead for three years, but every exhibition included a sprinkling of works by prominent deceased artists. Shannon, Thaulow, and Rico illustrate the difficulty of assigning a definite nationality to many late nineteenth-century artists. Shannon was born in the United States and moved to London at the age of sixteen but, unlike Whistler who emigrated at twenty-one, was always considered an English rather than an expatriate American painter. Thaulow was a Norwegian and Rico a Spaniard, but both rose to fame in Paris, and throughout their careers they were indifferently assigned to both France and their native countries.

In 1898 the Department of Fine Arts again bought two American paintings — Gari Melchers's *A Sailor and His Sweetheart* (figure 35) and William Merritt Chase's *Did You Speak to Me?* The department also acquired two examples of the popular Glasgow School — Alexander Roche's third-prize-winning *The Window Seat* (figure 36) and E. A. Walton's *The*

*Shepherd* (figure 37), which had won an honorable mention; as well as *After the Day's Work* by the English Realist Frank Bramley. Mindful, perhaps, of the mounting discontent with sales reported by the Paris advisory committee, the department bought no fewer than four French paintings: *Village on the Shore of the Marne* (figure 38) by the veteran Impressionist Alfred Sisley; *Evening at the Garenne-Bezons* by René Billotte, whom Beatty recommended to Carnegie the following year as "one of the strong modern painters"; *Twilight* by Albert Gosselin, a rising star of the older salon, who by the age of thirty-five had received the Legion of Honor and had been declared *hors concours*; and *Paysanne* (figure 39) by Jules Bastien-LePage, who had died in 1885.[89] From a stylistic viewpoint, 1898 might have been called the year of the Bastien-LePage School, for the realism of Melchers, Bramley, and the two Glaswegians had been deeply influenced by the departed master.

The imbalance between France and America was corrected in early 1899, when for the first time the Department of Fine Arts purchased paintings outside its own exhibition. It acquired George Inness's *The Clouded Sun* (figure 40) from the Thomas B. Clarke sale held at the American Art Galleries, New York, on 17 February 1899, thus securing a first-rate work by an artist considered by many to be the country's foremost landscape painter. Two months later the department bought Dwight Tryon's *May*. Unable to persuade Charles Lang Freer to give up the first-prize-winning *Early Spring in New England*, the Fine Arts Committee asked Tryon to send two other paintings, *May* and *Sunrise in April*. Both were displayed in the gallery for several weeks in March while the committee decided which one to purchase, and the choice eventually fell to the former, which a local reporter described as "very similar to the gold medal picture."[90]

One of the more interesting features of the 1899 exhibition, according to a reviewer for *Brush and Pencil*, was the inclusion of several Italian works.[91] Contemporary Italian art was unfamiliar to the American public, and although the reviewer found it decadent and undistinguished the Department of Fine Arts took the opportunity to expand its range by acquiring *The Anaglyph of Trajan in the Roman Forum* (figure 41), a meticulously detailed finished study of architectural ruins by the elderly academic Luigi Bazzani. The department also acquired two thoroughly Impressionist urban scenes — Childe Hassam's *Fifth Avenue in Winter* (figure 42) which had won gold medals at Munich in 1892 and the World's

Columbian Exposition in 1893; and *Boulevard des Italiens, Paris* (figure 43) by Jean-François Raffaëlli, who had served so memorably on that year's jury.

Two of the prizewinners, both specimens of French Realism, entered the collection—André Dauchez's *The Boats*, which had taken third place; and Lucien Simon's *Portraits*, a group portrait of Dauchez and other French artists, which had won an honorable mention. The second American purchase from the exhibition was Henry Ossawa Tanner's *Judas*, a grim portrayal of the betrayer of Christ committing suicide by hanging. This acquisition catered to local curiosity (Tanner had been born in Pittsburgh and was black to boot) and gave the Carnegie galleries an example of a type of painting theretofore unrepresented, the academic religious narrative. As Ida A. Smith of the *Pittsburgh Post* observed, "No gallery is complete without some of these tragedies in oil and color."[92] Once again, French purchases had outnumbered American purchases, and once again the disparity was corrected after the close of the exhibition. In early 1900 the Department of Fine Arts bought Henry Ward Ranger's *An East River Idyll* at a sale of works from the William T. Evans Collection. This, like the pictures by Hassam and Raffaëlli, was a modern urban scene, very different from the autumnal woodland interiors with which Ranger was usually identified. The collection of Impressionist masters was enriched in 1900 with the purchase of Camille Pissarro's *The Great Bridge at Rouen* (figure 44), and *The Beach, Trouville*, a late work by the pioneer pleinairist Eugène Boudin, who had died in 1898.

As though to compensate somewhat for the dominant realism of these works, and of the permanent collection as a whole, the department also selected two pictures representative of the antirealist strain in late nineteenth-century art—*Aucassin and Nicolette* (figure 45), an exercise in Burne-Jones Pre-Raphaelitism by the British artist Marianne Stokes; and *The Wild Chase* (figure 46) by the German symbolist Franz Stuck. The latter purchase required a degree of courage on the part of the Fine Arts Committee, for the painting had received bad reviews from conservative and progressive critics alike. Charles Caffin, the progressive critic for both the *New York Evening Post* and *Harper's Weekly*, observed that its symbolism was impenetrably obscure, and its general significance was obviously "maniacal": "It smacks of the old trick of exploding a bomb to arrest attention," he wrote, "and the shock to one's feelings and the abominable oppression to one's nostrils are scarcely condoned by the virtuosity displayed in constructing the infernal thing or by the lurid beauty of the coloring it flings to view." Austin E. Howland echoed Caffin's remarks in *Brush and Pencil,* damning Stuck's work as "hideous," "maniacal," and "the effort of a trickster to attract attention." Ida Smith of the *Pittsburgh Post* was no less condemnatory: she described it as "the weirdest canvas that ever struck this gallery and got through," and she advised parents to keep their children away from it, lest they suffer nightmares forever after. Only Arthur Hoeber, who reviewed the exhibition as a special correspondent for the *New York Commercial Advertiser,* had anything good to say about it, finding it an original and thoughtful work despite its "novelty." The local press reported the news of its acquisition with something less than enthusiasm. The *Pittsburgh Times* called it "a rather weird thing" but added that the jury was rumored to have considered it for honors; the *Pittsburgh Dispatch* noted that artists had praised Stuck's handling of the misty gray clouds in the background, implying the existence of merits imperceptible to the unprofessional eye. Less charitably, the *Pittsburgh News* hinted that it had been bought solely because the artist belonged to a foreign advisory committee. In view of Beatty's problems with the Munich committee, and the fact that no German paintings had been bought to date, there may have been a grain of truth in that remark.[93] Mrs. Stokes's picture was much less controversial. Caffin mentioned it in passing as one of several academic works that "mislead the layman and afford little inspiration to the student," but few critics noticed it, and a writer for the *Pittsburgh Dispatch,* after observing the behavior of a Sunday gallery crowd, reported that it was the most popular of the new acquisitions.[94]

In 1900, the Fine Arts Committee also tried to buy the third-prize winner, Sergeant Kendall's sweetly sentimental *The End of the Day* (figure 47), but was disappointed to learn that it had already been sold. As a result, no American works were acquired from that year's exhibition. This omission was repaired by the purchase of two pictures in early 1901. Beatty finally discharged his debt of gratitude to John White Alexander by persuading the committee to buy *A Woman in Rose;* and Elihu Vedder's *The Keeper of the Threshold* (figure 48) was added to the collection shortly before the close of the Institute's fiscal year. The acquisition of this work, one of Vedder's most enigmatic mystical images, confirms that Beatty and the committee were particularly interested in antirealist art at that time. The work was no stranger to the Carnegie galleries, having appeared in the annual exhibition for 1898, when Charles Caffin described it as "deep and suggestive" but admitted that he had no idea of what it meant. Its second visit to the gallery, as part of a traveling loan exhibition of Vedder's paintings and drawings, was the occasion of its purchase. The department had to wait several months to take possession of it, because it first had to go to Chicago with the rest of the exhibition, then appear at the great Pan-American Exposition in Buffalo, where it received a gold medal.[95]

As previously mentioned, the only picture purchased from the 1901 exhibition, and the last to enter the ill-fated chronological collection, was *The Penance of Eleanor, Duchess of Gloucester*, Edwin Austin Abbey's rendering of a dramatic scene from the second part of Shakespeare's *Henry VI*. A splendid example of the sort of literary subject much beloved of the Royal Academy, it arrived in Pittsburgh fresh from winning a gold medal at Buffalo and was given the place of honor on the west wall of the central gallery. Charles Caffin, never fond of the academic, found it rather unimaginative but granted that it was "a clear and forcible realization of Shakespeare's meaning"; most out-of-town reviewers ignored it or gave it only a passing mention. However, the local press was ecstatic about it: the *Pittsburgh Leader* called it "the most striking canvas in the entire exhibition"; the *Pittsburgh Gazette* agreed that it was the best thing in the galleries and regretted that it was ineligible for honors owing to Abbey's position on the London advisory committee. Its purchase, even at the enormous price of $9,000, seemed altogether appropriate.[96]

Nevertheless, to have spent the entire acquisitions budget on a single work would appear to have been impolitic in view of the artists' dissatisfaction with the number of sales from Pittsburgh. The likeliest explanation for this behavior is that Beatty no longer cared. As we shall see, he was about to make an attempt to end the annual exhibition, an attempt that, had it succeeded, would have allowed him to devote his resources entirely to the permanent collection. He may well have regarded *The Penance of Eleanor, Duchess of Gloucester*, as the last picture his department would ever buy from an international exhibition in Pittsburgh.

# The Exhibition and the Public
## 1897–1901

### The Popular Response

ALTHOUGH ONE of Carnegie's major purposes was to bring sweetness and light into the lives of Pittsburgh's workers, the exhibition was by no means keyed to the working-class public. Like older exhibitions in other cities, the Carnegie annual celebrated its opening every year with a gala reception for the more affluent and notable section of the community. The "press view," held from seven to ten o'clock on the eve of the official opening, was so called, according to a writer for the *Pittsburgh Dispatch*, because "a few lone newspaper men were permitted to foregather with numerous artists, lawyers, doctors and manufacturers, and to timidly intrude into bevies of beauties, to tread where angels spread trains, frills, flounces and furbelows — traps for the unwary." The local press returned the favor by describing in richly glowing society-page gush the "groups of stylishly-gowned women and well-groomed men moving about among the tall masses of tropical plants on the divans; the frou-frou of silks and the hum of conversation." The gathering, we are assured, was aesthetically sophisticated enough to talk "more or less expertly of 'atmosphere,' 'tone,' and other things." All the same, one imagines that the young woman who exclaimed, "Oh, how gloriously brilliant!" upon entering the main gallery was more impressed with the spectacle of so much wealth and fashion than with the paintings on the walls.[1]

The official opening of the exhibition took place on Founder's Day.

The Founder's Day celebrations were necessarily less exclusive than Press View Night because the Institute's Music Hall where they were held could accommodate many more people than the galleries could; nevertheless, their character was distinctly unproletarian. This did not go unremarked. In 1897 a letter from "Pleb" appeared on the editorial page of the *Pittsburgh Leader* denouncing the Carnegie Institute's avowed populism as sheer humbug, because on Founder's Day a thousand seats in the Music Hall had been reserved for "the class of people known as the Four Hundred, the millionaires, the horse show faddists, and that other genera [*sic*], the 'dontcherknows.'" Until such reservations were abolished, he concluded, no "self-respecting poor man" should go near the Institute. Pleb's terminology was inaccurate (the Four Hundred was an East Coast phenomenon, and it is doubtful that there were as many as a thousand Pittsburghers whom the Astors and Vanderbilts would have regarded as social equals), but there were certainly a number of millionaires in the audience, and perhaps a few of those were the affected Anglophiles signified by the epithet "dontcherknows." The *Pittsburgh Post*'s description of a Founder's Day crowd as "a gathering of cultured men and women" may be taken to mean the same thing, with class admiration replacing class animosity.[2]

Judging from the published transcripts of the Founder's Day ceremonies, the workers (who in any event could not have left their jobs on a weekday afternoon) missed little in the way of enlightenment and entertainment. From two to four in the afternoon, the audience sat and listened to a series of speeches, usually beginning with an address by William Nimick Frew, and a report from Samuel H. Church, secretary of the board of trustees, detailing the marvelous progress made by the various departments of the Institute during the past year. They were followed by speeches from visiting dignitaries, including President William McKinley in 1897, the founder himself in 1898, Chinese ambassador Wu Ting Fang in 1900, and former president Grover Cleveland in 1901 (figure 49). These speeches invariably featured flattering remarks about Carnegie, Pittsburgh, and the Institute; even Minister Wu took the opportunity, in his address on "Educational Ideals in and out of China," to salute the city as "a modern Athens at the junction of the Allegheny and the Monongahela" that was destined to become "the admiration and envy of the world."[3]

Although Founder's Day was intended to celebrate the entire Institute, special emphasis was given to the Department of Fine Arts, and the elected jurors were often invited to speak. In 1899 Jean-François Raffaëlli delivered a gallically effusive speech on internationalism in art, and William Merritt Chase offended wealthy Pittsburghers by exhorting them to buy from the exhibition; in 1900 Anders Zorn lectured on the importance of the applied arts, suggesting that a medal of honor should be awarded to the most beautiful door handle as well as to the most beautiful painting; in 1901 John White Alexander denounced the large federal tariff against imported works of art, whereas the English juror Robert W. Allan diplomatically avoided polemics and praised the Institute as "the center of Art in the United States."[4]

The famous comedian Joseph Jefferson, who delivered a surprise address in 1899, should perhaps be included among the artists, for he was widely known to be a talented amateur painter and his humor on that occasion derived from the pretense that he was going to give one of his pictures to the Carnegie galleries. "I know you will all cherish the gift," he said, "especially when I tell you that my paintings have been repeatedly refused admission to the exhibitions of art in the large art galleries of this country." His jokes seem rather worse than his paintings conceivably could have been, but fashions in humor change; the trustees liked him well enough to invite him back in 1901 and 1902. The Fine Arts Committee also liked him well enough to hang a loan exhibition of his work in the spring of 1900.[5]

At some point in the proceedings, often toward the end, the prize-winners of the annual exhibition were announced. William Nimick Frew normally performed this office, but in 1897 it was turned over to President William McKinley. When the speeches and announcements were finished, the audience went to the galleries, where they could meet the guests of honor and examine the pictures until the general public was admitted at five o'clock. It was on one such occasion that Minister Wu expertly deflated the pretensions of an unidentified art critic whom he had asked to show him a particularly good picture and to explain why it was excellent. The critic was just warming up to a highly technical explanation when Wu interrupted him: "Did you ever paint a picture?" "No, Sir," replied the critic, whereupon Wu grunted and walked away.[6]

What, then, was done to educate the toilers, that their lives might become more susceptible to sweetness and light? Very little. Indeed, very little was done to educate any class of society. Press View Night and Founder's Day were not informational events; even the artists' addresses were largely uninformative about the state of contemporary art. Had one faithfully attended every Founder's Day from 1897 to 1901, one would have learned from Raffaëlli that there was a style called Impressionism that had had difficulty getting itself accepted twenty years before but that was now practiced worldwide, and from Zorn that there were people who wanted to apply the principles of high art to objects of everyday use. And that would have been all.

Nowadays, a major exhibition begets an abundance of lectures, tours, symposia, and other activities, as well as a thick catalogue full of scholarly and critical essays; but in the 1890s this educational apparatus was still in its most rudimentary stages. Yet it is impossible to accuse John Beatty of insincerity when he declared in 1902, "It has been the policy of the Department, from the very inception of the work, to place great importance on its educational influence upon our own people," or when he predicted several years earlier that the Carnegie Institute would "become one of the greatest educational influences in America."[7] What little was done by the Institute in Pittsburgh was more than was done by the major exhibitions of New York, London, and Paris.

Beatty was primarily, almost exclusively, interested in educating Pittsburgh's young people. "From influencing young minds through love of beauty, almost unconsciously, results ensue which shall uplift the character in future years and place the whole individual on a higher plane"; this, he told an interviewer in 1900, constituted in itself "the great good of the art galleries." The following year, in an address delivered to a group of school principals, he stressed the importance of influencing people's tastes when they were young and impressionable — "young people form opinions, old people assert them," he said — and emphasized the practical advantages to be derived from developing the aesthetic sensibilities: "Now, since the overwhelming majority of your boys and girls will enter the vast field of manufacture, the cultivation of knowledge of the beautiful in form and color becomes important. A keen appreciation of the graceful, of the appropriate and proper proportions of objects of artistic beauty will be found helpful in a thousand ways."[8]

As early as the 1895 loan exhibition, Beatty had urged the local art schools to suspend their afternoon sessions and instead send their students to view the paintings. Following the 1896 exhibition, he could report with satisfaction that "nearly all the educational institutions of Pittsburgh in which art is taught sent school parties on specially appointed days, and a number of the city ward schools and public schools of the near neighborhood were represented during the period of exhibition by large delegations of students." There were no guided tours, and for the next few years the teachers were left to their own devices, assisted occasionally by Beatty, who would lecture school groups when his schedule, and presumably his inclinations, permitted.[9]

Finally, in October 1900, Jennie Ralston, head of the Fifth Avenue High School's normal department, suggested that Beatty give guided tours to the students on a regular basis. Teachers of both drawing and English, she wrote, were interested in such tours, and, a true child of her age, she trotted out the supposedly beneficial influences of art in support of her idea: "Such a policy would exert its influence for uplifting not only upon the students, but also through the students a great good might be effected upon the parents." A few days later Beatty met with a committee representing the academic and normal departments of the Pittsburgh high schools, and he agreed to conduct two-hour tours for "advanced students" (high school juniors and seniors) twice a week until the close of the annual exhibition (figure 50). These tours were described as "informal talks," but their informality did not involve intimacy—a typical tour group comprised between one hundred and two hundred teachers and pupils. Beatty also arranged to lead tours for the Allegheny public schools, for private schools, and arts organizations.[10]

After 1900 these school tours became a permanent feature of the annual exhibitions. Ernest Knaufft, writing in the *Review of Reviews* in 1903, praised them as a unique local phenomenon, thanks to which "the Carnegie Galleries are attended by more young people than any other art gallery in the United States." On 9 November 1909, speaking at the dedication of the Museum of Fine Arts building in Boston, Beatty boasted that "the impressionable, eager, knowledge-seeking young people of Pittsburgh have a broader knowledge of modern art than the young people of any other city in America." His pride in this achievement was all the more justifiable in that he accomplished it single-handedly. It was not until 1913 that the Fine Arts Committee secured the services of a guide, and Beatty ceased to add the duties of docent to those of director.[11]

Beatty's educational ideas were unquestionably progressive for his day, but they affected few people. The major beneficiaries were high school students, and at the turn of the century a secondary education was still the exception rather than the rule for the average American.[12] Tours were also offered to arts organizations, but these were composed of students, amateur and professional artists, and upper-middle-class aficionados who already possessed at least a basic knowledge of contemporary painting. For most of those who entered the Carnegie galleries, the only source of information was the ten-cent catalogue, and this, though somewhat less terse than the usual nineteenth-century catalogue, was hardly adequate to the purpose. It gave the names of the artists and the titles of their works; it provided a few facts about each artist, such as place of birth, place of residence, organizational affiliations and honors; it included photographs of some of the paintings and some of the painters. Its most educational feature was the bibliography, printed at the end, listing books and articles that the interested gallery-goer could consult at the Carnegie Library. Here, for example, is the bibliography for Claude Monet published in the 1900 catalogue:

> Bell's Representative painters of the nineteenth century, p. 145–148
> Brownell's French art, p. 124–132; 134–137
> Moore's Modern painting, p. 84–88
> Muther's History of modern painting, v. 2, p. 769–770
> Van Dyke's Modern French masters, p. 167–174
> Century, v. 44, p. 696
> Pall Mall magazine, v. 21, p. 209 (June, 1900)

This is a good, short English-language bibliography for its time, and anyone who took the trouble to read the items listed in it would have come away with a pretty fair understanding of Monet, although extensive reading in an accompanying list of more general works would have been necessary to understand Impressionism as a whole.

It is unlikely, however, that many casual visitors to the exhibition had the time and motivation to do the recommended reading, and improbable to the highest degree that the workers that Carnegie hoped to enlighten could benefit from it in any way. Certainly, few of Carnegie's own employees could have done so. Both the exhibition and the library were free to everyone, but the cost of the catalogue and trolley fares to and from Oakland — for the Institute had been built in an affluent middle-class neighborhood — would have strained the budgets of all but the most highly paid millworkers. Even those who had the money (and, of course, an adequate level of literacy) would not have had time for a course of study: the twelve-hour days and seven-day weeks common in the steel industry allowed scant leisure for intellectual recreations. *The Pittsburgh Survey*, a detailed account of the city's working class published in six volumes between 1909 and 1914, described the plight of a steelworker who was ripe for cultural elevation but grossly overworked: "He cannot go out and feel much like work the next day. He usually goes to lectures at the Carnegie Library [a small neighborhood library, not the great Institute], but to little else. No man who works twelve hours, he says, has time or energy to do much outside of his work. His life is lived in the mill." By way of contrast, the contemporary settlement house exhibitions of New York and Boston, which aimed solely at bringing art to the masses and were unencumbered with ambitions of becoming American salons, were far more accessible, in every sense, to their audiences. They were situated in working-class neighborhoods; they sold "explanatory catalogues," rich with comments and quotes, for two cents apiece; and they offered many free lectures and tours.[13]

Although virtually nothing was done to educate the general public, Beatty maintained that cultural enlightenment was making great strides among his fellow Pittsburghers:

> The first year . . . there were great crowds of people who simply walked through the rooms to look about them. Curiosity was the main incentive of their coming, and they went away with only a hazy idea of a lot of pictures, most of which could not even be clearly recalled. As the years passed by, however, there was a gradual change, and I believe now that the majority of visitors to the exhibits see and appreciate the main points of each exhibit. Pictures are looked at with more intelligence, and in art, as in all else, intelligent understanding is the key to real appreciation.

When Beatty made this observation in 1900, it had already become habitual with him. As early as 1896, he had been impressed by a "manifest tendency on the part of the people to critically study the works with the purpose of deriving the greatest possible amount of instruction and pleasure"; as late as 1914 he was still remarking "the studious and thoughtful interest of the people" who had "come to remain, to study and to enjoy in a degree which was not so apparent in the early years of our work."[14]

How, precisely, had this increase in the public's "intelligence" been achieved? Beatty nowhere specifies the means. Apparently, simply looking attentively at pictures whose quality had been guaranteed by a jury of eminent artists was enough to effect the hoped-for improvement. In fairness to Beatty, it should be noted that this view was not peculiar to him: most nineteenth-century writing on the elevating influence of art has little to say about such practical measures as lectures or explanatory catalogues, assuming that the mere sight of a work of art will call this influence into operation. Indeed, the aesthetic theories of Kant, Schopenhauer, and other well-known philosophers had long since made this view intellectually respectable, if not convincing.

In order to show that the annual exhibition was reaching the masses, Beatty frequently cited attendance figures. As Helen Horowitz points out in *Culture and the City*, cultural philanthropists of the period usually resorted to head counts to prove that they were accomplishing their missions, as if large numbers could somehow be equated with a high degree of spiritual uplift. Charles L. Hutchinson, president of Chicago's Art Institute and a great believer in the Gospel of Art, attached as much significance to attendance records as did Beatty and was said to review these figures personally every day.[15]

It took Beatty several years to fully acquire this numerical faith: in his 1897 report he was content to observe that the attendance for 1896 was "very large," and it was not until 1899 that he began throwing out numbers of impressive magnitude and seeming precision. During the first two weeks of the 1898 exhibition, he wrote, 40,860 persons had passed through the galleries. Regarding this as "a reasonably fair average attendance," he estimated that about 240,000 people had visited the exhibition and called this "an unprecedented showing." The 1899 exhibition was even less precedented: 52,654 during the first two weeks, 300,000 in all (a figure slightly exceeding the estimated population of Pittsburgh at that time). This would mean that about a thousand Pittsburghers passed through the galleries every hour, which seems improbable on the face of it.[16]

At this point, however, we begin to doubt the reliability of Beatty's figures for other reasons, for on 1 January 1900 he told the *Pittsburgh Post* that the total attendance had been "perhaps 200,000," not 300,000, and that this was a record. Similarly, he stated in his fourth annual report that catalogue sales had risen by 10 percent since 1898, and by 30 percent since 1896, but a few months later he told an interviewer for *The Library* that catalogue sales had risen by 33 percent every year since 1896. The annual report for 1903 confirms our doubts. In 1902, wrote Beatty, the exhibition had drawn 138,172 people, making it "the best-attended exhibition to date." This report includes a list of the attendance figures for the first two weeks of every exhibition after 1897, and in each case the figure is half or less of the figure originally given. Beatty admitted the unreliability of the figures, attributing it to the lack of a mechanical means for registering the tally. Following the 1904 exhibition, which, because of the ongoing expansion of the Institute building, was held in a temporary free-standing structure, he observed that for the first time the attendance records were accurate. In the old building, he said, people who had been counted would leave the galleries to visit the library and the museum, then return to the galleries and be counted again, thereby inflating the figures.[17]

The local press affords us some vivid glimpses of the popular response to the exhibition. Pittsburgh's newspapers were generally much attracted to the Gospel of Art, either from genuine conviction or because it offered a convenient angle from which to cover the exhibition, and as a result they occasionally sent reporters to observe how the public was behaving in the galleries, to see if the Gospel was finding an audience and having an effect. Their observations confirm Beatty's claims that the exhibition was well attended. This was especially true of Sunday, the only day of the week when most people were free from work. On Sunday, 6 November 1897, "the crowds poured up every stairway in a manner that made rigid control impossible; the guards simply directed the course of the stream and let it take its way." By four o'clock, two hours after the gallery opened, the entire supply of catalogues was sold out. On Sunday, 19 November 1899, the crowd was so thick that "it was almost impossible to get up the stairs," and it was extremely difficult to view the pictures until the guards persuaded everybody to move in the same direction. Two weeks later there was "almost a crush" by four o'clock, despite a spell of inclement weather that discouraged many people from going out. On most Sundays, and occasionally on weekdays, the crowds were swelled by out-of-towners who had arrived on special excursion trains from other parts of western Pennsylvania, as well as from Cincinnati and Cleveland. It should not be supposed, however, that all these people descended upon Oakland solely or primarily to expose themselves to the uplifting influence of art. On the contrary, the fall chrysanthemum show at Phipps Conservatory, a short walk from the Institute, always drew the largest crowds, and the exhibition was only a secondary attraction. For most people, a typical Sunday outing began with a tour of the conservatory, continued with a visit to the galleries and the museum, and concluded with a free organ recital in the Institute's Music Hall.[18]

Reporters liked to emphasize the social diversity of the exhibition crowd. For example, the *Pittsburgh Times* reported in 1899 that the visitors to the galleries included "the classes that work and the classes for whom they work. There were men who wore suits of jean and blue woolen shirts, with a cheap felt hat as a topper, and there were men who had broadcloth coats and glistening silk hats and patent leather shoes." In 1900 Frances Parry of the *Pittsburgh Dispatch* pointed to

> the millionaire, looking over the catalogue of prices; the student from the art institute, studying values and colors through half-closed eyes; Aunt Maria from the country, whose principal comment is "Well, I declare!"; the mechanic with his best girl, standing in awkward but appreciative silence at a bad angle with the prize picture; finally, there are school children of all ages sprinkled in liberally.[19]

The conspicuous presence of the working class stands in sharp contrast to its no less conspicuous absence in today's exhibitions of contemporary art. There were fewer competing amusements in the late nineteenth century, and most important, the art of the day was more universal in its appeal: attractive landscapes and charming genre pieces, although their finer points might be grasped only by connoisseurs, could easily be appreciated by the unrefined and ignorant. Nevertheless, the majority of those who came to receive Carnegie's infusion of sweetness and light were solidly middle class. "The crowds are almost invariably well-dressed," wrote a reviewer for the *Pittsburgh Post,* "and the better class people predominate."[20]

According to the security guards, women — many of them art students — outnumbered men by at least eight to one. Although there is no reason to doubt the liberal sprinkling of children mentioned by Frances Parry, the guards disliked unsupervised children on account of their "insane desire to touch pictures," and they tried to direct them to their "proper place," the museum of natural history. Lower-class children were regarded as particularly objectionable. Late one Friday afternoon in November 1899, George Harlow of Wilkinsburg saw a guard turn away three small boys whose clothes betrayed their poverty. When Harlow, presumably bristling with the same indignation that later prompted him to send a strong letter to Beatty, asked if the exhibition was not open to the public, the guard replied, "It is to gentlemen, but these boys did not even have on clean shirts." Beatty's response to Harlow, and therefore his opinion of the practice, has not been preserved. Although his educational interests focused on high school students, he was concerned to reach younger children, and he implemented several programs toward this end, including an annual exhibition of art by pupils of the Pittsburgh public schools (1901), the distribution to schools of photographs of works in the permanent collection (1902), and a weekly children's art hour, comprising a lecture and a visit to the galleries (1913). All the same, he may have preferred to discourage a few potential working-class geniuses than to run the risk of vandalism and pickpocketing.[21]

It is usually difficult, if not impossible, to reconstruct the popular response to the major exhibitions of the past; the opinions of critics are preserved, while those of the casual viewer are lost beyond recovery. However, the early Carnegie annuals are a partial exception, thanks to the local press. From time to time, an editor would assign a reporter or a reviewer to wander around the galleries and record the fugitive remarks of the exhibition-goers. The evidence gathered from such eavesdropping does not on the whole support Beatty's contention that Pittsburghers were becoming more knowledgeable and sophisticated in matters of art, but it must be kept in mind that the reporters were primarily interested in gathering funny remarks and amusing anecdotes: a quiet, intelligent conversation would have made colorless copy. Although the local papers tended to echo Beatty in their editorial comments, the reporters assigned to the galleries often reached different conclusions. In 1898, after studying the public's response to that year's prizewinners, a reporter for the *Pittsburgh Times* wrote that "Pittsburgh may be educated in some art, but in painting, as a day at the Institute will show, there are many sadly neglected educations." After a similar experience in 1900, a reporter for the *Commercial Gazette* stated flatly that Beatty was wrong and that Pittsburghers had acquired no great knowledge of art. A more hopeful reporter for the *Pittsburgh Times* observed in 1899 that "people are trying to get an understanding of the ideas of the artists" but had to admit that their attempts were "sometimes rather amusing" and frequently led to "discouraging remarks being made."[22]

> It is the tiny bit of woodland orchard, with an old, gnarled apple tree,
> and a swing falling from its branches, which brings a smile and a tear
> to the eye. It is the sunny kitchen, where rows of pies are baking, or
> mayhap a group of kittens catching at the sunbeams, which carries
> the memory back swiftly to olden days when such a kitchen repre-
> sented the paradise of home to the onlooker; and the dimpled smile of
> a baby, which may have been scornfully rejected by the judges, wins
> its unerring way to the public heart.

This is how a writer for the *Pittsburgh Dispatch* characterized the popular taste of 1899, before going on to give a detailed account of the works that had won public favor. That year's prizewinners are notably absent from the list; however, the *Portrait of a Child* by Frank Benson, whose *The Sisters* took second prize, was pronounced "too sweet for anything" by many women, some of whom expressed a wish "almost to kiss" the subject's pretty little feet. An earlier article in the *Pittsburgh Dispatch* informs us that *The Sisters*, a portrait of two little girls, was also "showered with admiration everyday." In general, the most highly esteemed paintings were those that featured children: such as Robert Vonnoh's *Little Louise*, "with her demure blue eyes and sweet mouth looking like a closely folded rose bud"; Charles Proctor's *Grandpa*, in which an old man blows smoke rings from a pipe to amuse a child; and Frederick Freer's *Nursery Rhymes*, showing a young mother with her baby on her knee. Indeed, the Proctor and the Freer were prime favorites of the exhibition, and although their appeal was largely to women, men were by no means unresponsive to them. Andrew Carnegie liked *Grandpa* well enough to buy it; and a "huge man, who would almost bow his head at a seven-foot door," was deeply touched by *Nursery Rhymes*. "There now, Mother, is that real?" he said. "It just makes me see you holdin' Harry on your knee, and tellin' him about the man that jumped into the bramble bush." Men especially admired Charles Courtney Curran's *Building a Dam*, a scene of boys frolicking in a stream, and would linger in front of it to reminisce about their own childhood exploits.[23]

To the average exhibition-goer of 1899, subject counted for almost everything, nuances of color and brushwork for little or nothing. Often, though, they were struck by a particularly convincing bit of realism. A winter landscape impressed them because "it looks so cold"; an autumn landscape because the effects of light looked "just like real sunshine." One woman declared that the fire glowing on the hearth in Frank Bramley's *A Mute, Inglorious Milton* "actually seems to burn," a quality that made it, in her opinion, the best thing in the show. The smoke rings in *Grandpa* fascinated everybody. They also responded to the occasional gimmick. Gari Melchers's *Young Mother* was at first mistaken for a Madonna because a copper plate behind her head resembled a halo. When the true nature of this halo was discovered, it aroused "a sort of interest in the picture which casual viewers might not otherwise feel."[24]

Beatty confessed to an interviewer in 1900 that the prizewinning paintings rarely found favor with the general public. First-prize winners, he said, were often "absolutely ignored by the public, save as a butt for ridicule," and this had been especially the case with D. W. Tryon's *Early Spring in New England* in 1898.[25] Contemporary observations confirm the truth of Beatty's statements but do not support his opinion that the situation was improving. A reporter who stationed himself near the 1898 prizewinners and listened to what people were saying about them recorded only a single favorable remark about *Early Spring in New England*, from a man who appeared to be knowledgeable about art. More typical was the high school girl who exclaimed "The idea!" and likened it to the advertising signboard across the street from her house; or the bewhiskered old man who declared, "I'm a son-of-a-gun"; or the loudly opinionated man who said, "Ain't it absurd? There's no life in that thing; the trees are scrawny, uninviting things, and the grass ain't natural. I don't want to say anything bad against this place, but I don't see how a man with a conscience could give a prize to a picture like that." Most typical, perhaps, were two women who did not like it but assumed that it had to be good if it had won a prize and who spent several minutes earnestly studying it from every possible angle and distance in a fruitless endeavor to appreciate its fine points. The second-prize winner, Childe Hassam's *The Sea*, and the third-prize winner, Alexander Roche's *The Window Seat*, fared somewhat better in the popular estimation, but not much. A "learned young man" preferred the Hassam to Tryon but added that both were Impressionist works, and therefore disagreeable to him. A young woman who had tried and failed to see the merits of Hassam and Tryon cautiously said, "I suppose the merit lies in the fact that these pictures introduce an entirely new school of art, which, of course, would make a true artist enthusiastic over them." Her own lack of enthusiasm was obvious. *The Window Seat* was censured for its size — many people thought it was too small to warrant a prize — and for the loose, painterly brushwork that made it difficult to read at close range. A woman who had found it confusing on close inspection decided that it was "pretty nice" after seeing it from a distance, but she still felt that there were many superior pictures in the exhibition. The honorable mentions fared best of all: according to the reporter, both *The Shepherd* by E. A. Walton and *Roses* by John F. Weir were extremely popular with the masses.[26]

As mentioned before, the only popular picture among the 1899 prize-winners was Frank Benson's *The Sisters*; however, the others do not appear to have aroused any considerable degree of adverse criticism. Beatty may have had this in mind when he said that the public's response to the prizewinners was improving. If so, the events of 1900 proved him wrong: the average exhibition-goer disliked both the first-prize winner, André Dauchez's *The Kelp Gatherers*, and the second-prize winner, Ben Foster's *Misty Moonlight Night* (figure 51). Both were somber, tonal works, belonging to a class of painting for which the public had little taste; both were condemned as "disappointing" and untrue to nature. But women adored the third-prize winner, Sergeant Kendall's *The End of the Day*, one of several popular mother-and-child subjects (including one by the infallible Frank Benson) exhibited that year. Men liked pictures with animals in them, especially Winslow Homer's *Hound and Hunter* and Benson's *Wild Fowl Alighting*. According to the guards, the most popular painting in the galleries was Anders Zorn's *Portrait of Mrs. Grover Cleveland*. Its appeal, observed a reporter for the *Pittsburgh Commercial Gazette*, had nothing to do with Zorn's talent and fame as an artist, everything to do with the celebrity of Frances Folsom Cleveland, who in 1886 had become America's youngest First Lady, and the only one to be married in the White House. Another big attention-getter was Franz Stuck's *The Wild Chase*, not because it was liked, but because it was so weird and offered so many opportunities to make disparaging remarks. References to pink elephants were overheard, and many viewers called it "a horrid thing."[27]

The 1901 first-prize winner fared as badly in the public eye as that of the previous year. Alfred Maurer's *An Arrangement* was particularly disliked. "Will there ever be a first prize picture of which our mothers and great-aunts will approve?" asked Henry Nickleman, reviewer for the *Pittsburgh Gazette*. He then illustrated his point by quoting the opinions of "Edna, a stenographer," and her friend Myrtle: "It's nothing in the world, Myrtle, but a girl sewing the binding on her skirt," cried Edna, her tone indicating amazement and disappointment. Her reaction, wrote Nickleman, arose from her inability to accept such a trivial and unemotional subject as worthy of art: "If the girl were leaning over to pick up a child, or to solemnly burn love letters, or to weep beside a bier, both Edna and Myrtle would have found the picture resplendent with beauty, they would really have experienced pleasure in looking at it." They also disliked the third-prize winner, Edmund Tarbell's *The Venetian Blind* (figure 52). This picture "puzzled and altogether confounded" them; they found the light unrealistic and the title misleading: they had expected a Venetian scene. The nude model's artificial pose prompted one old man to suggest that "she would sleep easier if she rested her back against that sofa instead of putting her feet there." But Edna, Myrtle, and everyone else were delighted with Elizabeth Ahrens's *Sewing — A Portrait*. This was due, in part, to the homely sentiment conveyed by Ahrens's grandmotherly model, in part to Ahrens's being a humble art student who had unexpectedly won a major award. The picture's plain oak frame attracted almost as much attention as the picture itself, for it was said that poor Miss Ahrens, unlike the more famous and prosperous artists displayed in the gallery, could afford no better. Next in popularity was Edwin Austin Abbey's *The Penance of Eleanor, Duchess of Gloucester*, whose scale and drama apparently compensated for an absence of that cuddlesome sentiment so often found in the most popular works. Another favorite was *A Portrait* by Cecilia Beaux. Edna admired it, said Nickleman, "not for its exquisite painting, but for certain Ladies' Home Journalish mannerisms that have become more and more marked in Miss Beaux's work of late years" — a slighting reference to the artist's skill in depicting fashionable toilettes.[28]

It would be belaboring the obvious to say that these published observations do not reveal any appreciable growth in the aesthetic sophistication of the general public during the early years of the Carnegie annuals. And yet one cannot wholly disagree with the reporter who wrote, "To listen to the comments of these crowds is equivalent to putting aside the cynical conviction that art is misunderstood by the masses."[29] Their understanding was certainly imperfect, but the distance between their taste and that of the cognoscenti was in many ways shorter than it is today. The writer who referred to "the dimpled smile of a baby, which may have been scornfully rejected by the judges" tried to emphasize this distance and badly overstated it. The baby's dimpled smile could not have appeared in the exhibition at all unless the judges had accepted it, the Fine Arts

Committee borrowed it, or a juror or foreign advisor painted it. The last possibility was by no means the least likely: of the artists whose work found special favor with the public, Abbey and Walton were foreign advisors, and Benson, Beaux, Freer, Homer, Vonnoh, and Zorn were elected to the jury more than once during their careers. Most of the popular painters ranked high in the esteem of critics and colleagues; many were among the more progressive artists of their day.

The public had trouble accepting the more extreme manifestations of Impressionism and Tonalism but objected less to modern technical innovations than to the emotionally neutral subjects they were so often allied with. Edna and Myrtle, to whom a Whistleresque treatment of light and form must have been quite a new thing, had nothing to say against this aspect of *An Arrangement:* it was the commonplace subject that disappointed them, and Nickleman believed that an infusion of drama or sentiment would have sufficed to make it delightful to them. Frank Benson was a leading American Impressionist, but by applying Impressionism to sporting scenes and children he established himself as a popular favorite. The women who wanted to kiss the little feet in Benson's *Portrait of a Child* and who cooed with admiration at the *Little Louise* of Robert Vonnoh, another leading Impressionist, may have been insensible to the peculiar beauties of the artists' techniques, but they were not misunderstanding the artists' intentions; on the contrary, they were giving responses that the artist had consciously strived to elicit. As we shall see when we examine the published reviews of the Carnegie exhibition, the trend toward formalism and the corresponding devaluation of the subject had not advanced so far by the turn of the century as to make "sentiment" a dirty word in the critical vocabulary. Critics often praised sentiment in art and, just as often, deplored its absence. Even so progressive a critic as Charles Caffin could censure young American painters for producing too many pictures that were "nothing more than studies of light as it filters through muslin curtains, creeps between the slats of Venetian blinds, or in full sunshine pours over the lace caps of peasant women or the white gowns of first communicants."[30] There was still a broad common ground on which the sophisticate and the unsophisticated could meet.

The response to Dagnan-Bouveret's *Christ and the Disciples at Emmaus* (figure 53) shows the existence of this common ground in an area where one would be surprised to find it today. This painting was introduced to Pittsburgh at the 1898 exhibition, but it was not a regular entry; rather, it had been purchased from the artist in August 1897 by Henry Clay Frick and his wife and donated to the Department of Fine Arts in July 1898 as a memorial to "their little girl Martha, who has fallen asleep." The piece had already been successfully exhibited in London and Paris; and Dagnan-Bouveret, hoping for a similar success in America, took the trouble to provide a written statement in which he explained that it was an attempt to bring a traditional religious subject up to date, that the subsidiary figures in modern dress (himself and his wife and child) were inspired by medieval and Renaissance donor portraits, that the woman and child were shown kneeling because they were still capable of faith, whereas the man was full of doubt and therefore unable to kneel.[31]

So far, there is nothing in this that might not be paralleled today in the exhibition history of a particularly clever installation. It is doubtful, however, that the installation would become the theme of Sunday sermons in the city's churches. This is precisely what happened to *Christ and the Disciples at Emmaus*. The Reverend Henry T. McClelland of the Bellefield Presbyterian Church made it the basis for a discourse on human and divine fellowship; the Reverend D. Dorchester of Christ Methodist Episcopal Church praised it for proclaiming "the surpassing glory of the divine spirit" and credited it with having "a distinctly higher spiritual tone than any religious picture that ever came to America." The Reverend G. H. Humason of the Lincoln Avenue Methodist Episcopal Church not only declared that the picture would "do as much for humanity in this city as any pulpit"; he revealed that the Carnegie Institute had been inspired by God to turn wealth into a means of spiritual enlightenment. "Take hold firmly of the hand your Creator has influenced Mr. Carnegie and his associates to reach toward you," he concluded, "and climb up for comfort and enjoyment into the higher rooms of your being." The only sour note was struck by the Reverend E. H. Ward of St. Peter's Protestant Episcopal Church: he vastly admired Dagnan-Bouveret's staring fin-de-siècle Christ, but he considered the modern figures "painfully grotesque" and wished they could be "blotted from the canvas."[32]

## The Critical Response

In 1899 William Nimick Frew thanked the daily papers for "the continued and hearty assistance" they had given to the Carnegie Institute, and especially to the annual exhibition.[33] These thanks were well deserved: the local press was an excellent publicity agent. The Institute had only to issue a press release for it to appear in every one of the city's papers; every circumstance surrounding the exhibition was reported in minute detail, and the reports were almost invariably favorable. For the majority of Pittsburghers who did not attend Beatty's guided tours, and who lacked the leisure and incentive to read the books and articles listed in the catalogues, the press provided a convenient, if not profound, source of information, thereby helping to further the Institute's mission. The national press, though less interested in minutiae than the local press, was also extremely supportive.

One can hardly speak of an international press in connection with the Carnegie annuals. European journals regularly printed notices of the prizewinners but nothing more; even the cosmopolitan *Gazette des Beaux Arts*, which frequently reviewed exhibitions outside its native France, rarely extended its sights as far as America, and it never touched on Pittsburgh. The only article of any significance to appear on the other side of the Atlantic was a piece published by the English critic D. Croal Thomson in the December 1898 number of the *Art Journal*. Thomson's purpose was not to review that year's exhibition but to give his British readers the most flattering possible introduction to the new artistic enterprise being undertaken in Pittsburgh. He liked almost everything about the Carnegie galleries, from their physical appearance (illustrated with photographs) to the method of selecting the international jury, and he predicted that they would transform Pittsburgh into a leading cultural center:

> It may be anticipated that as years go on we shall hear more and more of the Carnegie Galleries, and if the name of the city in which they are situated, Pittsburgh, sounds in British ears unpoetic, if not absolutely prosaic, yet as artistic associations gather around it, it is likely that ideas of a more elevated character will be accepted.

His sole complaint, albeit a mild one, was that the annual exhibitions were too general: he thought it would be more interesting to feature the artists of one particular country or school each year. In view of Thomson's enthusiasm, it is not surprising to learn that he was personally acquainted with Beatty, having first met him in London in 1896, and was apparently on friendly terms with him. In February 1899 he sent Beatty a copy of the relevant issue of the *Art Journal*, together with a genial letter in which he expressed the hope that his article would "do the Institute good on this side, where the prejudices are difficult to overcome."[34]

It would be an exaggeration to say that American art criticism at the turn of the century was synonymous with the name of Charles Caffin, but the ubiquity of his voice and the frequency with which it was heard sometimes give that impression. Caffin wrote for no fewer than three prestigious publications: *Harper's Weekly*, the *International Studio* (that is, the text of the British *Studio* bound up with a separately written and printed American supplement), and the *New York Evening Post*. His views were thus disseminated through a large-circulation general-interest magazine, an influential art journal, and one of the leading newspapers of the country's acknowledged art center. He was a force to be reckoned with. Fortunately for Pittsburgh's reputation, Caffin was an enthusiastic supporter of the annual exhibition, praising it year after year for its variety, high standards, complete representation of contemporary trends, and comfortably compact size. "The trustees of the Carnegie art galleries," he wrote in 1898, "have put themselves at the head of the art movement not only in America, but also in Europe." From 1898 to 1901 his only complaint about the exhibition as a whole was that it had been rather unattractively hung in the latter year, so as to produce "a bewildering patchwork of pattern and color in which good is as often skied as the indifferent is hung upon the line." Nevertheless, he felt that the exhibit was superb.[35]

Apart from this single instance of bad hanging, the annual exhibition could do no wrong in Caffin's eyes, and he blamed the artists, not the management, for whatever flaws he perceived. Was the foreign contribution a bit deficient in 1900? Caffin believed it was, but he added, "it must be acknowledged that this yearly gleaning from foreign harvests is a very difficult task, involving incredible work and much disappointment"; the fault lay with the Europeans, who were "loath to send their pictures so far and to part with them so long." And despite the general deficiency in this category, the Glasgow School and the French Impressionists were well represented. Was the American contribution similarly lacking in 1901? Caffin thought so, and he blamed American artists for failing to support the exhibition. He had heard it said that the Fine Arts Committee and the juries discriminated against American art, that in the past too many awards had gone to foreigners instead of to the native artists in whose interests the exhibition was supposedly founded, but he dismissed these criticisms as narrow and provincial. He argued that Americans had received their fair share of prizes and that, in any event, the Institute's mission was to encourage the national art indirectly by educating and broadening the public's understanding and taste. Addressing this same point earlier, in 1898, he had observed that "an understanding public is as necessary to the spread of art as good painters, and an understanding of what is being done at home is likely to be broader and deeper when it grows out of an extended comparison of many men and many manners."[36]

Caffin's reviews were already displaying that love of the new that in later life led him to praise the Armory Show and embrace the works of such Modernists as Picasso, Picabia, and Brancusi. He was contemptuous of the few academic works exhibited at Pittsburgh, dismissing them as misleading to the layman, uninspiring to the student, and "opposed to most of the principles upon which American art is firmly establishing itself." He wholeheartedly admired the Impressionists, both foreign and native, and whenever he explicitly described a painting as belonging to this school it was invariably in a favorable context. Edmund Tarbell's *My Family*, for example, was "a sunny bit of Impressionism"; Raffaëlli's *Boulevard des Italiens, Paris* was "a piece of brilliant Impressionism"; the purest exponents of the style such as Pissarro, Monet, and Childe Hassam were almost beyond reproach. Asked how Pittsburghers might better appreciate their annual exhibition, Caffin advised the utmost broadmindedness: they must rid themselves of their preconceptions about how things should be represented, he said, and try to look at a picture from the artist's own point of view.[37]

Caffin liked sentiment in art and often singled out for praise paintings that had also won the approval of the general public. He admired the ever popular Frank Benson's "infinite tenderness for the little ones," commended the "sentiment of flowers" that informed John Ferguson Weir's *Roses*, and felt that the "beautiful feeling" in Sergeant Kendall's *The End of the Day* amply atoned for certain technical faults he found in it. Caffin was, however, far more attuned to subtle nuances of expression than the average viewer and far more responsive to formal qualities. According to the press, the average exhibition-goer regarded Tryon's *Early Spring in New England* as peculiar and unnatural, but Caffin considered it a masterpiece: "The picture is painted with a matured knowledge, the values represented to a nicety and the various features chosen with a full sense of balance. . . . In addition to its technical excellence, the scene is full of a personal feeling; it speaks to the imagination as well as to the sense."

Similarly, though neither Alexander Roche's *The Window Seat* nor Ben Foster's *Misty Moonlight Night* touched the emotions of the public, Caffin detected "a feeling of pensiveness and tranquility" in the former and "a beautiful subtlety of expression in rendering the immaterial charm of night" in the latter. At times, expressive power could make up for formal weakness, as in Kendall's bronze-medal winner or Thomas Eakins's *The Thinker: Portrait of Mr. Louis N. Kenton* (figure 54), which he considered "uncompromisingly repellant as a picture," but "as a study of human character, extremely fascinating." Less frequently, formal strength could redeem an absence of sentiment. Childe Hassam's *The Sea* appealed solely to the eye and lacked "poetical suggestion," and Edmund Tarbell's *The Venetian Blind* was merely "a studio study of a partially nude model seated on a sofa," yet both impressed him as superb paintings on account of their technical brilliance. Nothing less than brilliance in one area could compensate for weakness in the other, however. The virtues of the first- and second-prize winners of 1901 were not, in Caffin's view, sufficient to balance their defects. Although Maurer was unquestionably a gifted painter, *An Arrangement* failed to "reveal the possession of any motive beyond a technical one," and Caffin believed that only the absence that year of so many prominent artists had enabled it to win a prize. Elizabeth Ahrens's *Sewing—A Portrait* was "very sincere and intimate," but "a plodding work" from a technical viewpoint, "almost painfully methodical, austere in color, and quite undistinguished for style." It, too, was unworthy of a prize, despite its great appeal to the public.[38]

*Harper's Weekly* was the only general-interest magazine to review the annual exhibition. All the other reviews at the national level appeared in specialized art publications such as the *Criterion*, the *International Studio*, *Brush and Pencil*, and the *Art Interchange*. With the exception of the *Art Interchange*, these magazines were uniformly well disposed toward the exhibitions. The Carnegie annuals received their most elaborate treatment from the Chicago-based *Brush and Pencil*, which, beginning in 1898, printed a long review every December, copiously illustrated with photographs of the prizewinners and other notable works. On the whole, these reviews make pretty dull reading, tending like so many reviews of the period to degenerate into lists of artists and paintings with short, perfunctory comments on each. One misses the spirit and the well-marked personality that distinguish Caffin's writings. Yet the reviews are not without value, for they exemplify a moderate school of American taste, neither so progressive and cosmopolitan as Caffin's nor so conservative and nationalistic as that of the *Art Interchange*.

Although the *Brush and Pencil* reviewers appreciated Tonal works, such as the paintings of Tryon and many of the Glasgow group, they often looked askance at Impressionism. They did not condemn it outright, nor were they wholly unaccepting of it, especially in its less extreme manifestations, but they approached warily, fearful lest their sensibilities be assaulted. For Caffin, the "Monet-like technique" of Childe Hassam's *The Sea* compensated for its lack of feeling; for an unidentified critic of the *Brush and Pencil*, the technique was an additional defect:

> It must be a picture of color, for it certainly has no charm either of line or mass. Modern this certainly is, and arranged with the seeming purpose of confounding and refuting all previous laws of composition. . . . One cannot help but feel that the loftiest traditions of art are hardly maintained by a portrait of a rocking chair with a not-too-solid figure in it, whose head is so much a secondary consideration that it is not revealed at all by the camera [that is, the accompanying photographic reproduction]. Red, blue, and yellow may captivate, but form, expression, and line are not wholly out of date.

Nevertheless, the writer called Hassam "courageous" and approved of the broadmindedness that the jury had displayed in honoring his work. "Such a spirit," he declared, "is worthy of notice, and gives hope of a free and unbridled development in our art here." This opinion was not shared by Henry C. Payne, who, in a short essay published a month later, expressed profound dissatisfaction with the award to Hassam, as well as the awards to Alexander Roche and E. A. Walton. All three, he complained, were typically modern in their superficial handling of the human figure. They treated it merely as a decorative object; their image of life was "stripped of all its high dignities of thought and feeling, and [had] become a series of painter's models."[39]

Frances B. Sheafer, who reviewed the exhibition in 1899, did not dwell on the subject of Impressionism, but she betrayed her attitude toward it by remarking that although Frank Benson was "undoubtedly of the Impressionist persuasion," he knew how to "paint real, living breathing children—children one would like to know." Clearly, she shared Payne's view that Impressionists were normally incapable of expressing personality and sentiment, and she regarded Benson as an exception to the rule. Bias was more overt in the writing of Austin E. Howland, who reviewed the exhibition in 1900 and in 1901. In 1900 he remarked that there had been many more Impressionist works on display the previous year, "some but a trifle out of normal, and others little more than mere suggestions of pictures." In 1901 he again noted a relative paucity of Impressionists and added that the jury had done its work conscientiously, producing less dissatisfaction with its decisions than in former years. Dissatisfaction with the jurors' actions and an abundance of Impressionism were obviously linked in his mind. However, he was not invariably and unalterably opposed to the style. Henri Le Sidaner's *Light,* which won an honorable mention in 1901, was a "distinctly Impressionist" work; nevertheless, Howland thought it was very good.[40]

A nationalist strain, usually somewhat muted, ran through the pages of the *Brush and Pencil.* Although Sheafer described Italian painting as decadent and Howland made the same observation about the Germans, there was little actual hostility toward foreign art; rather, there was a conviction that it was in some ways alien to American sensibilities and that American artists should avoid succumbing to its influence. This view was explicitly stated in an 1898 editorial in *Brush and Pencil,* in which the awarding of a first prize to Tryon, and the similar honor won two years earlier by Winslow Homer, were seen as extremely encouraging for the development of American art. National art, argued the editor, C. F. Brown, must be founded on national themes, for affection improves art and the deepest affection attaches to native things. Homer and Tryon were "loyal and true"; that is, they stayed at home and painted American subjects, unlike the many expatriates, who were "losing a distinctive quality in their work which a long, patient, and even suffering existence in their home country might give them." Too much of their work, he complained, consisted of "Brittany peasants, Dutch children, bizarre effects and a general rehash of things that have been done a thousand times by men who can put the right flavor into them." These same ideas informed the criticism of Austin E. Howland. Why, he wondered in 1900, had the gold medal gone to André Dauchez's *The Kelp Gatherers,* instead of to Ben Foster's *Misty Moonlight Night* or Sergeant Kendall's *The End of the Day?* Dauchez's picture was by no means bad, and it demonstrated "a phase of French art which is well worth careful study and which Americans have had comparatively little opportunity to see," but the second- and third-prize winners had "the added charm of home scenes" and should have been preferred for that reason. A year later, he characterized modern French art as elegant, charming, and stylish "reflections of well-bred Parisian society," but therefore "foreign to American ideas and sympathies."[41]

In contrast to the mild nationalism of *Brush and Pencil,* the eagle fairly screamed in the pages of the *Art Interchange.* Initially favorable to the Carnegie galleries, the tone of its reviews darkened in 1896 ("Mr. Carnegie's noble intentions have miscarried through the inexperience and incapacity of those intrusted with their carrying out") and by the end of 1897 had degenerated into vitriolic abuse. The magazine's "Observer" did not object to the quality of the work displayed in the annual exhibitions; indeed, he neglected to mention paintings at all. Rather, he objected to the international character of the exhibition: foreign artists were being hung in Pittsburgh, foreign artists were receiving awards from a jury that included foreign members, and this in his view constituted an intolerable disservice to American art. "Several years ago," wrote the Observer in December 1897,

> much was said for the generosity of Mr. Andrew Carnegie in establishing his "Fund for the encouragement of American Art," and great results were predicted from it; but in view of the reckless misdirection of affairs in Pittsburgh the "encouragement of American Art" part of the plan is proving little less than a ridiculous farce that is bringing the institution into discredit.

For one thing, there had been no sales in 1896; for another, the American artists were being outnumbered by the foreigners: he claimed that of 243 paintings currently on display, only 80 were by "our artists." "The great mistake seems to be that the management held the exhibition in this country at all. They should have carried it direct to European shores with all of its 'encouragement,' for, held on this side of the ocean, it only proves a discouragement." Apparently the Observer's definition of an American artist excluded expatriates, for he complained that only one of that year's five prizewinners lived in this country, even though three of the five were citizens of the United States. He also complained that too much money was being spent "to bring a few painters over from Europe to pass judgement on the work of our men and give eclat to the affair." He suggested that prizes be eliminated and the greater part of the endowment be used to purchase paintings chosen by a jury of reputable, presumably native, artists. Above all, he urged the Institute to stop "racing over the earth asking men to send their pictures, bribing them with false hopes and promises, even paying ocean passages and travel expenses to get a few conspicuous artists to come to Pittsburgh with their work." International exhibitions, he concluded, were all very well, but the Carnegie Institute was not the place for them. If the management could not recognize that fact, "let us hear no more about the 'Encouragement of American Art' at Pittsburgh."[42]

The *Art Interchange* was not the most prestigious magazine of its kind, being aimed at amateurs, at the genteel hobbyists for whom it reproduced patterns for china painting, embroidery, and decorative stencils, and at the rabble of minor artists upon whose feeble productions it unfailingly doted. Ben Foster, unquestionably an artist of the first rank (he won the silver medal in 1900 and was elected to six juries from 1903 to 1912) told Beatty that he and his colleagues never read it. Beatty rarely bothered to reply to attacks in the press, and he probably would have ignored the December 1897 review if it had not been given wider publicity in the New York newspapers, or if it had always been printed with editorial disclaimers. The *New York Evening Post*, for example, characterized it as "the usual trade vaporings in favor of protection" and went on to say, "The offensiveness of this utterance is only equalled by its pettiness. Such paltry parochialism is not talked on the other side of the Atlantic when American artists make successes and carry off honors, and one is ashamed to read it in an American periodical." The *New York Times*, however, reprinted the Observer's remarks in a slightly condensed version without comment and without even a bare indication that they were being quoted from another publication. The casual reader would have taken these opinions for the *New York Times*'s own — and the *New York Times* counted for a great deal more than the *Art Interchange*.[43]

Assuming that Ben Foster, who sometimes reviewed exhibitions for the *New York Evening Post*, was responsible for that journal's strongly pro-Pittsburgh stance, Beatty sent his reply to Howard Russell Butler with instructions to deliver it to Foster. Butler also conveyed Beatty's reply to Andrew Carnegie. Although Foster had not written the remarks in the *New York Evening Post*, he regarded the Observer's criticism as a "waspy, ignorant attack" and lost no time in picking up the letter and urging his managing editor "to publish it as promptly and prominently as possible." This was done. In his rebuttal, Beatty accused the *Art Interchange* of printing "reckless and inaccurate statements" and described the entire article as "manifestly untrue." According to the Observer, only 80 works by Americans appeared in the exhibition. This was false: there were 130 American works, slightly over half the total number of pictures hung. According to the Observer, no paintings had been sold in 1896. This, too, was false: the Institute had purchased several works. (Naturally, Beatty neglected to mention that there had been no private sales, which is doubtless what the Observer had in mind.) It was also untrue that the Institute had paid the traveling expenses of several well-known artists in order to induce them to bring their works to Pittsburgh: the jurors were elected by the contributors, and all submissions to the exhibition had been entered before the results of the election had been announced and the jurors notified. As to the implication that American artists were being slighted in favor of their foreign brethren, Beatty firmly denied this. The exhibition included only 130 American pictures for the simple reason that only 130 American pictures had been judged worthy of admission. Had foreign artists been excluded, the jurors would not have admitted more American works until the number had been brought up to 243; instead, the exhibition would have consisted entirely of the 130 accepted American works. Beatty's letter appeared in both the *New York Evening Post* and the *New York Commercial Advertiser*; it did not, however, appear in either the *New York Times* or the *Art Interchange*. The latter's response was to say nothing at all about the Institute until January 1902, when it published a short item about Carnegie's interest in the career of young George Carspecken.[44]

Outside Pittsburgh, newspaper coverage of the annual exhibition was sparse during the earliest years. Full-scale reviews were rare; brief notices of the jury elections and of the prizewinners were common, sometimes elaborated with such comment about the general character of the exhibition as the writer could safely make without going to the trouble of actually visiting Pittsburgh.[45] Carnegie may have hoped to create the American Salon, but to the editors of New York, Boston, Philadelphia, and Chicago it was a local affair: Pittsburghers did not read their papers, and their readers were not about to flock to Pittsburgh, so it merited hardly more than a passing nod. In 1897 William A. Coffin, art critic for the *New York Sun*, bluntly informed Beatty: "My editors do not think it worthwhile from a newspaper point of view to go to Pittsburgh to review the exhibition." It was true, he added, that he frequently reviewed exhibitions in Boston, but that was because many Bostonians read the *Sun*.[46]

The little that was published outside Pittsburgh was usually favorable, if superficial. The most florid tribute was penned by Charles Ault, secretary of the Western Artists Association and an occasional contributor to the exhibition, for his column in the *Cleveland Plaindealer:* "Down where the busy waters of the Allegheny and the Monongahela unite and make the torpid Ohio flood," he wrote, "smoke-crowned Pittsburgh now enjoys an exhibition of the world's contemporaneous art, the like of which, in its representativeness, is not to be seen anywhere." He remembered when there had been "carping critics who sneeringly pointed out the inevitable failure of the enterprise," but they had been given the lie, and he urged doubting Clevelanders to take "a few hour's ride from their own Cimmerian darkness" and see for themselves the proof of its success.[47]

This is not to say that there were not occasional, albeit infrequent, outbursts of nastiness. The chief of these was an article by the pseudonymous "Nemo" that appeared in the *Philadelphia Item* in November 1901. Although Nemo had journeyed to Pittsburgh for Press View Night, he was less interested in discussing the paintings than in launching a virulent diatribe worthy of the *Art Interchange* against the management of the Carnegie galleries. His remarks were antiforeign, anti–New York, even anti-Philadelphia. Good pictures by American artists, he charged, had been "crowded out" so that inferior pictures by European artists could be hung, a procedure that could "hardly be called aiding American art." Whereas the *Art Interchange* had complained in 1896 that only fifty New Yorkers had been accepted, Nemo considered thirty-five New Yorkers too many, especially as they were members of "the New York clique . . . which runs in such burlesques of nature as 'foggy' Ben Foster's Close of Day, and Maurer's Arrangement, which is little more than an imitation of Japanese art." He believed that this clique had used improper influence to gain admission, and he was certain that the Philadelphians (all of whom were in one way or another associated with the Pennsylvania Academy of Fine Arts) had done likewise. The slightest taint of the Pennsylvania Academy was enough to damn an artist in Nemo's estimation: Robert Henri, a former student there, should not have been accepted; Cecilia Beaux, a former student and current faculty member, was "degenerating"; Edwin Austin Abbey, whose only sin was to have studied there briefly in 1868, was not a first-rate artist, merely a designer. "I think if Mr. Carnegie knew how the Carnegie Exhibitions were being managed, he would hardly be pleased, for Mr. Carnegie is a fair man." It requires only the most cursory reading between the lines to recognize in Nemo a failed artist who preferred to blame his failure on preference and underhanded machinations rather than on his lack of talent. Beatty did not dignify these assertions with a rebuttal.[48]

The lack of publicity in New York was a cause of particular concern to the management of the Carnegie galleries. New York was where the country's most important artists lived and worked, and they would not participate fully in the exhibition unless they were convinced that it was a worthy showcase for their pictures. As the press could not be relied upon to do this, the management decided in 1898 to take matters into their own hands by arranging a public relations event that they hoped would compel the New York art community to pay attention to Pittsburgh. Early that year or late in the preceding year, in the wake of the bad publicity generated by the *Art Interchange*, Willbur Reaser — a New York artist whose work had just been purchased for Carnegie by the special committee — suggested to William Nimick Frew that the Institute might do well to sponsor a visit by the city's leading artists and critics to the next exhibition. Frew communicated with Carnegie, who was abroad at that time, and on 4 February 1898 informed Beatty that the founder was enthusiastic about the idea. "It would be the greatest honor we have yet achieved for Pittsburgh," Carnegie told Frew, "barring one: the President's coming." He thought that the Pennsylvania Railroad would give them very low rates for the excursion and offered to contribute himself.[49]

By the end of August Frew had secured half-price round-trip fares ($10.50) from the Pennsylvania Railroad, and Reaser had written to say that the arrangements were complete and those who wished to take part in the trip could register at the Macbeth Galleries. It is not clear from the correspondence whether Reaser was referring to the excursion that took place in early December, to a second excursion that was planned for late December, or to both. The second trip had to be canceled owing to lack of interest, and Carnegie's suggestion in the fall of 1898 that he pay the half-price fares himself hints that the response to the first trip was disappointingly feeble. Frew realized that Carnegie was eager to have the trip come off as planned but discouraged his suggestion on the grounds that "we would be showing ourselves too anxious."[50]

On the morning of 9 December 1898, a special car bearing twenty-two New York notables arrived at Pittsburgh. Most of them were artists; many of them were high-ranking officials in art societies. The party in-

cluded Howard Russell Butler and W. Bailey Saxon, president and trea-
surer of the American Fine Arts Society, respectively; H. B. Snell, presi-
dent of the New York Watercolor Club; J. O. Brown, president of the
Watercolor Society; Frederick Crowninshield, acting president of the
Society of Mural Painters; and Charles DeKay, secretary of the Fine Art
Club. Among the better-known artists were Eastman Johnson, Dwight W.
Tryon, Will Low (who had been a member of the jury the year before),
Frederick Dielman, Frederick A. Bridgman, H. Bolton Jones, and R.
Swain Gifford. John LaFarge, president of the Society of American Art-
ists, also made one of the party, but he traveled separately and arrived in
Pittsburgh a day earlier. Missing from the group were the representatives
of the press whom the Institute had hoped to attract. Two of the visitors —
Charles DeKay and Samuel Isham — frequently wrote about art; neither,
however, reviewed the Carnegie exhibitions before or after the trip.
Among the other artists, it is possible that some occasionally penned
unsigned reviews, but none were prominent critics, and the published
accounts of the trip do not identify any of them as being connected with
the press.[51]

Upon their arrival, the New Yorkers were welcomed at the station by
Beatty and several members of the Fine Arts Committee. From then on,
they were shown the lavish hospitality — what one local paper termed
"the inevitable program" — usually accorded to the elected jurors. There
were tours of the art gallery, library, and museum; a special organ recital in
the Music Hall; a concert by the Pittsburgh Orchestra; visits to the county
courthouse designed by H. H. Richardson and to Carnegie's steel mills;
and a succession of lunches, teas, and dinners. The program of activities
covered two days, though not all the participants chose to stay that long.
The New Yorkers praised the exhibition, as one might have expected: to
have done otherwise would have seemed ungrateful. John LaFarge pronounced it the equal of the Royal Academy; Frederick Bridgman declared
it "the best modern exhibition in the world." Dwight Tryon called it "the
best show in the country" — a somewhat self-serving remark, as he had
just taken the first prize. Walter Cook, one of the four architects in the
party, thought the design of the gallery space ideal, surpassing anything he
had seen in New York (figure 55).[52]

Carnegie and the Fine Arts Committee were satisfied enough with
the 1898 excursion to want to repeat it in a different context the following year. On 13 August 1899, William Nimick Frew told John B. Cauld-

well, director of the American fine arts exhibition for the 1900 Paris Exposition, that it would be "a great scheme" to have the jury appointed to select American paintings for Paris visit the upcoming exhibition as guests of the committee. This, he said, would "stir up the painters" to send their best work to Pittsburgh — and he might have said that it would also stir up a great deal of publicity and would support the exhibition's claim to be the American Salon. That Carnegie was privy to this scheme is hinted at by Frew's remark that "we have always a good friend to fall back on" should the committee find itself short of funds for such an excursion. Cauldwell initially approved the idea but soon had second thoughts that prompted him to reject it. It would create "complications" with Boston, Chicago, and Philadelphia, he told Frew, implying that the art institutions in those cities would resent any special attention given to Pittsburgh.[53]

After 1898 there was a gradual increase in the amount of coverage that the Pittsburgh exhibition received in the New York press. The 1898 excursion may have contributed to this in some small way, but the likeliest reason is simply that with the passage of time the exhibition was becoming an established fixture in the American art world, and therefore of greater interest to New Yorkers. In 1899 the critic for the *Independent* actually took the trouble to visit Pittsburgh and wrote a glowing review in which he declared that all the works on display spoke "the language of good painting" and that the city was indeed emerging as a major art center: "One is so impressed by the abounding energy of the civic life! Art should rise here as it did in Greece, Florence, Venice and Holland, on the surge of a people's awakening." That year's review in the *New York Times* was, by comparison, a model of impassive terseness; however, it included comments on the appearance of the galleries and remarks on previously unexhibited works, indicating that the writer had also visited Pittsburgh.[54]

The following year saw the publication of the first extensive review in the *New York Commercial Advertiser*. Arthur Hoeber, acting as the paper's special correspondent, expressed some distaste for "garish" Impressionist paintings and questioned the advisability of awarding prizes, "since in their distribution much injustice is bound to ensue," but he found the exhibition as a whole unusually rich in good and interesting work and characterized it as being "of an advanced and progressive nature, well worth study." In this same year, the *New York Evening Post* expanded its coverage of the Carnegie exhibition. In previous years Charles Caffin had written a single review, but in 1900 he wrote two full-length notices, the second appearing a few days after the first.[55]

In November 1901, Beatty complimented Samuel Swift, art critic of the *New York Mail and Express*, on having done his "whole duty" by the Carnegie Institute, and by American art as well. What Swift had done was to write the longest review of the exhibition to appear in any out-of-town newspaper up to that date. It comprised four separate notices: the first, published on 7 November 1901, was a general overview; the remaining three, published on 11, 13, and 14 November, dealt with figure painting, landscape, and portraiture, respectively. In addition, there was a short notice in the paper's illustrated weekend supplement. Although Swift was a little inclined to overemphasize the trite thesis that American art was forceful, vigorous, rudely honest, full of strong feeling (whereas European art was elegant, polished, and deficient in sentiment), he applauded innovation wherever it occurred and thoroughly sympathized with the methods and goals of the Carnegie exhibitions. He could not grant Pittsburgh the status of major art center: the predilection of its wealthier citizens for slickly academic portraits by Theobald Chartran proved, in his estimation, that it was "still practically virgin soil from the art point of view." He was encouraged, however, by the belief that these same citizens were no longer as fond of Bouguereau as they had been before the Institute "lit the lamp of art education five years ago," and he noted optimistically that enthusiasm for art had now become a matter of municipal pride. Despite his reservations, Swift felt that "something near akin to a miracle" had happened in Pittsburgh.[56]

The *New York Sun* and the *New York Commercial Advertiser* also printed lengthy reviews in 1901. The *Sun*'s review was divided into three parts, two of which dealt separately with the American and the foreign pictures; and although the anonymous reviewer used critical commonplaces such as "sentiment," "sincerity," and "poetry" in a vague and thoughtless manner, he was at least well disposed toward the exhibition, praising its high standards and the opportunity it gave art students to keep in touch with the latest European movements. The *Commercial Advertiser* published two notices: the first was a long but rather undistinguished review by an unidentified staff correspondent; the second was an attempt to explain why the Carnegie annual had, in the writer's opinion, a higher average level of quality than any other exhibition in the world. Both the jury system and the Carnegie fortune were cited, but the lion's share of the credit went to John Beatty for his experience, seasoned judgment, and personal involvement.[57]

Beatty no doubt found these remarks gratifying, and he must have been pleased with the general tenor of that year's reviews; nevertheless, he was still dissatisfied with the press coverage in New York. On 8 January 1901, the New York muralist and landscape painter Robert Reid wrote to say that he was "a bit discouraged" about sending to Pittsburgh: "Never a word do I hear of my pictures from the moment they leave till they get back here — what's the use?" Beatty urged him not to lose interest — "We need the help of every able man in America" — and assured him that the press had been filled with notices of his work. "Perhaps," he suggested, "you take old fogey New York papers."[58]

For many New York reviewers, the most striking thing about the Carnegie exhibition was its having been situated in the provincial hinterland. "It should, of course, be in New York instead of Pittsburgh," observed Samuel Swift, "but it was quite open to Mr. Carnegie to establish such an exhibition where he chose." Occasionally, a note of defensive local pride was struck, as when a critic for the *Commercial Advertiser* wrote in 1898 that "notwithstanding the claims recently put forward by Pittsburgh as an art center, New York must be reckoned with when it comes to a question of the aesthetic happenings of the year." However, most critics made use of the rising prominence of Pittsburgh to expose the shortcomings of New York, and the *Commercial Advertiser* itself, in 1901, declared that "New York would do well to take a lesson from this Carnegie show."[59]

It was clear by the mid-1890s that the National Academy of Design had failed to become the American equivalent of the Royal Academy of Art. In 1897 the *International Studio* compared the quality of the paintings at the Carnegie Institute to the quality of those at the National Academy, very much to the detriment of the latter, but few reviewers bothered to be so explicit: their remarks were predicated on the assumption that the "fall displays of the official society are not as a rule famed for their excellence." Commenting on an address to the New York Art Students League in which John White Alexander had warned that the metropolis was falling behind the times, the *New York Evening Post* admitted in 1901, "The aesthetic traveler who would gain a fair idea through the public exhibitions not only of the current art of Europe, but also of the best in American art, might do well . . . to omit New York and betake him direct to

Philadelphia and Pittsburgh." The reason for this, according to the *Evening Post,* was not that culture was moving westward or that Pittsburgh and Philadelphia were extraordinarily enlightened; rather, it was because the provincial cities were not established art centers. Organizing committees in New York had to deal with hundreds of local artists, all eager to exhibit and many personally known to the committee members. As a result, the committees could not be as selective as they might wish, and the quality of their exhibitions declined.[60]

Other commentators pointed out that New York, being a large and active art center, had a plethora of societies and dealers in competition for pictures, making it impossible to get together a single first-rate exhibition, while a city like Pittsburgh could skim the best work from New York's many small exhibitions and bring them together in a single place. Charles M. Kurtz reported in May 1900 that "meetings" were being held in New York to remedy the situation, with the intention of inaugurating an international exhibition like the Paris Salon. He did not say who was involved in these meetings (leading artists? presidents of societies?), but in any event they produced no tangible results.[61]

It will be obvious to anyone who has read this far that the press coverage in Pittsburgh was voluminous in the extreme; indeed, it would have been impossible to reconstruct the early history of the Carnegie exhibitions without drawing upon the copious documentation provided by the local press. Pittsburgh had eight daily papers in the late 1890s (today it has only one), and they all published reviews, special features, and a multitude of short items relating to the exhibitions. Many of the shorter items, such as those announcing the sending of invitations or the arrival of foreign works at the gallery, appeared in a number of papers in virtually identical form and typically included optimistic remarks by Beatty about the quality of the upcoming show. Clearly, these were press releases from the Institute, as were certain longer items such as the biographies of the jurors that appeared after their election. Among the usual special features were interviews with Beatty, Frew, Caldwell, and the more sociable jurors; observations on the popular response to the paintings; accounts of Press Night and Founder's Day; and reprints of favorable out-of-town reviews. Occasionally, there were indifferent attempts at humor, such as the comic verses of the *Pittsburgh Leader*'s Arthur Burgoyne, caricatures of the paintings by "Johnston the Cartoonist" (figure 56), and the purported aesthetic views of Goosti, a monkey at the Highland Park Zoo.

From time to time there were also purely informative and theoretical pieces having only a general bearing on the exhibition, such as L. M.'s attempt to explain Impressionism to Pittsburghers, Anna Woodward's account of the Paris Salons, and an imaginary dialogue debating the validity of religious subjects in modern art.[62]

Carnegie hoped to turn Pittsburgh into a great American art center, but the press, inflamed with local pride, often seemed to believe that this hope had already been fulfilled. Arthur Burgoyne expressed this attitude in verse:

> Blue stockings once were wont to snub
>   our town, then low of station,
> And point to Boston as the hub
>   and center of creation.
> They'd warn us in a tone serene
>   to bow before our betters,
> High rollers in the lofty sphere
>   of arts refined and letters.
>
> But things have changed. Our town to-day
>   Bostonian fame is sharing,
> To higher ground we've made our way,
>   and azure hose we're wearing.
> There's not a single soulful fad
>   wherein we're not indulging,
> And since the novel turn we've had
>   the town with brains is bulging.
>
> In art New England in the rear
>   is left far distant lagging,
> Our prize exhibit every year
>   discounts Bostonian bragging.
> Yes, Boston's nose is out of joint
>   (confound her ostentation!)
> Since Pittsburgh is the central point
>   of art adjudication.
>   . . . . . . . .
> Then glory to this good old town
>   so rapidly advancing

> In all the things that bring reknown,
> applause and praise entrancing.
> Great the reward that someday we
> will harvest for our striving,
> And Boston — well, she ought to be
> rejoiced that she's surviving.

Burgoyne's tongue was doubtless in his cheek, but the editor of the *Pittsburgh Chronicle-Telegraph* could solemnly write: "Pittsburgh, almost before the world has heard of the effort made here, has leapt to a foremost station among the art centers of Christendom."[63]

Even when it did not rise to the heights of boosterism, the local press was overwhelmingly favorable toward the exhibition. Uncomplimentary notices were rare after 1896, although they did occur. Albert F. King's scathing remarks, published in the *Pittsburgh Dispatch* in November 1899, have already been discussed. Several months earlier, the *Pittsburgh Leader* had printed some extremely derogatory comments in an article whose ostensible purpose was to announce the forthcoming reinstallation of the permanent collection in the galleries. The anonymous writer wrote in the same vein as the *Art Interchange*'s controversial review of December 1897. He charged that Carnegie's desire to encourage American art had "either been entirely lost sight of or bluntly ignored" and that the exhibition had thereby become "a blight upon the best that our artists could do by becoming an 'open door' to all the studios of the old world." A singularly misinformed critic, he identified the Scottish painter E. A. Walton as an American and the American-born English painter J. J. Shannon as a Scotsman. He also labored under the misconception that cash prizes had been abolished in 1897, allowing the entire endowment to be used to purchase "those works that please the fancy of the Fine Arts Committee." Beatty forbore to correct him in detail and simply pointed out that, contrary to his assertions, American artists were dominant in the permanent collection.[64]

These two articles, together with James Fairman's *Essays on Art*, were the only wholesale condemnations of the Carnegie galleries to appear in the local press after the furor surrounding the "business man's jury" of 1896, and they were in no way representative of journalistic sentiment. Yet Fairman's essays — originally published as a series of eleven articles in the *Pittsburgh Dispatch* during the last two months of 1897 and reissued as a bound pamphlet in 1898 — warrant closer consideration, not because they were typical but because they constitute the single longest review ever written of a Carnegie exhibition, and they speak with a strongly individual voice quite unlike that of the average Pittsburgh critic.

James Fairman is one of those minor nineteenth-century artists whose careers, insofar as they are discoverable, lead to sober reflections on the futility of aspiration — one of those artists whom one occasionally stumbles upon in out-of-the-way places, who fairly bristle with powerful personalities and great pretensions, yet who remain shadows in the end, their lives and works lost in obscurity. We learn a few things about Fairman from a pamphlet published in London in 1880, apparently a promotional effort by a dealer or by Fairman himself. He was born in Glasgow in 1826, son of a Swedish father (the surname was originally Fehrman), and emigrated to New York with his widowed mother in 1832, attended evening classes at the National Academy of Design in the 1840s, and in the 1850s combined the practice of art with the study of law and a career as an Abolitionist platform speaker. He served in the Union army during the Civil War until he was invalided out after distinguishing himself for gallantry at the Battle of Fair Oaks in 1863. He then returned to painting in New York and apparently enjoyed some success as a lecturer on art. According to the *Biograph,* a British publication, he was "recognized as the most brilliant and instructive art lecturer in America." (This seems inflated, but perhaps the English writer was inclined to accept the artist's word for his American reputation.) In 1871 Fairman traveled to the Holy Land, then spent the rest of the decade in Europe, living for several years each in Düsseldorf, Paris, and London. His one-man show at London's Conduit Street Gallery in 1879 earned him a glowing review from the *Art Journal* in which he was praised for his "exact knowledge regarding the physical phenomena of nature." From 1880 to 1897 he passes altogether from the historian's view and shortly thereafter disappears altogether. The *Essays on Art* definitely establish his presence in Pittsburgh in 1897, but we do not know when or why he went there. A history of the city published in 1898 notes: "The recent work of James Fairman has attracted the attention of all lovers of art in Pittsburgh. Many of his paintings rank with the best that have been produced in the United States in recent years." If this claim were true, it seems strange that the artist is utterly unknown to students of nineteenth-century American art and has even escaped the notice of specialists in western Pennsylvania's regional art. The 1880 pamphlet identified him as a landscapist and mentioned several works by name, including *Jerusalem from the Mount of Olives* (measuring six by nine feet), and *Christian and Hopeful Viewing the Gates of the Celestial City, from the Delectable Mountains* (eleven by seven and a half feet), the latter illustrating an incident from Bunyan's *Pilgrim's Progress*. Clearly, his taste had been formed by the more gargantuan type of Hudson River School landscape, already out of fashion by 1880.[65]

Fairman begins his review (which runs to eighty pages in the bound pamphlet) by proclaiming perfect allegiance to the most idealistic goals of the gallery's founders. With florid eloquence he describes the elevating power of art and the ennobling, refining effects that the gallery will have upon "the toiling masses of our people"; he believes that steelworkers can be turned into artists or, as he puts it, "can be made to coin the beautiful and true in the realm of thought by the talismanic power of an education that can be placed within the reach of the humblest."[66] However, when he comes to deal with the exhibition itself, it becomes plain that he regards it as a defective instrument of enlightenment. Conservative to the core, he sees the gallery as dominated by "the most recent European, especially French, mannerisms of conception and execution." These mannerisms represent a "departure from the academic methods of the past," and to depart from academic methods is, in Fairman's view, to abandon all fidelity to natural appearances.[67]

He will not allow any of the prizewinners the least merit with regard to subject, expression, composition, drawing, modeling, color, or technique: to him they are all frankly abominable, and he can only account for the jurors' actions by appealing to "morbid imagination."[68] He has a particular dislike for Winslow Homer, whom he accuses of "a careless, superficial piece of rough painting" and a "neglect of nature and obliviousness of optical laws." Homer's early work of the 1860s, such as *Prisoners from the Front*, wins his admiration, but for him Homer is one of those "artists of native power, early promise and creditable possibilities, whose careless and presumptuous moods forfeit a creditable career and who degenerate in the atmosphere of their self-complacency."[69]

Fairman releases his fiercest invective upon James McNeill Whistler: the face of Pablo de Sarasate reminds him of a "dead subject on a slab in the morgue"; the whole figure is "ghastly and repellent, having no suggestion of the genus homo outside of Dante's Inferno." He affects to mistake Whistler's other contributions for the "accidentally exposed plates of some Kodak novice, who had 'developed' them into first-class Whistler pictures."[70] The artists both in and out of the exhibition that Fairman favors are French academics such as Bouguereau, Gérôme, Cabanel, and Benjamin-Constant or the more academic of the non-French painters such as Abbey, Alma-Tadema, George de Forest Brush, Will H. Low, F. A. Bridgman, and George Hitchcock. He is more inclined, however, to discuss his dislikes than his likes.

Fairman concludes that the exhibition has been "a depressing failure," and he places the blame squarely on its organization. Most of his remarks betray a resentment toward the leaders of his profession that must arise, one suspects, from his own failure to win recognition in his field. Certainly, he is obsessed with the idea that famous artists are continually scheming to spoil the chances of their more skilled but lesser known colleagues. Accordingly, Fairman insists that the exhibition can be salvaged only by prohibiting artists from either electing or serving upon the juries and by making an established reputation of no consequence in determining the acceptance of the artist's work. If by this he means that Beatty should refrain from inviting specific artists, we have already seen that an invitation from Beatty was by no means a guarantee of acceptance. Fairman also recommends eliminating the taint of profit: there should be no cash prizes or sales. One of his suggestions, that scholars be employed to give lecture tours of the exhibitions, anticipates the docent program that was established years later.[71]

When the essays were published in pamphlet form, the editor of the *Pittsburgh Dispatch* pronounced them to be "among the clearest and most virile specimens ever contributed to the American press." Nevertheless, the *Pittsburgh Dispatch* carried no more reviews by Fairman and never became identified with his ultraconservative viewpoint. With the exception of the *Pittsburgh Post*, none of Pittsburgh's newspapers had clear, consistent critical voices or positions. Reviews were usually unsigned, and if a note to Beatty from the *Pittsburgh Times* informing him that a particular staff member had been "assigned to cover the collection for us this year" reflects a general practice, the absence of consistency is not surprising: a single paper may have employed several different critics within the span of a few years. Nor is it impossible that several papers sometimes used a single critic. This certainly happened in 1901, when the *Pittsburgh Leader* and the *Pittsburgh Commercial Gazette* published reviews that, although not precisely identical, expressed the same opinions in words that were closely similar, at times exactly the same.[72]

The *Pittsburgh Dispatch*, *Pittsburgh Post*, and *Pittsburgh Leader* may have featured longer and more expertly written reviews than their competitors, but it cannot be said that the local critics ever rose to conspicuous brilliance. On the other hand, it cannot be said that they were markedly inferior to those in other cities: if Pittsburgh did not produce a Ruskin or a Baudelaire in the 1890s, neither did New York. Pittsburgh's critics, like their fellows elsewhere, more or less adroitly manipulated such terms as "poetry," "atmosphere," and "sentiment"; their reviews tended to become long lists of artists and titles, each qualified with a short descriptive phrase such as "a beautiful conception," "effectively handled," or (perhaps the most common) "very interesting"; they were happiest and most eloquent when dealing with narrative paintings whose subjects they could describe at length. Their views were generally middle-of-the-road. They normally liked the prizewinners, even if these were not their personal favorites; they could accept technical innovations in paintings when the subjects were pleasing; they recoiled only from the most extremely progressive work and sometimes even showed signs of dawning acceptance. Sophie G. Keenan, who covered the exhibition for the *Pittsburgh Press* in 1899 and 1900, was fairly representative in this regard. In 1899 she loathed Degas and likened John Twachtman's *The Waterfall* to "huckleberry jam curdled with milk and a little turned"; in 1900 she noted that "the vehement Impressionism" of previous years appeared to be mellowing, commended Degas for some finely painted heads, and admitted that "even Twachtman is milder and less fermented."[73]

The best, if only because the most vivid, of the local critics was Ida Adeline Smith, whose signed reviews appeared in the *Pittsburgh Post* from 1899 until 1907, when she died at the age of forty-seven. A native of Pittsburgh, Smith studied at the School of Design for Women, then went on to further her education at the Art Students League in New York and the Académie Julian in Paris. After returning to Pittsburgh, she taught art at the Thurston Preparatory School and at the Pennsylvania College for Women, and she earned a solid local reputation for her portraits of children.[74]

Her reviews of the Carnegie exhibitions are remarkable for their personal style and their colloquial vigor and avoidance of artsy affectation. Here, for example, is Smith expressing her delight with one of George de Forest Brush's mother-and-child portraits:

> Here is real high art. The men who scrub the floors can see it, and artists who are painting day by day can see it also. This is true art. Nobody needs to try to like this. Nobody needs someone to explain it. Hurrah! hurrah! that such a picture can be painted! It makes the heart rejoice. Just wait till you all see it.

Her enthusiasm was always unmistakable, as were her distinctly populist leanings. She frequently urged her readers to trust their own instincts, to form their own judgments, and to resist being cowed by those of the recognized experts. Referring to the well-known fact that paintings hung on the line were, in the opinion of the jurors, the best in the show, Smith exhorted the average Pittsburgher:

> Look aloft! Look up — not down! Do not let yourself be discouraged in admiring the top line. We will perhaps in twenty years become an "Art Center" if we will only look and think for ourselves. If we people of Pittsburgh will study and learn and keep our brains cool and clear, unmoved by the foreign jumping-jacks and New York fakirs, after a while we, the people, will become intelligent. Be not like dumb, driven cattle.[75]

Smith's views on art were not, on the whole, very different from those of Charles Caffin. Like Caffin, she appreciated purely technical and formal qualities, even the most progressive of her day, but attached great significance to subject and expression. She could, for example, praise Cecilia Beaux (figure 57) for her handling of the medium, yet censure her for a lack of feeling: "Alas, that one who could paint that dress so deliciously that it makes the blood tingle should care no more for the human soul in a picture than for the jeweled necklace."[76]

The same mixture of admiration and dissatisfaction informed her estimates of Degas and John Singer Sargent. Of a work by Degas she wrote, "Somebody has said that the three great things are line, mass, and color. That isn't true, of course, but if it were, then this fragment would be fine; and it is fine. You want some other things, though, don't you, dear reader?" She also found Sargent, for all his accomplishments, similarly lacking in depth:

It is a curious study to watch the rise of admiration for Mr. Sargent in any human mind. The earnest student grows more and more enthusiastic until he reaches a wild climax of adoration. Then, as he studies farther and thinks deeper and begins to look for more subtle qualities, his admiration settles into a calm, judicious delight, and he can see that there is a lack at times, and that unless this great man lives and grows for many years, he will not have fulfilled his promise.[77]

However, Smith was hardly Caffin's equal in sophistication. She tended to coo and burble over portraits of adorable children; and she occasionally revealed a streak of moralism that today sounds conventionally Victorian, as when she advised Franz von Stuck "to take himself in hand and attend to religious principles." She was deeply offended by Stuck's "ugly" portrait of Beethoven in the 1901 exhibition:

> Beethoven must have had an occasional noble thought. He must have been kind of uplifted when he was composing. He could not have been plotting murders all the rest of his life. Yet this portrait would imply as much. That is not fair to do poor Beethoven like that, for he is dead now and cannot strike back. A low-minded painter ought to be wiped off the earth, for it is the grandest profession of this old world.[78]

Whereas Caffin was captivated by the subtle poetic charms of Dwight Tryon's landscapes, Smith was wholly immune to them: she wrote of "the inane fields of Tryon" and was "almost tempted to make a pun about his Tryon another subject." Caffin would doubtless have found this remark regrettably Philistine — perhaps self-consciously so, for Smith's populism was not without a touch of affectation — but anyone who has seen a large number of Tryons will appreciate its justice. And it must be said that Smith's taste was neither dainty nor weak-stomached. Thomas Eakins was a favorite of hers because of the unvarnished realism that so many of her contemporaries found unpalatable. "His 'Crucifixion' is a fine piece of realism," she wrote in 1900, "so real that one cannot bear to look at it" (figure 58). Yet its unbearable qualities were precisely those that made it admirable to her.[79]

To anyone who has read any considerable amount of local press coverage of the early Carnegie exhibitions, Smith's most refreshing trait is her refusal to pay the customary obeisance to the founder and his glorious ideal of turning Pittsburgh into an art center. She frequently pointed out that Pittsburgh was neither a great art center nor in a fair way of becoming one. And although she did not mention Carnegie and the Institute's wealthy trustees by name, she poured scorn on the pretensions of rich men who dared to meddle with art:

> There is a tendency on the part of Pittsburghers to speak condescendingly of the [Pan-American] exhibition because they have seen a number of the pictures at the Carnegie. This is part of our pure Pittsburgh spirit. The same thing makes us think that we are an art center, and loudly bray to the world that we have the greatest show on earth. How long shall this last? How long must the masses be patronized by the wealthy classes? Will the time never come when the man who has spent his life making money and sold his birthright of poetry for the pottage of the world — when this man shall be made to take off his shoes before entering the temple of art?[80]

At the conclusion of her review for 1900, Smith put her finger firmly upon a conspicuous defect in the idea of transforming Pittsburgh into another London or Paris through the influence of the annual exhibitions. The "old man" is undoubtedly the landscapist George Hetzel, whom we earlier saw regretting his career in Pittsburgh and who had died the previous year:

> Now the thing that is hard to bear is when people tell us Pittsburgh is an Art Center because this exhibition is the greatest one in the world. The only way that this will ever become an Art Center is through the humble studios of our dear town. The artists who live and die here and who teach the children are the ones who really set the pace. Many gallant painters have settled in our midst and gone away in a few years. Some have had to struggle on here and have died with broken hearts. We know one old man, dearly loved by all the brush people, who lost courage and was glad to die. When a thousand like him have suffered and gone, then we will be an Art Center. Until then let us wait patiently and bear with grace the bitter sayings of them who brag in lofty places and who speak of things beyond them as far as love of beauty is beyond the greed of gold.[81]

The point is just: an art center produces art, it does not simply play host to it. The Carnegie exhibitions, despite their high quality and the effusive rhetoric surrounding them, did nothing, apart from providing a little inspiration and giving a seasonal boost to the small local art market, to ensure that Pittsburghers would themselves produce art of a similar quality. In this respect, they failed to live up to the expectations of Carnegie and the city's promoters. This is not to say, of course, that the exhibitions were a worthless undertaking. It is time now to address the questions of what they actually accomplished and to what extent their achievement measured up to the publicized goals of their organizers.

✃ 5 ✄

# The Achievement of the Early Internationals

O N 20 MARCH 1902, the Fine Arts Committee announced that the annual competitive exhibitions were to be discontinued. A special loan exhibition would occupy the galleries in the last two months of 1902, and competitive exhibitions would be held every other year thereafter, with loan exhibitions in the alternate years. The loan exhibitions, it was explained, would further the Institute's educational mission by exposing Pittsburghers to a broader range of art than the competitive exhibitions could provide. Moreover, the quality of the latter would improve, for the Fine Arts Committee had noticed that "the present-day artists cannot contribute first-class work every year." The editor of the *Pittsburgh Post* appeared to be uncomfortable with this announcement. After all, he reflected, the annual exhibitions had been very good for local pride. Nevertheless, he assured his readers that the committee members were intelligent, that their decision was "probably" wise, and that the Carnegie annuals were not to be eliminated altogether, but simply transformed into biennials.[1]

The loan exhibition took place as scheduled and, if Beatty's figures are reliable, was the best-attended exhibition up to that time. It consisted of 155 paintings, all but four from private collections and nearly two-thirds from the Pittsburgh area. As in 1895, most of the pictures were by nineteenth-century artists, many of them still alive and at the height of their powers.[2] Had the committee's original decision been adhered to, the

215

following year would have seen a competitive exhibition like those held from 1897 to 1901. However, on 6 March 1903 the committee decided to modify its plan: there was to be an elected jury as before, and the usual prizes were to be awarded, but the invitations were to be limited to American artists living in the United States. This plan, carried out, turned an international exhibition into a smaller, purely American one, thereby reducing the expense and the effort needed to mount it. The diminished scope was to some extent camouflaged by running the exhibition concurrently with a traveling exhibition organized by the International Society of Sculptors, Painters, and Gravers, which included works by European and expatriate American artists.[3]

As late as March 1904, the future of the annual exhibitions was still in doubt. In his report for the year ending 31 March 1904, Beatty did not recommend resuming them, even in an Americans-only form: the exhibitions, he wrote, had been very successful, but they had outlived their usefulness and were consuming resources that might be better spent on the permanent collection. "I think it more than probable," he concluded, "that a union of effort on the part of several great American institutions can be secured, with a common object of providing an important international exhibition every year." Beatty did not work this plan out in detail, but it seems likely that he envisioned an arrangement whereby the Carnegie annual would be hosted by a different institution every year, in which case the burden might fall to Pittsburgh only twice a decade or so. At the end of his report, Beatty listed the names of all the artists who had exhibited at the Carnegie galleries from 1896 to 1903. He did not give a reason for doing so, but the valedictory mood is unmistakable.[4]

The unsettled status of the exhibition from 1902 to 1904 is, at first sight, a bit puzzling. Barring a few difficulties with artists and foreign advisors, the exhibition was running smoothly in 1901 and was receiving excellent reviews. Yet suddenly its whole future was being called into question. The obvious explanation is that Beatty himself was making an effort to discontinue it. In 1899, as we have seen, he told the press that the permanent collection was far more important to him than the exhibition, and in the spring of 1900 he flatly informed the Fine Arts Committee that as long as they insisted upon having the exhibition they could not expect to have a first-rate collection. Moreover, Beatty's duties were onerous, and in 1899 they nearly crushed him. During an interview with the *Pittsburgh Dispatch* in January 1899, he had revealed a disinclination to spend the usual two months traveling abroad. He did not believe, he told the reporter, that it would be necessary to visit Europe that summer; everything could be easily arranged from Pittsburgh. But he admitted that the Fine Arts Committee wanted him to go, and the committee had its way; Beatty went.[5]

When the exhibition opened the following autumn, Beatty, stricken with what the *Pittsburgh Dispatch* called an "illness closely bordering on nervous exhaustion," was unable to attend. "I guess I have been too ambitious — at least too continuous in my effort," he told Carnegie. "The doctor says, 'plain nerve exhaustion,' and that I had better go slow for a while." After spending several weeks recuperating in the country, he returned to Pittsburgh on 5 December 1899 to discuss that year's purchases with the Fine Arts Committee; but the next day's papers reported that he was ill again and that the meeting had been canceled.[6] Clearly, the annual exhibitions exacted a tremendous toll from Beatty. And it was not a toll that he paid gladly; there were, he felt, more important things to be done.

Beatty did not succeed in relieving himself of his burden, however. The details of his effort to do so have not been preserved, but it is easy enough to understand why Carnegie and the Fine Arts Committee would have been unwilling to give up the annual exhibition. It cost Carnegie only what was to him a negligible sum of money, and no labor at all. In return, it provided him with a highly publicized philanthropic venture that was linked to some of the highest-sounding ideals of the age. A good permanent collection might have been of equal or greater benefit to the community, but it would have attracted less attention and thus would have been less satisfying to a man who reveled in his image as a public benefactor. As for the committee members, their easy labors on behalf of the exhibition were rewarded with opportunities to share the limelight with world-famous artists and to congratulate themselves on a job well done.

In any event, the annual exhibitions were restored in 1904 and continued with occasional hiatuses — in 1906, due to the expansion of the Institute; from 1915 to 1919, due to World War I; in 1932, due to financial difficulties — until 1939, after which they were suspended for ten years because of World War II and its aftermath. When they were resumed in 1950 they ceased to be annual: the intention was to make them biennial, but after 1952 they became triennial and remained so until they were discontinued for reasons of expense after 1970. The exhibitions were revived in 1982 on the triennial plan. Over the years, their organization has changed completely from the plan worked out in 1897. After Beatty retired in 1921, his successor, Homer Saint-Gaudens, replaced the elected jury with a smaller, appointed one (1922), abolished the foreign advisory committees (1927), and relieved the jury of its admissions functions (1933). In 1967 Gustave von Groschwitz replaced the long-standing system of awards (which by 1955 had grown to include five numbered prizes, five honorable mentions, a garden club prize, and a popular prize) with a system of six equal prizes. Three years later Leon A. Arkus abolished the jury of awards and all prizes.[7]

The long—if sporadic—life of the exhibitions does not mean that Beatty was wrong to regret their influence on the permanent collection. Today's visitor to the Carnegie Museum of Art may well be inclined to agree with him, for the collection, although rich in works of art from the period covered by the exhibitions, is conspicuously poor in older works. One has only to compare it to Kansas City's Nelson-Atkins Museum of Art, for example—a younger but in many ways comparable institution that was not burdened with hosting a would-be American Salon—to realize how much is missing. No doubt a great deal of money was spent in Pittsburgh on merely temporary installations that might have been used toward lasting acquisitions.

All the same, it would be unfair to blame the weaknesses of the collection entirely on the exhibitions. Some of the blame must surely attach to the falling-out that occurred between Carnegie and Henry Clay Frick during the winter of 1899–1900.[8] Had the two not quarreled, Frick's collection might have stayed in Pittsburgh to form part of the present Carnegie Museum of Art instead of going to New York, and this in itself would have repaired many of the deficiencies in the permanent collection. When he and Carnegie were on good terms, Frick was always happy to make a loan or a donation to the Department of Fine Arts. In June 1896, for example, he urged Beatty to "take anything of mine you like for November." But in September 1899, when his relations with Carnegie were beginning to chill, he told Beatty that he was unable to lend any paintings, because his wife was unwilling to part with them. Thereafter, he refused all requests for loans, invariably giving the same reason.[9] The quarrel was a bitter one, and it is understandable that Frick wanted nothing to do with an institution founded with Carnegie's money and bearing Carnegie's name.

It must be kept in mind, however, that Beatty's views did not necessarily coincide at all points with those of Carnegie and that the present permanent collection does not appear deficient if seen in light of the latter's original intentions. Carnegie explicitly disavowed any desire to create a gallery that would house every period of art: such galleries were entirely proper, he observed in his 1895 dedication speech, but he immediately went on to announce that "the field for which the gallery is designed begins with the year 1896."[10] In that speech and in other recorded statements, he constantly emphasized that the Carnegie gallery existed for the benefit of contemporary and future art, not for the art of the past. Although his pet project of a chronological collection proved abortive, the collection as it stands today is very much what he hoped it would become — a survey of modern, especially American, art from the 1890s to the present.

And what of Carnegie's other hopes, the great ambitions of which he spoke so resoundingly in Founder's Day addresses and which were echoed by the exhibition's organizers, by the press, by visiting jurors and other notables? What progress did the early annual exhibitions make toward his goal of turning Pittsburgh into a major art center, bringing sweetness and light to its toiling masses, and promoting the development of American art?

Pittsburgh obviously did not become a major art center, and it showed no signs of developing into one during the late 1890s. In retrospect, it is hard to imagine how the annual exhibitions were supposed to accomplish this feat. The rather vague reasoning seems to have been along the following lines: "Paris and London have important exhibitions and are major art centers; therefore, if Pittsburgh has an important exhibition, it will become a major art center too." This was putting the cart before the horse. London and Paris had been the cultural, no less than political, capitals of their respective nations for centuries before their first public exhibitions were thought of; it was their existing artistic preeminence that had created these exhibitions, and not the other way around. Pittsburgh, on the other hand, had never been more than the cultural capital of western Pennsylvania, a region undistinguished for its achievements in the arts. Major art centers invariably had large numbers of major artists and would have had them even without annual exhibitions: indeed, New York had not had a large annual exhibition of any real importance since the decline of the National Academy of Design, yet its position as the art center of the country remained unchallenged. In this respect, Pittsburgh was vastly inferior not only to New York but to Boston and Philadelphia as well. There were certainly artists working in the city of Pittsburgh, and some of considerable talent, but none of international or national reputation. The frequent reminders in the press that John White Alexander, Mary Cassatt, and Henry O. Tanner were Pittsburgh-born were, in effect, attempts by local pride to compensate for this deficiency. There was very little in Pittsburgh upon which to build an art center.

In point of fact, the Carnegie exhibitions did not even attempt to build upon the slight foundations that Pittsburgh offered. The New York critic Samuel Swift underscored an essential truth about them when he remarked that Carnegie had been free to establish them wherever he chose: the exhibitions were *in* the city but in no sense *of* it.[11] Had Carnegie chosen to move them down the Ohio River to Cincinnati, their character would not have been altered in the least. The same artists who exhibited in Pittsburgh would have sent their pictures to Cincinnati; the elected jurors would have traveled a few hundred miles further west and made the same decisions in Ohio that they made in Pennsylvania; and no doubt the Cincinnati artists, with the exception of Frank Duveneck and a few others, would have had as little success in passing the juries as did their upstream counterparts. Given the policy of displaying only the best contemporary painters, it was inevitable that the exhibition would be alienated from the existing art community of whatever city it was located in, unless that city were already a major art center.

How, then, were the exhibitions to create a local Renaissance? This question was never discussed explicitly, but the idea runs through all the scattered commentary that the exhibitions' influence was to be primarily inspirational: the sight of so many masterpieces assembled in the Institute's galleries would inspire the local youth to pursue careers in art. This begs the further question of how the local youth were to go about fulfilling their ambitions once these had been sufficiently inflamed. In the 1890s their only option was to leave home and seek instruction on the East Coast or abroad. Pittsburgh had art schools at that time, but none possessed the prestige commensurate with the pretensions of a would-be art center, and the Institute did not try to correct this defect. The Car-

negie Institute of Technology (now Carnegie Mellon University), organized in 1912, included an art department that was to become one of the
more reputable in America, but it owed nothing to Beatty or the Fine
Arts Committee, and very little to Carnegie himself. Carnegie — whose
leading biographer has described him as "rather indifferent to the only
institution of higher education to bear his name" — opposed the creation
of the department until a local artist and teacher, Martin Leisser, persuaded him that instruction in the fine arts would promote good industrial
design.[12] Today, such instruction is available at all of Pittsburgh's universities and colleges, but this is also true of virtually every other university
and college in the country, and no credit can be given to the annual
exhibitions.

There is no reason to believe that the Carnegie exhibition was a more
effective instrument for furthering the Mission of Art than it was for
turning Pittsburgh into an art center. Here again we enter a realm of
glittering vagueness where it is difficult to lay hold of anything substantial. The idea appears to have been that looking at pictures would awaken
a love of beauty in the hearts of the beholders, which would eventually
color their entire beings and improve their manners, minds, and characters. Did such transformations actually occur? It is impossible to say, but
nobody ever noted that Pittsburghers were generally more refined and
spiritually elevated than the inhabitants of cities that did not enjoy the
benefits of an annual exhibition.

To appreciate the shallowness of Carnegie's thinking in this area, one
need only compare it to that of his contemporary, the great English designer and poet William Morris. Morris was hardly Carnegie's inferior
when it came to preaching the Gospel of Art: one of his chief "claims for
decent life" was nothing less than "a beautiful world to live in."[13] Morris
realized, however, that a beautiful world could not be achieved solely
through the sporadic and limited efforts of well-meaning philanthropists
but would require the complete reconstruction of society upon a more humane plan, a plan that would make the existence of multimillionaires like
Carnegie impossible. We can imagine what a socialist of the Morris stamp
might have said to Carnegie after hearing his fine sentiments aired in a
Founder's Day address: "You compel men under the threat of starvation to
work long hours of the most unrelenting drudgery under conditions that
are at best unpleasant and at worst dangerous. You give them only enough
leisure to sleep, eat, and propagate; you pay them only enough wages to

secure the barest animal necessities of life; and you are always looking for ways to pay them less and work them harder. You then spend a tiny fraction of the profits that you have sweated from them on a gallery full of pictures that you have allowed them neither the time nor the education to appreciate, and expect the mere act of gazing upon painted canvases to fill their dreary lives with "sweetness and light.' You, Mr. Carnegie, are either a fool or a hypocrite."

These charges could not easily be dismissed. Carnegie's idealistic professions of concern for "the toilers of Pittsburgh" must ultimately be judged by the grim realities of Homestead, a steel town just three miles distant from the elegant art gallery in Oakland. After a bloody strike in the summer of 1892, in which the Amalgamated Association of Iron and Steel Workers failed to resist Henry Clay Frick's union-busting tactics, Homestead had been left wholly at the mercy of the Carnegie Steel Company. And what did the great philanthropist make of it? "The town was as squalid and unlovely as could well be imagined," wrote Hamlin Garland in 1894, "and the people were mainly of the discouraged and the sullen type to be found everywhere where labor passes into a brutalizing stage of severity." In 1900, when the annual exhibition had been spreading enlightenment for five years, Charles Spahr, a journalist who lived in Homestead for several weeks, described the inhabitants as "cheerless almost to the point of sullenness" and the general atmosphere as "at times heavy with disappointment and hopelessness."[14] Apparently Carnegie did not choose to make Homestead a realm of sweetness and light, nor even of simple kindness. He did, however, give it a magnificent library.

Had Carnegie been reproached with the disparity between his philanthropic ideals and his actual practice as an employer, he might have replied that his hands were tied: he could not treat his employees better than his competitors treated theirs without being worsted in the marketplace, and the only remedy for this was social legislation that would compel all employers to behave alike. Carnegie actually made this argument in an interview published in the *Northern Daily News* (Aberdeen, Scotland) in September 1891. It is a sound argument — in fact, a common socialist argument of the period — but it must be remembered that Carnegie led the pack in underpaying and overworking and that other industrialists had to treat their employees worse in order to compete with him.[15]

Alternatively, he might have shifted his ground and argued that his philanthropic endeavors were primarily intended to benefit the potential geniuses among the working classes. In his view, poverty and hardship spurred such persons to higher achievement, and his duty was not to remove their incentive by providing them with debilitating luxuries like decent wages and indoor plumbing, but to inspire them to self-improvement.[16] Perhaps the early annual exhibitions had this effect. Perhaps the crowds that passed through the galleries included some working-class youths who went on to better their lot; perhaps the paintings themselves inspired them with notions of beauty that made them all the more determined to escape from ugliness and squalor. We simply do not know. If our temperaments happen to be less sanguine than Carnegie's, we are apt to ponder the fate of those potential geniuses who required gentler nurturing, and who lacked the strength, aggressiveness, and luck to free themselves from the blighting environment created by the Carnegie Steel Company and other industrial giants. What happened, we wonder, to the young Homestead steelworker who told Charles Spahr that he wanted an education more than anything else, but that his twelve-hour workday left him too exhausted to study?[17] Here was a man who wanted to better himself and would have eagerly taken advantage of the resources supplied by Carnegie, had he not had the misfortune to work for Carnegie.

Are we to conclude, then, that Carnegie was being hypocritical when he spoke of giving spiritual enlightenment to the people of Pittsburgh? Joseph Frazier Wall, the most insightful and judicious of Carnegie's biographers, faced a similar question when considering the contrast between his subject's expressed benevolence toward labor and his actual treatment of workers. According to Wall:

> The answer lies in Carnegie's lifelong quest to reconcile the Radical egalitarianism of his Dunfermline childhood with the capitalistic success that he enjoyed in manhood. For his own peace of mind he had to believe that he had not betrayed the faith of his fathers when he became a multimillionaire and an employer of tens of thousands of men. He once wrote that of all the lines in Robert Burns's poems he loved, the one that meant the most to him was "Thine own reproach alone do fear." Indeed, Carnegie was so confident of his own abilities that it was the only reproach he *could* fear. But fear it he did, and somehow he had to justify his kind of life to himself.[18]

To the extent that the effort to reconcile irreconcilables involved him in blindness, evasion, superficiality, and delusion, Carnegie may be considered a fool, but he was certainly no hypocrite. The idea of the Mission of Art was one in which he could sincerely believe, and if the idea as generally formulated strikes us today as long on platitudes and short on genuine substance, we can be sure that Carnegie was unable to see it in that light—it served too many of his inner needs for him to seriously question it or think about it critically. On the other hand, Beatty—whose own inner needs were different—was more interested in bringing the Mission of Art to middle-class high school students, whose upbringing and education had prepared them to receive it. Perhaps he even agreed with a most un-Carnegian remark made by Childe Hassam at the 1902 Founder's Day celebration: "Of course you cannot make good art popular. . . . But you can develop the taste of the few who want to know, and are allowed to know her secrets."[19]

Carnegie hoped that the annual exhibitions would provide encouragement to American art, and in later years Beatty came to view this as their single greatest achievement. Speaking at the dedication of the new Museum of Fine Arts building at Boston on 9 November 1909, he told his audience, "Fourteen years ago American art was not adequately estimated or fairly appreciated by the American public. The impression prevailed, especially among purchasers of paintings, that the works of European artists were more important, artistically, than those produced by American painters." The Carnegie Institute, however, had been a "potent force" in changing all that: "Year after year, some hundred and fifty paintings representative of the ablest masters of Europe were mingled with a like number representing the strongest men of America," until it was "demonstrated to the most obtuse . . . that our American art is equal in quality and spirit to the very best modern art in the world."[20]

Was this true? Did the American public of 1895 generally undervalue the work of American artists? and did the Carnegie exhibitions help to bring about a reevaluation? Popular perceptions are notoriously difficult to pin down. According to Beatty, among the most important agents of change were the reviewers, who took advantage of this unparalleled opportunity to compare American and European painting and then influenced public opinion through their writings. However, the reviews published during the 1890s present a different picture. Not one of the critics gave the faintest indication of having revised his estimate of American art as a result of viewing the Carnegie exhibitions; none showed the least awareness of a tendency for Americans to slight the work of their compatriots, or even addressed it as an issue. Comparisons between European and American art were few and rarely went beyond broad generalizations about the former's being refined and mannered, at least in its French mode, and the latter's being honest and forceful. There was no question that both were equal in quality. To the minority who complained that it was unfair to include so much foreign work in an exhibition intended to benefit Americans, Charles Caffin pointed out that the cause of American art had long since been won:

> If American art were in its infancy there might be some point in the assertion. The child would feel awed in the presence of the man. But in the same breath it is asserted that our native art has passed this stage, and can hold its own in the world. If so, why need it fear competition? As a matter of fact, it need not.

Although some critics treated the American paintings separately from the foreign, many did not and mixed them together indiscriminately. The press coverage as a whole was colored by the assumption that the public were interested in the artists of their own country. That Caffin's 1901 review for *Harper's Weekly* omitted all mention of foreign works suggests that he and his editors believed their readers to be far less concerned with these than with the American works.[21]

Although the critics appreciated the international aspect of the Carnegie exhibitions, there is no reason to suppose that they lacked other opportunities to compare American and European art. This may have been true of a few of the lesser local reviewers, but the influential New York–based critics — and even most of the Pittsburghers — demonstrated a familiarity with both foreign and native contemporary art that extended far beyond the galleries in Oakland. For example, much of Caffin's account for the *New York Evening Post* of the foreign works exhibited in 1900 dealt with what was missing from the collection: the works of La Thangue and Stanhope Forbes did not represent the most recent developments of their styles; the Italians were represented only by Laurenti and Pictor, who offered "poor consolation" for the absence of Morbelli, Tito, Joris, and Maria; Souza-Pinto was too Parisian to represent Portugal and should have been supplemented with Malhon, Salgado, and Columbano; Norway was represented only by Thaulow, and Denmark was not represented at all, although its art was "more fascinating than much in Europe."[22]

Caffin had obviously learned a great deal from traveling abroad, and this would have been true of the leading critics and of the affluent cognoscenti in general. For determined art lovers who could afford to indulge their tastes (and this was the only section of the public whose opinions on the relative merits of American and European art could possibly have any effect), there were other opportunities as well. They could frequent the dealers, especially those in New York, who handled a wide range of foreign art; they could attend the small exhibitions held at private clubs, many of which were open to nonmembers; they could travel to the large exhibitions held in Boston, Philadelphia, Chicago, and St. Louis, where foreign works were often displayed, if not so abundantly as at Pittsburgh.

The idea of encouraging American art could be taken in the narrower sense (expressed most clearly by the *Art Interchange*'s Observer) of encouraging American artists by awarding them prizes, providing a market for their work, and generating useful publicity. The early exhibitions were not particularly effective in supplying this type of encouragement nor were they designed to be. Prizes were generally awarded to well-known artists, American and European, to whom they could have been little more than pleasant additions to reputations already securely established. The spotlight of publicity tended to pick out those celebrated figures who had long been accustomed to its glare, while leaving in the dark those lesser artists who would have had more to gain from it. Although the Fine Arts Committee prided itself upon a democratic policy of allowing anyone to submit to the juries, its desire to create a select exhibition of the best and most representative specimens of contemporary art produced a bias toward the most successful painters, who were least in need of encouragement. It is true that in 1901 the first and second prizes went to virtual unknowns — Alfred Maurer and Elizabeth Ahrens — and that young George Carspecken had been hung on the line, but these were exceptional occurrences and were widely recognized as such. Charles Caffin assumed that the prizes would have been awarded quite differently had not an unusually large number of prominent artists failed to contribute that year.[23]

Carnegie's dream of founding an American Salon that would exert a potent influence upon American art was already something of an anachronism by the 1890s. The great official exhibitions of Europe were not what they had been fifty years earlier: their power had been sapped by rival exhibiting bodies, many avowedly secessionist, and by the rise of the private dealer, and it would continue to diminish in the twentieth century. This same situation obtained in America, with the difference that no single exhibiting body ever achieved complete and unquestioned dominance. Beatty's behavior toward the artists was, as we have seen, more often that of a humble petitioner who hoped they would send their nicest pictures to Pittsburgh than that of a powerful exhibition director whose favor or disfavor might materially affect their careers. He realized that his success depended on their goodwill, and that they could easily take their work elsewhere.

A far more influential, and certainly far more controversial, exhibition might have been created had Beatty anticipated the 1913 Armory Show by introducing to America the works of those artists who have come to be known as the Post-Impressionists. Carnegie and his trustees would no doubt have taken a dim view of this, but Beatty could have justified their inclusion on the ground of Carnegie's own hope "that the pictures exhibited from time to time will be of all schools," that is, on the ground that the exhibition had a duty to be fully representative of contemporary trends.[24] The Paris advisory committee might also have raised difficulties, but Beatty could have avoided these by arranging to receive works as special loans subject only to the action of the Fine Arts Committee. The presence each year of several extremely avant-garde paintings would have added spice to the exhibition without sinking it as a whole in the critical and popular esteem; they would have drawn a great deal of attention, especially from persons given to the pleasures of outrage and indignation, and would probably have won a few passionate advocates among those who were determined to keep up with the latest thing from Paris, whatever that might be. If, however, Beatty ever visited the annual Salon des Indépendants, where such works were displayed, he left no record of having done so. As far as can be determined, he had no awareness at all of the Post-Impressionists. It is curious that, in the entire mass of documentation pertaining to an exhibition that purported to show a full range of American and European painting and was praised for its completeness, there is not so much as a faint allusion to those tendencies that are today regarded as having been of the first importance in the art of the 1890s.

We must conclude, then, that the organizers of the exhibition failed to achieve their highest purposes. We must not, however, characterize the exhibition as a failure on that account. Nothing could be more usual than for a great public benefaction to be tricked out with glowing ideals tailored to the fashion of the age, ideals about which nobody thinks clearly or critically, ideals that, as a few minutes of clear critical thought would reveal, the benefaction cannot fulfill. The utility of these ideals, apart from giving a cosmetic luster to the enterprise in hand, lies in their power to inspire and sustain the labors of the benefactors. The ideals expressed at the founding of the Carnegie annual exhibition appealed to patriotism (encouragement of American art), local pride (transformation of Pittsburgh into an art center), and a belief in the Mission of Art (elevation of the toiling masses). Although the first of these ideals could not have been realized by the exhibition as it was actually organized, and the other two could not have been realized by any exhibition, no matter how ingeniously it may have been conceived, yet there is no doubt that Carnegie, with his weakness for euphoriant superficialities, found them truly inspiring and would not have created the exhibition without the motivation that they provided. Beatty's diplomatic manners were too inscrutable to allow us to ascertain the precise extent to which he shared these ideals: we know that he came to disagree with the means employed to realize them and that his position required from him a closer attention to the practical side of things than to the theoretical, but he publicly subscribed to them and there is no reason to believe that he did not, with some personal modifications and reservations, accept them as his own. In any event, the fact that the exhibition fell short of reaching its most exalted goals does not mean that it accomplished nothing, or even that more immediate and prosaic goals were not brilliantly achieved.

The most brilliant achievement was the establishment of a free annual exhibition of contemporary art in Pittsburgh. Although this was not enough in itself to make the city "interesting" in the sense approved by Matthew Arnold, it certainly made the city more interesting than it had been. Pittsburgh had had exhibitions before, but these had been largely mediocre affairs, depending as they did upon contributions from local artists and collectors, and none had been associated with a permanent gallery. Something better had long been desired by the more cultivated citizens, and it was precisely this that Carnegie's philanthropy and Beatty's direction supplied.[25] It is true that the exhibition engrossed resources that might have been spent to more lasting effect upon the permanent collection; nevertheless, for the art-loving Pittsburgher of modest means it was a magnificent feast after long years of famine, offering him for two months of every year a quantity and variety of first-rate painting previously available only to the fortunate few who had money and leisure enough to permit frequent trips to the East Coast and Europe. Beatty himself, when pointing to the effect that the exhibition was having on the permanent collection, had to acknowledge that the growth of the latter would have been "slow under any circumstances" and could not have given such "immediate benefit to the people living now."[26]

We need not believe in the Mission of Art to accept the idea that a life is richer and better for having art in it than it would be without art, and that anything that puts art into lives is to that extent a good thing. From this point of view, the annual exhibition was definitely a good thing; it succeeded year after year in putting a great deal of art into a great many lives — succeeded better at this, in fact, than the Carnegie International of the present day. Eyewitness accounts of the 1890s tell us that the galleries were crowded on weekends, sometimes so densely crowded that the security guards had to direct the flow of traffic. The 1991 International presented quite a different weekend scene: the galleries were, by comparison, sparsely populated, and it was not unusual to see only three or four people at a time in a single large room. Even allowing for the greater sizes of the works of art (mostly installations) displayed in 1991, the contrast is striking and instructive. It shows, in the most graphic way possible, that the annual exhibitions of the 1890s were truly popular, whereas their modern successors are not. One reason for this is that many more inexpensive amusements are available to late twentieth-century Pittsburghers, the most inexpensive of them being to sit at home and watch actors pretend to do exciting things on television.

Another reason is that the exhibition is no longer free. In the 1890s a person with no existing interest in art who had come to the Institute to use the library, view the natural history collection, or listen to a free organ recital, could wander at no cost through the galleries — moved by nothing more than idle curiosity or a desire to kill time — and perhaps have an interest awakened. This is precisely what Carnegie hoped would happen. Today, the visitor to the galleries must already have an interest in art sufficiently awakened to justify paying an admission fee.

The most important reason, however, is that contemporary art has itself ceased to be popular. In the 1890s a painting by a leading master frequently excited the same degree of admiration in both the ignorant and the knowing. The former admired, for example, a portrait of a child because the subject was pretty and adorable; the latter also appreciated these qualities but were sensitive to the formal means whereby the artist had expressed them. This common ground has disappeared during the past century, with the result that art created for the knowing utterly fails to provide the ignorant with any of the pleasures that they expect from art. If one visits a working-class or lower-middle-class Pittsburgh home, one typically finds a few pictures (for the most part commercial reproductions) on the walls, and these almost invariably depict pleasant landscapes and seascapes, flowers, attractive children and adults in period and ethnic costume, religious scenes, and the like. The taste of the average Pittsburgher, in common with that of the average North American and Western European, remains very much what it was in the 1890s. The entire range of late Modernism, from Jackson Pollock to Anselm Kiefer, can hardly be said to exist for most people except as an object of scorn, and there are many for whom even such early Modernists as Matisse and Picasso are a bit on the edge. When the founders of the Carnegie Institute proposed to bring art to the people, they had at their disposal an art that the majority of people could accept. The organizers of today's International have lost this advantage and find themselves — despite an educational apparatus of lectures, tours, and special events that Beatty would have envied — preaching to the converted while most of the population is left out in the cold.

Although the creation of an annual exhibition that delivered the goods, so to speak, was the major achievement of its founders, there were other, less tangible, benefits that bore some relation to the founders' loftier aspirations. An awareness of one of these benefits was much in the mind of the *Pittsburgh Post* editor who, uneasy at the prospect of even a temporary discontinuation of the annual exhibitions, observed in 1902 that they had had an excellent effect on local pride. Having seen how enthusiastically the press embraced the idea of Pittsburgh as an art center, praised the Carnegie exhibition as the finest in the country, perhaps in the world, and quoted the flattering, often envious comments of out-of-town reviewers, we can well believe it. This enthusiasm, which at times exceeded the bounds of reason as well as those of modesty, becomes understandable when we realize how little Pittsburghers had to be proud of in the late nineteenth century. Unless they were disposed to brag about the accomplishments of the steel industry, they had virtually nothing: their city was known to the world as a smoky, dirty, uncultured mill town, whose dominant aspect Carnegie's idol Herbert Spencer aptly summed up with the word "repulsiveness."[27] To be able to point to something so manifestly unrepulsive as an exhibition of art, juried by leading artists and praised by leading critics, and say, "This, too, is Pittsburgh" was immensely satisfying to them. Of course, when Carnegie told a Founder's Day audience in 1914 that Pittsburgh had come to be more widely known as a "fostering mother of Fine Arts" than as a "great workshop," he was indulging in a characteristic piece of exaggeration.[28] As any longtime resident can attest, the image of a provincial industrial city persisted into the 1970s, only to be replaced by the image of a provincial Rust Belt city. But these negative images have long been mitigated, at least in some quarters, by the fame of certain of the city's cultural and educational institutions; and to Carnegie belongs the credit of giving the city its first source of nonindustrial distinction.

The Carnegie exhibition could no more affect the development of American art than it could turn Pittsburgh into a major art center, but it could make a genuine contribution to national pride — not to the sort of national pride that expressed itself in the mindless, militaristic jingoism of the Spanish-American War, but to the sort that expressed itself in a quest for cultural excellence. To those who attached their patriotism to this quest, the late nineteenth-century proliferation of art schools, galleries, and societies throughout the country, especially in what New Yorkers and Bostonians had long regarded as the benighted hinterland, was extremely heartening. Many of the nation's great regional museums were founded between 1880 and 1900, sometimes in cities that had within living memory been rough frontier settlements, and many a small town could boast an "Academy of Fine Arts" or an "Art Association" where persons hungry for enlightenment could hear lectures on topics ranging from the frescoes of Domenico Ghirlandaio to the war paintings of the Russian Realist Vassili Vereschagin.[29]

The Carnegie exhibition, being the only American exhibition that attempted year after year to mount a comprehensive survey of contemporary Western art and to challenge comparison with the great annual exhibitions of Europe, became a major participant in this movement. Americans were inclined to take the comparison seriously: a writer for the

*Review of Reviews* declared in 1903 that artists both at home and abroad had come to regard the Carnegie annual as "one of the events of the year," second in importance only to the Salon and the Royal Academy; and more than one critic, as we have seen, considered the Pittsburgh show superior in quality to its rivals in Paris and London.[30] The scant attention that it received from the overseas press and the difficulties that Beatty encountered with certain European masters indicate that the comparison was not altogether admitted on the other side of the Atlantic; nevertheless, enough leading foreign artists contributed to make the comparison plausible to hopeful American eyes and to lift the exhibition out of the realm of the provincial in European eyes. "The first time I went to Europe," Beatty told an interviewer in 1899, "an artist who has a painting in the Luxembourg asked me, 'Is not Pittsburg in Australia?'. Now there is neither artist nor student in these countries who does not know the Carnegie galleries by name."[31] New York would have been the natural and expected location for a would-be American Salon, but the establishment of the Carnegie exhibition in a city unknown to the world of art made its rapid rise to fame more striking and more expressive of the cultural aspirations of the entire nation. The higher manifestations of civilized life, it seemed to say, would no longer cling to the Eastern Seaboard, and the hope expressed in 1895 by Charles Eliot Norton — that "the very energy displayed in the attainment of material things may indeed, now that the means of culture have been so abundantly secured, exhibit itself in acquiring the culture itself" — was beginning to be fulfilled.[32]

# APPENDIX A

## Prizewinners at the Carnegie Annual Exhibitions, 1896–1901

### 1896

|  |  |
|---|---|
| First Prize ($5,000) | Winslow Homer, *The Wreck* |
| Second Prize ($3,000) | Gari Melchers, *The Shipbuilder* |
| Gold Medal | John Lavery, *Lady in Brown* |
| Silver Medal | Jean-François Raffaëlli, *Notre Dame, Paris* |
| Bronze Medal | Cecilia Beaux, *Ernesta* |

### 1897

|  |  |
|---|---|
| Medal of the First Class | James J. Shannon, *Miss Kitty* |
| Medal of the Second Class | Fritz Thaulow, *The Arques at Ancourt — Evening* |
| Medal of the Third Class | J. Alden Weir, *Face Reflected in a Mirror* |
| Honorable Mention | Louis Paul Dessar, *Mending the Nets* |
| Honorable Mention | Wilton Lockwood, *The Violinist* |

### 1898

|  |  |
|---|---|
| Medal of the First Class | Dwight W. Tryon, *Early Spring in New England* |
| Medal of the Second Class | Childe Hassam, *The Sea* |
| Medal of the Third Class | Alexander Roche, *The Window Seat* |
| Honorable Mention | E. A. Walton, *The Shepherd* |
| Honorable Mention | John F. Weir, *Roses* |

### 1899

|  |  |
|---|---|
| Medal of the First Class | Cecilia Beaux, *Mother and Daughter* |
| Medal of the Second Class | Frank W. Benson, *The Sisters* |
| Medal of the Third Class | André Dauchez, *The Boats* |
| Honorable Mention | Lucien Simon, *Portraits* |
| Honorable Mention | John H. Twachtman, *The Waterfall* |

## 1900

Medal of the First Class   André Dauchez, *The Kelp Gatherers*
Medal of the Second Class   Ben Foster, *Misty Moonlight Night*
Medal of the Third Class   William Sergeant Kendall, *The End of the Day*
Honorable Mention   Robert W. Allan, *All Hands on Deck*
Honorable Mention   Julius Olsson, *Waterfall in Winter*
Honorable Mention   W. Elmer Schofield, *Twilight*

## 1901

Medal of the First Class   Alfred H. Maurer, *An Arrangement*
Medal of the Second Class   Elizabeth W. Ahrens, *Sewing — A Portrait*
Medal of the Third Class   Edmund C. Tarbell, *The Venetian Blind*
Honorable Mention   Henri Le Sidaner, *Light*
Honorable Mention   Mary L. Macomber, *The Hourglass*

# APPENDIX B

## Juries of Award, 1896–1901

In 1896 the Fine Arts Committee acted as the jury of award. From 1897 to 1905 John Caldwell, chairman of the Fine Arts Committee, served as president of the jury of award.

### 1896

John Caldwell
William McConway
William Nimick Frew

S. D. Warmcastle
Joseph R. Woodwell
D. T. Watson

A. Bryan Wall
Edward M. Bigelow

### 1897

#### American

Frank W. Benson (Salem, Mass.)
Cecilia Beaux (Philadelphia)
William M. Chase (New York)
Frank Duveneck (Cincinnati)

Winslow Homer (Scarboro, Maine)
John LaFarge (New York)
Will H. Low (Bronxville, N.Y.)
Edmund C. Tarbell (Boston)

#### Foreign

John M. Swan (London)

Edwin Lord Weeks (Paris)
[American national residing abroad]

### 1898

#### American

William M. Chase (New York)
Frederick W. Freer (Chicago)
Wilton Lockwood (Boston)
Edmund C. Tarbell (Boston)

John H. Twachtman (Greenwich, Conn.)
Frederick P. Vinton (Boston)
Robert W. Vonnoh (Rockland Lake, N.Y.)
J. Alden Weir (New York)

#### Foreign

John Lavery (London)

Fritz Thaulow (Paris)

## 1899

### American

Edwin H. Blashfield (New York)
William M. Chase (New York)
Charles H. Davis (Mystic, Conn.)
Thomas Eakins (Philadelphia)
John J. Enneking (Boston)
Frederick W. Freer (Chicago)
Wilton Lockwood (Boston)
Robert W. Vonnoh (Rockland Lake, N.Y.)

### Foreign

Jean-François Raffaëlli (Paris)
William Stott (London)

## 1900

### American

Frank W. Benson (Salem, Mass.) [unable to serve because of illness]
Kenyon Cox (New York)
Charles H. Davis (Mystic, Conn.)
Thomas Eakins (Philadelphia)
John J. Enneking (Boston)
Frederick W. Freer (Chicago)
Eugene A. Poole (Pittsburgh)
Frederick P. Vinton (Boston)

### Foreign

Alexander Harrison (Paris) [American national residing abroad]
Anders L. Zorn (Mora, Sweden)

## 1901

### American

John W. Alexander (New York)
Frank W. Benson (Salem, Mass.)
Thomas Eakins (Philadelphia)
Frederick W. Freer (Chicago)
Winslow Homer (Scarboro, Maine)
Clarence M. Johns (Pittsburgh)
John LaFarge (New York) [unable to serve because of illness]
Robert W. Vonnoh (Rockland Lake, N.Y.)

### Foreign

Robert W. Allan (London)
Edmond Aman-Jean (Paris)

# NOTES

Unless otherwise stated, all cited correspondence is addressed to John Beatty. The original correspondence is the property of the Archives of American Art, Smithsonian Institution, Washington, D.C. It may be consulted on microfilm through the Archives of American Art and at the Carnegie Museum of Art.

Many of the newspaper articles cited in the text are preserved in the William Nimick Frew Scrapbooks in the Pennsylvania Room of the Carnegie Library of Pittsburgh. Although they are invaluable aids to research, they are themselves unpaginated and do not give original page numbers. To have repaired this omission in the present work would have been impossible without sacrificing most of the convenience that the scrapbooks afford; however, turn-of-the-century newspapers were much shorter than those of today, and anyone wishing to consult a particular article will find no difficulty in doing so with the information provided.

## Preface

1. G. Weisberg, "Tastemaking in Pittsburgh: The Carnegie International in Perspective, 1896–1905," *Carnegie Magazine* 56, no. 10 (July–August 1983): 20.

## Chapter 1

1. Cited in J. F. Wall, *Andrew Carnegie* (New York, 1970; reprint, Pittsburgh, 1989), 225.

2. A. Carnegie, *The Autobiography of Andrew Carnegie* (Boston and New York, 1920), 339.

3. A. Carnegie, "The Advantages of Poverty," *Nineteenth Century* 29 (March 1891), reprinted in *The Gospel of Wealth and Other Timely Essays*, ed. Edward Kirkland (Cambridge, Mass., 1962), 64. Wall discusses in detail Carnegie's relationship to Social Darwinism in *Carnegie*, 376–97, 814–15.

4. A. Carnegie, "The Best Use of Wealth," in *Miscellaneous Writings of Andrew Carnegie*, ed. Burton J. Hendrick (Garden City, N.Y., 1933), 2:209–10.

5. Carnegie, *Autobiography*, 338; Wall, *Carnegie*, 815–16; B. J. Hendrick, *The Life of Andrew Carnegie* (Garden City, N.Y., 1932), 2:253–54.

6. A. Carnegie, "The Gospel of Wealth," in *The Gospel of Wealth*, 39, 43 (this essay first appeared in the June and December 1889 numbers of the *North American Review* as "Wealth" and "The Best Fields for Philanthropy"); Carnegie, "The Best Use of Wealth," 210–11.

7. Leisser quoted in Anna Jane Phillips, "Patriarch of Pittsburgh Art Finds Life Lots of Fun at 91," *Pittsburgh Post-Gazette*, 29 July 1936, in Agnes Way Scrapbook, Carnegie Library of Pittsburgh, 76; Carnegie, *Autobiography*, 143; A. Carnegie, address delivered on 11 April 1907, in *Memorial of the Celebration of the Carnegie Institute at Pittsburgh, Pennsylvania, April 11, 12, 13, 1907* (Pittsburgh, 1907), 60.

8. Carnegie, New York, to William N. Frew, Pittsburgh, 24 October 1894, quoted in Wall, *Carnegie*, 817.

9. See the detailed account in N. Harris, *The Artist in American Society* (New York, 1966), 159–86.

10. American Art-Union, *Transactions for the Year 1844* (New York, 1845), 10, quoted in R. Stein, *John Ruskin and Aesthetic Thought in America, 1840–1900* (Cambridge, Mass., 1967), 11.

11. G. Bissell, "Art and Education," *Municipal Affairs* 6, no. 2 (June 1902): 185–86.

12. M. Remick, "The Relation of Art to Morality," *Arena* 19 (April 1898): 493.

13. A. Duganne, *Art's True Mission in America* (New York, 1853), 17, quoted in Harris, *Artist in American Society*, 184; H. Beecher, "Be Generous of Beauty," in *Eyes and Ears* (Boston, 1862), 282, 284.

14. J. Addams, "Successful Efforts to Teach Art to the Masses: The Art-Work Done by Hull-House, Chicago," *Forum* 19 (March–August 1895): 615.

15. M. H., "Art and the People," *Harper's Weekly* 37 (29 April 1893): 395. For working-class art exhibitions, see also "The East Side Loan Exhibition," *Critic* 20 (25 June 1892): 357; A. Bernheim, "Successful Efforts to Teach Art to the Masses: Results of Picture-Exhibitions in Lower New York," *Forum* 19 (March–August 1895): 610–14; R. Lynes, *The Taste-Makers* (New York, 1954), 157–59.

16. C. L. Hutchinson, report as Sunday school superintendent, 1882, in notebook (Hutchinson Papers, Newberry Library, Chicago), 34. Carnegie was familiar with Hutchinson's philanthropic endeavors: in a letter to Hutchinson dated 30 April 1901, he expressed his "interest and admiration for the good work a band of you—all cordial friends—are doing for Chicago" (Hutchinson Papers, Chicago Historical Society).

17. C. L. Hutchinson, "Art: Its Influence and Excellence in Modern Times," *Chicago Saturday Evening Herald*, 31 March 1888, quoted in H. L. Horowitz, *Culture and the City* (Lexington, Ky., 1976), 75, 76 (Horowitz provides an illuminating analysis of Hutchinson's views [74–83]).

18. C. L. Hutchinson, "The Democracy of Art," *American Magazine of Art* 7 (1916): 399, quoted in Horowitz, *Culture and the City*, 206.

19. Hendrick, *Carnegie*, 1:243.

20. Carnegie, *Autobiography*, 307.

21. M. Arnold, *Culture and Anarchy*, in *Works* (London, 1903–1904), 6:225–26.

22. A. Carnegie, *Triumphant Democracy* (New York, 1886; reprint, New York and London, 1971), 321.

23. Ibid., 318–27.

24. Ibid., 339.

25. K. Vanderbilt, *Charles Eliot Norton* (Cambridge, Mass., 1959), 126–32, 206–08.

26. M. Arnold, *Mixed Essays*, in *Works* (London 1903–1904), 10:37; *Letters of Matthew Arnold*, 2:396, quoted in Wall, *Carnegie*, 444; Arnold, "Civilisation in the United States," in *Five Uncollected Essays*, ed. K. Alcott (Liverpool, 1953), 53–55 (first appeared in *Nineteenth Century* [April 1888]); Arnold, "A Word About America," in *Five Uncollected Essays*, 21 (first appeared in *Nineteenth Century* [May 1882]).

27. A. Carnegie, New York, letter to the president and trustees of the Carnegie Institute, October 1897, quoted in Wall, *Carnegie*, 817.

28. Rudyard Kipling, *American Notes* (New York, 1889), 215.

29. J. J. Ingalls, "Lessons of the Fair," *Cosmopolitan* 16 (1893–1894): 142–43.

30. P. Bourget, "A Farewell to the White City," *Cosmopolitan* 16 (1893–1894): 135.

31. W. Besant, "A First Impression," *Cosmopolitan* 15 (1893): 533.

32. Will Low, *A Painter's Progress* (New York, 1910), 251.

33. See John C. Van Dyke, "Painting at the Fair," *Century Magazine* 48 (May–October 1894): 439–44. Although Van Dyke believed that Europe was generally on the wane, he did not think that America would supersede her entirely. Scandinavia, in his view, also held great promise.

34. Carnegie, "Best Use of Wealth," 214–15. See also Carnegie's letter dated 2 January 1896 to the board of trustees of the Carnegie Institute, in *Carnegie Fine Arts and Museum Collection Fund: Constitution and By-Laws of the Board of Trustees Together with Mr. Carnegie's Letter and Deed of Trust* (Pittsburgh, 1907), 1–2.

35. Carnegie, "Best Use of Wealth," 214; *Carnegie Fine Arts and Museum Collection Fund*, 1. The quotation is from Carnegie, *Triumphant Democracy*, 327.

36. William N. Frew, quoted in "Men to Buy Works of Art," *Pittsburgh Post*, 1 January 1896, 2. Carnegie, speech delivered at Pittsburgh in November 1989, in *Founder's Day, 1898, at the Carnegie Institute* (Pittsburgh, 1898), 18.

37. "Future of Art in Pittsburg," *Pittsburgh Dispatch*, 30 December 1894, 17.

38. The duties of the Fine Arts Committee are specified in article 3, sections 2–8, of the constitution and bylaws of the board of trustees. See *Carnegie Fine Arts and Museum Collection Fund*, 12–14.

39. Carnegie, letter to Frew, 2 February 1896.

40. Carnegie, "Best Use of Wealth," 213–14.

41. Arnold, *Culture and Anarchy*, 42.

42. Carnegie, "Best Use of Wealth," 217.

43. "Private Pictures May Be Exhibited," *Pittsburgh Leader*, 24 December 1899.

44. Quoted in Edgar Munhall, *Masterpieces of the Frick Collection*, with an introduction by Harry D. M. Grier (New York, 1970), 4.

45. For A. B. Wall and J. R. Woodwell, see P. Chew and J. Sakal, *Southwestern*

*Pennsylvania Painters, 1800–1945* (exhibition catalogue, Westmoreland County Museum of Art, Greensburg, Pa., 27 September–29 November 1981): 134–36, 150–54. For J. Caldwell, see Obituary, *Pittsburgh Bulletin* 59, 27 November 1909, 13; "Art Galleries Receive a Loan of Fine Pictures," *Pittsburgh Dispatch*, 1 August 1901. For H. C. Frick, see Munhall, *Masterpieces of the Frick Collection*, 3–5. For D. T. Watson, see J. W. Jordan, *Encyclopedia of Pennsylvania Biography* (New York, 1914), 1:270–72; "Art and Book Sales Past and to Come," *American Art News* 15, 14 April 1917, 7. For W. McConway, see G. I. Reed, *Century Cyclopedia of History and Biography of Pennsylvania* (Chicago, 1904), 2:101; "William McConway," *Pittsburgh Index* 39, 9 November 1918, 4; and F. C. Harper, *Pittsburgh of Today* (New York, 1932), 5:743–45. For W. N. Frew, see J. W. Jordan, *Encyclopedia of Pennsylvania Biography*, 9:193–96. For J. M. Clark, see J. W. Jordan, *Encyclopedia of Pennsylvania Biography*, 6:2184–85. For J. G. Holmes, see J. Fleming, *History of Pittsburgh and Environs* (New York and Chicago, 1922), 152. For E. M. Bigelow, see *The City's Blue Book: Councilmen and City Officials of Pittsburgh* (Pittsburgh, 1904–1905), 5; A. P. Moore, *The Book of Prominent Pennsylvanians* (Pittsburgh, 1913), 18; Obituary, *Pittsburgh Bulletin* 73 (9 December 1916): 23.

46. See M. K. Olds, *John Wesley Beatty: Artist and Cultural Influence in Pittsburgh* (Masters dissertation, University of Pittsburgh, 1953).

47. J. W. Beatty to H. K. Porter, 13 October 1894; Porter to Beatty, 17 October 1894.

48. "Essays on Our Leading Citizens: John Wesley Beatty," *Harpoon*, May 1913, 7; Lila Hetzel, "Biography of George Hetzel" (1946; Carnegie Library of Pittsburgh); John O'Connor Jr., *The History of the Pittsburgh International, Carnegie Institute, 1896–1952* (Pittsburgh, 1952), 1; Olds, *John Wesley Beatty*, 24.

49. W. B. Morris, "Director John W. Beatty and His Work," *Pittsburgh Press*, 14 April 1901; "Essays on Our Leading Citizens," 8.

50. Morris, "Director John W. Beatty."

51. J. W. Beatty, *The Relation of Art to Nature* (New York, 1922), 1.

52. "Old Favorites Will Return," *Pittsburgh Dispatch*, 7 September 1913 (CMOA Biographical Files); J. W. Beatty, "The Modern Art Movement," *North American Review* 219 (1924): 263.

53. See, for example, "John W. Beatty Talks of Art," *Pittsburgh Dispatch*, 26 January 1899, an account of a lecture given at Pittsburgh's Twentieth Century Club, in which he speaks of truth to nature as the vital element in a painting and urges both Realists and Impressionists to seek more of it.

54. Beatty, *Relation of Art to Nature*, 69–70. Quotations are from ibid., 5–6, 15.

55. K. Cox, *The Classic Point of View* (New York, 1911; reprint, 1980).

56. J. W. Beatty, "The Art Gallery," *Dedication Souvenir of the Carnegie Library* (Pittsburgh, 1895), 46.

57. "Men to Buy Works of Art," *Pittsburgh Post*, 1 January 1896, 2.

58. J. Caldwell, Atlantic City, 25 February 1897.

## Chapter 2

1. Beatty to Porter, 13 October 1894. Beatty quoted in "First Fall Exhibit," *Pittsburgh Leader*, 1 November 1896, 5.

2. Art Society of Pittsburgh, circular letter, 8 July 1895 (CMOA Archives); "Many Paintings Rejected," *Pittsburgh Times*, 7 November 1895, 2. See also L. R. Beck, Philadelphia, 20 August 1895; E. W. Brainerd, Boston, 13 September 1895.

3. I. M. Gaugengigl, Boston, 13, 18 August 1895; E. Tarbell, Boston, n.d. [summer 1895]; J. W. Alexander, New York, n.d. [ca. August], 2, 7, 9 October 1895; W. Shirlaw, New York, 7 August, 7, 19 September 1895; W. A. Coffin, New York, 2, 8 September 1895.

4. W. A. Coffin, New York, 8 September 1895; J. W. Beatty, *Eleventh and Twelfth Annual Reports of the Director of Fine Arts for the Years Ending March 31, 1907, and March 31, 1908* (Pittsburgh, 1908), 38; Beatty, *Fourteenth Annual Report of the Director of Fine Arts for the Year Ending March 31, 1910* (Pittsburgh, 1910), 25.

5. Alexander, New York, n.d. [ca. August 1895]; G. D. Brush, New York, 29 September, 4 October 1895.

6. Mrs. G. Vanderbilt, Bar Harbor, Maine, 24 July 1895; J. D. Rockefeller, Cleveland, 25 July 1895.

7. G. W. Elkins, Philadelphia, 24 July 1895; C. L. Hutchinson, Chicago, 13 July, 30 August, 20 September 1895.

8. For an account of the critics' visit, see "Critics Are Pleased," *Pittsburgh Dispatch*, 5 November 1895, 2. For the architecture and history of the Carnegie Institute, see J. D. Van Trump, *An American Palace of Culture* (Pittsburgh, 1970). The 1895 dedication souvenir includes essays by the architects (Longfellow, Alden, and Harlow) and the decorator (Elmer Ellsworth Garnsey), which describe the building's appearance in 1895.

9. D. C. Thomson, "The Carnegie Art Gallery," *Art Journal*, December 1898, 353; A. Hoeber, "Pictures in Pittsburg," *New York Times*, 10 November 1895, 29.

10. "Critics Are Pleased," *Pittsburgh Dispatch*, 5 November 1895, 2.

11. Hoeber, "Pictures in Pittsburg," *New York Times*, 10 November 1895, 29. Trumble quoted in "Praise from a High Source," *Pittsburgh Dispatch*, 18 November 1895, 4.

12. The *New York Journal* and the *Philadelphia Record* reviews are quoted in "Mr. Carnegie's Gift," *Pittsburgh Dispatch*, 8 November 1895, 4.

13. F. Weitenkampf, "Art in Pittsburgh," *Art Interchange* 35 (July–December 1895): 141.

14. "In the Art Gallery," *Pittsburgh Dispatch*, 5 November 1895, 2; Beatty, "The Art Gallery," 46–47.

15. Hoeber, "Pictures in Pittsburg," *New York Times*, 10 November 1895, 29.

16. T. W. Dewing, Windsor, Vt., 16 August 1896; H. W. Ranger, East Lyme, Conn., 10 September 1896.

17. Art Society of Pittsburgh, circular letter, 8 July 1895 (CMOA Archives); Alexander, Paris, 17 April 1896.

18. "In the Art Gallery," *Pittsburgh Chronicle-Telegraph*, 5 November 1895, 3; "His Pictures Rejected," *Pittsburgh Chronicle-Telegraph*, 6 November 1895, 1.

19. "The Carnegie Art Exhibit," *Pittsburgh Press*, 6 November 1895, 9; "Where Artists Disagree," *Pittsburgh Chronicle-Telegraph*, 1; "Art and Anger Make Trouble," *Pittsburgh Post*, 4; "Many Paintings Rejected," *Pittsburgh Times*, 2 (all 7 November 1895).

20. H. S. Stevenson, Pittsburgh, 20 April 1896.

21. "All Records Broken," *Pittsburgh Dispatch*, 2 December 1895, 2; "To Stimulate Art Culture," *Pittsburgh Post*, 3 January 1896, 2.

22. Carnegie, New York, to Frew, 17 April 1896, quoted in full in "In the World of Art," *New York Times*, 26 April 1896, 22.

23. "More Cash for the Art Fund," *Pittsburgh Post*, 2 April 1896, 1; "Premium on Art," *Pittsburgh Leader*, 20 April 1896, 4; "Prize Offers," *Pittsburgh Dispatch*, 20 April 1896, 3; "In the World of Art," *New York Times*, 26 April 1896, 22.

24. "Prize Offers," *Pittsburgh Dispatch*, 20 April 1896, 3.

25. Beatty to Harry V. Allison, New York, 4 May 1896; A. J. Bell, San Jose, Calif., to A. Carnegie, New York, 13 April 1896.

26. "In the World of Art," *New York Times*, 26 April 1896, 22.

27. "More Cash for the Art Fund," *Pittsburgh Post*, 20 April 1896, 1; "In the World of Art," *New York Times*, 26 April 1896, 22.

28. F. D. Millet, New York, 5 May 1896; T. S. Clarke, New York, 22 April 1896; E. A. Abbey, Fairford, Glos., 31 May 1896; E. A. Abbey to William Burling Abbey, 9 June 1896, quoted in E. V. Lucas, *Edwin Austin Abbey, Royal Academician* (New York, 1921), 2:299.

29. Alexander, Paris, 23 July, 3, 14 September 1896.

30. Alexander, Paris, 3 September 1896; George Hitchcock, Egmond-am-Zee, Holland, 22 August 1896.

31. Alexander, Paris, 3 September 1896; "Pittsburg's Art Treasures," *Pittsburgh Post*, 29 November 1896, 7; "Artists not Suited," *Pittsburgh Leader*, 6 December 1896, 9.

32. "Gotham Artists Feel Aggrieved," *Pittsburgh Dispatch*, 2 November 1896, 5; "New York Artists Mad," *Pittsburgh Leader*, 3 November 1896, 7.

33. W. S. Budworth and Son, New York, 12, 13, 14, 16 October 1896 (CMOA Archives); Alexander, Paris, 13 September 1896.

34. Beatty, quoted in "Art and Science," *Pittsburgh Chronicle-Telegraph*, 3 November 1896 (William J. Holland Scrapbook, 1895–1897, Library of the Carnegie Museum of Natural History).

35. "Pittsburgh Art Exhibition," *Art Interchange* 37 (July–December 1896): 148.

36. Entry forms for 1896 (CMOA Archives).

37. Stuart MacDonald, "Art in Saint Louis," *Harper's Weekly* 39 (12 October 1895): 976–77; "Art in Saint Louis," *Harper's Weekly* 41 (23 October 1897): 1064.

38. Alexander, Paris, 17 April 1896.

39. J. Herlitz, Munich, 11 September 1896.

40. C. M. Kurtz, St. Louis, 27 October 1896; List of foreign works exhibited in St. Louis, with Beatty's selections marked, filed with 1896 entry forms (CMOA Archives).

41. "Pittsburgh Art Exhibition," *Art Interchange* 37 (July–December 1896): 148.

42. The lower estimate appears in ibid., and in John Angus MacKay, "The Standard Is High," *Pittsburgh Times*, 4 November 1896, 2. The higher number is in J. N. Fort, "Pictures Under Cover," *Philadelphia Item*, 25 November 1896, reprinted in *Pittsburgh Press*, 27 November 1896, 9. A typewritten list of works accepted and rejected filed in the CMOA archives with the 1896 entry forms confirms the figure given by Fort.

43. Harrison S. Morris, Philadelphia, 12 May, 10, 16, 21 November 1896. The original entry forms give a 12 December closing date, but many are accompanied by separate printed slips, signed by the artists, allowing their works to be exhibited until 1 January.

44. See, for example, Kenneth Frazer, New York, 16 November 1896; and Charles Paul Gruppe, Rochester, N.Y., 2, 16, 19 November 1896. The term "preferred exhibition" is used by Henry Mosler, New York, 11 January 1897, with "preferred" heavily underlined.

45. Frederick Freer, Chicago, 10, 17, 18, 24 November 1896.

46. Fort, "Pictures Under Cover"; "The Observer," *Art Interchange* 38 (January–June 1897): 18.

47. See Horatio Walker, Windsor, N.H., 20 August 1897; Kenyon Cox, New York, 5 April 1897.

48. "The Carnegie Art Gallery," *New York Times*, 6 November 1896, 5; "Pictures at Pittsburgh," *Harper's Weekly* 40 (14 November 1896): 1120; *Philadelphia Inquirer* review reprinted in "Art and Artists," *Pittsburgh Dispatch*, 13 December 1896, 26; I. M. McDougall, "Great Art Exhibit," *Chicago Evening Post*, 7 November 1896, reprinted in "Praise from the West," *Pittsburgh Times*, 16 November 1896, 3; "Pittsburgh Art Exhibition," *Art Interchange* 37 (July–December 1896): 147–48.

49. "First Fall Exhibit," *Pittsburgh Leader*, 1 November 1896, 5; John Angus MacKay, "The Standard Is High," *Pittsburgh Times*, 4 November 1896, 2; "Art at Carnegie Hall," *Pittsburgh Leader*, 5 November 1896, 4; "Treasures in High Art," *Pittsburgh Post*, 5 November 1896, 2; "Was a Happy Day for Mr. Carnegie," *Pittsburgh Dispatch*, 6 November 1896, 3. For the popularity of Fildes's *The Doctor*, see Arts Council of Great Britain, *Great Victorian Pictures* (1978 exhibition catalogue), 36.

50. W. G. Kaufmann, "First Annual Exhibitions of the Pittsburgh Carnegie Art Gallery," *Pittsburgh Dispatch*, 22 November 1896, 12.

51. L. M., "Manet and His School," *Pittsburgh Dispatch*, 15 November 1896, 4.

52. John Angus MacKay, "Twenty Freak Pictures," *Pittsburgh Times*, 7 November 1896, 4.

53. "Largest of the Season," *Pittsburgh Times*, 27 November 1896, 3.

54. "Will Soon Be Removed," *Pittsburgh Leader*, 24 November 1895, 5.

55. "Art Needs Encouragement," *Pittsburgh Dispatch*, 6 November 1896, 3; "Pittsburg's Art Treasures," *Pittsburgh Post*, 29 November 1896, 7; J. W. Beatty, *First Annual Report, January 13, 1897*, 2.

56. C. M. Kurtz, New York, 16 November 1896; H. S. Morris, Philadelphia, 10 November 1896.

57. C. Beaux, Philadelphia, 14 October 1896.

58. "Pittsburg's Art Treasures," *Pittsburgh Post*, 29 November 1896, 7. See David Brody, *Steelworkers in America* (New York, 1970), 43–44, for the wages of steelworkers in 1895 and 1900.

59. A. Burgoyne, "All Sorts," *Pittsburgh Leader*, 16 November 1896, 10.

60. "Pittsburg's Art Treasures," *Pittsburgh Post*, 29 November 1896, 7; "Like a Summer Day," *Pittsburgh Dispatch*, 23 November 1896, 8.

61. "$500 for an Art Guess," 10 November 1896, 1, 7; "The *Times* Art Prizes," 10 November 1896, 4 (both in *Pittsburgh Times*).

62. "That $500 for a Guess," *Pittsburgh Times*, 11 November 1896, 1; "All After That $500," *Pittsburgh Times*, 12 November 1896, 1; "Yesterday the Big Day," *Pittsburgh Times*, 13 November 1896, 3; "Pictures Will Be Marked," *Pittsburgh Dispatch*, 13 November 1896, 2; "Crowds Become Larger," *Pittsburgh Times*, 14 November 1896, 7; "Pictures All Marked," *Pittsburgh Times*, 16 November 1896, 3.

63. Fort, "Pictures Under Cover"; "New Paintings Hung," *Pittsburgh Times*, 28 November 1896, 7.

64. "All After That $500," 12 November 1896, 1; "Distinguished Guests," 21 November 1896, 7; "Scholars See the Pictures," 12 December 1896, 3 (all in *Pittsburgh Times*).

65. "The Best Works Here," 25 November 1896, 3; "The Galleries Crowded," 7 December 1896, 2 (both in *Pittsburgh Times*).

66. "Amateur Art Critics," 15 November 1896, 3; "Among the Pictures," 20 November 1896, 3 (both in *Pittsburgh Times*).

67. "Divided into Twenty-eight Parts," *Pittsburgh Times*, 15 December 1896, 1.

68. "Art Prizes Awarded," *Pittsburgh Times*, 5 December 1896, 1; "Pittsburg's Liberal Gifts to Painters of the World," *Pittsburgh Dispatch*, 5 December 1896, 3.

69. The design of the medal is discussed in a letter from J. C. Platt, treasurer of the Tiffany Glass and Decorating Company, New York, to John Caldwell, 23 June 1896.

70. "Treasures in High Art," 5 November 1896, 2; "Pittsburg's Art Treasures," 29 November 1896, 7 (both in *Pittsburgh Post*).

71. "Art News and Notes," *Pittsburgh Leader*, 8 November 1896, 9.

72. "Art Notes," *New York Sun*, 4 December 1896, 7.

73. "Artists Not Suited," *Pittsburgh Leader*, 6 December 1896, 9.

74. For the public reaction to the prizewinners, see "Art Prizes Awarded," 5 December 1896, 1; "Divided into Twenty-eight Parts," 15 December 1896, 4 (both in *Pittsburgh Times*).

75. "Artists Not Suited," *Pittsburgh Leader*, 6 December 1896, 4; "The Observer,"

*Art Interchange* 38 (January–June 1897): 18. ("Carnegie Gallery Prizes," *New York Times*, 6 December 1896, 1, is a typical out-of-town announcement of the winners.)

76. Alexander, Paris, 7 December 1896; Gari Melchers, Detroit, 19, 24 December 1896; S. H. Church to Beatty, 15 January 1897; Beatty to Melchers, 16 January 1897.

77. Alexander, Paris, 27 January 1897.

78. "Home from Paris," *Pittsburgh Dispatch*, 18 November 1896, 2; telegram from C. L. Freer, Waldorf Hotel, New York, 5 December 1896; "Bronzes Nearly Ready," *Pittsburgh Dispatch*, 8 March 1897.

79. Alexander, Paris, 13 September 1896; H. Johnston, Hotel Duquesne, Pittsburgh, n.d. [November 1896].

80. Beatty, *First Annual Report*, 4, 5.

81. J.-F. Raffaëlli, Paris, to Carnegie, New York, 18 January 1897. See also Raffaëlli's remarks to Beatty, 18 December 1896.

82. "Large Sum for an Art Gallery," 2 January 1896, 5; "In the World of Art," 26 April 1896, 22 (both in *New York Times*).

83. A. Harrison, Pont Aven, 1 January 1897; G. Hitchcock, Holland, 14 December 1896, 10 January, 14 February 1897; Guinchard et Fourniret, Paris, 27 November 1896; G. Boldini, Paris, 30 December 1896.

84. Alexander, Paris, 7 September 1897.

85. Beatty, *First Annual Report*, 2–3.

## Chapter 3

1. "A Great Art Gallery," *Pittsburgh Times*, 22 January 1897, 1; "The Chronicle of Arts," *Pittsburgh Leader*, 24 January 1897, 9.

2. H. R. Butler, typescript, n.d. [late 1896].

3. "A Great Art Gallery," *Pittsburgh Times*, 22 January 1897, 1; "The Chronicle of Arts," *Pittsburgh Leader*, 24 January 1897, 9; "Art Plans for Pittsburgh," *New York Times Saturday Review of Books and Art*, 30 January 1897, 4–5.

4. Carnegie quoted in "The Chronicle of Arts," *Pittsburgh Leader*, 24 January 1897, 9. "Art Plans for Pittsburg," *New York Times Saturday Review of Books and Art*, 30 January 1897, 4–5; "The Chronicle of Arts," *Pittsburgh Leader*, 24 January 1897, 9.

5. Detailed descriptions of the plan appear in "The Carnegie Institute," *New York Times Saturday Review of Books and Art*, 3 April 1897, 4, and in "Portfolio of Arts," *Pittsburgh Leader*, 18 April 1897, 12.

6. "Great Artist Will Pass upon Rare Paintings," *Pittsburgh Dispatch*, 20 September 1899; A. Carnegie, "The Progress of Eighteen Years," in *The Eighteenth Celebration of Founder's Day* (Pittsburgh, 1914), 15–16; J. Caldwell, Atlantic City, 25 February 1897.

7. Carnegie, *Triumphant Democracy*, 318. Detaille story quoted in *Memorial of the Celebration of the Carnegie Institute at Pittsburgh, Pennsylvania*, 60–61.

8. See, for example, "Artists' Jury for Pittsburg," *New York Times*, 30 September 1897, 5 ("the operation of this original and democratic plan is being watched with intense interest by artists everywhere"); the speech given by S. H. Church, secretary of

the board of trustees, on 3 November 1897, in which he describes the jury plan as "the most original and democratic ever devised" (*The Second Celebration of Founder's Day* [Pittsburgh, 1897], 15); and "American Studio Talk," *International Studio* 3 (October 1897): iv, where the jury plan is again described as "original and democratic."

9. For the salon jury, see Elizabeth Gilmore Holt, *The Art of All Nations, 1850–1873* (Garden City, N.Y., 1981), 2–5, 78, 112, 265; Jacques Lethève, *Daily Life of French Artists in the Nineteenth Century* (New York and Washington, 1972), 109–10; Geraldine Norman, *Nineteenth-Century Painters and Paintings* (Berkeley and Los Angeles, 1977), 87–88; John Rewald, *The History of Impressionism* (New York, 1961), 452. For the Society of American Artists, see Eliot Clark, *History of the National Academy of Design, 1825–1955* (New York, 1954), 106–07.

10. W. L. Palmer, Albany, N.Y., 24 August 1901; Beatty to Palmer, 31 August 1901.

11. "Artists' Jury for Pittsburg," *New York Times,* 30 September 1897, 5; W. Macbeth, New York, 2 December 1897; F. Freer, Chicago, 29 April 1898; Alexander, Paris, 2 February 1898; F. Benson, Boston, 4 February 1898; E. A. Abbey, Fairford, Glos., 16 February 1898; E. L. Weeks, Paris, 25 February 1898; W. Gay, Paris, 4 March 1898; G. Hitchcock, Egmond-am-Zee, Holland, 17 March 1899.

12. G. Hitchcock, Egmond-am-Zee, Holland, 17 March 1899; H. W. Ranger, East Lyme, Conn., 24 May 1899 (see also his letters of 10 September 1896, 26 March 1898, 28 October 1899, and 12 September 1900).

13. F. Benson, 4 February 1898; W. McConway, 24 July 1897; Beatty to McConway, 26 July 1897.

14. D. W. Tryon, New York, 17 April 1897; Beatty to Tryon, 20 April 1897; Tryon, South Dartmouth, Mass., 24 April, 3 August, 3 September 1897.

15. Tryon, South Dartmouth, Mass., 1 September 1898; R. Knoedler, Paris, 8 August 1898; Tryon, South Dartmouth, Mass., 30 September 1898.

16. R. C. Minor, New York, 20 April 1897; C. S. Pearce, Paris, n.d. [late winter, 1898]. The figures for 1901 appear in Beatty's *Sixth Annual Report,* submitted 1 April 1902, 7. Of the 509 works received by the jury, 357 were considered for acceptance, honors, and position; 45 for acceptance and position; 80 for honors and position; 6 for honors only; and 21 for position only. The works not considered for acceptance were those that had already been accepted by the foreign advisory committees.

17. "American Studio Notes," *International Studio* 9 (November 1899): xx; H. S. Morris, Philadelphia, 3 October 1900.

18. Austin E. Howland, "The Pittsburgh Art Exhibition," *Brush and Pencil* 7 (December 1900): 130; Alexander, Paris, August 1898; J. B. Cauldwell, New York, 19 August 1899.

19. Alexander, Paris, 2 February 1898.

20. For the William Stott story, see "Are Ready for Their Hard Work," *Pittsburgh Press,* 12 October 1899; "Work of Artists Is with the Jury," *Pittsburgh News,* 12 October 1899. (The one juror with whom Stott was unacquainted was William Meritt Chase.) For the Frank Duveneck story, see J. W. Beatty, "Recollection of an Intimate Friend-

ship" (1923–1924), in Lloyd Goodrich, *Winslow Homer* (New York, 1944), 219. For the Cecilia Beaux story, see Cecilia Beaux, *Background with Figures* (Boston and New York, 1930), 211–12.

21. For "honor and distinction," see W. Homer to Thomas S. Clarke, May 1897, quoted in Goodrich, *Winslow Homer*, 140–41. For "Mr. Beatty," see Frank Benson, quoted in Goodrich, *Winslow Homer*, 152. According to Beatty, Homer "was always prompt in attendance, quick in his decisions, and earnest in the performance of every official duty, even to the point of objecting to any interruption of the work." For the stands of corn, see Beaux, *Background with Figures*, 212.

22. Goodrich, *Winslow Homer*, 152, 167–68; "Carnegie Is Adding to Art Collection," *Pittsburgh Dispatch*, 12 October 1901; "Marvelous Energy Astonished Them," *Pittsburgh Leader*, 18 October 1901.

23. "Pittsburg Art Is Praised by Famous Judges," *Pittsburgh Dispatch*, 12 October 1899; "Are Ready for Their Hard Work," *Pittsburgh Press*, 12 October 1899; "Center Is Here Says Raffaëlli," *Pittsburgh Post*, 14 October 1899. Carnegie's views on Anglo-American reunification are set forth in "A Look Ahead," *North American Review* 156 (June 1893): 685–710.

24. "Pictures from Pittsburg for Paris Salon," *Pittsburgh Dispatch*, 16 October 1899; "Discoursed on Art," *Pittsburgh Commercial Gazette*, 17 October 1899; "Carnegie Art Exhibit About Ready to Open," *Pittsburgh Dispatch*, 31 October 1899; W. M. Chase, "The Utility of Art," in *The Fourth Celebration of Founder's Day* (Pittsburgh, 1899), 27–29; "Founder's Day Celebration a Big Success," *Pittsburgh Dispatch*, 3 November 1899, 1, 6, 7; "Stimulating Interest in Big Addition," *Pittsburgh Dispatch*, 4 November 1899, 6.

25. J.-F. Raffaëlli, "Beautiful Gems of Art Described by a Master," *Pittsburgh Dispatch*, 2 November 1899, 7. For his addresses to the Art Students League and the Twentieth Century Club, see "Pictures from Pittsburgh for Paris Salon," *Pittsburgh Dispatch*, 16 October 1899; "Discoursed on Art," *Pittsburgh Commercial Gazette*, 17 October 1899; "No Girl Model," *Pittsburgh Dispatch*, 24 October 1899. For his Founder's Day speech, J.-F. Raffaëlli, "The International Idea of Art," *The Fourth Celebration of Founder's Day* (Pittsburgh, 1899), 26–27.

26. "Will Be Ready for Jury," *Pittsburgh Post*, 11 October 1899; "Pictures from Pittsburgh for Paris Salon," *Pittsburgh Dispatch*, 16 October 1899. For Pittsburgh women, see "Sketches Made from Interior of a Carriage," *Pittsburgh Dispatch*, 20 October 1899; "No Girl Model," *Pittsburgh Dispatch*, 24 October 1899; editorial, "A Typical American Girl," *Pittsburgh News*, 24 October 1899; "Northside Girl for His Model," *Pittsburgh Post*, 26 October 1899; "Has Chosen No Model," *Pittsburgh Leader*, 26 October 1899; "Painting It for the Show," *Pittsburgh Post*, 27 October 1899; "Carnegie Art Exhibit About Ready to Open," *Pittsburgh Dispatch*, 31 October 1899.

27. "The Art Center," *Pittsburgh Leader*, 11 October 1899; "Pictures from Pittsburg for Paris Salons," *Pittsburgh Dispatch*, 16 October 1899; "A Pittsburg Picture," *Pittsburgh Leader*, 18 October 1899; "Famous Artist Will Paint Here," *Pittsburgh Post*, 18 October 1899; "Sketches Made from Interior of a Carriage," *Pittsburgh Dispatch*, 20 October

1899; "No Girl Model," *Pittsburgh Dispatch*, 24 October 1899; "Painting It for the Show," *Pittsburgh Post*, 27 October 1899; "Carnegie Exhibit About Ready to Open," *Pittsburgh Dispatch*, 31 October 1899.

28. "Exhibition Pictures Painted on the Spot," *Pittsburgh Press*, 19 October 1899; " 'Oh, We Have a Great Variety of Weather Here, Mr. Raffaëlli,' " *Pittsburgh Chronicle-Telegraph*, 19 October 1899; Arthur Burgoyne, "All Sorts," *Pittsburgh Leader*, 16 October 1899. For the attempt to interest Raffaëlli in the East End, see "Sketches Made from Interior of a Carriage," *Pittsburgh Dispatch*, 20 October 1899; "Painting It for the Show," *Pittsburgh Post*, 27 October 1899. For the remarks on Press Review Night, see "Pittsburg's Intelligence and Culture Were There," *Pittsburgh Dispatch*, 1 November 1899, 2.

29. R. Allan, London, 2 December 1901. During his stay in Pittsburgh, he said that the jury system came "as near perfection as possible" and that he was proud to claim Carnegie as a "brother Scot" ("The System of Awards Praised by Juror Allan," *Pittsburgh Dispatch*, 8 November 1901). For Alexander Harrison, see A. Harrison, Pont Aven, 1 January 1897; Percival Phillips, "Two Jury Members for Art Exhibit Reach America," *Pittsburgh Dispatch*, 8 October 1900; "Leave for Pittsburg To-Day," *Pittsburgh Post*, 10 October 1900; "Art Jury Takes First Glance at Carnegie Gems," *Pittsburgh Dispatch*, 12 October 1900; A. Harrison, Chicago, n.d. [November–December 1900].

30. For Thaulow, see "Praise from Thaulow," *Pittsburgh Commercial Gazette*, 12 September 1899; "Thaulow's Views of Us," *Pittsburgh Times*, 12 September 1899; "Art and Artists," *Pittsburgh Leader*, 17 September 1899. For Weeks, see E. L. Weeks, "Art Exhibition at the Carnegie Institute, Pittsburg," *Harper's Weekly* 41 (20 November 1897): 1153–54; Weeks, New York, 11 November 1897.

31. J. Lavery, New York, 9 October 1898, and London, 9 November 1898, 19 July 1899; G. Hitchcock, 17 March 1899; John Lavery, *The Life of a Painter* (Boston, 1940), 241–42.

32. For Homer, see Philip C. Beam, *Winslow Homer at Prout's Neck* (Boston, 1966), 154. The anecdote was told by Edmund Tarbell, who also served on the 1897 jury. For Raffaëlli, see "Americans Winners," *Pittsburgh Post*, 21 October 1899. For "Madder Brown," see "Patricio," Letter to the Editor, *Pittsburgh News*, 27 October 1899.

33. The jury process is most fully described in "Jury of Award Being Impaneled," *Pittsburgh Post*, 11 October 1900, and Clarence Johns, "The Jury and Its Methods," *Pittsburgh Index*, 9 December 1901.

34. F. Benson, Boston, 4 February 1898.

35. H. W. Ranger, 12 September 1900; "American Studio Talk," *International Studio* 3 (1897–1898): viii.

36. "Art and Artists," *Pittsburgh Dispatch*, 24 September 1899. Frank Brangwyn, although elected, was unable to serve because of a recent illness (F. Brangwyn, London, 30 September 1899) and was replaced by another Englishman, William Stott. [Samuel Swift], "The Three Prizewinning Pictures Shown at Carnegie Institute, Pittsburg," *New York Mail and Express Illustrated Saturday Magazine*, 9 November 1901.

37. Samuel Swift, "Pittsburg Art Show," *New York Mail and Express*, 7 November

1901 (CMOA Archives); A. L. Merritt, London, September 1899; G. H. Boughton, Cambridge, England, 8 August 1900.

38. M. J. Heade, St. Augustine, Fla., 4 September 1897; M. Knoedler and Company, New York, 4 October 1901; Beatty to Knoedler and Company, 12 October 1901; R. S. Gifford, New York, 12 May 1899.

39. W. T. Mossman, "Carnegie Art Show," 3 November 1897, 14; "Pittsburg Artists," 21 March 1897, 12; "The Works of Local Artists," 20 January 1901 (all in *Pittsburgh Leader*).

40. "The Art Association," 7 March 1897, 14; "Pittsburg Artists," 21 March 1897, 12; "The Works of Local Artists," 20 January 1901 (all in *Pittsburgh Leader*). See also Beatty's offer on 14 February 1898 to Charles Walz, secretary of the association, and Walz's reply of 1 March 1898.

41. H. S. Stevenson cited in "The Works of Local Artists," *Pittsburgh Leader*, 20 January 1901.

42. This view was expressed in an editorial, "The Jury at Work," *Pittsburgh Chronicle-Telegraph*, 13 October 1899.

43. "Painting the Impressionistic," *Pittsburgh Leader*, 18 March 1900.

44. "Ridicules the Great Raffaëlli," *Pittsburgh Leader*, 26 November 1899. King was against the whole idea of the annual exhibitions from the start. In 1894 he had said that Carnegie's endowment ought to be used primarily to purchase at least one painting a year from every competent local artist ("Future of Art in Pittsburg," *Pittsburgh Dispatch*, 30 December 1894, 17). He also hoped that the Fine Arts Committee would not be dominated by "men with so-called 'high art' ideas, whose imaginative powers are so wonderfully developed that they are able to see upon a canvas a beautiful, fleecy group of Washington County sheep where the ordinary observer sees but a pile of stones; who see merit only in the work of such masters as Diaz, Daubigny, Corot, etc." This was an attack on A. Bryan Wall, whose favorite subject was flocks of Washington County sheep and whose style was derived from "Diaz, Daubigny, Corot, etc." According to the 1899 interview, King's own tastes ran to the academicism of Gérôme, Alma-Tadema, and Bouguereau.

45. E. W. Ahrens, Philadelphia, 9 November 1901. For Maurer, Ahrens, and Carspecken, see C. H. Caffin, "The Sixth Annual Exhibition, Carnegie Institute," *Harper's Weekly* 45 (23 November 1901): 1184; Caffin, "American Studio Notes," *International Studio* 13 (December 1901): xxxix–xlviii; A. E. Howland, "Pittsburgh's Sixth International Art Exhibition," *Brush and Pencil* 9, no. 3 (December 1901): 134, 143; Swift, "Pittsburg Art Show," *New York Mail and Express*, 7 November 1901 (CMOA Archives); Swift, "Portraits in Pittsburgh," *New York Mail and Express*, 14 November 1901; Swift, "The Three Prizewinning Pictures," *New York Mail and Express Illustrated Saturday Magazine*, 9 November 1901; "Carnegie Pictures," *New York Commercial Advertiser*, 8 November 1901; "Picture Exhibition at Pittsburgh," *New York Sun*, 8, 12, 14 November 1901; "Art Display at the Big Institute Is the Best Yet," *Pittsburgh Dispatch*, 7 November 1901; Ida A. Smith, "The First Glimpse," *Pittsburgh Post*, 7 November 1901;

"List of Paintings to Be Exhibited at the Carnegie Galleries," *Pittsburgh Times*, 22 October 1901.

46. "Carnegie's Liberality," *Philadelphia Item*, 22 November 1901; "Editorial Comment," *Art International* 48 (January 1902): 12; "Artistic Career Is Quickly Killed," *Pittsburgh Gazette*, 18 July 1905, 5.

47. Carnegie, New York, telegram to Frew, Pittsburgh, 4 November 1895, quoted in Wall, *Carnegie*, 817.

48. F. Benson, Salem, Mass., 7 October 1897; J. De Camp, Boston, 14 December, ca. 16 December 1897; J. Sharp, Cincinnati, 20 September 1898. The French artist Jules Meunier told Beatty (29 June 1901) that he had decided against sending his *Bathers* after someone told him that it might be considered shocking, but he was referring to American prudishness in general rather than to Pittsburgh prudishness in particular.

49. Pearce, Paris, 30 October 1898.

50. E. A. Abbey, Fairford, Glos., 2 December 1897.

51. F. D. Millet, Broadway, Glos., 9 October 1901.

52. Pearce, Paris, 3 October 1901.

53. G. Weisberg, "Tastemaking in Pittsburgh," *Carnegie Magazine* 56, no. 10 (July–August 1983): 25.

54. Writing from Eragnez-Barincourt on 9 June 1898, Pissarro told Beatty, "It is understood that I cannot accept, for the reasons I have explained to you, your invitation to take part in the jury of which you spoke to me." A few days later, writing to his son Lucien, Pissarro described Beatty as "a charming man" and informed him of the invitation, adding, "Naturally I declined, out of principle." C. Pissarro, Paris, to L. Pissarro, 18 June 1898, in C. Pissarro, *Letters to His Son Lucien*, ed. John Rewald (Santa Barbara, 1981), 422.

55. Alexander, Paris, 10 September 1897; Guinchard et Fourniret, shipping agents, Paris, 8 September 1899.

56. J. W. Beatty, *Report of the Director of the Department of Fine Arts to the Fine Arts Committee, 22 July 1897*, 2; M. Cassatt to H. S. Morris, Philadelphia, 29 August 1904, quoted in Frederick A. Sweet, *Miss Mary Cassatt, Impressionist from Pennsylvania* (Norman, Okla., 1966), 166. According to Alexander, 10 September 1897, "old Puvis" failed to attend because "he is off on his wedding tour, the giddy young thing." Cassatt explained to Harrison S. Morris that she had accepted the appointment "only because Whistler suggested it," and that her principal motive had been to persuade the Carnegie Institute "to buy some really fine Old Masters to create a standard. In this hope I was naturally disappointed."

57. Beatty to Pearce, 18 September 1900; Pearce, Paris, 6 October 1900.

58. Pearce, Paris, 3 October 1901.

59. J. Saint-Germier, Biskra, Algeria, 29 November 1901; M. Demont, Paris, 7 October 1901; H. Martin, Paris, January 1902; P. Dannoye, Paris, 10 October 1901; Pearce, Paris, 3 October 1901.

60. Pearce, Paris, 30 October 1898 (see also 6 October 1900, 3 October 1901); Alexander, Paris, 7 September 1897.

61. W. Gay, Paris, 16 September 1898; A. F. King, "Ridicules the Great Raffaëlli," *Pittsburgh Leader,* 26 November 1899; A. Woodward, "The Paris Salon and Its Pictures," *Pittsburgh Dispatch,* 4 February 1900; Frew quoted in "Stimulating Interest in Big Addition," *Pittsburgh Dispatch,* 4 November 1899, 6; Guinchard et Fourniret, Paris, 8 September 1899.

62. Alexander, Val-de-la-Haye, France, 22 September 1898, Paris, 25 February 1900, and New York, 27 March 1901; Beatty to Alexander, 29 March 1901. For one of Alexander's typical effusions on the Pittsburgh exhibition, see "Finest of the Year," *Pittsburgh Commercial Gazette,* 29 November 1898.

63. Alexander, Paris, ca. March 1900; Beatty to Alexander, 22 March 1901.

64. M. Fisher, London, 30 October 1898; A. East, London, 28 August 1898; J. M. Hamilton, London, 30 September 1898; G. Sauter, London, 17 October 1898; F. D. Millet, Broadway, Glos., 7 September 1899.

65. Dicksee and Company, London, 15, 22 September 1897; H. H. La Thangue, 21 September 1897. For other instances when paintings requested by Beatty were rejected, see R. Bunny, Finistere, 16 September 1897; H. Muhrman, London, 16 September 1897; M. P. Lindner, Dordrecht, Holland, 17 September 1897; F. Brangwyn, London, 21 September 1897; G. Sauter, London, 17 October 1898.

66. J. W. Beatty, *Report of the Director of the Department of Fine Arts to the Fine Arts Committee,* 1; H. Muhrman, London, 16 September 1897.

67. F. Brown, London, 27 July 1901.

68. Beatty to F. von Lenbach, Munich, n.d. [late May–early June] 1900; T. Rosenthal, Munich, 5 September 1900; C. Marr, Munich, 9 September 1900; Beatty, Paris, to C. Marr, Munich, 29 June 1901.

69. C. Marr, Munich, 29 August 1897, 9 September 1900; T. Rosenthal, Munich, 5 September 1900. For accounts of damage, see E. Friant, Paris, n.d. [June 1897]; G. Courtois, Paris, 30 May 1898; G. H. Herlitz, shipping agent, Munich, 18 April 1899; C. Fairchild, New York, 9 January 1900; Dicksee and Company, shipping agent, London, 7 February, 9 March 1900, 14 March, 29 October, 12 December 1901; F. Bridgman, Divonne-les-Bains, France, 22 August 1900; H. Breckenridge, Philadelphia, 10 October 1900, 24 January 1901; La Société des Beaux-Arts, Glasgow, 28 February 1901.

70. C. Marr, Munich, 9 September 1900.

71. "Loud with Their Praise," *Pittsburgh Dispatch,* 15 November 1895, 4.

72. F. Bridgman, Divonne-les-Bains, France, 22 August 1900; W. McEwen, secretary, Paris Society of American Painters, n.d. [late winter 1898]; W. H. Low, Bronxville, N.Y., 13 October 1898; A. L. Merritt, Andover, England, September 1899.

73. "Bought Some More Pictures," *Pittsburgh Dispatch,* 15 December 1896, 9; Editorial, "The Art Galleries," *Pittsburgh Post,* 16 December 1896, 4.

74. Beatty, *Second Annual Report of the Director of the Carnegie Institute Department of*

*Fine Arts,* 1 April 1898, 6; Beatty, letter to A. Carnegie, New York, 20 February 1899; Beatty, letter to W. A. Reaser, New York, 21 February 1901.

75. Carnegie and his wife spent the entire period from May 1897 to October 1898 in Europe (Wall, *Carnegie,* 719). "Carnegie Views the Paintings," *Pittsburgh News,* 18 November 1899.

76. "Many Pictures Sold," *Pittsburgh Dispatch,* 28 January 1899 (this article appeared with minor variations in the *Pittsburgh Chronicle-Telegraph, Pittsburgh Commercial Gazette, Pittsburgh Press,* and *Pittsburgh Times* for the same date); B. Foster, New York, to H. C. Frick, Pittsburgh, 2 March 1898; W. A. Reaser, New York, 17 February 1901; Beatty to Reaser, New York, 21 February 1901.

77. Beatty to A. Carnegie, n.d. [November 1899]; "Fine Paintings Sold," *Pittsburgh Commercial Gazette,* 1 January 1900.

78. "Carnegie Pleased," *Pittsburgh Leader,* 13 November 1900; "The Many-Sided Carnegie," *Pittsburgh Times,* 16 February 1901; "Artists Realized $18,319," *New York Times,* 18 January 1902, 1.

79. "Fine Arts Committee Meets," *Pittsburgh Times,* 10 January 1899; "Many Pictures Sold," *Pittsburgh Dispatch,* 28 January 1899; "Fine Paintings Sold," *Pittsburgh Commercial Gazette,* 1 January 1900; "Master Works of Art to Stay in Pittsburg," *Pittsburgh Dispatch,* 6 January 1900; H. H. Gallison, Boston, 23 November 1900; J. P. Downie, Glasgow, 21 December 1900; "Pittsburgers Buy Pictures," *Pittsburgh Post,* 18 January 1901; R. Vonnoh, Rockland Lake, N.Y., 28 October 1901; Beatty to E. Aman-Jean, Paris, 30 December 1901; "Artists Realized $18,319," *New York Times,* 18 January 1902, 1.

80. J. A. Israel, "Art in Pittsburgh," *Pittsburgh Dispatch,* 20 December 1896, 12. This was a frequent complaint among provincial American artists. It often appeared, for example, in the pages of *Arts for America,* published by the Chicago-based Central Art Association. In 1898 Ralph Clarkson, a prominent portraitist, excoriated those "who love Chicago and who will not admit that it is second in anything; yet they spend much time away from here, and money on works of art no better and ofttimes not as good as what they might find here." See R. Clarkson, "The Art Situation in Chicago," *Arts for America* 7 (1898): 270; also "How to Make Chicago an Art Center," *Arts for America* 7 (1897): 107, and Charles Francis Browne, "Chicago, 1897," *Arts for America* 7 (1898): 300–02.

81. W. M. Chase, "The Utility of Art," in *The Fourth Celebration of Founder's Day* (Pittsburgh, 1899), 28–29; "Founder's Day Celebration a Big Success," *Pittsburgh Dispatch,* 3 November 1899, 1, 6, 7; "Stimulating Interest in Big Addition," *Pittsburgh Dispatch,* 4 November 1899, 6.

82. "Art Stores Busy," *Pittsburgh Leader,* 27 December 1896, 5; "Annual Exhibit Greatly Assists Local Art Trade," *Pittsburgh Dispatch,* 30 October 1899, 12; "Artists and Their Work," *Pittsburgh Dispatch,* 12 November 1899.

83. Beatty, London, to Carnegie, Skibo Castle, Scotland, 28 June 1899; "Europe Will Be Searched for Art Treasures," *Pittsburgh Dispatch,* 23 May 1900.

84. See Beatty, *Second Annual Report*, 1 April 1898, 4; *Third Annual Report*, 1 April 1899, 5; *Fourth Annual Report*, 1 April 1900, 1–2.

85. *Eighth Annual Report*, 1 April 1903, 10; *Fifteenth Annual Report*, 1 April 1911, 28–29; *Eighteenth Annual Report*, 1 April 1914, 11–12; *Twentieth Annual Report*, 1 April 1916, 16; *Twenty-fifth Annual Report*, 1 July 1921, 17; *Twenty-sixth Annual Report*, 1 July 1922, 9, and Letter of Transmittal.

86. Carnegie, "The Best Use of Wealth," 213. *Carnegie Fine Arts and Museum Collection Fund: Constitution and By-Laws of the Board of Trustees Together with Mr. Carnegie's Letter and Deed of Trust* (Pittsburgh, 1907), 12–13.

87. Typescript (March 1944) of extracts regarding the chronological collection from the minutes of the board of trustees (Carnegie Institute, MOA Archives); Beatty, *Sixth Annual Report*, 1 April 1902, 2.

88. Beatty, undated memorandum regarding revision of Carnegie Institute bylaws, ca. 1919–1921; "American Painters Are Given High Rank in Paris," *Pittsburgh Post*, 9 July 1900.

89. Beatty to A. Carnegie. n.d. [November 1899].

90. "Have Two Tryon Pictures," *Pittsburgh Times*, 2 March 1899.

91. Frances B. Sheafer, "The Pittsburgh Exhibition," *Brush and Pencil* 5, no. 3 (December 1899): 129.

92. Simon's work met a singularly unhappy fate: on 28 December 1904, while traveling to an exhibition at the Art Institute of Chicago, it was destroyed in a train wreck at Sherwood, Ohio. See V. A. Clark, "Collecting from the Internationals," *Carnegie Magazine* 56, no. 5 (September–October 1982): 22. A feature article in the *Pittsburgh Leader* focused on Tanner's success in "overcoming the impediment of race prejudice and compelling recognition" ("Artist Tanner Is Native Pittsburger," 14 January 1900). [I. A. Smith], "Six Paintings Will Stay Here," *Pittsburgh Post*, 6 January 1900.

93. C. H. Caffin, "The Pittsburgh Exhibition—First Notice," *New York Evening Post*, 2 November 1900, 7; Howland, "The Pittsburgh Art Exhibition," *Brush and Pencil* 7 (December 1900): 143; Ida A. Smith, "Lovers of Fine Art Attend Press View," *Pittsburgh Post*, 1 November 1900; A. Hoeber, "Pittsburg's Exhibition," *New York Commercial Advertiser*, 2 November 1900, 7; "Four Pictures Purchased for Carnegie Galleries," *Pittsburgh Times*, 17 January 1901; "Sale of Art Works," *Pittsburgh Dispatch*, 18 January 1901; "Pictures Chosen," *Pittsburgh News*, 17 January 1901.

94. C. H. Caffin, "The Pittsburgh Exhibition—Second Notice," *New York Evening Post*, 6 November 1900, 5; "Very Few Pleasure Seekers Were Out," *Pittsburgh Dispatch*, 14 February 1901.

95. S. Kendall, New York, n.d. [November–December 1900]; C. H. Caffin, "The Pittsburg Exposition," *New York Evening Post*, 4 November 1898, 5; "Vedder Canvas for the Gallery," *Pittsburgh Post*, 7 April 1901.

96. Caffin, "American Studio Notes," *International Studio* 13 (December 1901): xlii; Howland, "Pittsburg's Sixth International Art Exhibition," *Brush and Pencil* 9, no. 3 (December 1901): 137–38; "Society Got a First Peep at the Paintings,"

*Pittsburgh Leader,* 7 November 1901; "Press View of the Galleries," *Pittsburgh Gazette,* 7 November 1901.

## Chapter 4

1. W. T. Mossman, "Carnegie Art Show," *Pittsburgh Leader,* 3 November 1897; "Pittsburg's Intelligence and Culture Were There," *Pittsburgh Dispatch,* 1 November 1899, 2.

2. "Pleb," Letter to the Editor, *Pittsburgh Leader,* 2 November 1897; "Crowds Viewed Prize Pictures," *Pittsburgh Post,* 3 November 1899, p. 2.

3. Wu Ting Fang, "Educational Ideals in and out of China," *The Fifth Celebration of Founder's Day at the Carnegie Institute* (Pittsburgh, 1900), 17.

4. J.-F. Raffaëlli, "The International Idea of Art," and W. M. Chase, "The Utility of Art," in *The Fourth Celebration of Founder's Day at the Carnegie Institute* (Pittsburgh, 1899), 23–29; A. Zorn, "Art Comprehension and Application," in *The Fifth Celebration of Founder's Day at the Carnegie Institute* (Pittsburgh, 1900), 29–31; J. W. Alexander, "Our Tariff Against Art," and R. W. Allan, "A Word About the Institute," in *The Sixth Celebration of Founder's Day at the Carnegie Institute* (Pittsburgh, 1901), 28–33.

5. J. Jefferson in *The Fourth Celebration of Founder's Day at the Carnegie Institute* (Pittsburgh, 1899), 34–35; *The Sixth Celebration of Founder's Day at the Carnegie Institute* (Pittsburgh, 1901), 34–36; *The Seventh Celebration of Founder's Day at the Carnegie Institute* (Pittsburgh, 1902), 34. In a letter to Beatty dated 4 May 1900, Jefferson promised to paint a large picture for the galleries, but nothing ever came of this.

6. *The Second Celebration of Founder's Day at the Carnegie Institute* (Pittsburgh, 1897), 30–31; "President Proclaims the Winners," *Pittsburgh Post,* 4 November 1897; "Reception by President," *Pittsburgh Dispatch,* 4 November 1897; "Pittsburg's Great Day," *Pittsburgh Times,* 4 November 1897; "Wu's Message to Americans," *Pittsburgh Leader,* 1 November 1900.

7. Beatty, *Seventh Annual Report,* 1 April 1903, 10; Beatty, "Art Relation of Carnegie Institute," *Pittsburgh Dispatch,* 18 October 1899.

8. G.M.I., "A Talk with John W. Beatty About the Carnegie Art Gallery," *Library,* 8 September 1900; "Art Study for Public Schools," *Pittsburgh Press,* 14 April 1901.

9. "Will Soon Be Removed," *Pittsburgh Leader,* 4 November 1895, 5; Beatty, *First Annual Report,* 13 January 1897, 2.

10. J. Ralston, Pittsburgh, 24 October 1900; "Students Will Study Art in Local Galleries," *Pittsburgh Dispatch,* 12 November 1900; "Study of Fine Paintings," *Pittsburgh Commercial Gazette,* 15 November 1900; Beatty, *Fifth Annual Report,* 1 April 1901, 8–9; *Sixth Annual Report,* 1 April 1902, 11.

11. E. Knaufft, "Fine Arts at the Carnegie Institute, Pittsburgh," *American Monthly Review of Reviews* 28, no. 6 (December 1903): 681–82; Beatty, "International Exhibitions," paper read at the dedication of the Museum of Fine Arts building, Boston, 9 November 1909, reprinted in *Fourteenth Annual Report,* 1 April 1910, 37–38; Beatty, *Eighteenth Annual Report,* 1 April 1914, 21–24.

12. According to figures from the U.S. Department of Education's National Center for Education Statistics (cited in the 1991 *World Almanac*, 207), only 3.3 percent of all school-age Americans were enrolled in public high schools. The comparable figure for 1987–1988 was 30.2 percent.

13. *The Pittsburgh Survey*, cited in Brody, *Steelworkers in America*, 34–39, 43–48, 93–94. For the exhibitions in New York and Boston, see "The East Side Loan Exhibition," *Critic* 20 (25 June 1892): 357; M. H., "Art and the People," *Harper's Weekly* 37 (29 April 1893): 394–95; "The East Side Free Art Exhibition," *Critic* 26 (11 May 1895): 346–47; A. C. Bernheim, "Results of Picture Exhibitions in Lower New York," in "Successful Efforts to Teach Art to the Masses," *Forum* 19 (July 1895): 610–14.

14. G. M. I., "A Talk with John W. Beatty About the Carnegie Art Gallery," *Library*, 8 September 1900; Beatty, *First Annual Report*, 13 January 1897, 2; *Eighteenth Annual Report*, 1 April 1914, 9. See also *Third Annual Report*, 1 April 1899, 3; "Art Exhibition Brings Much Mail," *Pittsburgh Dispatch*, 30 January 1899; "Art Viewers Break Attendance Records," *Pittsburgh Post*, 5 December 1899; "Pittsburgers Break Record," *Pittsburgh Post*, 1 January 1900; *Sixteenth Annual Report*, 1 April 1912, 11.

15. Horowitz, *Culture and the City*, 105–06.

16. Beatty, *First Annual Report*, 13 January 1897, 2; *Third Annual Report*, 1 April 1899, 3; "Remarkable Attendance," *Pittsburgh Leader*, 11 November 1899; "Art Viewers Break Attendance Records," *Pittsburgh Post*, 5 December 1899; "300,000 Saw the Pictures," *Pittsburgh Times*, 30 December 1899; "Best Yet Held," *Pittsburgh Dispatch*, 1 January 1900.

17. "Pittsburgers Break Record," *Pittsburgh Post*, 1 January 1900; Beatty, *Fourth Annual Report*, 1 April 1900, 3; G. M. I., "A Talk with John W. Beatty," *Library*, 8 September 1900; *Seventh Annual Report*, 1 April 1903, 12–13; *Eighth Annual Report*, 1 April 1905, 13.

18. "Many Park Attractions," *Pittsburgh Times*, 7 November 1898; "Great Crowds Thronged the Art Galleries," *Pittsburgh Dispatch*, 6 November 1899, 5; "Remarkable Attendance," *Pittsburgh Leader*, 11 November 1899; "Art and Artists," *Pittsburgh Leader*, 12 November 1899; "Crowds Break Record," *Pittsburgh Times*, 13 November 1899; "Excursions Were Big," *Pittsburgh Times*, 20 November 1899; "The Best of All," *Pittsburgh Commercial Gazette*, 20 November 1899; "Rain and Mud Discouraged Park Visitors," *Pittsburgh Dispatch*, 4 December 1899; "Many Saw the Pictures," *Pittsburgh Chronicle-Telegraph*, 12 November 1900; "Pittsburgers at the Art Galleries," *Pittsburgh Post*, 25 November 1900; "Art Exhibition Will Draw Large Crowds Until Close," *Pittsburgh Post*, 29 December 1901.

19. "Crowds Break Records," *Pittsburgh Times*, 13 November 1899; F. Parry, "Secluded Art Gems," *Pittsburgh Dispatch*, 3 December 1900. For similar descriptions, see "Great Crowds Thronged the Art Galleries," *Pittsburgh Dispatch*, 6 November 1899, 5; "Twenty Thousand People Visited the Institute," *Pittsburgh Dispatch*, 5 November 1900.

20. "Pittsburgers at the Art Galleries," *Pittsburgh Post*, 25 November 1900.

21. "Lovers of Nature Find It Difficult to Concede Painters the Right of Distortion," *Pittsburgh Times*, 10 November 1899; "Pittsburgers at the Art Galleries," *Pittsburgh Post*, 25 November 1900; G. R. Harlow, Wilkinsburg, 18 November 1899. For the public school art exhibitions and distribution of photographs, see Beatty, *Sixth Annual Report*, 1 April 1902, 10–12; for children's art hour, see *Eighteenth Annual Report*, 1 April 1914, 26.

22. "Popular vs. Artistic Ideas," *Pittsburgh Times*, 4 November 1898; "The Art Show," *Pittsburgh Commercial Gazette*, 7 November 1900; "Lovers of Nature Find It Difficult to Concede Painters the Right of Distortion," *Pittsburgh Times*, 10 November 1899.

23. "The Pictures Best Beloved of the People," *Pittsburgh Dispatch*, 3 December 1899.

24. "No Diminution of Crowds," *Pittsburgh Dispatch*, 19 November 1899.

25. G. M. I., "A Talk with John W. Beatty," *Library*, 8 September 1900.

26. "Popular vs. Artistic Ideas," *Pittsburgh Times*, 4 November 1898.

27. "The Art Show," *Pittsburgh Commercial Gazette*, 7 November 1900; "Pittsburgers at the Art Galleries," *Pittsburgh Post*, 25 November 1900.

28. "People Peer at Prize Pictures and Praise Them," *Pittsburgh Dispatch*, 9 November 1901; H. Nickleman, "The Philistine in the Art Gallery," *Pittsburgh Gazette*, 17 November 1901; "Abbey's Picture Much Admired," *Pittsburgh Press*, 24 November 1901.

29. "No Diminution of Crowds," *Pittsburgh Dispatch*, 19 November 1899.

30. C. H. Caffin, *The Story of American Painting* (New York, 1907), 269.

31. H. C. Frick to Frew, 9 July 1898; "H. C. Frick's Great Gift," *Pittsburgh Times*, 4 November 1898.

32. "Disciples at Emmaus," *Pittsburgh Times*, 7 November 1898; "Religion in Art" and "Carnegie Institute," *Pittsburgh Commercial Gazette*, 7 November 1898; "A Clerical Criticism," *Pittsburgh Commercial Gazette*, 21 November 1898.

33. W. N. Frew, "Preparing for the Big Art Exhibit," *Pittsburgh Post*, 10 September 1899.

34. D. C. Thomson, "The Carnegie Art Gallery," *Art Journal* (December 1898): 353–55; D. C. Thomson, London, 1 February 1899.

35. C. H. Caffin, "Art in Pittsburg," *Harper's Weekly* 42 (12 November 1898): 1104; Caffin, "The Pittsburg Exhibition — First Notice," *New York Evening Post*, 2 November 1900, 7.

36. C. H. Caffin, "The Pittsburg International Exhibition," *Harper's Weekly* 44 (17 November 1900): 1083; Caffin, "The Pittsburgh Exhibition — Second Notice," *New York Evening Post*, 6 November 1900, 5; Caffin, "The Sixth Annual Exhibition," *Harper's Weekly* 45 (23 November 1901): 1184; Caffin, "American Studio Notes," *International Studio* 12 (December 1901): xxxix; Caffin, "Art in Pittsburg," *Harper's Weekly* 42 (12 November 1898): 1104.

37. M. W. Brown, *The Story of the Armory Show* (New York, 1963), 129, 145, 154.

C. H. Caffin, "International Exhibition," *Harper's Weekly* 43 (11 November 1899): 1149; Caffin, "The Pittsburgh Exhibition — First Notice," *New York Evening Post*, 2 November 1900, 7; advice to Pittsburghers quoted in "Pittsburg Art Display Stands Alone on Merit," *Pittsburgh Dispatch*, 1 November 1899, 2.

38. Caffin, "The Pittsburgh Exposition," *New York Evening Post*, 4 November 1898, 5; Caffin, "Pittsburg International Exhibition," *Harper's Weekly* 43 (11 November 1899): 1149; Caffin, "The Pittsburgh Exhibition — First Notice," *New York Evening Post*, 2 November 1900, 7; Caffin, "The Pittsburgh Exhibition — Second Notice," *New York Evening Post*, 6 November 1900, 5; Caffin, "The Pittsburg International Exhibition," *Harper's Weekly* 44 (17 November 1900): 1083; Caffin, "The Sixth Annual Exhibition," *Harper's Weekly* 45 (23 November 1901) 1184; Caffin, "American Studio Notes," *International Studio* 13 (December 1901): xxxix.

39. "The Exhibition at the Carnegie Galleries," *Brush and Pencil* 3, no. 3 (December 1898): 168, 173; H. C. Payne, "Life the Accuser," *Brush and Pencil* 3, no. 4 (January 1899): 222–23.

40. Sheafer, "The Pittsburgh Exhibition," *Brush and Pencil* 5, no. 3 (December 1899): 133; Howland, "The Pittsburgh Art Exhibition," *Brush and Pencil* 7, no. 3 (December 1900): 139; Howland, "Pittsburg's Sixth International Art Exhibition," *Brush and Pencil* 9, no. 3 (December 1901): 134.

41. C. F. Brown, "The Editor," *Brush and Pencil* 3, no. 3 (December 1898): 192; Sheafer, "The Pittsburgh Exhibition," 136; Howland, "The Pittsburgh Art Exhibition," *Brush and Pencil* 7, no. 3 (December 1900): 133–34, 143; Howland, "Pittsburg's Sixth International Art Exhibition," *Brush and Pencil* 9, no. 3 (December 1901): 138.

42. "The Observer," *Art Interchange* 38 (January 1897): 18; "The Observer," *Art Interchange* 39 (December 1897): 140–41. For favorable notices, see Frank Weitenkampf, "Art in Pittsburgh," *Harper's Weekly* 35 (December 1898): 141; "The Observer," *Art Interchange* 36 (January 1896): 16; "The Observer," *Art Interchange* 36 (June 1896): 150.

43. B. Foster, New York, 4 January 1898; "Art News," *New York Evening Post*, 24 December 1897, 5; "Encouragement of American Art," *New York Times Illustrated Weekly Magazine*, 26 December 1897, 15. The review was also reprinted in the *New York Commercial Advertiser*, 29 December 1897, 7, without editorial comment but with the source clearly stated.

44. B. Foster, New York, 4 January 1898; H. R. Butler, New York, 10 January 1898; Beatty's letter printed in "Art News," *New York Evening Post*, 31 December 1897, 5, and "In the Art World," *New York Commercial Advertiser*, 6 January 1898, 7.

45. See for example, "Art Notes," *New York Sun*, 5 November 1897, 7; "In the Art World," *New York Commercial Advertiser*, 6 November 1897, 18. The Department of Fine Arts cooperated with out-of-town newspapers by sending them the names of the prizewinners in advance of Founder's Day, so that they could publish them on the day itself. The papers agreed not to print them before they were officially announced in Pittsburgh, but the *Chicago Evening Post* violated this agreement in 1899 and 1900 by

printing them the day before (J. Kelly, managing editor, *Chicago Tribune*, 8 November 1900).

46. W. A. Coffin, New York, 4 November 1897.

47. C. H. Ault, "Art Notes," *Cleveland Plaindealer*, 4 December 1898, 5.

48. "Pittsburgh Art Exhibition," *Art Interchange* 37 (July–December 1896): 148; Nemo, "Art in Pittsburg," *Philadelphia Item*, 9 November 1901, 6.

49. Frew, New York, 4 February 1898.

50. Frew, New York, 23 August 1898; W. A. Reaser, New York, 30 August, 20 December 1898; W. Macbeth, New York, 22 December 1898; Frew, New York, n.d. [September–October 1898].

51. "Art Party Here Today," *Pittsburgh Dispatch*, 9 December 1898; "New Yorkers Are Greatly Astonished," *Pittsburgh Dispatch*, 10 December 1898. See also (all 9 December 1898) "Visiting Artists," *Pittsburgh Chronicle-Telegraph*; "Art Exhibit Honored," *Pittsburgh Leader*; "Attracts Great Artist," *Pittsburgh News*; "Men of Fine Arts Will Be Guests," *Pittsburgh Post*; "New York Artists," *Pittsburgh Press*; "Artists at the Institute," *Pittsburgh Times*.

52. "New Yorkers Are Greatly Astonished," *Pittsburgh Dispatch*, 10 December 1898; "World-Known Artists' Praise for Pittsburg," *Pittsburgh Post*, 10 December 1898; "Artists Sing Our Praises," *Pittsburgh Dispatch*, 11 December 1898.

53. Frew, Point Pleasant, N.J., to J. B. Cauldwell, New York, 13 August 1899; Cauldwell to Frew, 16, 18 August 1899.

54. "Pittsburg as an Art Center," *Pittsburgh Press*, 21 November 1899, reprinted from the *New York Independent*; "Incidents and Events," *New York Times Saturday Review*, 4 November 1899, 750.

55. Hoeber, "Pittsburg's Exhibition," *New York Commercial Advertiser*, 2 November 1900, 7; Caffin, "The Pittsburgh Exhibition—First Notice," *New York Evening Post*, 2 November 1900, 7; Caffin, "The Pittsburgh Exhibition—Second Notice," *New York Evening Post*, 6 November 1900, 5.

56. Beatty to S. Swift, New York, n.d. [late November 1901]. S. Swift, Art Show," *New York Mail and Express*, 7 November 1901, 7; Swift, "The Three Prizewinning Pictures," *New York Mail and Express Illustrated Saturday Magazine*, 9 November 1901, 3; Swift, "Pittsburg's Art Show," *New York Mail and Express*, 11 November 1901, 5; Swift, "Art in Pittsburg," *New York Mail and Express*, 13 November 1901, 5.

57. "Picture Exhibition at Pittsburg: First Notice," *New York Sun*, 8 November 1901, 7; "Picture Exhibition at Pittsburg: Second Notice—The American Pictures," *New York Sun*, 12 November 1901, 7; "The Exhibition at Pittsburg: Concluding Notice—The Foreign Exhibits," *New York Sun*, 14 November 1901, 5. "Carnegie Pictures," 8 November 1901, 5; "The Art World," 16 November 1901, 11 (both in *New York Commercial Advertiser*).

58. R. Reid, New York, 8 January 1901; Beatty to Reid, 10 January 1901.

59. S. Swift, "The Pittsburg Exhibition," *New York Mail and Express*, 21 May 1901,

5; "The Art World," *New York Commercial Advertiser*, 31 December 1898, 11; "The Art World," *New York Commercial Advertiser*, 16 November 1901, 11.

60. "American Studio Notes," *International Studio* 3 (December 1897): viii; "The Art World," *New York Commercial Advertiser*, 5 November 1898, 5; "Pittsburg Leads in Art," *Pittsburgh Dispatch*, 8 April 1901, reprinted from the *New York Evening Post*. (Alexander's address is reported in "Pittsburg's Lead in Art Affairs," *Pittsburgh Chronicle-Telegraph*, 4 April 1901.) For a typically derogatory review of the National Academy of Design, see "The Autumn Academy," *New York Evening Post*, 24 November 1896, 7.

61. L. A. Frere, "Pictures Praised," *Pittsburgh Dispatch*, 13 November 1899, reprinted from *Criterion*; C. M. Kurtz, "American Salon Is Now Proposed," *Pittsburgh Leader*, 6 May 1900.

62. "Goosti Goes to Art Show," *Pittsburgh Post*, 6 November 1899, 6; L. M., "Manet and His School," *Pittsburgh Dispatch*, 15 November 1896, 4; A. Woodward, "The Paris Salon and Its Pictures," *Pittsburgh Dispatch*, 4 February 1900; "Details of a Combat with a Philistine," *Pittsburgh News*, 18 November 1899.

63. A. Burgoyne, "All Sorts," *Pittsburgh Leader*, 3 November 1897; Editorial, "Worthy of the President," *Pittsburgh Chronicle-Telegraph*, 30 October 1897.

64. "Next Exhibition," *Pittsburgh Leader*, 12 March 1899; Beatty quoted in "Americans Abroad," *Pittsburgh Dispatch*, 19 March 1899.

65. *Biographical Sketch of Col. James Fairman, the American Artist and Art Lecturer, from the London "Art Journal" and "Biograph"* (London, 1880), 1–8; E. Wilson, ed., *Standard History of Pittsburg, Pennsylvania* (Chicago, 1898), 865.

66. J. Fairman, *Essays on Art* (Pittsburgh, 1898), 5–9.

67. Ibid., 10–13.

68. Ibid., 14–17.

69. Ibid., 55–56.

70. Ibid., 59.

71. Ibid., 64–67.

72. Editor's note, in Fairman, *Essays on Art*, 2; unsigned note from the *Pittsburgh Times*, 2 November 1898; "Society Got a First Peep at the Paintings," *Pittsburgh Leader*, 7 November 1901, and "Press View of the Galleries," *Pittsburgh Commercial Gazette*, 7 November 1901.

73. S. G. Keenan, "Art Jury and the Public," *Pittsburgh Press*, 19 November 1899; Keenan, "This Year's Art Show of High Even Standard," *Pittsburgh Press*, 1 November 1900.

74. Obituary, *Pittsburgh Bulletin*, 1 June 1907, 15.

75. I. A. Smith, "Art Show Is Ready," *Pittsburgh Post*, 2 November 1899.

76. Smith, "The First Glimpse," *Pittsburgh Post*, 7 November 1900.

77. For Degas, see Smith, "Art Show Is Ready." For Sargent, see Smith, "Lovers of Fine Art Attend Press View," *Pittsburgh Post*, 1 November 1900.

78. Smith, "The First Glimpse."

79. Smith, "Art Show Is Ready"; Smith, "Lovers of Fine Art Attend Press View."

80. Smith, "In the Art Galleries," *Pittsburgh Post*, 15 September 1901.

81. Smith, "Lovers of Fine Art Attend Press View."

## Chapter 5

1. "Step Forward in Local Art," *Pittsburgh Post*, 20 March 1902; Editorial, "This Year's Art Exhibition," *Pittsburgh Post*, 22 March 1902.

2. Beatty, *Seventh Annual Report*, 1 April 1903, 10–13, 24–27.

3. Beatty, *Eighth Annual Report*, 1 April 1904, 10–11.

4. Ibid., 9–10, 19–25.

5. "Art Exhibition Brings Much Mail," *Pittsburgh Dispatch*, 30 January 1899; "Director Beatty Going Abroad," *Pittsburgh Post*, 27 April 1899.

6. "Great Crowds Thronged the Art Galleries," *Pittsburgh Dispatch*, 6 November 1899; Beatty to Carnegie, n.d. [ca. November–December 1899]; "Art Viewers Break Attendance Records," *Pittsburgh Post*, 5 December 1899; "No Selections Made," *Pittsburgh Dispatch*, 6 December 1899.

7. For the later history of the Carnegie exhibitions, see O'Connor, *The History of the Pittsburgh International*; L. A. Arkus, *Retrospective Exhibition of Paintings from Previous Internationals*, exhibition catalogue, Department of Fine Arts, Carnegie Institute, Pittsburgh, 5 December 1958–8 February 1959, n.p.; V. A. Clark, "Collecting from the Internationals," *Carnegie Magazine* 56, no. 5 (September–October 1982): 16–20. Although the International Series of one-man retrospectives held in 1977 and 1979 was publicized as being in some way connected with earlier exhibitions, no real connection is discernible.

8. For details of the rupture between Frick and Carnegie, see Wall, *Carnegie*, 714–64.

9. H. C. Frick, Pittsburgh, 29 June 1896, 13 September 1899, 3 October 1900, 3 July 1902.

10. Carnegie, "The Best Use of Wealth," 215.

11. Swift, "The Pittsburg Exhibition," *New York Mail and Express*, 21 May 1901, 5.

12. Wall, *Carnegie*, 864. Leisser story is in A. J. Phillips, "Patriarch of Pittsburgh Art Finds Life Lots of Fun at 91," *Pittsburgh Post-Gazette*, 29 July 1936.

13. W. Morris, "How We Live and How We Might Live," *William Morris: Stories in Prose, Stories in Verse, Shorter Poems, Lectures and Essays*, ed. G.D.H. Cole (London, 1948), 585.

14. H. Garland, "Homestead and Its Perilous Trades," *McClure's Magazine* 3 (June, 1984): 3–5; C. B. Spahr, *America's Working People* (New York, 1900), 146–47. For an account of the Homestead strike and its aftermath, see Wall, *Carnegie*, 537–82.

15. See Wall, *Carnegie*, 391–92. For a discussion of Carnegie's leading role in reducing labor costs and increasing the length of the workday, see Brody, *Steelworkers in America*, 2–7, 27–49.

16. This idea appears throughout Carnegie's writings, most notably in the article

"The Advantages of Poverty," published in the March 1891 number of *Nineteenth Century*.

17. Spahr, *America's Working People*, 154.

18. Wall, *Carnegie*, 523.

19. C. Hassam, "The Carnegie Institute in the American Art Movement," in *The Seventh Celebration of Founder's Day* (Pittsburgh, 1902), 37.

20. Beatty, "International Exhibitions," in *The Carnegie Institute: Annual Report of the President of the Board of Trustees for the Fiscal Year April 1, 1909–March 31, 1910* (Pittsburgh, 1910), 34–39.

21. Caffin, "Art in Pittsburg," *Harper's Weekly* 42 (12 November 1898): 1104; Caffin, "The Sixth Annual Exhibition," *Harper's Weekly* 45 (23 November 1901): 1184.

22. Caffin, "The Pittsburgh Exhibition—Second Notice," *New York Evening Post*, 6 November 1900, 5.

23. Caffin, "The Sixth Annual Exhibition," *Harper's Weekly* 45 (23 November 1901): 1184.

24. Carnegie, "The Best Use of Wealth," 214.

25. See, for example, the exchange of views published in the *Pittsburgh Telegraph* in November 1877 (Agnes C. Way Scrapbook, Carnegie Library of Pittsburgh, 9, 23–24, 30), in which the city's low state of culture was lamented and a "free salon of fine art" proposed as the most promising remedy.

26. Beatty, *Second Annual Report, 1 April 1898*, 4.

27. H. Spencer, *Autobiography* (New York, 1904), 2:468.

28. A. Carnegie, "The Progress of Eighteen Years," in *The Eighteenth Celebration of Founder's Day* (Pittsburgh, 1914), 14–15.

29. For a contemporary review of this phenomenon, see "The Field of Art," *Scribner's Magazine* 20, no. 5 (November 1896): 649–52.

30. E. Knaufft, "Fine Arts at the Carnegie Institute, Pittsburgh," *Review of Reviews* 28, no. 6 (December 1903): 680, 684.

31. Beatty quoted in "Art Exhibition Brings Much Mail," *Pittsburgh Dispatch*, 30 January 1899.

32. C. E. Norton, lecture notes for 6 May 1895, quoted in Vanderbilt, *Charles Eliot Norton*, 201.

# BIBLIOGRAPHY

John Beatty's annual reports to the board of trustees are indispensable to the study of the early Carnegie exhibitions. The first six reports, covering the years from 1896 to 1901, are preserved in typescript at the Carnegie Museum of Art. This series of reports includes a report presented by Beatty to the Fine Arts Committee on 22 July 1897, in which he discusses the formation of the foreign advisory committees. After 1902 Beatty's reports were printed and bound together with those from the directors of the Carnegie Institute's other departments. These can be consulted at the Carnegie Library of Pittsburgh.

Also indispensable is the correspondence of the Department of Fine Arts. The original correspondence is in the Archives of American Art, Washington, D.C. Microfilms are held by the Carnegie Museum of Art and the Archives of American Art.

From 1896 on, the Carnegie Institute published complete transcripts of its annual Founder's Day programs. These can be most easily consulted at the Carnegie Library of Pittsburgh. The catalogues of the annual exhibitions are widely available in public, university, and museum libraries.

To keep the bibliography to a reasonable length, I have omitted most of the hundreds of items cited from local newspapers. Many of these from 1897 to 1911 are conveniently preserved in the scrapbooks compiled for William Nimick Frew, first president of the board of trustees. These are held by the Pennsylvania Room of the Carnegie Library of Pittsburgh.

## Selected Bibliography

Adams, Henry, Kenneth Neal, et al. *American Drawings and Watercolors in the Museum of Art, Carnegie Institute*. Pittsburgh, 1985.

"American Studio Notes." *International Studio* 3 (December 1897): v–viii; 9 (November 1899): xx.

"American Studio Talk." *International Studio* 3 (October 1897): iv.

Arnold, Matthew. *Works*. 10 vols. London, 1903–1904.

———. *Five Uncollected Essays*. Edited by Kenneth Alcott. Liverpool, 1953.

Arkus, Leon. *Retrospective Exhibition of Paintings from Previous Internationals*. Exhibition catalogue. Department of Fine Arts, Carnegie Institute, Pittsburgh, 1958.

"Art for the People." *Outlook* 63, no. 11 (11 November 1899): 626–27.

"Artists' Jury for Pittsburg." *New York Times*, 30 September 1897, 5.

"Art News." *New York Evening Post*, 24 December 1897, 5; 31 December 1897, 5.

"Art Notes." *Chicago Times-Herald*, 5 November 1898, 4.

"Art Notes." *New York Sun*, 4 December 1896, 7; 7 November 1897, 7.

"Art Plans for Pittsburgh." *New York Times Saturday Review of Books and Art*, 30 January 1897, 4–5.

"The Art World." *New York Commercial Advertiser*, 5 November 1898, 5; 31 December 1898, 11; 10 November 1899, 5; 16 November 1901, 11.

Ault, Charles H. "Art Notes." *Brush and Pencil* 3, no. 4 (January 1899): 255. Reprinted from the *Cleveland Plaindealer*, 4 December 1898, 5.

Beam, Philip C. *Winslow Homer at Prout's Neck*. Boston, 1966.

Beatty, John W. "The Art Gallery." In *Dedication Souvenir of the Carnegie Library*. Pittsburgh, 1895.

———. *The Relation of Art to Nature*. New York, 1922.

———. "American Art at Paris." *American Review of Reviews*, (November 1923): 532–37.

———. "Recollections of an Intimate Friendship." (Written 1923–1924.) In Lloyd Goodrich, *Winslow Homer* (New York, 1944), 207–26.

———. "The Modern Art Movement." *North American Review* 219 (1924): 251–64.

Beaux, Cecilia. *Background with Figures*. Boston and New York, 1930.

Beecher, Henry Ward. *Eyes and Ears*. Boston, 1862.

Bissell, George E. "Art and Education." *Municipal Affairs* 6, no. 2 (June 1902): 185–88.

Brody, David. *Steelworkers in America: The Non-Union Era*. New York, 1970.

Brown, Charles Francis. "The Editor." *Brush and Pencil* 3, no. 3 (December 1898): 192.

Caffin, Charles H. "The Pittsburgh Exposition." *New York Evening Post*, 4 November 1898, 5.

———. "Art in Pittsburgh." *Harper's Weekly* 42, no. 2186 (12 November 1898): 1104, 1106.

———. "Pittsburg International Exhibition." *Harper's Weekly* 43, no. 2238 (11 November 1899): 1149.

———. "The Pittsburgh Exhibition—First Notice." *New York Evening Post*, 2 November 1900, 7.

———. "The Pittsburgh Exhibition—Second Notice." *New York Evening Post*, 6 November 1900, 5.

———. "The Pittsburg International Exhibition." *Harper's Weekly* 44, no. 2291 (17 November 1900): 1083.

———. "The Sixth Annual Exhibition, Carnegie Institute." *Harper's Weekly* 45, no. 2347 (23 November 1901): 1171, 1184.

———. "American Studio Notes." *International Studio* 12 (December 1901): xxxix–xlviii.

——. *The Story of American Painting*. New York, 1907.

Carnegie, Andrew. *Triumphant Democracy*. New York, 1886; reprint, New York and London, 1971.

——. *The Autobiography of Andrew Carnegie*. Boston and New York, 1920.

——. *Miscellaneous Writings of Andrew Carnegie*. Edited by Burton J. Hendrick. 2 vols. Garden City, N.Y., 1933.

——. *The Gospel of Wealth and Other Timely Essays*. Edited by Edward C. Kirkland. Cambridge, Mass., 1962.

"Carnegie Art Exhibition." *New York Times*, 20 May 1901, 7.

"The Carnegie Art Gallery." *New York Times*, 6 November 1896, 5.

*Carnegie Fine Arts and Museum Collection Fund: Constitution and By-Laws of the Board of Trustees Together with Mr. Carnegie's Letter and Deed of Trust*. Pittsburgh, 1907.

"Carnegie Gallery Prizes." *New York Times*, 6 December 1896, 1.

"The Carnegie Institute." *New York Times Saturday Review of Books and Art*, 3 April 1897, 4.

"Carnegie Jury of Awards." *New York Times*, 28 September 1901, 3.

"Carnegie Pictures." *New York Commercial Advertiser*, 8 November 1901, 5.

"Change in Carnegie Art Jury." *New York Times*, 1 October 1899, 25.

Chew, Paul A., and John A. Sakal. *Southwestern Pennsylvania Painters, 1800–1945*. Exhibition catalogue. Westmoreland County Museum of Art, Greensburg, Pennsylvania, 1981.

Clark, Vicky A. "Collecting from the Internationals." *Carnegie Magazine* 56, no. 5 (September–October 1982): 16–27.

*Dedication Souvenir of the Carnegie Library, Pittsburgh*. Pittsburgh, 1895.

"The East Side Loan Exhibition." *Critic* 20 (25 June 1892): 357.

"Encouragement of American Art." *New York Times Illustrated Weekly Magazine*, 26 December 1897, 15.

"Essays on Our Leading Citizens: John Wesley Beatty." *Harpoon*, May 1913, 7–8.

"The Exhibition at the Carnegie Galleries, Pittsburgh, Pennsylvania." *Brush and Pencil* 3, no. 3 (December 1898): 167–75.

Fairman, James. *Essays on Art*. Pittsburgh, 1898.

Fort, J. N. "Pictures Under Cover." *Philadelphia Item*, 25 November 1896, 8. Reprinted in the *Pittsburgh Press*, 27 November 1896, 9.

Garland, Hamlin, with A. C. Bernheim and Jane Addams. "Successful Efforts to Teach Art to the Masses." *Forum* 19 (March–August 1895): 606–17.

Goodrich, Lloyd. *Winslow Homer*. New York, 1944.

Harris, Neil. *The Artist in American Society*. New York, 1966.

Hendrick, Burton J. *The Life of Andrew Carnegie*. 2 vols. Garden City, New York, 1932.

Hetzel, Lila. "Biography of George Hetzel." Typescript, c. 1946. Art Department, Carnegie Library of Pittsburgh.

Hoeber, Arthur. "Pictures in Pittsburg." *New York Times*, 10 November 1895, 29.

———. "Pittsburg's Exhibition." *New York Commercial Advertiser*, 2 November 1900, 7.

Horowitz, Helen Lefkowitz. *Culture and the City: Cultural Philanthropy in Chicago from the 1880s to 1917*. Lexington, Kentucky, 1976.

Howland, Austin E. "The Pittsburgh Art Exhibition." *Brush and Pencil* 7, no. 3 (December 1900): 129–46.

———. "Pittsburg's Sixth International Art Exhibition." *Brush and Pencil* 9, no. 3 (December 1901): 129–45.

Hyatt, Will J. "Some Collections of Painting in Pittsburgh." *Art and Archaeology* 14, nos. 5, 6 (November–December 1922): 323–29.

"Incidents and Events." *New York Times Saturday Review*, 4 November 1899, 750.

"In the Art World." *New York Commercial Advertiser*, 6 November 1897, 18; 12 November 1897, 4; 29 December 1897, 7; 6 January 1898, 7.

"In the World of Art." *New York Times*, 26 April 1896, 22.

Knaufft, Ernest. "Fine Arts at the Carnegie Institute, Pittsburgh." *American Monthly Review of Reviews* 28, no. 6 (December 1903): 680–86.

"Large Sum for an Art Gallery." *New York Times*, 2 January 1896, 5.

Lavery, John. *The Life of a Painter*. Boston, 1940.

Lucas, E. V. *Edwin Austin Abbey, Royal Academician*. 2 vols. New York, 1921.

Lynes, Russell. *The Taste-Makers*. New York, 1954.

MacDonald, Stuart. "Art in Saint Louis." *Harper's Weekly* 39 (12 October 1895): 976–77.

———. "Art in Saint Louis." *Harper's Weekly* 41 (23 October 1897): 1064.

McDougall, I. M. "Great Art Exhibit." *Chicago Evening Post*, 7 November 1896, 5.

*Memorial of the Celebration of the Carnegie Institute at Pittsburgh, Pennsylvania, April 11, 12, 13, 1907*. Pittsburgh, 1907.

M. H. "Art and the People." *Harper's Weekly* 37 (29 April 1893): 394–95.

Morris, Harrison S. "Carnegie International Jury Awards Second Honors to Ellen W. Ahrens." *Philadelphia Press*, 8 November 1901, 5.

Morris, W. B. "Director John W. Beatty and His Work," *Pittsburgh Press*, 14 April 1901.

Munhall, Edgar. *Masterpieces of the Frick Collection*. Introduction by Harry D. M. Grier. New York, 1970.

Nemo [pseudonym]. "Art in Pittsburg." *Philadelphia Item*, 9 November 1901, 6.

"The Observer." *The Art Interchange* 36 (January 1896): 16; 36 (June 1896): 150; 38 (January–June 1897): 18, 70; 39 (July–December 1897): 110, 140–41.

O'Connor, John, Jr. "The Carnegie Institute International Exhibition." *Art and Archaeology* 14, nos. 5, 6 (November–December 1922): 301–11.

———. *The History of the Pittsburgh International, Carnegie Institute, 1896–1952*. Pittsburgh, 1952. Originally published as four articles in *Carnegie Magazine* 26, nos. 5–8 (May–October 1952).

Olds, Marion Knowles. *John Wesley Beatty: Artist and Cultural Influence in Pittsburgh*. Masters dissertation, University of Pittsburgh, 1953.

Payne, Henry C. "Life the Accuser." *Brush and Pencil* 3, no. 4 (January 1899): 222–23.

"Picture Exhibition at Pittsburg." *New York Sun*, 8 November 1901, 7; 12 November 1901, 7; 14 November 1901, 5.

"Pictures at Pittsburgh." *Harper's Weekly* 40 (14 November 1896): 1120.

"Pictures at the Carnegie Institute." *New York Times Illustrated Weekly Magazine*, 14 November 1897, 5.

"Pittsburgh Art Exhibition." *Art Interchange* 37 (July–December 1896): 147–48.

"Pittsburg's Art Exhibition." *New York Times*, 4 November 1898, 7.

"Pittsburg's Art Exhibition." *New York Times Illustrated Magazine Supplement*, 13 November 1898, 2.

Remick, Marie C. "The Relation of Art to Morality." *Arena* 19 (April 1898): 483–95.

Saint-Gaudens, Homer. "The Carnegie Institute." *Art and Archaeology* 14, nos. 5, 6 (November–December 1922): 287–301.

Sheafer, Frances B. "The Pittsburgh Exhibition." *Brush and Pencil* 5, no. 3 (December 1899): 125–37.

Smith, Ida A. "Art Show Is Ready," *Pittsburgh Post*, 2 Nov. 1899.

——. "Six Paintings Will Stay Here," *Pittsburgh Post*, 6 Jan. 1900.

——. "Lovers of Fine Art Attend Press View," *Pittsburgh Post*, 1 Nov. 1900.

——. "In the Art Galleries," *Pittsburgh Post*, 15 Sept. 1901.

——. "The First Glimpse," *Pittsburgh Post*, 7 Nov. 1901.

Spahr, C. B. *America's Working People*. New York, 1900.

Stein, Roger B. *John Ruskin and Aesthetic Thought in America, 1840–1900*. Cambridge, Mass., 1967.

Strazdes, Diana, et al. *American Paintings and Sculpture to 1945 in the Carnegie Museum of Art*. New York, 1992.

Swift, Samuel. "The Pittsburg Exhibition." *New York Mail and Express*, 21 May 1901, 5.

——. "Pittsburg Art Show." *New York Mail and Express*, 7 November 1901, 7.

——. "The Three Prizewinning Pictures Shown at Carnegie Institute, Pittsburg." *New York Mail and Express Illustrated Saturday Magazine*, 9 November 1901, 3.

——. "Pittsburg's Art Show." *New York Mail and Express*, 11 November 1901, 5.

——. "Art in Pittsburg." *New York Mail and Express*, 13 November 1901, 5.

——. "Portraits at Pittsburg." *New York Mail and Express*, 14 November 1901, 5.

Thomson, D. Croal. "The Carnegie Art Gallery." *Art Journal*, December 1898, 353–55.

Vanderbilt, Kermit. *Charles Eliot Norton: Apostle of Culture in a Democracy*. Cambridge, Mass., 1959.

Van Trump, James D. *An American Palace of Culture: The Carnegie Institute and Carnegie Library of Pittsburgh*. Pittsburgh, 1970.

Wall, Joseph Frazier. *Andrew Carnegie*. New York, 1970; reprinted Pittsburgh, 1989.

Way, Agnes C., Scrapbook of Press Clippings. Art Department, Carnegie Library of Pittsburgh.

Weeks, Edwin Lord. "Art Exhibition at the Carnegie Institute, Pittsburg." *Harper's Weekly* 41 (20 November 1897): 1153–54.

Weisberg, Gabriel. "Tastemaking in Pittsburgh: The Carnegie International in Perspective, 1896–1905." *Carnegie Magazine* 56, no. 10 (July–August 1983): 20–26, 40–41.

Weitenkampf, Frank. "Art in Pittsburgh." *Art Interchange* 35 (July–December 1895): 141.

# INDEX